THE EARTHLY PARADISE

The Garden of Eden from Antiquity to Modernity

THE EARTHLY PARADISE

The Garden of Eden from Antiquity to Modernity

Editor
F. Regina Psaki

Literary Editor
Charles Hindley

State University of New York Press

Cover artwork entitled "Creation of Animals" from *La Bible de Sens*. Old Testament. 21st Century, Royal Library of Torino, Italy.

Publication Data:

Psaki, F. Regina. *THE EARTHLY PARADISE: The Garden of Eden from Antiquity to Modernity*
ISBN 1-58684-159-9
March 2002 (first edition)

For information, contact

State University of New York Press, Albany, NY

www.sunypress.edu

Table of Contents

Editor's note

The essays contained in this volume constitute, not a continuous narrative of the history of how the Eden story in Genesis has been understood, but rather a series of snapshots taken at different moments in that history. They include examples of Christian, Jewish, and Islamic interpretations of Genesis in different periods, places and contexts. They address popular movements, learned exegesis, literary appropriations and modern theology and philosophy. They move from antiquity to the twentieth century, and span a spectrum from orthodox to heterodox interpretations of the Eden narrative. The goal of this collection is to represent each moment addressed in some detail; thus the picture the collection sketches, gains in depth and nuance what it loses in clarity and apparent coherence. Indeed, there is an obvious case to be made that overarching narratives are always achieved at the expense of accuracy and complexity, that the picture only "comes clear" by panning back from it to a very great distance, one which necessarily blurs the details and misses the exceptions to the general image.

All but three of the essays contained in this volume were originally written in Italian (two were written in English, one in French). The literary editor and first translator for the project is Charles Hindley, who provided English versions of those essays for whom no other translator is noted. It is difficult to appreciate the monumental nature of this task if one has not already done it; suffice it to say that without his contribution this collection would simply not have appeared.

Academic style in Italian and French differs not just formally but substantially from English style, however, and a second level of "translation" was necessary to make these essays more accessible to their new audience. Moreover, despite the edenic promises of computer technology, many a slip still occurs in transferring electronic documents from Italian-language formats to English-language ones (not to mention in transliterations from Arabic, Greek, and Hebrew). For formatting, troubleshooting, and homogenizing editorial protocols as far as possible, I thank Nicole Sundquist, who spent many hours resolving uncertainties of various kinds in this project. For expert layout and final design of the collection I thank Lori Howard of Black Sheep Design. William and Susan Piché sponsored the generous Piché Award in Arts and Sciences at the University of Oregon which permitted the collaboration of Sundquist and Howard, and I thank them sincerely. Last but not least, Pier Cesare Bori was the moving force behind this as behind so many research initiatives, and it has been an enriching experience for me to collaborate with him.

—F. Regina Psaki
The Giustina Family Professor
of Italian Language and Literature,
University of Oregon

Introduction

Pier Cesare Bori

1. This volume brings together the work of a group of scholars who meet regularly every year in Bertinoro, near Bologna, to discuss subjects relating to the history of the interpretation of biblical texts.

The scholars are specialists in various fields (the history of exegesis, philosophy, theology and literature), embracing Judaic and Islamic as well as Christian perspectives, and the group takes as its starting point the history of the interpretation of a specific passage or idea in the Bible.[1]

The subject chosen for 1995/1996 was "Paradise on Earth," which sums up the central idea and refers specifically to the second chapter of Genesis. Compelling work has already been done on this subject,[2] of course, but our own interest was not in the "next world," as the various paradisal typologies which have emerged in the course of history have understood it (McDannell-Lang, and Bernheim-Stavridès). Nor were we interested in the exploration of the original paradisal place, the "Garden of Delights," from the historical-exegetical point of view (Morris-Sawyer), or from that of the debate on its historicity and whereabouts (Delumeau). Our interest lay rather in the original condition of the human creature as it is presented in Genesis, as the image of what the human being had been (and is still) called upon to be, with all the connected relationships: man-woman, humanity-nature, and humanity-divinity.

---

[1] In 1993 the Prologue to John's Gospel (see *Annali di storia dell'esegesi* 11/1 [1994]) and in 1994/1995 the theme "In Spirit and Truth" (*'In Spirito e Verità.' Letture di Giovanni 4*, 23–24, ed. P. C. Bori [Bologna: EDB, 1996]).

[2] In particular, C. McDannell and B. Lang, *Heaven: A History* (New Haven and London: Yale University Press, 1988); P.-A. Bernheim and G. Stavridès, *Paradis Paradis* (with a general survey of the extra-biblical world) (Paris: Plon, 1991); J. Delumeau, *Une histoire du paradis. Le Jardin des délices* (Paris: Fayard, 1992); P. Morris and D. Sawyer, *A Walk in the Garden: Biblical, Iconographic and Literary Images of Eden* (Sheffield: JSOT, 1994).

Starting from this central point, the studies contained in this volume branch out in several directions, for the authors have reconstructed very different moments and contexts of the history of the interpretation of Genesis 2. It seems to me necessary, therefore, considering that most of the studies have to do with the history of Christian theology and Christian thought, to return briefly to that central point, as it is expressly articulated in the New Testament.

2. The interest of the New Testament and of Paul in the history of our origins is theological, and considers the idea of our original humanity as a necessary premise of eschatology. In the theological history of humanity, made up of a succession of creative interventions linked together, the last days are to be understood by understanding the first days. To fully understand the work of the Messiah it is necessary to start with Adam, from the corporate solidarity of all men with him and with his sin. It can then be understood how, through an inverse symmetry, from the new Adam may spring salvation for all.

> Wherefore, as by one man sin entered into the world, and death by sin; and so death passed upon all men, for that all have sinned: (For until the law sin was in the world: but sin is not imputed when there is no law. Nevertheless death reigned from Adam to Moses, even over them that had not sinned after the similitude of Adam's transgression, who is the figure of him that was to come. But not as the offence, so also is the free gift. For if through the offence of one many be dead, much more the grace of God, and the gift by grace, which is by one man, Jesus Christ, hath abounded unto many. (Rom. 5:12–15)

This central passage governs the entire New Testament interpretation of Genesis 2: an interpretation that depends rigorously on the realization of the Messiah that is at the heart of Christian writing (and here the work of Jakob Taubes must be recalled).

In another passage, 1 Cor. 15, Paul refers to the first Adam, and answers the questions he has been asked on the resurrection of the flesh and the way this will happen. Here it is not a case of explaining that through the obedience of One, all are saved (parallel to the sin of one alone, which condemned all). Rather, Adam's condition is only the first stage of humanity's bodily nature, the "psychic" stage. A further stage in the flesh is given, that of the second Adam, "celestial," spiritual, "incorruptible": "For since by man came death, by man came also the resurrection of the dead. For as in Adam all die, even so in Christ shall all men be made alive" (1 Cor. 15:21 ff.). These two points of view have in common the continuity between justification, sanctification and final resurrection, anticipated in the body of the Messiah: "the first man, Adam, became a living being, but the last Adam became spirit, giver of life" (15:23).

I would argue the absolute logical and theological priority of Romans 5 over 1 Cor. 15. On the substance of theological anthropology, Paul in 1 Cor. 15 says no more than he has said in Romans 5–8, leaving aside the expectation of the imminence of *parousia*, of the Second Coming.

3. Once the synthesis supporting Paul's work has been lost, two very different anthropologies can be developed from these two points of view about our original condition. A dualism can be discerned that seems to us more important, theoretically and historically speaking, than the distinction between theocentric and anthropocentric paradise traced by McDannel and Lang.

On the one hand there is Paradise as our original state, to which the Messiah as second Adam leads us back *here and now*, and indefectibly settles the humanity grafted on to his resurrected body. The reading of the entire context of Romans 5–8 in this way is fascinating, especially the passage of Rom 8:18–23 (to the groan of creation together with the groan of labor Eve, named Zoé, the mother of every living person, has condemned us). It is fascinating to read the quotation from Paul in the vision George Fox describes, his return to Paradise ("Now was I come up in spirit through the flaming sword into the paradise of God. All things were new, and all things gave another smell unto me than before, beyond what words can utter. I knew nothing but pureness, and innocency, and righteousness, being renewed up into the image of God by Christ Jesus, so that I say I was come up to the state of Adam which he was in before he fell...").

On the other hand, there is the paradisal condition as the *future* metamorphosis of the flesh, not to be had in the present, truly "in the beyond," with respect to the line traced by the *parusia*: the final extension, beyond the celestial goal of an earthly expectation and dynamism, towards "Eye hath not seen, nor ear heard, neither have entered into the heart of man, the things which God hath prepared for them that love him" (1 Cor 2:9, spoken in another context). The earthly garden is therefore the pure reflection of this earthly garden, as in Judaic eschatology, in which the celestial garden is the basis of the earthly one (Nachmanide). Monasticism, which also imagines itself as a return to Paradise, means this Paradise, which is of the beyond, and not—so to speak—this side of history, like the former. Paradise then takes the form, for historical existence, of something that has been lost and something that is before us, an object of nostalgia, of sighs, and of *Streben*, as for Goethe, "fulfilment is given by our eternal ascending" (see Destro, below).

4. Besides this dualism, I would point out briefly in conclusion another interesting development that takes place in the history of the reception of Paul's text. This is an interpretative gesture tending towards the secular, which originates precisely from taking the eschatological premise to its logical conclusion. It may then be noted that Fox's text itself, despite its rigorously Pauline basis, allows us to glimpse a possibility of religious-philosophical development.

> ...but as people come into subjection to the spirit of God, and grow up in the image and power of the Almighty, they may receive the Word of wisdom, that opens all things, and come to know the hidden unity in the Eternal Being.

A model of human completeness is outlined here, founded on the restoration of the divine image, and expressed in the knowledge of and dominion over creation. This is the anthropology of Pico della Mirandola that moves from a realized eschatology, from a humanity firmly planted in the middle of the rediscovered garden, with a christology so implicit as to appear dissolved into a discourse on the fulfilment and wholeness of humanity.

Where the eschatological, soteriological, Messianic reason is assumed wholly, it is taken for granted, and *this is precisely why* one can begin to talk confidently once again simply of *humanity* and of *human* nature.

The Anxiety of Eden

Stefano Levi Della Torre

By the end of the sixth day, the stormy creation process had flowed into an apparently quiet time and place: a time, the seventh day; a place, the Garden of Eden. Shabbat is the time of Eden and Eden is the place of Shabbat. Neither a dead place nor a dead time: once the world has been created, the relationship between the Creator and His creation remains suspended for it to continue to exist. The Seventh Day and Eden represent the pause within which the relationship exists and is processed. On the seventh day the Divine withdraws, leaving space and breath for the non-divine, i.e. for the creation:[1] the garden of Eden is the actual forge in which the co-ordinates of the relationship between God, humans and the world come into being.

Eden is the locus of splitting and of doubling, a crossroads and a choice. This is the narrative pattern of the second chapter of Genesis, a passage with fracture lines which will explode in Chapter 3 with the transgression of the forbidden fruit. Binary oppositions—day/night, wet/dry, high/low—are the imprinting in/of creation and eventually flow into the distinction between life and death and good and evil, to then flow back to the Creator Himself and His behavior as the creation impacts on Him. The seventh day is the first result of this flow back (Gen. 2:2): "On the seventh day Elohim ceased from all the work He had made and Elohim blessed the seventh day." God completed His work by resting: He added non-doing to doing, non-making to making (Rashi).[2] Completeness such as this is duality, a polarization between the seventh and the other days, but it is only when in contact with the Creation that duality invests God Himself: "On the day when Adonai Elohim made the earth and the sky" (Gen. 2:4). This is the first time God is described using two denominations: the tetragrammaton (Y H

[1] I am referring to the Cabalistic doctrine of Tzimtzum, by Isaac Luria (16th c.).

[2] Rashi of Troyes, Rabbi Solomon ben Isaac (1040–1105), the founder of an important school of exegesis, in L. Cattani, ed., *Commento alla Genesi* (Casale Monferrato: Marietti, 1985).

W H, read Adonai) and Elohim. According to aspect, God is Elohim (Justice) and Y H W H / Adonai (mercy and personal relationship). The world could not exist with Justice or Mercy alone: it is this refraction, the refraction of God in His creation, into these two aspects, that makes it possible. The divine action refracts into two terms: *bara'* and *'assa,'* to create and to make: "...as on the seventh day (on *Shabbat*) He rested from all the completeness he had created (*asher bara'*) to make (*la'assot*)" (Gen. 2:3): creation from nothing and the processing of what has emerged, virtually two moments of/in creation.

At this point in time, what is the world landscape like? It could be defined as bare: "There was neither a plant nor herb growing wild upon the earth, because the Lord God (Y H W H / Elohim) had sent no rain on the earth; nor was there any man to till the soil" (Gen. 2:5). However, this would appear to contradict what is said about the third day of the creation, in Gen. 1:12): "...the earth yielded fresh growth, plants,... trees bearing fruit...." I shall refer to the two terms of Gen. 2:5 (following Cassuto) to avoid this contradiction,[3] where "shrubs and herbs" are not to be seen as any two members of the plant world, but as two specific kinds: *siah* and *'essev,* thorns and thistles and gramineous plants. Thus the thorns and thistles and gramineous plants had not yet grown. These are the prototypes of cultivation, the former negative, the latter positive: thorns and thistles are weeds, the enemy of farming and cultivation, while gramineous plants are the object of cultivation and farming. The strength of this interpretation lies in the fact in Gen 2:5 it is immediately followed by "there was no man to till the soil" and in the conclusion that the opposition between thorns and thistles on the one hand, and gramineous plants on the other, had not yet arisen. The opposition in question emerges when God punishes Adam, saying: "Cursed is the ground by your fault... thorns and thistles shall it bring forth to you and you shall eat wheat (*'essev*) from the field" (Gen. 3:17–18).

[3] See U. Cassuto, *A Commentary on the Book of Genesis* (Jerusalem: The Agnes Press, 1944–1989), 101–103. Rashi proposes a different solution to the problem: on the third day plants remained near the opening, the surface of the soil, and only on the sixth day did they sprout and grow.

Says the Lord: as you have eaten the fruit thus knowing good and evil, likewise you will have to distinguish good in what you eat (gramineous plants) from evil (thorns). Like the woman who will generate in pain (Gen. 3:16), man will generate corn by bleeding in the bushes. However, this contrast is hardly felt at the threshold of Eden, and it will become apparent through the events taking place in Eden.

The word *'essev*, herb, was defined in the text as a gramineous plant. It appears to be the appointed food for both human beings and animals (Gen. 1:29–30). Animals and humans share it in a kind of communion; the animal nature of the human being nevertheless contains a divine element as well: "Adonai Elohim formed the *adam* of the dust of the ground, and breathed the soul *(neshamma)* of life into his nostrils and the *adam* received the breath *(nefesh)* of life" (Gen. 2:7). Animals, unlike human beings, had been supplied with *nefesh* but not with *neshamma:* human beings possess a double nature, they are hybrids living between the natural and the divine element, made of dust, but after His own likeness and image. The relationship between human beings and the other living beings that were supplied with *nefesh* is also double, twofold, as in Gen. 1:26: man "...shall have dominion over the fish of the sea, ...and over the fowl of the air, the cattle and the wild animals...." Rashi comments the double meaning of the verb *veirdu,* which means both "shall have dominion" and "shall fall down" as low as beasts, or lower. Rabbi Khanina said that if human beings are worthy they shall dominate, but if they are not worthy they shall not. Rabbi Ja'kov of Kefar Hanin said: "...what is after Our image dominates, what is not after Our image does not dominate" *(Genesis Rabbah* 8,12).

"In the beginning Elohim created heaven and earth" (Gen. 1:1). Maimonides translates this "heaven and earth" as "high and low" (*More' Nevukhim,* Book 2, Chapter 30). In the beginning God created the high and the low. Human beings are placed as the mediators between high and low thanks to their double nature, both earthly and heavenly. According to Rashi's commentary man's first action is consistent and unfolds in a prayer so that rain may fall on the earth: "When Adam was created he understood that the rain was necessary to the world and prayed for it. The rain fell and trees and buds sprung up." The invocation from below moves what is high up, just like smoke from a sacrifice (see *Zohar*, Bereshit 2, 35 a).

Genesis Rabbah 14,1 says that the rain—that is, the fertile relationship between the sky and the earth—is allowed to fall and the earth man himself is made of is mixed: "it is like one kneading dough, [who] first pours water and then mixes it" (Rashi). Steam rising from the earth and falling down onto it, the human being bridging high and low: this is the function of human beings in the world and the meaning of their existence. Four are their terrestrial features: eating and drinking; reproducing; evacuating; and dying. Likewise four are their heavenly features: upright position; speech; knowledge; and vision (*Genesis Rabbah* 8,11).

"Adonai Elohim formed man from the dust of the earth" (Gen. 2:7): according to Sanhedrin 38a, He collected the dust from the four corners of the earth so that wherever human beings may die, the earth will receive them in their grave, as if they are part of the soil itself. Human beings are not just the vertical mediation between high and low, but also the horizontal mediation between the world's multiplicity, *res cogitans* and *res extensa*. This centrifugal diverging interpretation which looks to the four corners of the earth is intertwined with the opposite centripetal and convergent one: God is thought to have taken the dust of the human being from that place of which it is said: "You shall make an altar of earth" (Ex. 20:24) (Rashi from *Genesis Rabbah* 14, 8). This is where the Sanctuary is: the man of earth, the altar of earth. The altar too is a point where the relationship between high and low focuses: the smells of the sacrifice, the smoke rising from the earth to the sky, and the altar itself with its four corners sprinkled with sacrificial blood as the ritual states: it radiates out horizontally to benefit the four corners of the world. Thus in the human being the vertical divine relationship refracts horizontally radiating throughout the creation, and in fact balancing it, as a comment in *Genesis Rabbah* 12,8 appears to suggest:

> God made man of earthly and heavenly substance, his body of earthly substance, his soul the heavenly one. This is why on the first day God created heaven and earth, on the second a firmament for heavenly beings, on the third He ordered: "Let... dry land appear" for the earthly beings; then on the

> fourth day He created lights for the heavenly beings and on the fifth He said "Let the waters come forth"—for the earthly beings. As a result on the sixth day He had to create a being made up of heavenly and earthly substances, least envy should arise among the results of the creation if either had received one day more than the other.

The vocation of human beings is to hold the various strands of the world together *by understanding them*: their two-fold nature, heavenly and earthly, makes it possible for them to reconcile the inherent antagonism of/in the creation, or indeed to exacerbate it, by fragmenting and generating confusion, as happened with the forbidden fruit and later with the Flood and the Tower of Babel.

Such is the being God placed in Eden, the Garden that He Himself had planted and made to grow. It differs from the third day when the earth grew plants and trees as ordered; God plants the Garden of Eden Himself, and the garden is God's creation, as is Adam. However, this is not a place of quiet: Adam is placed in the garden "to work it and look after it" (Gen, 2:15).[4] In the sequence of creation human beings are at the top of the pyramid of beings, but now man is in the center of a circle.[5] Whereas in this second chapter of Genesis, the acts are repeated, as if they follow the creation of man and are as it were a function of his. God creates and establishes an environment *for man*: the soil to cultivate, the animals, and woman. This anthropocentric or better still androcentric position is nevertheless ambiguous, as *Pirkei de Rebbe Eliezer* (Chapter 2) suggests:

> Adam stood upright and considered the high and the low... He was in God's likeness and his measure stretched from East to West. Looking at him all the creatures were struck by fear because they mistook him for the creator, and went to him to bow.

Idolatry, the animal nature of idolatry, originates in Eden and is rooted in the apparently centrality of man. "You shall be like Elohim," the tempting serpent will say in the chapter that follows.

---

[4] Another interpretation is based on a difference meaning of the verb *'avad*, to worship.

[5] See Gerhard Von Rad, *Genesi* (Brescia: Paideia Ed., 1978), Vols. 2–4, 93.

The order of relationships is worked out in Eden: it is first of all a hierarchical order, partly announced in Gen. 1:28, and enacted in the garden. Adam is entrusted with power over the animals that God "sent to man to see what he would call them" (Gen. 2:19), just as God Himself had named the elements of the universe and their temporal rhythms (Gen. 1:5–8–10). The act of naming is also an act of domination (see Num. 32:38, 2 Kings 23:24 and 2 Chronicles 36:4).[6] This is why human beings cannot name God. In the first version man and woman were created together and no hierarchy was established ("God created man in His likeness, He created them male and female," Gen. 1:27). In this version a hierarchy is established: the woman is drawn from Adam's side and she is named by him: "She shall be called woman, *ishah,* because she has been drawn from man, *ish*" (Gen. 2:23). And then: "Adam called his woman Eve, *Hava*" (Gen. 3:20). Differences between the divine and the human are established in Eden; the temptation to confuse them—idolatry—is a temptation which the serpent calls for. The temptation emerges and is shattered, but at the same time the hierarchy between man and woman is established, as are their roles. This anthropological process is shared by many other cultures, and in religious terms it could be seen as an escape from the mythological traditions of the Great Mother. In many archaic traditions the Mother is shapeless chaos. Some interpret the word *tehom,* the "abyss" of Gen. 1:2, as being derived from *Tiamat,* the Babylonian goddess of the waters. In the legend of Gilgamesh the goddess Aruru shaped human beings from clay. In the Sumer myths of origin the goddess Nammu is the sea-mother who generated earth and heaven.[7] Perhaps these notions filter through to Genesis, where the waters seem not to be created within ("At the beginning Elohim created heaven and earth"), but no mention of the waters (where the "spirit of God moved upon the face of the waters," Gen. 1:1–2) is made herein.

---

[6] See U. Cassuto, *A Commentary,* 130.

[7] See W. G. Lambert, *Ancient Cosmologies* (London: Allen and Unwin, 1975).

The original mother, as R. L. Rubenstein has said, is the same great cannibal that reabsorbs into herself, that devours the living and annihilates them in their graves. The mother goddess was two-faced, the loving life-giver and life-supporter, but also the dreadful ogress. In Judaism each significant crossing represents a choice between chaos and cosmos. Once the Goddess who generated the deepest chaotic distress was relinquished, the Jews confidently turned to the Lord of creation and to His laws.[8]

Genesis and some of the mythological themes of the Mediterranean area appear to have features of the male/female relationship in common. In the Gilgamesh legend a sacred prostitute transformed Enkidu—Gilgamesh's double—into a human being by giving him knowledge of himself through face-to-face (human) sexuality. In the Gilgamesh epic, Siduri is the goddess of knowledge and the garden is her kingdom. In Eden Eve leads Adam from nature to the knowledge of good and evil, to the discovery of his animal nakedness and the resulting need to cover his body. A serpent steals the herb of eternal youth from Gilgamesh, thus precluding immortality; in Eden the serpent's seduction precludes Adam and Eve from the tree of life (Gen. 3:24). Furthermore, fatal gardens are linked to the myth of female custody, such as the Garden of the Hesperides where the snake Ladon guards inaccessible fruits: Hercules, aided by Prometheus, steals into the garden to become immortal.[9] See also Mircea Eliade, *Traité d'histoire des religions* (Paris: Payot, 1948), ch. 8, which associates the Great Goddess and the tree of life in Egypt and Mesopotamia. Siduri and Calypso were also among

---

[8] Richard L. Rubenstein in *The Religious Imagination: A Study in Psychoanalysis and Jewish Theology* (Indianapolis: Bobbs Merrill, 1968).

[9] Karl Kerenyi, *The Gods of the Greeks* (*Die Mythologie der Griechen*, 1951) (New York: Thames and Hudson, 1979). "Aeschylus in the tragedy of *Prometheus Bound* gave Hercules an advisor and a seer in the person of the punished Titan, a benefactor of humankind" who stole fire from the sky to give it to human beings. "Assteas of Paestum describes the scene... with Calypso whose island belong to the same kingdom over the world's end to which the Garden of Hesperides belonged. She offered the dragon to drink from a cup; the dragon sips it and fails to see that a Hesperides is picking fruit and Hercules has been given one. These fruits were the property of the gods" (190).

the many theophanies of the Great Goddess which appear at the center of the world, in the *omphalos* next to the tree of life and the four springs in a garden. In Eden a woman takes the initiative and plays a Promethean role: she breaks the prohibition and gathers the divine element of knowledge for human beings.

In Eden the female element is originally the more active side, which later turns to subordination. As in other mythical gardens the tale is that of a progressive rotation, from female protagonism to male power.

The garden has a center and two trees are planted in it, of life and knowledge respectively (Gen. 2:19). As in the case of man, the garden is the place where the refraction of heaven falls on the earth: *vertically*, pathways towards the divine prerogatives, immortality and knowledge, like trees growing upwards; *horizontally* "a river flows out of Eden to irrigate the garden and from there splits to form four streams" (Gen. 2:10) to irrigate the world's regions.[10] The four rivers are the link between Eden and the earth which will be populated by the generations of human beings. Eden is immanent in the history and geography of civilizations: it is the hydraulic heart of the world.

The great riverscape seems to outline a map: Mesopotamia on one side, the Nile on the other (Rashi's interpretation of the Pishon River). These are the mother lands of Israel: Abraham leaves Mesopotamia with the first family of Jews. Egypt is the Lord's garden (Gen. 13:10) which Moses left with the people who had become a multitude. They have been lands of sorrow but also of homesickness, of yearning. The wealth of water is a lost paradise, and Eden, the land of departure with no return, the incubator of human history, is a well-watered garden, a superabundant oasis.[11] It is an original superabundance holding a pro-

---

[10] The rivers are the Pishon, the Gihon, the Hiddequel and the Ferat (Euphrates). Only the last of the four has been clearly identified. On this subject see the *Encyclopaedia Judaica* entry on Paradise (Jerusalem: Keter, 1971); Von Rad, 96–98; and Cassuto, 114–121. On Eden and its geographic position, see *Encyclopaedia Judaica*, 78.

[11] On the meaning of the word Eden, Cassuto rejects the Sumero-Accadic derivation from *edinu* (desert, steppe) and prefers the Hebrew word *aden* (to cool and regenerate). Eden thus means a well-watered place (Cassuto 107–108). He compares the garden in Genesis and the one in Ezekiel 28:11–19 and 31:8–9 (74–82).

phetic promise: "you will draw water joyfully from the salvation springs" (Isaiah 12:3).

A place, therefore, with a center, a great spring, perhaps an enclosure, access to which will be protected by the cherubim with their swords of fire, an enclosure crossed by the flow of the four rivers. Eden's layout could be described as a Mandala, an elementary shape, a pole, the world's axis branching out in four directions. It is the relationship between the one and the many: "The garden is the woman, the river penetrates her and sprinkles her; up to this time everything had been one, but as from this point there is separation, moving downwards: from here there is splitting" (*Zohar*, Ber. 2, 35).

"So the human being has become like one of us, because he knows good and evil" (Gen. 3:22). Indeed, the (male) human being was unique when he was created in God's image, according to Gen. 2: "but it is not good for him to be alone, I shall make him a help meet for him" (Gen. 2:18), and the woman was created from his side.

Now we can read the Biblical passage as a parable of the anthropocentric affirmation from its inception to its crisis: it peaks as human beings become nearly God-like, but it ends with man's de-centering, dividing the human into man and woman, expelling them from the center, from God's place.

The Mystical Architecture of Eden in the Jewish Tradition

Giulio Busi Eden

The "earthly Paradise" is not a place to be found in the Hebrew Bible. A long cultural process has in fact transformed the biblical "garden of Eden" into this deeply evocative space located between heaven and earth. The locution "terrestrial paradise" does not actually translate any biblical expression, but simply substitutes the *gan 'eden* of the Genesis—that can be interpreted, literally, as "pleasure garden"[1]—with a noun of Persian origin, "Paradise," and an adjective, "terrestrial," that has no exact equivalent in biblical Hebrew. Furthermore, in the metamorphosis from "Eden" to "Paradise," the explicit mention of pleasure, with its specific qualification of the "garden," has been erased.

The word "Paradise" (*pardes* in Hebrew), which can be found in other biblical books,[2] is in fact extraneous to the story of Adam. In Talmudic and Midrashic literature, the expression *gan 'eden* is constantly used to indicate the divine garden, while *pardes* invariably denotes a garden planted by man.[3] Thus, the "terrestrial Paradise" can be consid-

---

[1] The relationship between *'Eden* and "pleasure" is obvious. It is true that the biblical expression: *wa-yitta' gan be-'eden* ("and the Lord God planted a garden eastward in Eden," Gen. 2:8), implies a topographical meaning, and suggested the idea of a different etymology of the word. See L. Koehler, W. Baumgartner, *Hebräisches und Aramäisches Lexikon zum Alten Testament*, Dritte Auflage, 5 v. (Leiden 1967–1995), s.v. *'eden* II.

[2] *Cant.* 4.13; Neh. 2:8 and Eccl. 2:5.

[3] The most relevant exception to this use is the well-known episode of "the four that entered the *pardes*" (t*Hagigah* II.3, b*Hagigah* 14b and y*Hagigah* II.77b). In this case, the term refers to the attainment of a mystical goal, that has been explicitly identified with the *gan 'eden* by medieval Jewish authors (see Y. Liebes, *Heto shel Elisha'. Arba'ah she-nikhnesu la-pardes ve-tiv'ah shel ha-mistiqah ha-talmudit*, Jerusalem 1990[2] [1986[1]]). It must be noted, however, that the mention of the four "who entered" (*she-niknesu*) seems to be inappropriate to the idea of Eden, where one can be admitted, but certainly not enter, on one's own initiative (see Gen. 2:15: "And the Lord God took the man, and put him (va-yannihehu) into the garden of Eden"). The word *pardes* must therefore signify, in this passage, an inner experience that only alludes to the real entrance into the garden.

ered a creation of Western languages.[4] This locution, recalling the idea of another Paradise—the heavenly one—splits, so to speak, the single or unique paradise, as if the banishment of Adam had created another place. It seems that the splitting of human destiny also doubled that unique garden. In the Hebrew tradition, however, the garden remains unique. To understand this, it is necessary to go back to the primordial creation.

There is a symbolic space that separates, in Jewish exegesis, the secret of divine silence from the actual manifestation of creation. It is as though the scene were suspended in expectation of the event, which is at hand but still concealed. In this interlude, which precedes the expression of the divine will—i.e., before the Creator commences the creation of the world—seven entities make a crown around God. Fixed on an eternal background, hidden to worldly view, they exist only for the Lord's delight.

A passage from the *Midrash Tehillim* enumerates the antecedents of creation: "Seven things, by two thousand years, preceded the creation of the world: the Torah, the throne of glory, the garden of Eden, Gehenna, Repentance, the Sanctuary in heaven and the name of the Messiah."[5] At first this list looks heterogeneous, as it puts together four spatial images—the throne of glory, Eden, Gehenna and the Temple, considered in its supernal archetype—and two notions that refer to the historical and cultural identity of the Jewish people: the Torah and the name of the Messiah. Among the seven symbols there is only one dynamic element, expressed by the word *teshuvah*. *Teshuvah* means, literally, "return" and also, in an ethical sense, "repentance" or "conversion." In accordance with its literal value, *teshuvah* indicates, in medieval and modern kabbalistic literature, the movement that brings every thing and every being back to its supernal origin, i.e. to the *Sefirah* of intelli-

[4] As is well known, the Greek *paradeisos* translates *gan 'Eden* already in the *Septuagint*.
[5] Midrash Tehillim XC.12 (*The Midrash on Psalms,* trans. from the Hebrew and Aramaic by W. G. Braude [New Haven 1959], Vol. 2, 94).
[6] See, for instance, Moses Cordovero, *Pardes rimmonim,* (Cracow and Nowydwor, 1591), c. 174v (*Sha'ar 'erkei ha-kinnuyim* XXII).

gence (*Binah*), the first source of dualistic existence.[6] Foreshadowing kabbalistic symbolism, the presence of the word *teshuvah* in the *Midrash* list may therefore be interpreted as an allusion to the path that brings back the other six eternal entities to their original place, i.e. to the unchanging center of creation.[7] Although all seven symbolic images come from the same divine space, their differences mark the manifold path towards the center. In other words, each one of the eternal entities opens a door to comprehension and—in its own unique way—offers an access to divine immobility.

Among these different symbolic paths towards the heart of the cosmic architecture, the one represented by the garden of Eden traces perhaps the most direct and general route. The image of the garden is in fact linked to the Adamic tale, and therefore precedes the definition of any specific Jewish cultural dominion. In fact, it is no accident that in the symbolic chain of the seven entities Eden was preceded only by one more general and higher image: the throne of glory, which nevertheless strictly pertains to God. Thus, while the throne belongs to God (being his regal emblem), and the other five symbols are related to Hebrew identity, only the garden—open to Adam—features the scene of a welcome originally prepared for every man.

Many pages of rabbinical literature and later mystical writings assert the value of the garden as universal symbol of the center for all human beings. A passage of the *Zohar*, for example, reads:

---

[7] The meaning of *teshuvah* as a return to the celestial abode is already suggested by b*Yoma* 86a: "R. Levi said: Great is repentance, for it reaches up to the Throne of Glory, as it is said: *Return, O Israel, unto the Lord thy God* (*Os.* 14.2)." The word *teshuvah* is used, in the wider meaning of "return," also in *Gen. Rabbah* XXI.6 (*Pesiqta rabbati* VII and *Num. Rabbah* XIII.3): "R. Abba b. Kahana said: This teaches that the Holy One, blessed be He, opened for him the gate of return. *And now*: this can only refer to repentance, as you read, *And now, Israel, what doth the Lord God require of thee, but to fear the Lord thy God*, etc." (Deut. 10:12). Concerning the literal meaning of the Hebrew *petach shel teshuvah* compare *Cant. Rabbah* V.2 and the expression *sha'arei teshuvah* (e.g. in *Deut. Rabbah* II.12; this gate, through which pass the Jews who repented, is described in *Zohar hadash, Midrash Ruth*, 82d).

> When the Holy One, blessed be He, admitted him [*i.e.* Adam] to the garden of Eden, he was able to see and to know from there all the supernal secrets and every wisdom. He was therefore able to perceive the splendour of his Master.[8]

The entrance to the garden therefore symbolizes the human possibility of reaching a privileged vantage point from which a higher knowledge may be obtained.

Just as the artifice of anamorphosis presents an image distorted in such a way that it becomes visible only when observed from a special perspective, thus only the vantage point of the center permits us to understand the complexity of reality. The divine perspective alone actually allows an order to the design of creation, while any other vantage point deforms it. This means also that to be banished from the garden means to be removed from the center and to lose this vantage point.

According to the Jewish tradition, however, the exile from the garden is temporary, since an ineluctable force brings all souls back after death to their origin. However, the path of this return is twofold since it reflects an essential worldly dichotomy: the contrast between the Jewish people and the other Nations gives rise to the division of the ultramundane space of the garden in Eden and Gehenna, the former reserved to the children of Israel, the latter a dwelling of sorrow for other peoples. The apparently surprising idea of a unique symbolic center, which joins the abode of the just to that of the wicked, is justified by the conception that one unique power permeates reality. From the center, therefore, the mosaic of the cosmos moves and, at the same time, everything goes back to the center, nonetheless maintaining, in the final stasis, the principle of dichotomy that rules the universe. The return of Israel to Eden is a conscious process, traced out by the coherent symbolism of biblical prescriptions. The return of the Gentiles on the other hand appears to be a negative process, devoid of any consciousness, and passively undergone. In consequence, Gehenna too can be seen as a kind of specular image of Eden, almost a rhetorical negation, necessary only to give more value to the recompense reserved for the Jews. Even

---

[8] *Zohar* I.38a.

in their substantial difference of quality, the two places are extremely close to one another:

> Gehenna and Eden. What's the distance between them? A hand's breadth. Rabbi Yochanan says: [They are divided by] a wall. The Rabbis say: They are parallel, so that one should be visible to the other.[9]

Gehenna and Eden are as close as the distinction between good and evil, which is often so subtle as to be almost imperceptible. Nevertheless this difference, faint in appearance, becomes an untraversable distance, a barrier which divides—until the Last Judgment—the punishment of the wicked among the Nations from the enjoyment of the just among Israel.

The representation of the wall dividing these two portions of the garden translates a notion of moral character into an architectonic symbolism, in accordance with the rabbinical idea of the cosmos as an architectural structure. In the Midrashic and mystical texts the creation of the universe is compared, in fact, to the building of a house, in which God, as the supreme Architect, followed the plan dictated by His own wisdom.[10] The disposition of the cosmic building follows an archetypal pattern and gives rise to the terrestrial as well as to the heavenly dwelling, eternal and incorruptible.[11] A strict correspondence between high

---

[9] *Eccl. Rabbah* VII.14.3.

[10] The building symbolism is already common in the Bible: see, for instance, Isaiah 5:2; Amos 9:6; Psalm 78:69, 102.17, 127.1, 147.2 and in Prov. 8:29–30. As for the rabbinical literature, the relevant texts are: b*Hagigah* 12a, *Tanhuma, Be-ha'alotekha,* XI and *Num. Rabbah* XV.18. See also *Gen. Rabbah* I.1; *Tanhuma* (ed. Buber), *Pequde,* VIII; *Eccl. Rabbah* III.1.11; *Midrash Zuta to Cant.* I, where *boneh,* "builder" is one of God's epithets; *Alfa beta de-rabbi 'Aqiva* (A. Jellinek, *Bet ha-Midrasch. Sammlung kleiner Midraschim und vermischter Abhandlungen aus der ältern jüdischen Literatur,* 6 vols. [Leipzig 1853–1878], Vol. 3, 12–49: 18).

[11] See, for instance, *Zohar* II.226a: "R. Eleazar further discoursed on the verse: *A song of ascents; of Solomon. Except the Lord build the house, thy labour is in vain* (Psalm 127:1). This verse—he said—was uttered by Solomon at the time when, having begun to build the Temple he became aware that the work proceeded of itself, as it were, in the hands of the labourers. *Except the Lord*—he thus said—*build the house,* etc. This alludes to the statement that *In the beginning God created heaven and earth* (Gen. 1:1), and tells us that the Holy One, blessed be He, created and garnished this world and fitted it out with all its requirements, thus making it a House."

and low makes every part of the world reflect an equal design and a similar proportion in the mansion above.

In post-biblical Judaism, the structure of heaven is often imagined as a succession of buildings which grow, from heaven to heaven, ever more ethereal and bright. Behind their insurmountable walls is concealed the glory of the angelic ranks and divine splendor.

> In seven sanctuaries—we read for instance in the *Hekhalot rabbati*—dwells *Twtrwsy'y*, the Lord God of Israel, and one room is inside the other one; and at the gate of every palace there are eight guardians of the threshold, four at the right and four at the left of the door.[12]

Similarly, the Edenic space too is represented as a series of palaces, in which souls dwell in accordance with their dignity.[13]

It is interesting to recall that the idea of a welcome prepared for the just in the divine palace is rooted so deeply in the Hebrew tradition that it emerges unexpectedly in a passage of the Gospels:

> "In my Father's house"—says Jesus—"are many mansions: if it were not so, I would have told you. I go to prepare a place for you. And if I go and prepare a place for you, I will come again, and receive you unto myself; that where I am, there ye may be also" (John 14:2–3).[14]

The *many mansions* of the Father's house correspond to the seven buildings of Jewish medieval mysticism, that open one inside the other, marking a progressive enhancement of pleasures and ornaments until the peak of the seventh palace which, according to the *Zohar,* is "the most hidden and concealed of all. In the center there is a column of many colors: green, white, red and black. When the souls ascend, they enter this palace, each one assuming its appropriate color.[15]

To the seven Edenic mansions correspond as many dwellings of darkness and suffering, that transform the indistinct abyss of Gehenna into an articulated negative architecture:

---

[12] *Synopse zur Hekhalot-Literatur,* eds. P. Schäfer et al. (Tübingen, 1981), 206.

[13] See already the *Midrash Konen,* in Jellinek, *Bet ha-Midrasch,* v. 2, 23–39: 28 ff.

[14] Compare Eccl. 12:5: "Because man goes to his eternal home [*el bet 'olamo*], and the mourners go about the streets.

[15] *Zohar* I.39a–b.

> We have therefore demonstrated that there are different degrees and palaces in the side of impurity as well as in the side of holiness.... There are seven palaces, corresponding to the seven names of Gehenna.[16]

Thus, the palaces of Gehenna are the result of transgressions, and the matter of which they are made is the darkness which accompanies every act of arrogance. Moreover, a line of malignant spirits stands before the dark architecture, each one watching over a particular entrance, corresponding to a different level of impiousness. Unlike the archangels of light, who jealously guard the doors of heaven, these evil archons push the wicked towards a dwelling that opens wide like a precipice.

In the pages of Hebrew literature, then, the architectonic metaphor of the ultramundane space represents a fundamental symbolism, in which images clearly explain the idea of recompense and punishment. The wall that in the *Midrash* divides the two halves of the garden, as well as the number of palaces of Gehenna and Eden described in the *Zohar*, and the disposition of the seven eternal entities inside the heart of the Edenic space, all interpret the same basic idea: the garden is nothing more than a part of the larger heavenly mansion, a closed space enshrined in a wider architectural project. The rural scenery of the biblical tale has been transformed. The primordial garden, apparently located by Genesis in an abstract background, appears suddenly surrounded by the majestic structure of the divine palace. As a matter of fact, the garden of Eden is the heart of the heavenly palace, and Adam its guardian. Inside the architecture of the palace, the garden naturally has the function of the delightful place where God goes for a walk *in the cool of the day* (Gen. 3:8). The "pleasure" to which the Hebrew word *'eden* alludes, then, means first of all the delight of God, while anyone else looking at the garden may only perceive the reflection of that pleasure.[17]

---

[16] *Zohar* II.263a.

[17] This is why the *kabbalah* identifies Eden with *keter 'elyon*, the supernal Crown, the highest and most hidden among the *Sefirot*. See, for instance, Cordovero, *Pardes* cit., c. 163v: "the true Eden is in the supernal Crown [...] the Eden is only above; if sometimes a lower Eden is referred to, it does not mean that any one among the lower *Sefirot* can be properly termed Eden."

Being the place of divine delight, Eden becomes also, in the Jewish tradition, the abode of royalty. The disposition of the seven eternal entities shows that rabbinical literature puts the throne of God in the heart of the garden, which is the focal center of the entire representation of Eden as well as of the still space which precedes the creation. Thus the garden, at the center of which stands the throne of glory, is the royal audience room, which only those admitted to the sovereign's presence can enter. It is the appointed place for the meeting between God and the people who come before Him. In the garden God talks to Adam, and in the garden He waits for the souls who come back to Him. No doubt the historical model closest to this is the *apadâna* of the Persian sovereign,[18] the pavilion of the royal palace in which the King of kings sat in his throne to receive his subjects.[19] In some texts of the Jewish tradition the link which ties the description of the divine audience room to the earthly royal one is clearly shown. For instance, in the *Pirkei De Rebbe Eliezer,* an early medieval *Midrash,* we can read: "[God] let Adam into his *apadâna,* as it is written: *And put him into the garden of Eden to cultivate it and to keep it*" (Gen. 2:15).[20]

The depiction of the garden of Eden, as it appears in the second chapter of Genesis, can therefore be compared to a scene taken from very close up, with a short-focus lens: moving back a little way the garden becomes visible in its spatial location, surrounded by the marvelous walls of the divine palace.

---

[18] The Hebrew term *appeden,* a loan-word from Persian, is mentioned in Dan. 11:45,: *Ohole appadeno* ("the tents of his pavilion").

[19] On the characteristics of the royal *apadâna* see, for instance, the description given by M. Dieulafoy (*Le livre d'Esther et le palais d'Assuérus,* in "Revue des études juives," *Actes et conferences* 1 (1888), CCLXV–CCXCI). Dieulafoy identifies the biblical *bitan* (located in the palace of Ahasuerus, in Esth. 1:5, 7:7 and 7:8) with the *apadâna.* It is interesting to note that the *Zohar* (II.196a) considers equal *bitan* and *gan 'Eden*: "[At midnight] the Holy One, blessed be He, enters the garden of Eden, for He finds no comfort until He goes there to have joyous communion with the souls of the righteous. This is the allegorical meaning of the verses: For we are sold, I and my people.... Then spoke the King... Who is he...? And the King arose in his wrath from the banquet of wine and went into the garden of the pavilion (*el ginnat ha-bitan* [Esth. 7:4–7])." For a Midrashic description of the *bitan* see *Esther Rabbah* II.6.

[20] *Pirkei De Rebbe Eliezer* XII.

The Ambiguity of Eden and the Enigma of Adam

Gaetano Lettieri

To limit oneself to providing raw materials and a synthesis of some Jewish and Christian interpretations of Eden obviously means resigning oneself to approximations. It means touching on various decisive theological perspectives without going deeply enough into them, and identifying the exegesis of Adam in Eden in Hebrew-Christian theology with protology *tout court*, and therefore with the most intimate theology. The prehistory of the creation, and in particular its culmination in Man, is in fact, theologically speaking, a privileged mirror of the eternal nature of God itself, the image of His original intention, the only foundation for a later theodicy. The articulation of the divine nature in dialectically distinct powers accounts for the double name of God, i.e., *theos* (the name of mercy: God is the Father who gives Himself to the creature) and *kyrios* (the name of sovereignty: God is Law, which orders and punishes to convert from difference to unity). This articulation should be explained starting from the need to harmonize the logic of participation (in the intimacy of love) and the logic of theodicy (the necessary metaphysical difference and creatural subordination). God is therefore confessed as the harmony of opposites, of the good of creation and the evil that is in any case subordinate to and finalized to this good.[1] In addition, eschatology and—in the Christian texts—Christology are immanent in the anthropology of Eden not only as a reconstitution of lost integrity postulated by the faultless creational intention of God, but also as an overcoming of an original lack of definition, of an original imperfection even, which can be removed and fulfilled only through divinity. God Himself overcomes His motionless and extrinsic lordship over Eden by taking on Himself the responsibility for the sins of man and of the world.

---

[1] See *Somn.* XXVI.162; *Mutat* III.15–26; *Her.* XXXIV.166; *Quod Deus Sit Immutabilis* XVI.75–XVII.81; *Plant* XX.85–89. On this, see N. A. Dahl and A. F. Segal, "Philo and the Rabbis on the Names of God," in *Journal of the Study of Judaism*, 9 (1978), 1–28; and A. M. Mazzanti, "*Theos* e *Kyrios*. I 'nomi' di Dio in Filone di Alessandria," in *Studi storici religiosi*, 5 (1981), 15–31.

The interpretations of Eden turn out, not surprisingly, to be many and varied. Eden as an absolutely perfect beginning, as the immanence of the created in God Himself, and therefore as an identity to be recovered; Eden as a prison of gratified desire, as an order or ontological system transcended by desire, absolute and fiendish stasis from which we must free ourselves; Eden as the place of full maturity, of human lordship (and therefore implicitly of man's own self-sufficient pride); Eden as the place of mankind's childhood, if not of an idiotic innocence, of a paralyzing ecstasy before the transcendence of natural beauty, in an abandon which prevents or precedes the reawakening of consciousness; Eden as a joy which is only apparent because unstable and undetermined or indefinite; Eden as the place of the human-divine passion, as the place or cryptic image of the tragic, intradivine split.

So what meaning can be given to the luxurious and, as it were, hypnotic perfection of the beauty of the garden, the innocent nudity of the body of Adam and a nature with no secrets for him, and the motionless flowing of the waters? Can Eden be a paradoxically atheistic or Godless place precisely in its being the total immersion of the creature in God, where the lack of distance itself can mean the absence of the recognition of divine transcendence? Is not sin therefore less the Hegelian awareness of the intradivine absoluteness of the finite, than the shadow itself or else the trace of having the qualities of a creature and its infinite distance from God? In this sense, is not Eden paradoxically the place of stasis, or rather of gifts and grace gone into hiding? Is it not therefore the place of the anguished solitude of the liberty of the creature, a freedom lost even before sin, precisely because abandoned to its own devices?[2]

---

[2] In the vast literature on Gen. 2–3 I would single out the extensive analysis in O. H. Steck, "Die Paradieserzählung, Eine Auslegung von Genesis 2,4b–3,24," in *Wahrnehmungen Gottes im Alten Testament* (Munich 1982), 9–116; see too the recent synthesis of P. Morris and D. Sawyer (eds.), *A Walk in the Garden: Biblical, Iconographical and Literary Images of Eden* (Sheffield 1992). For a quick summary of Christian exegesis of Eden of the first three centuries, see ch. 15 in A. Orbe, *Introducción a la teología de los siglos II y III* (Rome 1987), 255–268. On Patristic exegesis of Gen. 1:26–27 and 2:7, see R. M. Wilson, "The Early History of the Exegesis of Gen. 1:26," in *Studia Patristica*, 1 (Berlin 1957), 420–437; G. Visonà, "L'uomo a immagine di Dio.

1. Adam *Redivivus* or New Adam? The Gospel of Mark, the Ebionites, and Paul

The Gospel of Mark presents the figure of Jesus by now adult with a very veiled, not always recognized[3] and yet theologically decisive identification with the new Adam:

> And it came to pass in those days, that Jesus came from Nazareth of Galilee, and was baptized of John in Jordan. And straightway coming up out of the

---

L'interpretazione di Gen. 1,26 nel pensiero cristiano dei primi tre secoli," in *Studia patavina*, 27 (1980), 393–430; S. Raponi, "Il tema dell'immagine somiglianza nell'antropologia dei Padri," in E. Ancilli, *Temi di antropologia teologica* (Rome 1981), 241–341; A. Hamman, *L'homme image de Dieu. Essai d'une anthropologie chrétienne dans l'Église des cinq premiers siècles* (Paris 1987).

The enigmatic complexity of the biblical text is shown by the wildly contradictory nature of the most recent interpretations. See, for example, J. van Seters, "The Creation of Man and the Creation of the King," in *Zeitschrift für die Alttestamentliche Wissenschaft*, 101 (1989), 333–341; M. Hutter, "Adam als Gärtner und König (Gen. 2,8–15)," in *Biblische Zeitschrift*, 30 (1986), 258–262; J. F. A. Sawyer, "The Image of God, the Wisdom of Serpents and the Knowledge of Good and Evil," in *A Walk in the Garden*, 64–73; T. Stordalen, "Man, Soil, Garden: Basic Plot in Genesis 2–3 Reconsidered," in *Journal for the Study of the Old Testament*, 53 (1992), 3–26; D. P. Wright, "Holiness, Sex and Death in the Garden of Eden," in *Biblica*, 77 (1996), 305–329; G. Anderson, "Celibacy or Consummation in the Garden? Reflections on Early Jewish and Christian Interpretations of the Garden of Eden," in *Harvard Theological Review*, 82 (1989), 121–148.

[3] See however J. Daniélou, *Sacramentum futuri. Études sur les origines de la typologie biblique* (Paris 1950), 8–9, and R. Pesch, *Das Markusevangelium* (Freiburg im Breisgau 1997), 2/e. See also two interesting recent contributions: C. Grappe, "Bâpteme de Jésus et bâpteme des premiers chrétiens," in *Revue d'histoire et de philosophie religieuses*, 73 (1993–1994), 377–393; U. Mell, "Jesu Taufe durch Johannes (Markus 1,9–15) zur narrativen Christologie vom neuen Adam," in *Biblische Zeitschrifte*, 40 (1996), 161–178. Justin already perfectly picks up the adamite reference in the connection between baptism and temptation: see *Dialogue with Trypho* 103,6; see too Irenaeus, *Adversus Haereses* V.21.2. Already in the *Testament of Levi* the prophecy of the Messiah was actualized in the waiting for the return of paradisal blessedness: "He will open the doors of paradise and ward off the sword pointing at Adam. He will give the tree of life to the saints to eat and on them the spirit of holiness will alight" (XVIII, 10–11). On the evolution of Judaic messianism in the Greek age, and especially on its adamite characterization, see W. Bousset, *Die Religion des Judentums im späthellenistischen Zeitalter* (Tübingen 1926), 261. On the relation between Adam in Eden and Jesus in the wilderness, see Ambrose, *Exp. Ev. Luc.* IV, 82–98.

> water, he saw the heavens opened, and the Spirit like a dove descending upon him: And there came a voice from heaven, saying: Thou art my beloved Son, in whom I am well pleased. And immediately the spirit driveth him into the wilderness. And he was there in the wilderness forty days, tempted of Satan; and was with the wild beasts; and the angels ministered unto him.

There seem to be systematic analogies between the protohistory of the Genesis Adam and the baptism of Jesus as the origin of the new creation. First, the re-emergence of Jesus (nude?) from the waters of life reactualizes the waters of Eden, above all the descent of the Spirit (the same vital breath of Gen. 2:7) on the waters (see Gen. 1:2 and the paradisal river in Gen. 2:10). The waters of Genesis also figure the symbol of the chrism, the messianic Spirit (see Isaiah 61:1–2) and the new alliance between God and man represented by the dove of Noah (see Gen. 8:11: the dove returns with an *olive* branch).[4] The above-cited reopening of the heavens and the divine voice which reaffirms the reacquired perfect offspring, the glorious "being in (His) image" of the man Jesus in whom God is pleased recalls Isaiah 42:1 and 63:11–19 and

---

[4] This would be enough to reject S. Gero's hypothesis in "The Spirit as a Dove at the Baptism of Jesus," in *Novum Testamentum*, 18 (1976), 17–35, which considers the descent of the Spirit and the appearance of a dove as dependent on two originally separate traditions. Mell, *Jesu Taufe*, 174–177, basing himself entirely on Philo, *Her.* XXV,126, interprets the dove as a symbol of Sophia (Spirit): "In der Person Jesu, so das Bild des Geistes als Taube, hat Gottes gütige Schöpfungsweisheit ihren Ort gefunden" (176). On the relation in Judaism between Spirit and water symbolism (starting from Gen. 1:2), and on its messianic significance, see F. Manns, *Le symbole eau-esprit dans le judaïsme ancien* (Jerusalem 1983); see esp. 113–120, devoted to "the testaments of the twelve Patriarchs." On the dove as symbol of the Spirit of God (by the Palestinian *midrasim* significantly identified with the spirit or the soul of Adam or of the Messiah) in the rabbinical tradition, see L. Ginzberg, *The Legends of the Jews*, I–VII (Philadelphia–New York 1909–1938), Vol. V, 7, note 15; see too *ibid.*, the rabbinical identification of the Spirit of God who wings above the waters with the soul of Adam, in which are contained all the souls of all men (see Numenius, in Porphyry, *De Anthro. Nympharum* 10=fr. 30 Des Places), or with the soul of the Messiah himself, considered by Ginzberg as a reaction to the Christian interpretation of Gen. 2, referred to the Holy Spirit.

above all Psalm 2:7, where a reference to the creation of Adam seems to be possible, as fulfilling the "it was very good" of Gen. 1:31.

If at first sight these analogies may appear forced or dubious, they gain strength from the analogies, a good deal more evident, concerning the episode of the temptation of Jesus. This temptation is the other inseparable side of the baptism for the synoptic tradition: Jesus is pulled away violently from the Spirit (an analogous and contrary movement to that of the expulsion from paradise) and placed for forty days[5] in the closed-in and lonely place of Satan's temptation (the desert is the image of Eden turned upside down, the place fit for the punishment capable of taking away the sin of Adam). Jesus lives in the peaceful company of the wild animals where the original harmony of creation is recovered, together with Adam's lordship over the beasts (See Gen. 1:26 and, in an eschatological perspective, Isaiah 11:6–8 and 65:25).[6] In the desert Jesus is served by (receives nourishment from?) the angels,[7] which corresponds

---

[5] In the *Book of the Jubilee* 3,9, Adam waits forty days before being introduced into Eden: "And after forty days were completed for Adam in the land where he was created, we brought him into the garden of Eden so that he might work it and guard it" (trans. O. S. Wintermute, in J. H. Charlesworth, ed., *The Old Testament Pseudepigrapha*, II [New York 1985], 59). Cfr. A. Orbe, "Los primeros 40 dias de Adán," in *Gregorianum*, 46 (1965), 96–103.

[6] One of the consequences of Adam's sin is the enmity between man and beasts, man having lost the glory of the divine image; see *The Life of Adam and Eve, Apocalypse (of Moses)* 10–11; *The Life of Adam and Eve, Vita* 37–38. The recovery of Adam's state is a mark of the Messiah: "And the wild beasts will come from the wood and serve man, and the asps and dragons will come out of their holes to subject themselves to a child. And women will no longer have pain when they bear, nor will they be tormented when they yield the fruits of their womb" (*2 [Syriac Apocalypse of] Baruch* 73,6–7), trans. A. F. J. Klijn, in J. H. Charlesworth, ed., *The Old Testament Pseudepigrapha*, I, [New York 1983], 645–646).

[7] The *Life of Adam and Eve, Vita 4* is interesting here: once expelled from paradise, Adam and Eve "walked searching for nine days and found nothing such as they had had in Paradise, but only such as animals eat. And Adam said to Eve: 'The Lord apportioned this for animals and beasts to eat, but for us there used to be the food of angels. But it is just and fitting for us to lament in the sight of God who made us. Let us repent with a great penitence; perhaps the Lord God will be forbearing and pity us and provide for us that we might live'" (trans. M. D. Johnson, in *The Old Testament Pseudepigrapha*, II, 258).

to the information we have in some Judaic apocrypha of the angels as servants and dispensers of food to the pre-lapsarian Adam.[8]

The paradisal symbolism and eschatological significance of the scene of the messianic baptism, and of the temptation in the desert, are definitively proved by references to certain passages in Isaiah:

> "Until the spirit be poured upon us from on high, and the wilderness be a fruitful field, and the fruitful field be counted for a forest. Then judgment shall dwell in the wilderness, and righteousness remain in the fruitful field. And the work of righteousness shall be peace, and the effect of righteousness quietness and assurance forever. And my people shall dwell in a peaceable habitation, and in sure dwellings, and in quiet resting places." Isaiah 32:15–18

> "For the Lord shall comfort Zion: he will comfort all her waste places; and he will make her wilderness like Eden, and her desert like the garden of the Lord..." (Isaiah 51:3)[9]

Starting with the baptism on the Jordan, then, it is possible to discern behind some passages of Mark the germinal cell of what is well and truly a *Geistchristologie.*[10] Certainly the ideology is more complex than a mere adoptionistic Christology: the Holy Spirit is the *dynamis,* the transcendent divine force which, united with Jesus at the Jordan, frees man from subjection to the demon. Decisive on this in Mark 3:22–30 are the harsh and tortured words of Jesus against those (including his kin) who do not recognize within and beyond the man Jesus the presence and action (redemptive and exorcistic) of the Spirit of God, blaspheming against it. I therefore propose that Mark 3:31–35, where Jesus

---

[8] On the angels as guardians and dispensers of the food of the trees of paradise, see *The Life of Adam and Eve, Apocalypse (of Moses)* 7.

[9] See Isaiah 29:17: Lebanon is eschatologically transformed by God into a paradisal garden. See 1 Kings 17:2–6; 18:19–40 and 19:4–8; 2 Kings 2:1–25, on the Jordan as the place where the prophetic investiture occurs; on the place near the Jordan where Elijah is fed by the ravens; on the forty days of Elijah in the desert nourished by the angels; on Mount Carmel as the place of the theophany (New Eden?); on the revelation of God as (Elijah's) spirit which descends on the prophet Elisha, and on the prophet Elijah seized with the spirit.

[10] On the *Geistchristologie*, see M. Simonetti, "Cristologia pneumatica," in *Augustinianum*, 12, (1972), 201–232, now also in *Studi sulla cristologia del II e III secolo* (Rome 1993), 23–52.

refuses to acknowledge his mother and his earthly brothers, implies originally a christological confession concerning the Holy Spirit (feminine in Hebraic) as true celestial mother of Jesus.[11] Jesus has become at baptism a new creature, the perfect Son of God—the first among many brothers—in whom the divine Spirit-Mother has just assumed a new identity.[12]

In spite of many differences it is interesting to link these Marcian-like features of adamitic *Geistchristologie* to a Judeo-Christian Christological tradition which we can, however approximately, define as Ebionite.[13] Ebionite Christology appears in the first place within the

---

[11] This interpretation of the gospel episode seems to me an assumption behind the doctrine of the Ebionites referred to us by Epiphanius, *Panarion* I,30,14,5: "'They deny his humanity, on the basis of the Savior's words, if you please, when he was told, 'Behold, thy mother and thy brethren stand without,'—'Who are my mother and my brethren?'" (trans. F. Williams, *The Panarion of Epiphanius of Salamis*, I [Leiden–New York–Copenhagen–Cologne 1987], 131). This interpretation is explicitly advanced by the Gnostic Gospel of Thomas (*NH* II,2) 99,101=49,21–50,1; see in this sense the Gospel of Philip (*NH* II,3) 80=70,22–33. But on the Holy Spirit as mother of Christ, see again the quotation from *The Gospel of the Jews* reported by Origen, *InIoh* II, 87–88.

[12] See E. Norelli, *L'Ascensione di Isaia. Studi su un apocrifo al crocevia dei cristianesimi* (Bologna 1994), ch. 7: "Tradizioni pneumatologiche retrostanti ad *AI* 3,26–28," 175–182. The doctrine (attested to by the *Ascension of Isaiah* and by the *Shepherd of Hermas*) of the competition between the (unique) Holy Spirit and the (many) demon spirits to occupy the heart of man (on demoniac possession see *Pseudo-Clementines, Hom* IX, 9; *Recogn* IV, 15–16) presupposes for Norelli a Pneuma-Sarx Christology, testified to e.g. by the V similitude of the *Shepherd of Hermas* (177); the gift (not to be contaminated) of a new breathing into the believers of the Spirit is related especially to the reception of baptism (180). Unfortunately Norelli does not deal with the passages in question in Mark.

[13] In my opinion Ebionism cannot be considered as a mere adoptionism, but must be recognized as a particular Cristology "from on high," where the identity of the Holy Spirit (with its ambiguous nature of divine power and supreme angelic creature, or in its identifiability with the pre-existing Adam-Christ) is certainly not comparable to that of the divine *Logos* hypostatically clearly distinct, nor is it even to be considered as merely "impersonal," as A. Orbe argues in his chapter devoted to the Ebionites in *Cristologia gnóstica. Introducción a la soteriología de los siglos II y III* (Madrid 1976), I, 351–379, esp. 361. The only exception for Orbe is that of the *Pseudo-Clementines*: "La teoria del *verus propheta* podria iluminar la preexistencia 'relativa' del Jesús ebioneo.

present corpus of the *Pseudo-Clementines*: Jesus is simply a man who deserves, for his obedience to the Law of the Father, personal and extraordinary union with the Holy Spirit. Such union is the gift of the blessing of the Messiah, identified with the pre-existing Christ, the Archangel-archetype of man who is the Adam of Eden, anointed with the oil of the tree of life[14] and invested with the triple chrism (royal, priestly and prophetic):

> When God had made the world as Lord of the universe, he appointed chiefs over the several creatures.... He set, therefore, an angel as chief over the angels, a spirit over the spirits, ...a man over men, who is Jesus Christ.... Although indeed he was the Son of God, and the beginning of all things, He became man; Him first God anointed with oil which was taken from the wood of the tree of life. From that anointing therefore He is called Christ. Thence, moreover, He Himself also, according to the appointment of his Father, anoints with similar oil every one of the pious when they come to His kingdom..., so that their light may shine, and being filled with the Holy Spirit, they may be endowed with immortality.[15]

The archetypal nature of Christ-Adam brings him very close to the perfect and impeccable "man in (His) image" of Philo, in an intermediate position between God Himself (or His Logos) and the sinning "moulded man." Indeed the First Man, the True Christ, descended into Jesus

---

Entre la preexistencia como Verbo personal o Hijo de Dios y la absoluta no-preexistencia de Jesús, habría lugar a introducir la intermedia, como *verus propheta* (resp. *verus Christus*)" (365); significantly however the paragraph in question is entitled "Al margen del ebionismo." See again A. Orbe, *La unción del Verbo, Estudios valentinianos III* (Rome 1961), 229–323, and esp. the conclusions at 322–323. For an adoptionist reductionism of the Ebionite doctrine, see J. Daniélou, *Théologie du Judéo-Christianisme. Histoire des doctrines chrétiennes avant Nicée* (Paris 1958), 68–76, esp. 75–76.

[14] On the paradisal tree of life as olive tree from which derives the solemn and priestly chrism, see *On the Origin of the World* (*NH* II,5 and XIII, 2) 110,8–111,8 and *EvPhil* 92=73,15–19. It may be remembered that in *EvPhil* 91=73,9–15, the cross on which the man Jesus dies is identified with the tree of life grown in the "paradise" planted by the father, the carpenter Joseph. On the identical nature of the tree of life and the redemptive cross, see *Epistle of Barnabas* 12,5; Justin, *Dialogue with Trypho* 86,1; *AdDiognetum* 12,7–8 and above all Clement of Alexandria, *Stromateis* V, 11,72.

[15] *Pseudo-Clementines, Recognitiones* I, 45 (trans. T. Smith, in *The Ante-Nicene Fathers*, Vol. VIII [Grand Rapids 1970], 2); see I,19 and III, 17–28.

at the Jordan, is the same Adam created in God's "image and likeness,"[16] entirely without sin,[17] remaining firmly in the garden of Eden, anointed by the Holy Spirit released by the tree of life. This Adam, impeccable and absolutely obedient to the Law of the Father, is also the True Prophet, or the identical Spirit or Christ who is incarnated in the prophets throughout the history of the salvation of Israel:

> If any one do not allow the man fashioned by the hands of God to have had the Holy Spirit of Christ, how is he not guilty of the greatest impiety in allowing another born of an impure stock to have it? But he would act most piously, if he should not allow to another to have it, but should say that he alone has it, who has changed his forms and his names from the beginning of the world, and so reappeared again and again in the world, until coming upon his own times, and being anointed with mercy for the works of God, he shall enjoy rest for ever. His honour it is to bear rule and lordship over all things, in air, earth, and waters. But in addition to these, himself having made man, he had breath, the indescribable garment of the soul, that he might be able to be immortal. He himself being the only true prophet, fittingly gave names to each animal, according to the merits of its nature, as having made it. For if he gave a name to any one, that was also the name of that which was made, being given by him who made it. How, then, had he still need to partake of a tree, that he might know what is good and what is evil, if he was commanded not to eat of it? But this senseless men believe.[18]

---

[16] See *Pseudo-Clementines, Hom* I,62, in which impeccable Adam is identified with the Image and the Likeness of God; see also *Hom* III,17.

[17] In reference to the negation of the sin of Adam, see the same non-Ebionite *Epistle of the Apostles*, 31: "To Adam was given the power to choose one of two things; he chose the light and placed his hand upon it. But the darkness he left behind him, and put it away from him." On the insuperable glory of Adam (also post-lapsarian?), see Ecclesiasticus 49:16: "Shem and Seth were glorified among men, but Adam is superior to every living creature;" see above all Wisdom 10:1–2: "Wisdom it was who kept guard over the first father of the human race, created alone as he was; after he had sinned she saved him and gave him the strength to rule over all things;" on this see J. E. Fossum, "Jewish Christian Christology and Jewish Mysticism," in *Vigiliae Christianae* 37 (1988), 260–287 and esp. 276–280; on the fortunes of Adam in the post-biblical Judaic literature see S. N. Lambden, "From Fig Leaves to Fingernails: Some Notes on the Garments of Adam and Eve in the Hebrew Bible and Select Early Postbiblical Jewish Writings," in *A Walk in the Garden*, 74–90, esp. 77–79.

[18] *Pseudo-Clementines, Hom* III, 20–21.

The Judaizing Christology attested to by the Ebionite components of the actual *Pseudo-Clementines* therefore recognizes an impeccable Adam, identified with the Christ–Holy Spirit who descends from heaven and anoints with the oil of the tree of life the sons of God (those who carry out his Law to perfection).[19] The garden is therefore the entire history of the salvation of Israel, and the original sin of the protoplast is only a heretical gloss leading to disastrous theological consequences. It is interesting to compare with this authentic Eden Christology not only what we find in the *Elenchos* (attributed to Hippolytus) on the spread in Rome of the Elkasaite tradition,[20] but above all that concerning Theodotus the Tanner of Byzantium (condemned by Victor of Rome between 189 and 199), and Theodotus the Money-Changer,[21] capable in any case of illuminating a persistent Roman Judeo-Christian christological tradition.[22] The first Theodotus, the Tanner, identifies Christ with the Spirit come down from on high on to Jesus immersed in the Jordan, but significantly denies that this Christ is God Himself.

---

[19] On the complex question of the stratification in the *Pseudo-Clementines*, see the original study by J. Rius-Camps, "Las Pseudoclementinas. Bases filológicas para una nueva interpretación," in *Revista Catalana de Teologia*, 1 (1976), 79–158.

[20] See *Elenchos* IX, 3,13–14; in the age of Callistus, Alcibiades at Rome spread the doctrine of a book of Elkasai, where the Son of God is identified with an angelic Man of colossal proportions (Adam as Macranthropos) and the Holy Spirit with an angelic Woman (an angelic Eve?) of similar size. In addition, the Elkasaite doctrine not only expected a scrupulous respect for the Law, anabaptism and ritual bathing, but transmitted the doctrine of the metemsomatosis of Christ; see J. E. Fossum, *Jewish-Christian Christology*, 270–275. For a broader view of the Elkasaite phenomenon, see G. P. Luttikhuisen, *The Revelation of Elchasai. Investigation into the Evidence for a Mesopotamian Jewish Apocalypse of the Second Century and its Reception by Judeo-Christian Propagandists* (Tübingen 1985).

[21] Hippolytus, *Elenchos* VII, 23–24.

[22] It is perhaps possible to reconstruct, in agreement with what was argued by the anonymous antimonarchian quoted by Eusebius in *Historia Ecclesiastica* V, 28,1–6, a Roman Ebionite tradition (not in the Harnackian sense of merely adoptionist) from the Gospel of Mark (of Roman composition?) to Theodotus the Money-Changer. On the two Theodotuses, see M. Simonetti, "Il problema dell'unità di Dio a Roma da Clemente a Origene," in *Studi sulla cristologia del II e III secolo* (183–215). See esp. 190, n. 40 on Theodotus the Tanner, where his basic theological doctrine of the de-

Theodotus the Money-Changer, a disciple of Theodotus the Tanner, identifies the Spirit Christ that descends on Jesus in the Jordan not with God the Father, but with a mysterious being "in (His) image," a detail which is in my opinion decisive. It allows us to suggest that the Christ from on high may be precisely the true prophet Adam,[23] the man created in the image of the divine transcendent *dynamis* identified with the

---

scent of the superior/higher Christ to the man Jesus at the Jordan is considered extraneous to the original Ebionite-Adoptionist Christology and therefore attributed to a Gnostic influence. In my opinion, on the contrary, Theodotus' Christology corresponds perfectly to that proposed by the fifth similitude of the Roman *Shepherd of Hermas* and to the Christology of the *Gospel of the Ebionites*. In a similar way, Theodotus the Money-Changer's Christology (see 191) is traced back to the affirmation of Christ as *nudus homo*, quite lacking Theodotus's decisive distinction between Jesus and Christ being "in the image" of the great power Melchisedek (and so archetype of Christ, "man in the image"), nor exploring the problem of the identity of Melchisedek (in reality celestial hypostasis for Theodotus). The fifth Similitude of the *Shepherd of Hermas* (LV, 2 and LVIII, 5–LIX, 6) figures the mission of Jesus in the world through a symbolism of the vineyard, an enclosed place of delights and of testing, an image of the garden of Eden. God entrusts his vineyard to a servant (the man Jesus) so that he may guard it and surround it with a fence; the servant surrounds the vineyard with a palisade (of angels). He cultivates it (pulling up the weeds until he is weary and sorrowful, see Gen. 3:17–18) and makes it bring forth fruit. The reward is the raising of the servant to the same level as the Holy Spirit, or in other words the union between human flesh and the pre-existing, divine living Spirit. Also in this similitude there seems to be the suggestion of the identification of Jesus with the new and pious Adam. It is no accident that the Eden symbolism in the *Shepherd of Hermas* is considerable: see the invaluable essay by L. Cirillo, "Erma e il problema dell'apocalittica a Roma," in *Cristianesimo nella storia*, 4 (1983), 1–31, esp. 15–25. For a Christology corresponding to that of the fifth Similitude of the *Shepherd of Hermas*, see Pseudo-Cyprian, *De montibus Sina et Sion*, IV, 1–3: "Christ carried in himself the flesh of Adam which was his figure (*figuralem*) and hung it on the wood; the flesh of the Lord from God the Father had the name of Jesus: the Holy Spirit that descended from the heavens from God, was called Christ, the Anointed of the living God, Spirit mixed (*mixtus*) with flesh: Jesus Christ."

[23] I therefore cannot share the hypothesis put forward by W. A. Löhr in "Theodotus der Lederarbeiter und Theodotus der Bankier– ein Beitrag zur römischen Theologiegeschichte des zweiten und dritten Jahrhunderts," in *Zeitschrift für die neutestamentliche Wissenschaft*, 87 (1996), 101–125.

Man archetype, the prophet Melchisedek,[24] considered by Philo himself to be one of the symbols or names of the Logos.[25]

In these Judeo-Christian Christologies Eden appears never to have been really lost. In their flawless image of Adam, the first and perfect creature of the goodness of God, the original incarnation of the divine Spirit, Israel—and therefore, in the universalistic Christian perspective, the whole of humanity—is always called, elected and justified. There is no original guilt, but only unfaithfulness to a Law always available (the historic reproposal of the Eden commandment)[26] that can alienate men

---

[24] Of great interest on this subject is the appendix (probably Christian: see Gianotto, *Melchisedek e la sua tipologia*, 45–46, note) to *2 (Slavonic Apocalypse of) Enoch* LXXI, 27–29: the child Melchisedek (conceived miraculously by a sterile woman without a carnal union with a man) is kidnapped by the angel Michael and placed "in the paradise of Eden;" Melchisedek, the true priest figure of Christ, is therefore Adam himself reborn, impeccable and immortal.

[25] On Philo's representation of the Logos as Melchisedek, see *LegAll* III, XXV, 79–XXVI, 82 and Gianotto, *Melchisedek e la sua tipologia*, 91–99. For an analysis of the different interpretations of Melchisedek in some Qumranic treatises (31–103) and the reductionist exegesis proposed for it by the Epistle to the Hebrews (105–152), see F. Manzi, *Melchisedek e l'angeleologia nell'Epistola agli Ebrei e a Qumran* (Rome 1997), esp. 261–271.

[26] In this sense Christ-Adam is Wisdom-Law in the sense of Prov. 3:18 and Eccl. 24:17–43, where in fact Wisdom is identified with the garden of Eden. For an analogous connection between Wisdom (Jerusalem, the Bride of Christ, the city where God makes His dwelling place with man) and Eden, see Rev. 21:1–22:5. For the rabbinical identification between the paradisal tree of life and the Torah, and for the identification of Eden (transcending paradise itself) with the place where God explains the Torah, see L. Ginzberg, *The Legends of the Jews*, Vol. I, 21 and 70; Vol.V, 30, n. 85; see too Vol. I, 81 ("Instead of the tree of life, God gave Adam the Torah, which likewise is a tree of life to them that lay hold upon her"), and Vol. V, 104–105, n. 95. See P. Morris's excellent essay, "Exiled from Eden: Jewish Interpretations of Genesis," in *A Walk in the Garden*, 115–166. In this perspective the entire Judaic religion, even the relation between Temple (new Eden) and Torah (new tree of life), is the renewal of the paradisal alliance between God and Adam. On the influence of these Judaic traditions on the theology and symbolism of the *Shepherd of Hermas*, see again L. Cirillo, "Erma e il problema dell'apocalittica a Roma," 16–21; on the correspondence between the *Shepherd of Hermas* and some of the Qumran texts, see esp. 21–22. On the paradisal commandment as general and universal Law and real knowledge of God, superior to the Mosaic Law, see Tertullian, *Adversus Iudaeos* 2,2–6; *Adversus Marcionem* I, 10,1.

from the original perfection of their progenitor whose justice, in Jesus Himself and in His Gospel, is again held up as an example of innocent, radical faithfulness to the just and provident Creator.[27]

Entirely different is Paul's perspective, in which any nostalgia for an originally lost perfection is absolutely lacking, entirely forgotten, or annulled when faced with the event of the cross and the resurrection of the Lord, generator of a time and a hope which are absolutely new. In Paul the adamite typology is utilized only to symbolize the absolute impossibility for human nature to be autonomous, and to exalt the extraordinary irruption of the Grace of God in Christ.[28] The Grace communicated in Christ is therefore wholly exceptional, subversive, and anarchic with respect to the order of creation of the Mosaic economy of the Law: it is, therefore, the irruption of a future both unexpected and by now irresistible, the experience of an absolute leap into the revelation of divine intentionality, and not the recovery of a lost perfection or reconstitution of an integrity which was in any case always naturally immanent in the creature.[29] The astonished

[27] The tradition of Syrian Christianity from the *Odes of Solomon* to Isaac of Nineveh seems to me to share continuity with this Judeo-Christian perspective, evocatively presented by P. Bettiolo in his essay, "Adam in Eden," in this volume.

[28] As is well known, Paul's only reference to paradise occurs in a mystical-eschatological, rather than protological, dimension (2 Cor. 12:4), as is the case with the only gospel reference in Luke 23:43. For an analysis of his apocalyptic debts and at the same time of the peculiarity of the Pauline ascent to the third heaven and thence to paradise (where the vision of God takes place) see C. Rowland, *The Open Heaven: A Study of Apocalyptic in Judaism and Early Christianity* (London 1982), 379–386; and A. T. Lincoln, *Paradise Now and Not Yet: Studies in the Role of the Heavenly Dimension in Paul's Thought with Special Reference to His Eschatology* (Cambridge 1981).

[29] On the theology of Pauline grace as theology of paradox, K. Barth is still essential: *Der Römerbrief* (Munich 1922), 2/e. On the Pauline theology of grace as supreme and irreducible apocalyptic-eschatological theology, as a real revolutionary theology, or rather a theology of the emptying of the worldly order of things (also in a messianic-political sense), see J. Taubes, *Die Politische Theologie des Paulus* (Munich 1993). On the other hand, on Pauline Christology as conscious neutralization of messianic hopes and as recovery of the Judaic-Hellenistic theologies of celestial mediation, see the weaker A. Chester, "Jewish Messianic Expectations and Mediatorial Figures and Pauline Christology," in M. Hengel and U. Heckel, eds., *Paulus und das antike Judentum* (Tübingen 1991), 17–89, esp. 65–78. On Pauline theology as the profound overcoming of the Judaic "covenantal nomism," see E. P. Sanders, "Jesus, Paul and Judaism," in *ANRW* II, 25–1 (Berlin–New York 1982), 390–450, esp. 429–450.

amazement before God who substitutes Grace for the Law, the entire ecumen for Israel, the nothingness of the pagans for what God Himself had elected as His own alliance (Rom. 9–11), almost as His own exclusive creature—this amazement suggests the absolute transcendence of Grace with respect to the entire creation. Creation remains by contrast closed into the vanity of creatural autonomy, slave of the "elements of the world" (Gal. 4:3). Similarly, the infinite, divine excess of Christ is compared to Adam, the Church as the body of Christ to the Eden of natural man.

A recent essay by G. E. Sterling[30] is remarkably important in this regard. For Sterling, the Pauline relationship between Adam and Christ (developed in part. in 1 Cor. 15:44–49 and in Rom. 5:12–21, but premised in Gal. 3:26–28 and Col. 3:9–11) is defined precisely by entering into conflict with an adamitic anthropology (supported by the Corinthians with whom Paul is polemicizing) of Judaic-Alexandrian origins. Paul reveals many points of contact with Philo's exegesis[31] of the double creation of man in Gen. 1:26–27 and 2:7, reworked by the Corinthians by starting from the Pauline interpretation of the Christian baptism (the baptismal incorporation in the only mystical body of Christ as the elimination of all the natural and worldly scissions: Gal. 3:26–28; Col. 3:9–11; Eph. 5:22–32). The peculiarity of the Pauline perspective, based in 1 Cor. 15:44–49 on a very singular exegesis of

---

[30] G. E. Sterling, "'Wisdom among the Perfect': Creation Traditions in Alexandrian Judaism and Corinthian Christianity," in *Novum Testamentum*, 37 (1995), 355–384. See too J. Jervell, *Imago Dei: Gen. 1, 26 im Spätjudentum, in der Gnosis und in den paulinischen Briefen* (Göttingen 1960) 294–295; D. R. MacDonald, "Corinthian Veils and Gnostic Androgynes," in K. I. King, ed., *Images of the Feminine in Gnosticism* (Philadelphia 1988), 276–292.

[31] Such a hypothesis had already been put forward by J. Daniélou. A strategic error by Sterling (364–367) must, however, be pointed out. In interpreting Philo, *LegAll* I, XII, 31–32, he identifies the celestial "man in (His) image" (generated and not molded) with the *pneuma* (or in other words the intellect proper to earthly man) breathed into Adam by God. In reality Philo keeps these two completely distinct, as can be seen in *LegAll* I, XIII, 33–34. On the other hand in *Deter* XXIII, 83–XXIV, 87, Philo openly identifies the *pneuma* insufflated by God (i.e., the soul of man) with the "image" of Gen. 1:26.

Gen. 2:7, consists in counterposing a charismatic-eschatological opposition to an ontological opposition. On the other hand, the dissident Corinthians identify the Spirit with a protognostic superior nature, so that their being celestial people depends on being incorporated in "the Man in (His) image" of Gen. 1.26. Christian baptism in this sense would be the enlightenment that reveals this natural incorporation. Paul interprets the spirit as Grace given by Christ—a new spiritual Adam, dispenser of living Grace—opposed to and not identified with the original Adam, who for Paul is an earthly and psychical sinner, and not celestial and spiritual.[32]

Adam is therefore the symbol of the fall of all human autonomy, whereas Christ is the transcendental act of Grace which is only realized in itself, and allows the authentic participation of Man in God. In this way Adam "is the figure of he who had to come" (Rom. 5:14), but a paradoxical figure, *sub contraria specie*, in the sense that to the sin and death of unique nature corresponds the redemption of Grace of the unique mystical body of Christ. The deepest sense of the Adamitic typology in Rom. 5:12–21 is therefore the same as the one that explains the relation between the past election of Israel, its being discarded in the present time, and its eschatological recovery through divine Grace only. "For God hath concluded them all in unbelief, that he might have mercy upon all" (Rom. 11:32). In Adam therefore the intrinsic vanity of any kind of nature is revealed, the universal invocation to the coming of Grace as the only meaning, the only reality that gives form to this unformed figure is still unconscious (Rom. 8:18–22).

But perhaps the culmination of the radically atypical Pauline Adam-Christ typology is Phil. 2:5–11. Adam and Eve's perverse sinning and

---

[32] On the scandalous Pauline interpretation of Adamitic typology, and on the paradoxical christological overcoming of the equation Law-Wisdom, see M. Hengel, *Der Sohn Gottes. Die Entstehung der Christologie und die jüdisch-hellenistische Religionsgeschichte* (Tübingen 1977), 2/e, 115–120. See too J. Daniélou, *Sacramentum futuri*, 9–12, who among other things insists precisely on the relationship between neo-Edenic anthropology and baptismal sacrament. On the patristic exegesis of the typology of the first and second Adam, see the ample excursus in R. L. Wilken, *Judaism and the Early Christian Mind: A Study of Cyril of Alexandria's Exegesis and Theology* (Yale 1971), 93–118.

desire to escape from death (Gen. 3:5), their proud desire to be as gods (Gen. 3:6), the fruit of their disobedience and unwonted appropriation, are opposed to Christ's renunciation (Phil. 2:6) of unwonted appropriation (a term completely out of place unless it presupposes an allusion to Adam's sin). To the sinner created of God (Gen. 1:26) is opposed the divine man (Phil. 2:6) who for Grace alone chooses to become like man (Phil. 2:7).[33] The exaltation[34] of the obedient acceptance of death on the part of Christ (Phil. 2:8) emerges in the unspoken but transparent comparison with the disobedience of Adam, as is confirmed by Rom. 5:19, where Adam is explicitly opposed to Jesus Christ. In the Christ-Adam opposition, the logic of the gift of divine Grace is opposed to the merely ontological logic of nature, to its autonomous *conatus essendi*. As in the extraordinary first two chapters of 1 Cor., God chooses the nothingness of the creation (which is Adam the fallen sinner himself) to demonstrate in Christ crucified the absolute creativity of His love.

What is the identity or return of Adam in Christ in Ebionitic christology, becomes in Paul an opposition or irreducible break. The Grace of Christ takes away the autonomy of nature (Grace is delivered to the creature, who appropriates it, and it then falls into oblivion) and Law (Grace become nature and ethnic-religious possession). Salvation does not come from having been created, nor from being pious Jews,

---

[33] On the relation between Phil. 2:6 and Gen. 1:26 see E. Peterson, "La libération d'Adam," in *Revue biblique*, 55 (1948), 199–214, esp. 208–211. Against the view of G. Quispel, "Ezekiel 1:26 in Jewish Mysticism and Gnosis," in *Vigiliae Christianae*, 34 (1980), 1–13, esp. 8–13, I believe that it is the *Poimandres* that interprets a Gnostic-Christian tradition depending on Phil. 2:5–11, which is a Pauline hymn, not pre-Pauline. On the relation between Pauline Christology and Gen. 1:26, the reference to Col. 1:15–18 cannot of course be overlooked; on this see J. E. Fossum, *The Image of the Invisible God: Essays on the Influence of Jewish Mysticism on Early Christology* (Göttingen 1995), 13–39 where, following Quispel, the hymn of Col. is made to depend on a pre-Christian Judaic doctrine of the celestial Man as Adam reclothed in divine glory, an exegesis of Ezech. 1:26.

[34] For the probable connection of Phil. 2:9 (the exaltation of Jesus through endowing him with the divine Name) with Judaic speculations on celestial Adam, see J. E. Fossum, *The Name of God*, 293–297.

but from having been visited by the Spirit which gives faith in the revelation of Christ. If the passage from the figure of Adam to Christ is a passage from the ontological to the charismatic, from nature to the coming of Grace, in an absolutely paradoxical reversal Adam has no value or sense in himself, but only as an invocation of Christ. Nature (psychical or natural man, of whom the first Adam is the type) is only a figure of Grace (of the second Adam, spiritual and celestial, in which the Grace of the Spirit has been universally breathed). Creation awaits from its first pulsations the redemption of Christ. Adam's sin itself seems to be none other than the provocation of the absolutely extraordinary redemption, of the eschatological new creation[35] that God reveals in Jesus Christ. In this perspective Eden can only be an unreal dimension. The imminent Parousia of Christ is the only true Eden, the only true revelation by God to mankind. In this sense, the Pauline paradise of Grace is for the natural man as lost and unreachable as the Eden of Genesis, present once more only because of the love of Christ—*spiritually* given back, yet nonetheless as unavailable Grace of God. This grace is not works, law, ethical behavior or religious purity, but a revolution of the world, a total uprooting and upsetting of nature, of creation itself: Sophia crucified, Adam crucified.

2. The Gnostics: Eden as Prison and Oblivion of *Deus Patiens*

The Gnostic exegesis of Eden, hypostatizing the Pauline dialectic between nature-law and grace in theological dualism,[36] drastically reverses the Ebionitic tradition. The key intuition of Gnosticism is the extreme extension of the Christological paradox, that is, the identity of the tangency in Jesus Christ of divine nature and human nature. I see Gnosticism as originally and essentially Christian and by no means docetistic, because characterized by a radical theopaschism. Gnostics

---

[35] On Christ as second Adam, revealer of the new creation, see D.F. Sawyer, "The New Adam in the Theology of St. Paul," in *A Walk in the Garden*, 105–116.

[36] See G. Quispel, "La conception de l'homme dans la gnose valentinienne," in *Eranos Jahrbuch*, 15 (1947–1948), 249–286, then in *Gnostic Studies* (Istanbul 1974), I, 37–57; S. Pétrement, *Le Dieu séparé. Les origines du gnosticisme*, ch. 6, "La liberté par la grâce," 259–297.

identify Christ the Redeemer not with the Ebionitic "impeccable Adam," and not only with the celestial "man in (His) image" of Philo, but also with the Adam who was a sinner, with the earthly "moulded man," having fallen and become prisoner of the body and of death.[37] (In other words, Gnostics identified Christ with the "Adam" who is Eve, earthly type of the Gnostic Sophia.) Sin in Eden is at the same time liberation from the Rulers' prison and the revelation turned upside-down of the intimate secret of the transcendent *Deus patiens*, of His paradoxical kenotic dynamism, generated by the Christian radicalization of the relation between a transcendent Father and a patient Son, between a hidden God of love and a God who died a sinner.

The eternal, intimate mystery of God is, for the Gnostics, the paradoxical, radical christological anthropomorphization of God, enacted in the passion and the fall of God in His Son, split into sin and the redemptive kenosis of the Son (of primordial Man, of the Logos, of Sophia). Consequently Eden, the garden of the motionless perfection of the creature, must be interpreted as a place of stasis, prison of the anarchical freedom of the Son, scene of the attempted removal of the scandalous dynamism of the Gnostic *Deus patiens*. Thus Eden does not merely represent the temporary triumph of the Demiurge, the abortive God of the cosmological order and of the legal prohibition, deceptively exalted by His absolute nature and power. More deeply, the history of

---

[37] See G. Lettieri, "Il fondamento cristologico del mito gnostico: la teofania sulle acque," in *Cassiodorus*, 1 (1995), 151–165: both in the most important Sethian texts of Nag Hammadi (*NH*, trans. J. M. Robinson, ed., *The Nag Hammadi Library* (Leiden–New York–Copenhagen–Cologne 1988), 3/e, and in those of the School of Valentinus and in the account of the barbelognostics in Irenaeus *(AdvHaer* I, 30), Gen. 1:26–27 and Gen. 2:7 refer to the transcendental divine apparition of the Redeemer Man, and to the imprisonment of the spiritual component of created man on the part of the Archons. My thesis is that this double-sided Gnostic anthropology is conceivable only if it depends on the synoptic stories of the baptism (interpreted as *kenosis* or decisive incarnation of the Son of God) of Jesus, so that the Christian-gnostic reinterpretation of the double primordial creation appears inseparable from that of the kenotic and redemptive baptism, the recreation of fallen man brought forward by the Gnostics into a precosmic dimension. See my forthcoming book *Deus patiens. L'essenza cristologica dello gnosticismo*.

extrapleromatic Eden reveals the Gnostic God's incapacity to keep within Himself (in His pleroma, in His fullness). The sin of Adam and Eve is the trace of the sin of Sophia (the passion of God personified), and therefore of the ambiguous christological expansion of love of the Gnostic pleroma outside of itself. Eden, conversely, represents the Father still imprisoned in Himself, wholly satisfied with His own lordship, or with His absoluteness, with being entirely free from relation with the *other*. Thus the exit from Eden is identifiable with the Gnostics' movement of liberation from the Rulers' imprisonment (Adam and Eve, chenotic image of the transcendent Son-Sophia, androgynous spiritual creature imprisoned by the Rulers). Furthermore, and above all, the exit from Eden is the kenotic movement of liberation of God from His own motionless absolute nature. It is a theological parricide mythically represented as the dethroning of the lordship of the Old Testament Demiurge by the serpent, symbol of the new God.[38] Therefore the history of sin does not coincide only with the history of salvation, and with the christological revelation of gnosis, but also with the decisive germinal intuition of the divine passion. The paradoxical redemptive kenosis of the Son is the other side of the kenosis of sin, so that in Christ (Sophia) God comes out of Himself; annihilates Himself, takes responsibility for the sins of the world, is treated as a sinner by God Himself, is raised on to the cross like a serpent, and is cursed and killed as blasphemer of God.

As Hippolytus' *Elenchos* (V, 19–23) informs us, the Gnostic Justin's *Book of Baruch*[39] is an obvious example of the Gnostic conception of paradise as a prison for Adam and for God Himself. Edem (Eden, the

---

[38] See *Testimonium Veritatis* (*NH* IX, 3) 45,23–49,7; Origen, *Contra Celsum* VI, 28; Porphyry, *Contra Christianos*, fr. 42 (Harnack); Julian, *Adversus Galilaeos* I, 5–16 (Neumann). On the "transformed value of the serpent of paradise in reference to Jesus as usurper of Jahweh"—especially with reference to gnosis and Marcion—see E. Bloch, *Das Prinzip Hoffnung* (Frankfurt 1959), Vol. II, ch. 53, the paragraph "Jesus und der Vater, Paradiesschlange als Heiland," 1493–1504; and *Atheismus in Christentum. Zur Religion des Exodus und des Reichs* (Frankfurt 1968), ch. 5, "Aut Caesar aut Christus."

[39] See M. Simonetti, "Note sul 'Libro di Baruch' dello gnostico Giustino," in *Vetera Christianorum*, 6 (1969), 71–89, esp. 82–85.

earth or Israel) is identified with a "semi-virgin," a being half-woman and half-serpent, or with the personification of original sin itself (Eve and the serpent responsible for the fall of Adam). Adam on the other hand is identified with Elohim, God the Father without prescience, who, still ignorant of transcendent Good, becomes infatuated with Edem. From the union between Elohim and Edem 24 angels are born, 12 paternal and good, 12 maternal and evil:

> "The multitude of all these angels together is Paradise," he says, concerning which Moses speaks, "God planted a garden in Eden towards the east," that is, towards the face of Edem, that Edem might behold the garden,—that is, the angels—continually. Allegorically the angels are styled trees of this garden, and the tree of life is the third of the paternal angels—Baruch. And the tree of the knowledge of good and evil is the third of the maternal angels—Naas. (*Elenchos* V, 21)

Once the world has been created, with the animals, the living beings from the bestial part of Edem (earth), then from the human part of Edem are moulded Adam and Eve, each one of whom is like "an image, and emblem (as well as) seal" of the union and the love between the Father and Edem. In an interesting variant of Philo's doctrine of a creation of man both angelic and divine, they receive the soul from Edem and the spirit from the Father. The world is then handed over to the twelve evil angels of Edem, divided into four groups called by the names of the four rivers of Eden. Paradise then is the image of the blind and merely natural power of the twelve Archons (or zodiacal signs), of the regular "circular dance" of time (the four seasons represented by the four groups of angels which succeed one another in the mastership of the earth)—the uninterrupted, monotonous flowing of evil in a world which is a prison.

But Elohim reveals the subversive transcendence of the Christian God with respect to creation and the necessity of its law. Having decided to push on beyond the confines of heaven, he sees the dazzling light of Good, who invites him to be seated on His right hand, showing that the Father is the Son of Good, called Lord by Elohim. After being abandoned by Elohim, Edem decides to take revenge by persecuting humanity, because humans are images of the Father. The earthly paradise therefore becomes the terrain of conflict between Baruch, sent as a savior by Elohim, and Naas, the serpent-tree of good and evil. Naas sexually seduces Eve and thence Adam by giving them his own fruit-seed to eat, and humankind is therefore expelled from paradise. Thus, the entire history of Israel is marked by the conflict between the redeeming action of Baruch (who through Moses and the prophets tries to liberate the divine spirit present in humanity) and the punishing actions of Naas (who succeeds in seducing the element of Edem present in every person, an element prone to sinning and subjection). Only the obedience of the man Jesus to the revelation of Baruch, an obedience observed right up to the death inflicted upon him by Naas, permits the abandonment of the body of Edem on the cross and the rejoining the Father.

> He [Jesus], however, leaving the body of Edem on the [accursed] tree, ascended to the Good One; saying, however, to Edem, "Woman, thou retainest thy son" (John 19:26), that is the animal and earthly man (1 Cor. 15:46 ff.). But [Jesus] himself, commending his spirit into the hands of the Father, ascended to the Good One. (*Elenchos* V, 21)

Only the passion and the death on the cross annihilate the Edem imprisonment, the earthly mixture of divine spirit and earthly spirit-body, freeing celestial Adam from his earthly or Edem double,[40] opening up to him his full identity with the supreme Good and with the Father "resurrected."

In the Sethian *Paraphrase of Seth*,[41] we find another identification of the prison of divine man with paradisal Eden. This is an allegory of the "polluted and baneful (and) disordered... impure womb"[42] of the

---

[40] The "man in (His) image" of Gen. 1:26, who is neither male nor female because androgynous, or absolutely simple and one, therefore represents the Gnostic divine transcendent Man, revealed by Christ to his elect: see *Naasseni*, in *Elenchos* V, 4 and above all the Gospel of Thomas 37 (*NH* II, 2) 39,27–40,2 (which probably depends on a passage in the *Gospel of the Egyptians*, conserved by Clement, *Stromateis* III, 13,92; for other passages see J. E. Ménard, *L'Évangile selon Thomas* [Leiden 1975], 113–115).

[41] *Elenchos* V, 13–17; see the parallel *Paraphrase of Shem* (*NH* VII, I).

[42] *Elenchos* V, 14; see V, 15. For a further identification of the womb with Eden, see the Simonian *Megale Apophasis* in *Elenchos* VI, 6–15, where paradise is interpreted as a symbol of human generation (esp. 14–15).

world originating from the union between the Darkness (the water, material and dark) and the divine Light and the Spirit poured out from on high. The Son, a ray of the perfect transcendent Light (the Father), descending into matter has remained imprisoned in the perfect Intellect (Adam) that the Darkness (the serpent demiurge identified with Jahweh) has generated to hold on to the Son. To recover the divine ray of Light imprisoned in Adam the prisoner of the womb (Eden), the supreme Light sends the celestial redeemer, "the perfect Word of supernal Light" (*Elenchos* V, 14). The latter penetrates into the womb-Eden in the likeness of the serpent (the phallus) to reach Adam the prisoner and free him, but—and this I consider to be of the highest importance—the womb-Eden is identified with the impure carnal womb of the Virgin Mary, where Christ Logos carries out His kenosis by making Himself flesh. The sin of Adam (the falling into the paradise-womb of the lower world) is repeated by (although in reality, according to the principle of inverse exemplarity, it is dependent on) the incarnation of the Logos, the kenosis in the paradise-womb of the world. The serpent, an ambiguous figure combining evil angel and wise liberator, precisely because he frees Adam from the imprisonment of Eden may be the symbol of the Logos who reveals the transcendence of the true fatherland.

The interpretation of Eden as Rulers' prison, as the place of oblivion of the only transcendent Father, is systematically dealt with in the ophitic-barbelo-gnostic or Sethian tradition. For example, in the fundamental information given by Irenaeus, *Adversus Haereses* I, 30 (esp. 6–9), the creation by Yaltabaoth and his bad Rulers of the man Adam, image of the transcendent "Man and Son of the Man," is carried out with the unconscious renunciation (secretly provoked by the Sophia Prunicos) to his creature of the divine power, of the spiritual breath earlier latent in Yaltabaoth. Paradise is therefore the Rulers' attempt to recover their own lost perfection through the imprisonment of a creature by now absolutely transcending its demiurge. It is no coincidence that paradise becomes the place for the erotic delights of the evil angels. Through the sexual possession of Eve (brought forth from Adam, but temporarily deprived of her spiritual power by Sophia Prunicos), the evil angels try to take possession of the spiritual nature hidden in their two anarchical creatures.[43] That is, they try (in vain) to see their spiritual creativity mirrored in them. The commandment not to eat of the tree of knowledge corresponds to the intention to subject Eve to Rulers' generation:

> But their mother (Sophia) cunningly devised a scheme to seduce Eve and Adam, by means of the serpent, to transgress the command of Yaltabaoth. Eve listened to this as if it had proceeded from the Son of God, and yielded an easy belief. She also persuaded Adam to eat of the tree, regarding which God had said that they should not eat of it. They then declared that, on their thus eating, they attained to the knowledge of that power which is above all, and departed from those who had created them. When Prunicos perceived that the powers were thus baffled by their own creature, she greatly rejoiced. (*Adv. Haer.* I, 30,7)

To the Adam who sins, Sophia reveals his paradoxical consubstantiality with God. The expulsion from paradise, however painful, therefore coincides with the liberation of the spirituals from the Rulers' limbo, from the divine desire of mere creative power. Thus Eden can be interpreted as the original absolute stasis of God, the autistic immobility in which God Himself cannot remain. In line with this, the serpent (Sophia) is the anxiety for knowledge and for hubris, and therefore the passion for otherness and for love which animates the eternal life of the Gnostic pleroma.[44] It is not by chance that the absolutely celestial paradise of the Gnostic pleroma (Valentinian and Sethian in particular) is a continuous gushing of alterity, a frenetic generation of aeons, all of them called by the Holy Spirit to participate in the su-

---

[43] On the paradox of an anarchical creature, entirely *nova*, transcending the Demiurge and the entire order of creation because secretly visited by the divine Spirit or identified with the transcending God himself, see, for example, the great Valentinian account in Irenaeus, *Adv. Haer.*, I, 1,1–8,5, esp. I, 5,5–6.

[44] Entirely corresponding to the Gnostic theo-anthropology is (if I may be allowed this anachronism) Hegelian anthropology: "Mankind, by taking the fruit of the tree of the knowledge of good and evil, has lost the form and the equalness with himself, and was therefore expelled from the condition of the innocent conscience, by nature which offered itself without requiring labour and by paradise garden of the animals" (G. W. F. Hegel, *Phenomenology of Spirit*, VII, 412).

preme perfection of the Father,[45] available for the recovery of Sophia herself.

In the texts of Nag Hammadi which can be traced to the Sethian tradition, the creation of man is almost always preceded, first, by the idolatrous, blasphemous position of the Archon, who pretends to be the One God, and second, by the pleromatic answer. From the pleroma descends a Voice which reveals the Name of the True God ("The Man and the Son of the Man"). Almost always the Voice is accompanied by the descent from the pleroma of a bright Image of Man, which is reflected in the primordial material waters, providing the Archons terrorized by the unforeseen theophany the model from which to create Adam.[46] To the idolatrous name of the solipsistic God-Archon (God the Creator transcending His creature, hence God who governs through a law which keeps the creature prisoner and subordinate in a preconstituted order), is christologically opposed the double name of Father and Son. This latter double name indicates the paradoxical and anarchical identity between the subjected or enslaved human creature who suffers and the God of Love, transcendent and Redeemer. So Adam is created "in the image" of the celestial Image descended from the pleroma, and "in the likeness" of the psychical Archons which mould him.[47] The creation of Adam therefore answers to the intention of the Rulers to take possession of the divine power Man which transcends them. But the result of the creation is a material-psychical abortion *ApocrIoh.* 15,5–19,14). Indeed only a direct intervention of the Savior Aeon—thanks to the deception practised on the Archon—allows the concentration in the creature "in (His) image" of the whole of the pneu-

---

[45] See, for example, *ApocrIoh* 4,20–9,20; significantly, celestial Adam is the aeon placed next to Christ, led into the intimacy of the secret relation between Father, Mother and Son, himself capable of generating aeons (Seth and his descendants) within the pleroma.

[46] *The Apocryphon of John* (*NH* II, 1 and IV, 1) 13,5–20,9.

[47] "And he (Yaltabaoth) said to the authorities which attend him, 'Come, let us create a man according to the image of God and according to our likeness, that his image may become a light for us...' And they said, 'Let us call him Adam, that his name may become a power of light for us'" (*ApocrIoh.* 15,1–4 and 11–13). See H.-M. Schenke, *Der Gott "Mensch" in der Gnosis*, ch. 3.

matic substance alienated outside of the pleroma. First concentrated in the unaware Archon himself, this substance is almost inadvertently breathed into Adam (Gen. 2:7), who thus becomes more divine, intelligent and brighter than his creators (*ApocrIoh.* 19:15–20:9). This provokes the envy of the Rulers and the beginning of Adam's persecution, but Adam is secretly defended by the transcendent Father. Christ-Sophia appears as Epinoia of light, the divine subject who descends into Adam himself to move him towards redemption. This conflict comes to a head in paradise and more specifically in the opposition between the Rulers' tree of life (which is death) and the tree of the knowledge of Christ. The Rulers drag Adam down into the place of the satisfaction of inferior desires, a place of the oblivion of his actual nature, of spiritual death:

> "And the Archons took him (Adam) and placed him in paradise. And they said to him 'Eat, that is at leisure,' for their luxury is bitter and their beauty is depraved. And their luxury is deception and their trees are goodlessness and their fruit is deadly poison and their promise is death. And the tree of their life they had placed in the midst of paradise... But what they call the tree of knowledge of good and evil, which is the Epinoia of the light, they stayed in front of it in order that he [Adam] might not look up to his fullness and recognize the nakedness of his shamefulness. But it was I [Christ] who brought about that they ate." (*ApocrIoh.* 21,16–25 and 22,3–9)

If the serpent (the creature of the Archons' Eden, as such dominated by their passions) remains evil, it unconsciously helps the work of redemption of Christ-Sophia (the other side of the serpent, personified in an eagle). The eagle (serpent) leads Adam to the expulsion which is at the same time his liberation from mortal prison, the spiritual reclothing of the nudity of his intelligence:

> "I [Christ] appeared in the form of an eagle on the tree of knowledge... that I might teach them and awaken them out of the depth of sleep. For they [Adam and Eve] were both in a fallen state and they recognized their nakedness. The Epinoia appeared to them as a light (and) she awakened their thinking." (23,26–35)

Some variations in the mythological scheme of the *Apocryphon of John* are introduced by the Sethian *Hypostasis of the Archons* (*NH* II,4). Adam is at the same time created "in the image" of the celestial Image which appeared on the waters, and moulded starting from the material substance proper to the Archons.[48] The psychical element is given to Adam by the demiurgical breath (see Gen. 2:7), but the persistence of the Archons in breathing their power into the creature "in (His) Image" is incapable of bringing it to life in imitation of the Image on the waters. Only the descent of the pleromatic Spirit is capable of breathing life into Adam, endowing him with a "living soul" (87,10–88,18). The archontic placing of Adam in paradise culminates in the prohibition (which the Archons impose unconsciously through the work of the transcending God) against eating from the tree of knowledge. This prohibition is in itself so ambiguous and tempting as to be perhaps considered in reality a message of liberation:

> "They [the Archons] do not understand what [they have said] to him [Adam]; rather, by the Father's will, they said this in such a way that he might [in fact] eat, and that Adam might [not] regard them as would a man of an exclusively material nature." (88,20–89,1)

The serpent, unlike what is claimed in the *Apocryphon of John*, is therefore interpreted as an earthly being, a creature of the Archons, into which however the "female instructing principle" descends temporarily, provoking the expulsion of Adam and Eve from Eden (see 89,31–91,11).[49]

---

[48] Remarkably similar is the anthropogony of *On the Origin of the World*: the new appearance of the pleromatic "Adam of light" at the lower level of the material world provokes the reaction of the Archons and the creation of Adam, "in the image" of the Rulers' body, and "in the likeness" of the Adam of Light (112,25–13,1); but the psychical Adam, partly brought to life by Sophia, is placed in paradise by the Archons. He cannot stand up, however, unless entirely brought to life and illuminated by the female spiritual principle, identified with the extraordinarily bright Eve, "the female instructing principle" and daughter of Sophia, and thus the reappearance of that "likeness" of the absolute bright Image; see 115,11–116,15.

[49] On *HypArch* 88,24–91,7, see P. S. Alexander, "The Fall into Knowledge: The Garden of Eden/Paradise in Gnostic Literature," in *A Walk in the Garden*, 91–104. This text limits itself to interpreting the peculiarities of Gnostic exegesis of Eden on the basis of a generic ontological dualism. For a masterly analysis of Gnostic, Judaic and Pagan materials on paradise (especially in the *OrMundi*), see the chapter "Éros et le paradis" in M. Tardieu, *Trois mythes gnostiques. Adam, Éros et les animaux d'Égypte dans un écrit de Nag Hammadi (II, 5)* (Paris 1974), 141–214. In *Evangelium Veritatis* (*NH* I, 3 and XII, 2) 18,22–31, the tree of the cross of Christ is identified with the tree as generator of life, and is therefore opposed to the Edenic tree of good and evil, generator of death.

In *The Second Treatise of the Great Seth* (*NH* VII, 2) the archontic creation of mankind is indissolubly connected to a precosmic theophany. "The descent upon the water, that is, the regions below" (50,16–17) coincides with the first incarnation of the Son, of the celestial Redeemer in a material body of man:

> I visited a bodily dwelling... The whole multitude of the Archons became troubled. And all the matter of the Archons as well as all the begotten powers of the earth were shaken when it saw the likeness of the Image, since it was mixed. And I am the one who was in it, not resembling him who was in it first. For he was an earthly man, but I, I am from above the heavens. (50,20 and 51,25–52,3)

The aim of the incarnation is to upset or amaze the Archons and to reveal the majesty of Man, image of the "Father of Truth, the Man of Greatness" (53,3–5), even outside of the pleroma. Evidently, the account presupposes a previous creation of the material man (Adam) as idol, bodily container, false image (ignorance) that imitates and at the same time imprisons the divine Man, revealed in a presupposed first theophany to the Archons as transcendent Name, or as celestial Image.[50]

> "But they [the Archons] who received the Name because of contact with ignorance—which [is] a burning and a vessel—having created it to destroy Adam whom they had made." (53,5–10)

Also: "For Adam was a laughing-stock, since he was made a counterfeit type of man by the Hebdomad" (62,27–29). But it is precisely the material Adam, despised by the Archons because so insignificant

---

[50] "The Majesty of the heavens, i.e., the Man of Truth, whose Name they saw" (57,6–9). The Name of Truth is the Son who reveals the unnameable Father: see the Valentinian *Evangelium Veritatis* 38,5–41,3; *ExcTh* 22,4–6; 26,1; 43,4; 86,2; Irenaeus, *AdvHaer* I, 21,3. A passage in *The Gospel of the Egyptians* (*NH* III, 2 and IV, 2) clarifies this relationship between Image, Voice, Name (the double name "the Man and the Son of Man"), and the anthropogonic account: "Then a voice came from on high, saying: 'The Man exists, and the Son of Man.' Because of the descent of the image above, which is like its voice in the height of the image which has looked out, through the looking out of the image above, the first creature was formed" (III, 59,1–10); see Tertullian, *Adversus Valentinianos* 24,2–25,3.

(see 53,35–54,13), who is paradoxically the hidden place of the revelation of the celestial Man, hence the creature transcending his material Creator.

The Valentinian exegesis of Gen. 1:26–27 and Gen. 2:7 proposes yet another variation on the relation between the image and likeness, and as they appear in the two anthropogonic accounts. In the great Valentinian account in Irenaeus, *AdvHaer* I, 1,1–8,5 (esp. I, 5,5–6) and in the Valentinian *Excerpta ex Theodoto* (51–56) handed down to us by Clement, the image is indeed interpreted as inferior when compared to the likeness. The former is related to the material nature, the latter to the psychical nature, identified with living spirit breathed on by the Demiurge. Spiritual nature is on the other hand generated by Sophia, who secretly inserts it in the material-psychical man created by the Demiurge precisely in the moment (Gen. 2:7) of the psychical, demiurgical insufflation (see also Hippolytus, *Elenchos* VI, 34,4–6; *EvPhil* 80=70,22–33). The man in (His) image, whose creation is narrated in Gen. 1:27, is therefore the man moulded from the mud of the earth, earthly and of flesh. Not admitted even into the demiurgic paradise (*Excerpta ex Theodoto* 51), he is destined to final annihilation. The man in (His) likeness, whose creation is narrated in Gen. 2:7, is on the other hand "the divine spirit (demiurgic)," the psychical man created in the demiurgic paradise. He is called to a free (even if naturally inferior) conversion to the transcendent God; whereas spiritual man is entirely separate, by nature predestined to salvation, citizen of the pleroma and not of paradise, *omousios* to Sophia and to God the Father himself, and not to the Demiurge.[51] On the other hand, Gen. 1:27 can also be re-

[51] See Irenaeus, *AdvHaer* I, 5,6 and *ExcTh* 50; Satorninos, in Irenaeus, *AdvHaer* I, 24,1; and the first fragment of Valentinus, recounted by Clement, *Stromateis* II, 8,36: the transcendent "pre-existing Man" inserts a spiritual nature superior to that of the Archons in the Adam they moulded "in the Name of the Man" (the celestial Voice-Image which functions as luminous model for the Archons is presupposed). I believe that Valentinus' fifth fragment (in Clement, *Stromateis* IV, 13,89–90), as well as the plausible cosmological interpretation of Clement, also demand a more profound anthropogonic interpretation: the image (Adam) is inferior (see *Stromateis* IV, 13,90) to the "living Face" (Clement *ExcTh* 10–12; 15; 23,4–5; *Stromateis* V, 6,34,1), to the

ferred not only to the spiritual man, but "to the best emission of Sophia" (*ExcTh* 21), mother of Christ Himself, "image of the Pleroma" (*ExcTh* 32). Thus baptism donates (or reveals, forming spiritually) to the spiritual man the "image of the celestial" (1 Cor. 15:49; see *ExcTh* 80), regenerating that divine androgynous identity that is the being, for its nature, image of the transcendent Father (*ExcTh* 21).

The Valentinian *Tripartite Tractate* (*NH* I, 5) again exhibits the usual adamitic tripartite anthropology: the Demiurge, that "the spiritual Logos moved invisibly" (104,32–34), creates the material man and breathes the spirit or psychical vitality into him, without noticing that the Logos endows its creature secretly also with "the first form... a Living Spirit and Breath of exalted aeons" (105,17 and 23–24). This endowment frees man from ignorance by giving him the knowledge of his celestial identity and of being begotten of "the Invisible" (105,25). So

> the first human being is a mixed formation, and a mixed creation... and a spiritual Word, whose attention is divided between each of the two (psychic and material) substances from which he takes his being. (106,18–25)

A tripartite distinction is therefore proposed between the spiritual tree of life, the psychical tree of the knowledge of good and evil, and the totality of the remaining edenic trees. The latter type of trees are justifiable, but trees of the demiurgical imprisonment, and thus of the spiritual death of a divine creature, transcending its material Creator: "Therefore, it is said that a paradise was planted for him (the first human being), so that he might eat of the food of three kinds of tree" (106,25–29). The Archons forbid the eating of both the spiritual and the psychical trees:

Name, to the Son, to the pre-existing Man revealed to the Archons. The Name, therefore, "has filled in the gap that was missing in the [material] creation" of the Archons, i.e., has inserted in Adam the spiritual seed (the likeness, in *Stromateis* IV, 13,90) which the first fragment treats. In effect, Clement explicitly asserts this anthropogonic interpretation in IV, 13,90,3–4. On the first Valentinus fragment, see J. Holzhausen, *Der "Mythos vom Menschen" im hellenistischen Ägypten*, 88–97, and the unconvincing analysis by C. Markschies, *Valentinus Gnosticus? Untersuchungen zur valentinianischen Gnosis mit einem Kommentar zu den Fragmenten Valentins* (Tübingen 1992), 13–53.

> Therefore they issued a command, making a threat and bringing upon him a great danger, which is death. Only the enjoyment of the things which are evil did he allow him to taste, and from the other tree with the double (fruit) he did not allow him to eat, much less from the tree of life. (106,35–107,6)

Corrupted by the evil serpent, however, man eats of the tree of good and evil and is consequently punished with expulsion from Eden and physical death. Once again, the logic of the Archons remains legalistic: the prohibition, the subordination of the creature in an intangible preconstituted order. The Logos itself, however, operates in such a way that its consubstantial creature must sin, be expelled, and know the alienation of death. Indeed, Eden remains the place of an enjoyment and repose which are fictitious and transient. It is the garden of appearances, of the likeness to the divine (and therefore idol of) perversion, the negation of the true, eternal, pleromatic reality:

> This is the expulsion which was made for him, when he was expelled from the enjoyment of the things which belong to the likeness and those of the representation. It was a work of providence, so that it might be found that it is a short time until man will receive the enjoyment of the things which are eternally good, in which is the place of rest. (107,19–26)

Only the knowledge of evil, the reuniting with good after the mortal alienation of sin, makes the divine creature really aware of his total identity, or rather of the ambiguous reality (absolutely divine and infinite, and yet defective, finite, impotent, sinful and mortal: see 74,18–81,7) of the Logos, of the eternally *patiens* Son of God, with whom real mankind is consubstantial.

> This the Spirit ordained when he first planned that man should experience the great evil, which is death, that is complete ignorance of the Totality, and that he should experience all the evils which come from this and, after the deprivations and the cares which are in these, that he should receive of the greatest good, which is life eternal, that is, firm knowledge of the Totalities and the reception of all good things. (107,27–108,4)

Therefore, the Gnostic Eden can be made the equivalent of the infernal gods of the Marcion of Irenaeus, *AdvHaer* I, 27,3.[52] The su-

[52] See the stimulating analysis by E. Norelli, "La funzione di Paolo nel pensiero di Marcione," in *Rivista biblica*, 34 (1986), 543–597, esp. 582–586. Norelli is perfectly right to point out the difference between the Gnostics and Marcion (585–586),

preme sin (free for Marcion, made rigid in a nature predestined to damnation for the Gnostics) is *not* to allow oneself to be tempted, to remain prisoners of a servile obedience, to shut out the anarchical revelation of grace that, beyond any law and any prohibition, proclaims the love (or identity itself for the Gnostics) that links the Father to sinning humanity. Gnosis is therefore the revealed knowledge (hypostatized in the Savior Jesus Christ, or in his female copies) that, beyond the apparent divisions, the transcendent divine and fallen humanity are one. What, then, is Gnostic sin, if not the law that divides God from humankind, good from evil, purity from sin? For in so doing the law generates hell and subordinates life in paradise to the alienating recognition of creatural incompleteness,[53] the extraneousness of the *other* with respect to the motionless absolute quality of a preconstituted order.[54] The true Gnostic paradise is instead identified with the absolute freedom of being the son, communicated by the cross of Christ, the only living gnosis of the absolute unity of love and of being between God and His creatures:

> "God [has planted] a garden.... This garden [is not the place where] they will say to me: '[Man, eat] this or do not eat [that, just as you] wish.' In the place where I will eat all things, is the tree of gnosis. That one killed Adam; but here, the tree of gnosis made men alive (*EvPhil* [*NH* II, 3] 84=71,22–72–3; see 92=73,19–27; 15=55,6–14). The law was the tree. It has power to give the knowledge of good and evil. It neither removed him from evil, nor did it

---

although in my opinion the differences of Gnostic natures must also be traced back to the Pauline opposition grace/law, which certainly becomes more rigid from a speculative perspective and is reduced to the opposition of metaphysical natures.

[53] See *OrMundi* 115,1–11: "When they (the Archons) had finished (the earthly) Adam, they abandoned him as an inanimate vessel, since he had taken form like an abortion, in that no spirit was in him;" the vessel-womb can be compared to paradise. Indeed, when the evil angels, having returned from Adam (though the latter had already secretly been endowed with a soul by the Sophia Zoe), "saw that Adam could not stand up, they were glad, and they took him and put him in Paradise. And they withdrew up to their heavens" (115,27–29).

[54] See in *Pseudo-Clementines, Recognitiones* II, 53 the Marcionite affirmation of the imperfection of the Adam created by the Demiurge, and the charge of falling into contradiction addressed to a God who first orders that the tree of good and evil shall not be eaten from, and then punishes humanity for having committed an evil act that Adam could not know about. See Augustine's answer to this, *DeGenLitt* VIII, 16,34.

set him in the good, but it created death for those who ate of it. For when he said, 'Eat this, do not eat that,' it became the beginning of death." (*EvPhil* 94=73,28–74,12)

—abridged by Shanta Kamath

Adam in Eden: The Difficult Discernment of the Perfect Life

Paolo Bettiolo

Ma anche le (cose) che fate secondo la carne
—queste sono spirituali.
Ignatius of Antioch, *Ephesians*, 8:2
[*But even the things you do according to the flesh,*
—these are spiritual]

1.

At the beginning of *The Concept of Dread*, Kierkegaard mocks the traditional "explanations" of original sin as meaning the first sin, the sin of Adam. He observes that since thought here "stumbled upon difficulties" in trying to accept the correctness of such explanations, which self-evidently refused to address the seriousness of the problem, it was necessary to devise "a way out" by introducing a "fantastic assumption," whose loss was the outcome of transgression, that *condition* of sin in which the sons of Adam find themselves.[1]

Kierkegaard insists repeatedly here on this *fantastic* berth for so much Christian speculation concerning our origins, and Adam in Eden: "The history of the human race acquires a fantastic beginning," a "state" that "is not found in the world." He continues: "Adam was fantastically put outside," so that "pious sentiment and fantasy got what it desired, a godly prelude." Again, "In a double way was Adam kept fantastically outside": in Catholicism, where the assumption was "dialectic-fantastic" (and he quotes the catechism of the Council of Trent, where it affirms that Adam lost "donum divinitus datum supranaturale et admirabile"); and in the reformed tradition ("Covenant Theology"), on the other hand, basing itself on a "historically fantastic" assumption (and he recalls "the [dramatically] imaginary notion of Adam acting as a representative of the whole human race"[23]).

[1] S. Kierkegaard, *The Concept of Dread*, trans. Walter Lowrie (Princeton University Press, 1957), 23. Further references will be noted parenthetically in the text.

The commonest interpretations of the biblical episode, whose writing is apparently characterized by "finite and vulgar consequentiality" also for Hegel, the great interlocutor of the Danish philosopher,[2] turn out to be "an ideal of the imagination"—"ein Ideal der Phantasie." Hegel also argued, however, in line with that demythification of the text (which runs from Aristobulus to Bultmann) to free it from its "speculative content," that "reason does not (however) allow itself to be led into error by these inconsistencies," thus finally finding within it that "eternal history of man" which is "the depth of the narration" itself (Hegel, 123). And the sense of the narration itself reveals, I would add, that "natural man is just what he shouldn't be:" "he is not free either for himself or towards external nature; he is the man of desire, of the boorishness of egoism, of dependence, and of fear" (Hegel, 97). The "naturalness and innocence" of such a paradisal condition, "however sweet it may be," argues Hegel, "a) is not without its horrible sides" (i.e., the "barbaric customs [human sacrifices]" associated with the gentle customs of so many peoples to whom "a milder climate" and a nature which "provided the means to satisfy physical needs" allowed a "sweet and benevolent" [Hegel, 98, 97] character,—evidently like Adam in Eden); "b) in general... lacks that universal self-awareness and those consequences and developments which make up the honour of the spirit" (Hegel, 98 [b]). In fact Hegel insists that: "those so mild empirical conditions of which we have spoken, even if they have moved us, must not be given a stage of perfection; we cannot even do this for human childhood" (Hegel, 99). Man "already has within himself an element of spiritual culture" (Hegel, 98): in Eden he is like a child, and even if, in growing up, he will seem to pass to "a worse stage, to becoming something else, to a fall from on high, from a divine idea, from a divine image" (Hegel, 104), even so he *has to* grow up. "Children are not guilty, but because they have no will, they are incapable of any responsibility" (Hegel, 107): man "must not be like a child; in this sense he must not be innocent."

---

[2] See G. W. F. Hegel, *Vorlesungen über die Philosophie der Religion II/2: Die absolute Religion*, (Hamburg, 1966), 100 and 122 respectively.

2.

An Eden as a place of the imagination, however crude its physical qualities may be, when not redeemed by thought: this would seem to be the Eden of the Scriptures and of tradition for Kierkegaard and Hegel, two of the crucial witnesses of modernity.

And yet fantasy and vulgarity, if they really are to be found in the Bible (at least at some of its levels), are much less in evidence than one might suppose from the ancient exegetic tradition that tries to clarify it. Since this essay will deal mainly with texts of Eastern Christianity, let us recall one of the first, which dates perhaps from the beginning of the second century and was Greek or Syriac in its first version: the *Odes of Solomon*. Here, in *Ode* 11, verses 16–19, the singer/bard says of the Lord:

> 16 And he brought me to his paradise,
> where (are) the riches of the Lord's delight.
> I saw mature and fruitbearing trees.
> And their crown was natural;
> their timber sprouts,
> and their fruits were laughing.
> From immortal earth their roots,
> and a river of joy watered them,
> and round about the earth of their eternal life.
> 17 And I bowed down to the Lord because of his glory.
> 18 And I said, "Blessed are they, Lord,
> those who are planted in your earth,
> and those who have a place in your paradise.
> 19 And they grow in the growth of your trees,
> and they have changed from darkness to light."[3]

There is not the slightest hesitation here about the trees being the sons of Adam, the righteous planted "at the mouth of the waters," as the psalm proclaims, at the "source of life," in the *eschaton*! Of course,

[3] The *Odes* are from the text published by M. Franzmann in *The Odes of Solomon—An Analysis of the Poetical Structure and Form* (Freiburg-Göttingen, 1991), here page 84 (for the Syriac text) and page 87 (for the integration of v. 16, which can be inferred from the Greek text). A presentation of the *Odes* can now be found in the introduction that M.-J. Pierre has added to his edition of the collection in *Les Odes de Salomon* (Turnhout, 1994).

the Eden of *in the beginning* is the *eschaton*, the Eden a later anonymous Syriac commentator, maybe later than Ephrem, but possibly earlier and already active at the end of the third century (his writings are rich, certainly, in Hebrew echoes), will forcefully declare to be "the Holy Church," or "the mercy of God which must be shed on all men."

Since God knew, in his prescience, what Satan had plotted against Adam, he placed him immediately in his mercy, as the blessed David sang: *Lord, you have been our dwelling place in every age* [Psalms 90,1—a further review of the text, which I shall return to later and call A, adds here "that is, you have made us in your mercy"]. And when he supplicates God [A adds: for the salvation of man], [David] says: *Remember your church, that you have possessed from the beginning* [Psalms 74:2], i.e. the mercy you must shed on our feeble offspring. Eden [is] the holy church, and the paradise that can be found in it is the inheritance of the rest and the region of life that God has prepared for the saints.[4]

On the other hand, in the third quarter of the fourth century, Ephrem, in whose school some suggest the author of *The Book of the Cavern* was formed, will not be reading the beauties of paradise very differently.[5] Certainly, for example, he will linger on a celebration of the vigorous physical growth, the sensitive beauty, of his welcoming trees.

---

[4] See *La caverne des Trésors—Les deux recensions syriaques*, Su-Min Ri (ed.) CSCO 486 (t) and 487 (v) (Louvain, 1987), here c. III v. 17–20, respectively to 27 (B) and 26 (A) for the text, and 13 (B) and 12 (A) for the translation. On the text, see my brief notes in "Lineamenti di patrologia siriaca," in *Complementari di Patrologia*, ed. A. Quacquarelli (Rome, 1989), 503–603, here 538–539.

[5] On Ephrem see S. Brock's excellent book, *The Luminous Eye—The Spiritual Vision of St. Ephrem* (Rome, 1985). The *Hymns on Paradise*, which I discuss below, have been edited by E. Beck in *Des heiligen Ephraim des Syrers Hymnen de Paradiso und Contra Julianum*, CSCO 174 (t) (Louvain, 1957). Available in a fine French translation, ed. R. Lavenant (with an introduction and notes by F. Graffin) in SC 137 (Paris, 1968), and in English, ed. S. Brock, in St. Ephrem the Syrian, *Hymns on Paradise* (New York: St. Vladimir's Seminary Press, 1990). They have been the object of an important study by N. Séd, "Les Hymnes sur le Paradis de Saint Ephrem et les traditions juives," *Le Muséon* 81(1968), 455–501.

He writes:

> "Should you wish/to climb up a tree,
> with its lower branches/it will provide steps before your feet,
> eager to make you recline/in its bosom above
> on the couch of its upper branches.
> So arranged is the surface of these branches
> bent low and cupped /—While yet dense with flowers—
> that they serve as a protective womb/for whoever rests there:"[6]

But further on he tells us: "All that you hear told/about this Paradise,/so pure and holy,/is pure and spiritual."[7]

And at once repeats: "since, even though it may appear terrestrial/ because of the terms used,/it is in its reality/spiritual and pure" (*Hymnen*, 155).

Indeed, he adds,

> "For him who would tell of it/there is no other means
> but to use the names/of things that are visible,
> thus depicting for his hearers/a likeness of things that are hidden.
> For if the Creator/of the Garden
> has clothed his Majesty/in terms that we can understand,
> how much more can his Garden/be described with our similes?
> (...)
> Do not let your intellect/be disturbed by mere names,
> for Paradise has simply clothed itself in terms that are akin to you;
> it is not because it is impoverished/that it has put on your imagery;
> rather, your nature is far too weak/to be able
> to attain to its greatness,/and its beauties are much diminished
> by being depicted in the pale colours/with which you are familiar." (*Hymns*, 155–156)

---

[6] *Hymnen* 9.3, 36 (here in the Brock version, *Hymns*, 137.) As can be seen, it is this interpretation of the *eschaton* as a return to a "pre-existence" that creates problems. Here I point out only that the *Hymns* of Ephrem are rich in images inferred from a non-"historical" world, and in particular from the vegetable kingdom, to indicate the perfect life. Adam, in sinning, is thrown out of the garden, whose boundaries are constituted by silent fig-trees, and at whose center stands the tree of life: from that moment his living diminishes, disturbed, among the wild beasts, from the agitation provoked by volitions or passions by no means animal, to find eventually annihilation and custody, dying, among the cold, hard stones (on these developments and on the traditions behind them, see Séd's article quoted above, in note 15).

[7] *Hymnen* 11.3, here 47; in the Brock version, *Hymns*, 155.

This is the message, then: the fullness of the senses of the kingdom ("fruits serve as their sky/flowers as their earth,"—"a cloud of fruits providing shade/for the head," "fruit to eat,/and fruit to quench the thirst;—to rinse the hands there is dew,/and leaves to dry them with after," "a garment of flowers/spread out beneath the feet..." [*Hymns*, 137–138]) have no substance whatsoever. If I may be allowed a quotation which will be useful later, the modern demand, inappropriately,

Is there no change of death in paradise?
Does ripe fruit never fall? Or do the boughs
Hang always heavy in that perfect sky,
Unchanging, yet so like our perishing earth,
With rivers like our own that seek for seas
They never find, the same receding shores
That never touch with inarticulate pang?
Why set the pear upon those river banks
Or spice the shores with odor of the plum?[8]

The question is inappropriate because such overabundance of good things, entirely full-bodied, shining, fleshed with vital juices, and irresistible, evaporate in their own matter. If the spirit, (which yet could do so), de facto "without its companion (the body)/... lacks true existence," and only in that has perception and life—it must also be said that "at the end/the body will put on" the beauty of the soul, "while the spirit shall put on/the very likeness of God's majesty."[9] So "bodies shall be raised/to the level of souls," and the spirit itself will be beyond itself, overwhelmed by "the waves of this joy," "as its faculties suck/at the breast of all Wisdom"— or, to quote the text exactly, "of Wisdoms."[10]

There is a taking leave of the body, then, in these texts; a taking leave of history, too — but not so much for fantastic worlds as for the kingdom, a kingdom whose dimensions are those indicated by Paul, in a verse often quoted in similar contexts: "Eye has not seen, nor ear heard, neither have entered into the heart of man, the things which God hath prepared for them that love him" (1Cor. 2:9).

---

[8] See Wallace Stevens, *Sunday Morning* VI, *Collected Poems* (New York: A. Knopf).

[9] See *Hymnen* 8.5 and 6, 34. Brock, *Hymns*, 143.

[10] *Hymnen* 9.21 and 23, 41 and Brock, *Hymns*, 143–144.

3.

The power of this leave-taking was known also to Kierkegaard. In *Either/Or*, through the pen of Judge William, an ethical Christian, celebrator of that unexpected salvation of the sensory in that spiritual life which in fact only Christianity introduces, — if he at first rejoices "that the God, who is spirit, loves also the love which is earthly,"[11] he is then led to recognize that "the God of the Christians, the God who is spirit, and is jealous of everything which is not spirit" (*Either/Or*, 49), and therefore to say, about his own Christian marriage, in which nevertheless in principle "the sensual is by no means denied, but rather ennobled":

> "I confess—it is wrong of me perhaps—that often when I think of my own marriage, the mental picture of it arouses in me an inexplicable sadness, for the fact that it will come to an end, that certain as I am that with her to whom I was united in marriage I shall live in another life, yet there she will be given to me in another way, that the contradiction which was a component in our love will be abolished. Yet it consoles me to know that I shall remember that with her I lived in the most heartfelt, the most beautiful relationship which human life affords. If I have any understanding of the matter, the defect of earthly love is the same thing as its advantageous quality, i.e., its partiality. Spiritual love has no partiality and moves in the opposite direction, constantly abhorring all relativities." (*Either/Or*, 62–63)

Now here we have a second feature of the difficult reception of the Biblical text, in shifting its meaning to *eschaton*: just as at first reading it seems to reflect a childlike dreaming (Hegel would have called it "animal"), now with the spiritualization of its interpretation it seems to make us melancholy for a lost creatural quality, rendered pointless.

What makes us uneasy is the passion for the present, the present of an individual alive in the "graceful" singularity of his/her history, a history the events of Christianity (at least in its Pauline version) has opened up. And it is the discernment of the *eschaton* as a discernment of the spirit, of what may be spiritual, which becomes central here.

Kierkegaard said of this passion against Hegelian allegory, for example, which resolved the individual into thought: "Man is immortal

---

[11] See S. Kierkegaard, *Either/Or*, rev. ed. H. A. Johnson (Princeton University Press, 1971), 21.

only because of knowledge; since only as a thinking being he isn't mortal, or in other words animal; but a pure, free spirit; the root of his life is knowledge, or thought...."[12]

Wallace Stevens, whose reservations regarding the fixed perfection of an eternal Eden I noted earlier, spoke in a late, rich letter of this same passion for the present, however unstable, or restless, *against the East*:

> While you are free to challenge the idea that the poets of antiquity in the East were not the same rollicking characters as the poets of antiquity in the West, I am no less free to reply that those in the East were so often lonely horsemen, hermits beside water falls, passengers on moonlit roads and men whose hearts were hollow, while those in the West were flirtatious young men that stood outside of the post office and picked up girls, sailors, tourists, and professors at Fribourg. Enfin, I refuse to take seriously the idea that living in a bamboo grove increases one's heft. If I lived in one for a week, I should be all elbows and knees at the end of that time."[13]

I would like to suggest here, in parenthesis, that this passion, as a passion for freedom to take a risk which is essential to it, also goes through the Origenian meditation on *eschaton*. Origen's questioning of himself on how one can endow stability in the determination of the *autoexousion* at the end of time, is not without point. Because if such a decision should turn out to be irrevocable through an act of divine abuse of power, the creature would have his essential difference taken away from him, which only freedom can guarantee, and with this the terms themselves of the creational act of God would be rendered futile: the production of a being in his image. But how can liberty otherwise be bound, in its intrinsic power of different resolution?[14]

I should note at this point that a passion of this kind is certainly older than Christianity. There are pages of Plato, for example, where the present, an impossible present, is, perhaps, his ultimate passion. Thus the myth in the *Politics* about the age of the world leads us to

---

[12] Hegel, *Vorlesungen uber die Philosophie der Religion*, 129.

[13] Wallace Stevens, *Letters of Wallace Stevens*, ed. M. Stevens (London, 1966).

[14] See briefly M. Simonetti in his introduction to Origen, *I Principi* (Turin, 1979), 71–71, and, among the texts of the Alexandrian referred to there, especially the decisive one in Origen, *Commento alla lettera ai Romani—Libri I–VII*, ed. F. Cocchini (Casale Monferrato, 1985), V,10, 298–300.

think that the best time for man is not that of God's government, when there was certainly no need, "so that there was nothing savage, nor did (men) devour each other, nor was there any war or conflict among them," nor even, it would seem, any interest in knowledge. The times of poverty, then, were happier times; the times in which unfortunately only in *individuals*, in impotence, as the *Laws* suggest, does that active awareness which makes man precious flourish more intensely. The individuals succumb to the obscurity of time, like Dion, perhaps. But coming to an end *in this way*—while operating *in spem contra spem*—they are at their finest, in the conjunction pursued freely, laboriously, and with extreme intelligence, of a fine living *in the present.*[15]

To return to our reflections on that critical text for *eschaton* which is the Genesis passage on Adam, in the awareness of the concerns recalled above within which there has been enquiry in modern times, I would like to continue with the recognition and discussion of at least one of the interpretative traditions, present from the earliest centuries in Christian texts.

4.

In an essay which, while not recent, still has much to tell us about Syrian asceticism, S. Brock was led to observe—in commenting on the hermitic, wild and frankly unpleasant features of early monasticism in Syria (as we can see from Ephrem's undoubtedly authentic texts)—that they emphasize, in their own way, the return of the Christian to the Adamitic state.[16] The monks lived in solitude, in desert places, perfect images of the Only-begotten, just like Adam and Eve. God was sufficient for them, in reality, so there was no need for others. Again, in such solitude Adam carried out the perfect will of God, and had a part in His spirit. Perhaps it could be said that in this way he was male and female, undifferentiated, one, in the incessant celebration of the celestial liturgy. When the desire to distinguish, or to divide things up into separate parts, entered into him, he lost his original familiarity with God:

---

[15] See especially K. Gaiser, *Plato's Metaphysic of History*, above all the first part.

[16] See S. Brock, "Early Syrian Asceticism," *Numen* 20 (1973), 1–19.

according to the traditions that Aphraates reports, he then abandoned the Father and Mother (God and his Spirit) to live with the woman created out of him, separate—no longer the sole one near the Sole One, no longer one near to the One, but made into the many.

In his *Exposition Against the Jews, on Virginity and Holiness*, Aphraates in fact writes:

> 10. We have heard the Law: *a man [shall] leave his father and his mother and shall cleave unto his wife: and they shall be one flesh* (Gen. 2:24). This is truly a great and excellent prophecy! Who leaves his father and mother from the time he takes a woman as wife? This is the sense (of the verses): man, when he has not yet taken a woman as wife, loves and honors God, his father, and the spirit of holiness, his mother, nor does he have any other love. But (this same) man, when he has taken a wife, leaves his father and his mother, the above mentioned, and his intellect joins to this world, and his intellect, his heart and his thought are drawn by God into this world and they love him and favour him, *as the man loves the wife of his youth* [Proverbs, 5:18], and the love for her is separate from that for his father and mother. 11. And (the Law) says: *they will become one flesh*—and it is true that, as man and wife become one flesh and one intellect, and the intelligence and the thought (of the man) move away from his father and mother, thus the man who has not yet taken a wife and remains single proceeds from his father with one spirit and one intellect.[17]

It should be noted that Gen. 2:24, on which Aphraates' exegesis turns, is the verse of the so-called second story of the creation: here Eve has already been generated! A little before the passage just quoted, in a paragraph to which the French translator gave the title "L'entrée du mal dans le monde," Aphraates had written:

> 9. The world, when it was virgin, was not impure, but after the rain fell on it, it made thorns grow [see Gen. 3:5 and 3:18]. Adam also, in his virginity, was pleasant and handsome, but after generating Eve, he did wrong and transgressed the commandment.[18]

---

[17] See *Aphraatis Sapientis Persae Demonstrationes*, ed. J. Parisot, PS 1 (Paris, 1894), and PS 2 (Paris, 1907), 1–489, here *Demonstratio* 18.10, 840. For an overall introduction to Aphraates see M.-J. Pierre: Aphraate le Sage Persan, *Les Exposés* I, SC 349 (Paris, 1988), 33–199.

[18] Aphraates' text is in PS 1, 837. See Pierre, in Aphraates, the Persian sage, *Les Exposés* II, SC 359 (Paris, 1989), 760.

Of the virginity of the earth, in a place in which Aphraates was meditating on the resurrection of the dead, an easier job than the one on the beginning, on creation, he had written (in a parenthesis): "it generated that which had not befallen in her, and when she did not conceive, it generated in her virginity. (...) Adam, in fact, was not seed that grew, he was not conceived and given birth to."[19]

So to an original fertile virginity, rendered fertile by God, is opposed a fertility of marriage which is actually prisoner of death. For the development of this last thought and to recapitulate the above themes, but also in connection with the teachings of the *Odes of Solomon* and the *Hymns of Paradise*, I reproduce here an ample selection of the meditation of Aphraates on the *eschaton*, and offer some further reflections on it.

> 12. In that region (eschatological Eden), [men] will forget this world. There they will have no needs, and they will love each other in the compassion that will be shed around. There will be no heaviness in their bodies, so they will fly with ease, *as the doves to their windows* [Isaiah 60:8]. There memories of evil will not be harbored in their minds, nor will anything impure rise in their hearts. Nor is there in that region the desire of nature: they will be weaned of every desire, because neither animosity nor immodesty will arise in their hearts. Also all that generates sin will pass away from them. In their hearts only reciprocal love will burn, no hatred will find its way into them.
>
> There they will not need to build houses, because they will live in fire, the dwelling place of saints.
>
> They will not have need to dress in clothes, because they will be dressed in eternal light.
>
> They will not need food, because they will sit at His table and will be nourished forever.
>
> There the air is desirable and magnificent, and its light splendid, magnificent and beautiful. There beautiful trees are planted, whose fruits do not diminish, whose leaves do not fall.
>
> (...)

[19] See PS 1, *Demonstratio* 8.6, here 372.

There no one loves his neighbour with excessive fear, but loves each and every one with enthusiasm, in the same way.

There they will not take wives nor generate children, nor will male and female be separated but all will be children of the Father who is in the heavens, as the prophet said: *Have we not all one father? hath not one God created us?* [Malachi 2:10].

13. And concerning what I have said, that there they will not take wives nor will male and female be separated,—our Lord and his apostle (themselves) have taught (this). Our Lord said: *But they which shall be accounted worthy to obtain that world, and the resurrection from the dead, neither marry, nor are given in marriage; Neither can they die any more; for they are equal unto the angels; and are the children of God* [Luke 20:35 and 36]. And the apostle said: *there is neither bond nor free, there is neither male nor female; for ye are all one in Christ Jesus* [Gal. 3:28].

In fact God separated Eve from Adam for generation, so that she become the mother of all. However, in that world there will be no female, just as in heaven there is no female, nor generation, nor commerce with desire. In that region there is no poverty of any kind, but only perfection and completeness: the old will not die nor the young become old, because the young take wives and generate children in the conviction that they will become old and die, so that when the fathers are dead, the children will take their place. All that, however, is (only) how it is in this world, because in that region there is neither need nor poverty, nor desire nor generation, nor end nor decease nor death, nor old age nor hatred, nor animosity nor zeal, nor work nor labour, nor darkness nor night nor lies.

In that region then there is no necessity, but it is full of light and life, of mercy and fulfilment, of satisfaction and joy and compassion/mercy, and of all the good promises, written and unwritten.

There, there is in fact what "eye hath not seen nor ear heard, neither have entered into the heart of man the things which God hath prepared for them that love him." [1Cor. 2:9][20]

Two features of this long quotation should be brought out; firstly the themes connected to the male/female opposition, and secondly those linked to having (or not having) clothes, a home, and work.

[20] Ibid. 22.12–13; 1013–1020.

5.

The features indicated above are obviously quite widespread in the Christian literature about our origins, and there are many studies concerning their many-sided complexities. Here I would like to recall a few individual aspects, beginning with a note I read in the margin to the *loghion* 114 of the *Gospel of Thomas*, in a recent study.[21]

That Gospel is generally dated at around the fifties of the second century, and is said to be the product of a group active in Eastern Syria, perhaps at Edessa. Some, like Theissen, have felt they perceived the result of a "modification" of the "ethical radicalism" or "of the praxis" of the tradition of the *loghia* of Jesus, in a "Gnostic or speculative radicalism... without practical consequences."[22] As Meeks sums it up, they read there the way in which "an eschatological ethos, adopted by prophets who called on the people to face an imminent transformation in their living worked by God, becomes a way of life that has to be made inner," in the perception that "the world itself is corrupt and kills" and to break away, if only in some way *in interiore homine,* is the only "life that procures salvation."[23]

These ideas concerning the beginnings and the evolution of themes linked to the preaching and eschatological behavior in Syria in the earliest Christian centuries may be kept in mind: they help, perhaps, to make more sense of what M. Lelyveld observes on the *loghion* of the Gospel, to which I referred above. One thing I spoke of there is the fate of Mary, whom Simon Peter wanted to expel from the group of disciples because "women are not worthy of the life," but whom Jesus drew to himself to make of her "a man, so that she too may become a living spirit, similar to you men," as he says to Peter, "because every woman who makes herself into a man will enter into the Kingdom of Heaven."

---

[21] M. Lelyveld, *Les Logia de la vie dans l'Evangile selon Thomas—A la Recherche d'une tradition et d'une rédaction* (Leiden–New York–Copenhagen–Cologne, 1987). The *loghion* 114 is reproduced, translated and commented on in ch. X of the book, under the title "the creation of woman," (138–143).

[22] See G. Theissen.

[23] See W. A. Meeks, *The Moral World of the First Christians* (Philadelphia, 1986), 108 and 105 respectively.

In commenting on these words Lelyveld is led to observe that the exclusion of the woman from Israel, to which Peter testifies (but also, I would add, the *way* she is admitted there by Jesus), can be understood only within "the loss of the sense of sacredness in earthly living" which characterizes the events of a sizeable part of the Judaic traditions in the time of middle Judaism, above all in its later phase.[24] So the conditions of the first Adam become increasingly those of a "celestial" life, and "the messianic infants" rediscover Adam one, and alone: the "*only created*" (by God), as Wisdom 10:1, says "alone like God," and *in this way* protected by his Wisdom; moreover, perhaps, as was suggested already, androgynous, and in *this* uniqueness the image of God.[25]

Lelyveld does grasp this, but I feel he does not insist on it sufficiently: this reading of Adam as heavenly, virgin, and who has not yet generated Eve, is radically alternative to that of Adam *ghenos*, or intelligible, in Philo's words; this reading that articulates the two stories of Genesis as successive moments of one historical event is something else with respect to the one that situates them in the perspective (Platonic, if you like) of the connection idea/sensory reality. Adam here is an existing being from the beginning, but it is an existence as it were *suspended.* A text of the Syrian ferment of the end of the fourth century, the *Liber graduum*, argues this very clearly. In 21,7, for example, we read:

> So Adam first was according to the perfect will of God, that which Jesus, in coming, showed in himself to whoever wished to be like him and be perfect, and looked at the heavens, and not at the earth, and rejoiced with the higher guardians, without care and without pain,—nor did he have to worry about food or clothes [see Matt. 6:25–31], but God Himself nourished him, as was right for the wealth of his gentleness, with bread from heaven [see John 6:31 ff.], as is written: Man *ate the food of angels* [Psalms 78:25]. And there

---

[24] See Lelyveld, *Les Logia*, 140, and in the same perspective, the notes of G. Garbini in *Cantico dei Cantici* (Brescia, 1992), particularly 320 ff., where the polemic of the Canticle's author against pr 1–9 is evident, against the tradition of knowledge, dominated by "a real phobia towards sex" (ibid. 321).

[25] "Messianic infant" ("enfant messianique") is Lelyveld's expression in *Les Logia*, the title of the first chapter of his study, 25–32. Similar developments, in relation to what Wisdom 10 says of Adam, are to be found in G. Scarpat, *Libro della Sapienza* II (Brescia, 1996), 278–279.

> was no work or pains of the body, as David also explained: *Because* the sons of man *rebelled against the words of God,*—those that had told them not to disobey my commandments—*and contemned the counsel of the most High*— that he wished them to be like angels—*Therefore he brought down their heart with labour; they fell down, and there was none to help.* [Psalms 107:11–12][26]

In fact in a previous section (21,2), the author had promised:

> And I will explain the way God first commanded Adam to be holy, perfect as the watchers and the angels in heaven, to dwell in spirit in heaven, with the angels, even though bodily he was on the earth, but naked of everything that is in it, having his intelligence wrapped in the glory of his Creator, while the earth is invisible to him.[27]

This is the heavenly life, a rapt life, careless of the world, which includes the emergence of the second feature; a life in the open, doing nothing, naked, as well as alone.

6.

There is no point in lingering for too long over this last theme. Like virginity or holiness, it is at least in part a theme found in the most ancient traditions (probably Judeo-Christian) of the churches of Syria, which Murray has studied in some depth with reference to the materials of a prebaptismal catechism, widespread in the various communities of the region, turning up in the writings of many authors.[28]

At the center of the latter are recalled, among other things, the words of the priest to the men of Israel, assembled before the battle in the "holy war"(Deut. 20:2–9); and the living experience of being a Christian is presented, in its inescapable opposition to the world, to its volition and to its behavior, as the *truth* of that war. So he who wishes to face the battle must be without home, woman and work. This is demanded of him by the single-minded concentration required by war; and it is demanded by the *state* from which he will move to the conflict,

---

[26] The *Liber graduum* is published by M. Kmosko in PS 3 (Paris, 1926); the passage quoted in the text is on pages 600,20–601,11. See also A. Kowalski, *Perfezione e giustizia di Adamo nel Liber graduum* (Rome, 1989).

[27] *Liber graduum*, 588,22–589,3.

[28] See R. Murray, "The Exhortation to Candidates for Ascetical Vows at Baptism in the Ancient Syriac Church," *New Testament Studies* 21 (1975), 59–80.

which would have no reason for existing unless he was on the point of becoming solitary/only begotten, like the Son, through baptism, in this way radically opposing himself to the world: "The single man is fitted for the struggle," Aphraates writes, thinking of Phil. 2:13–15, "because their face is set towards [what is] in front of them, nor do they recall what is behind them."[29]

And it is this living in abstinence, marginal to the world and devoted only to the anticipation of the celestial liturgy, to which even considerations like those in the *Liber graduum*, that counterpose the righteous and the perfect (the former placed under the law, because bound to worldly behavior, and the latter free from it), bear witness.[30] And the position of the former is the same as that of Adam the sinner, thrown out of Eden and now incapable of being guardian to the "entire will" of God; capable however of observing His later commandments, those which in his memory lead him to not do to others what he would not have them do to us.[31] The position of the latter, on the other hand, is that of Christ, perfect Adam, *emptied* of the world and, in it, only witness of the emptying/charity of God.[32]

The *Liber graduum*, it must be added, does not counterpose the two orders in a static way; nor does it say that the destiny of the righteous is one thing, that of the perfect another. As has been suggested, between the fourth and fifth centuries in Syria many and varied are the environments in which old forms of local asceticism and new statutes of monasticism, cenobitical and solitary, arriving from Egypt, are mixed together and reemerge in new forms. Old ecclesiologies, if not theologies, are thought out again, after contact with new doctrines concerning the "states of perfection," with results that are more or less consistent

---

[29] See PS 1, *Demonstratio* 7,18, here 341.

[30] On these themes see Kowalski's study in general, cited in note 26.

[31] See, for example, *Liber graduum* 1,4, here 18: "Adam, our father, fell from the pedestal of perfection and remained on the pedestal of justice, that (is): do not do unto anyone that which is hateful, and: as he wishes should be done unto him, so he should do to the men he comes up against."

[32] On the Adam-Christ relation, see Kowalski, *Perfezione e giustizia*, 110–115; on the chenosis/emptying, in relation to Phil. 2:6–7, see ibid. 138–140.

with the behavior and teachings of the so-called "great church."[33] The authors of the *Liber graduum* do not divide the community into words and acts, though they do bear witness to a tension, of which they are dramatically aware and which they know for its violent outcomes.[34] They cannot or do not know how to dissolve the terms either practically or theoretically, because the Adam in God is distracted from the world and can only say about it that it is transient, like the reality contained in it.

In the unease which such a figure could and can now bring on, does something re-echo that is not the mere melancholy/jealousy of an impassioned spirit?

Adam lives a suspended life, I said. This has to be interpreted, however. Kierkegaard also imagined an unreal life for the Adam before sin: he was then "not animal, but neither is he properly a man;" he was a spirit, yes, but a "dreaming spirit," that "is not yet posited as spirit;" he gave names to the animals, but "as... children when they are learning to recognize an animal on the ABC card,"[35] that is, quite superficially. Only in sin does he fully become man (*Dread*, 44). It is not like this for the ancient texts: what is set out for Adam there is positive living, before sin; a living that also has its own duration, to be conjectured, extrapolating from the biblical texts or from traditions related to them, sometimes in hours, sometimes even in a week.[36] It remains to be said, however, that his living, whether it be a question of days or hours, is in any case a lived experience taken out of history.

---

[33] See J. Gribomont, "Les Homélies ascétiques de Philoxène de Mabboug et l'écho de Messalianisme," *L'Orient syrien* 2(1957), 419–432.

[34] See the notes that Kowalski devotes to "Ambiente e datazione del *Liber graduum*" in *Perfezione e giustizia*, 213–222.

[35] Kierkegaard, *The Concept of Dread*, 44 and 42 respectively.

[36] On the traditions relating to those few hours that passed between creation and Adam's sin see W. F. Macomber, "The Theological Synthesis of Cyrus of Edessa, an East Syrian Theologian of the Mid Sixth Century," *Orientalia Christiana Periodica* 30 (1964), 5–38 and 363–384, here 14 note 1; on those that define the period in a week, see Lelyveld, *Les Logia*, 27.

The unease I mentioned is felt by the ancient sources themselves, that often cannot decide whether Adam was mortal or not, in the beginning;[37] that cannot decide whether the whole of history *ascends* to Jesus or *descends* to him, and that often present the two versions together, without deciding.[38]

I would like to offer at least one solution to this set or series of problems, which will have to be gone into more deeply in later work. My starting point for what follows are the writings of a late Nestorian monk, Isaac of Nineveh, who lived mainly between Qatar and Khuzistan in the second half of the seventh century.[39]

7.

Neither the consensus nor the polemics that marked the reception of Isaac's works should obscure the broadly traditional features of his writings, in which expressions and thoughts of previous literature—monastic, certainly, but also homiletic, exegetic, or theological—reappear in a balance precariously maintained between sometimes very different theses.

This is not the place to point out these extensive derivations. Suffice it to emphasize Isaac's full, strong conviction, which he shares with his sources, of the centrality of the experience of solitariness in the Christian tradition. This is consistent with the twin witnessing that characterizes it: first a witness for hope, a reason for the proclamation of the resurrection of the dead, that the solitary person carries out in the very act of renouncing the world (intending to show through this that it is not the untranscendable end of human living, that only God knows and gives[40]); second, a witness for the *absolute* novelty of the *eschaton*,

---

[37] See the notes in the introduction by K. Alwan and Jacques de Saroug, *Quatre homélies métriques sur la création*, CSCO 509 (Louvain, 1989), especially XXII–XXIII.

[38] See Macomber, *The Theological Synthesis*, 10 ff.

[39] See my introduction to a volume of his writings, *Discorsi spirituali ed altri opuscoli* (Magnano [BI], 1990), 9–44.

[40] On this feature of Isaac's teaching see discourse II of the so-called "first part" of his writings, that can be read in the English version edited by A. J. Wensinck, *Mystic Treatises by Isaac of Nineveh* (Amsterdam, 1923), 80–82.

that the world, the creature, cannot in any way comprehend, and that the solitary person testifies to extraordinarily by making himself void, rendering himself completely silent, in mute expectation.[41] But the two features are consistent with the Gospel only if held with charity[42]—and charity, "the power of the kingdom,"[43] is from the start the creative gesture of God, repeated in His delivering the Son to humiliation and death, which revives the world in its creatural quality and raises it to intimacy with the Creator, when one loves.[44] And perhaps this is the point in which Isaac takes up the tradition most strongly and at the same time is most innovative: that because of this there is no rule or path to be present to God, to be men of His presence, alive; there is only surrender, within which to be led to attempt the ever more rapid steps of a free walking onwards.[45] Humility—mercy, in fact—is the creature's only and indefinable path, which God Himself discovers.[46]

---

[41] On the transcendence of the future world to the creatural order and on the fact that one can have knowledge of it only through spiritual revelations, see for example *Capitoli della conoscenza* 3,56, in Isaac of Nineveh, *Discorsi spirituali*, 133–134; on worship, as the extreme act of man (and of the solitary person), see ibid. 1,20, 55.

[42] On charity as the distinctive feature of the Christian authenticity of the solitary life itself see discourse 81 of the "first part" of his writings, in the English version quoted above, *Mystic Treatises*, 379–381.

[43] See *Capitoli dell conoscenza* 4,78, in *Discorsi spirituali*, 183.

[44] *Capitoli*, 4,81, in *Discorsi*, 185.

[45] On the image of God as mother "who teaches her child to walk," see discourse 36 in *Discorsi ascetici*, 303. We can also recall here that for Isaac, Adam, who was mortal from the beginning, had not been created to stay in Eden, but to come out of it, so that he can write for example in *Capitoli della conoscenza* 3,2: "We are not mortal because we sin, but because we are mortal we were pushed towards sin" (see *Discorsi spirituali*, 119). "Disobedience did not bring the house of Adam towards death, nor did disobeying the commandment force them to leave paradise: it is certain that (God) did not create Adam and Eve so that they should stay in paradise, in a small area of the earth, but so they could *be lords* over all the earth" (see Gen. 1:28); he writes this in an important meditation on the subject of Gehenna which can be read in the "second part" of his writings, and which I have translated here from my own translation into Italian in *Discorsi spirituali*, 227–237, here 229.

[46] On the theme of humility in Isaac see discourse 82 of the "first part" of his writings, in *Mystic Treatises*, 384–389.

For the rest, only God can, and provides; He has loved this world, as it was, and it will be, unfailingly, through His grace; without this grace no one can do anything, unless they have received it from Him.[47]

Melancholy proceeds in each and every one, from wanting to define a condition, a thought, a work of salvation; in wishing to privilege something over/against something else, while "the Truth is hidden in its being to everything created, and those beings gifted with reason through him, live a long way off from it"—all of them.[48]

All existences are finished, for themselves; but God is open to all of them, if they give themselves to Him. It is difficult to adhere to the modesty that such propositions require; they strip away every ambition, but both the modern and the ancient feel love for this stripping away, and confess:

"Denn Armut ist ein grosser Glanz aus Innen..."[49]

---

[47] See Isaac's slightly younger contemporary Simon of Taibuteh, in *Libro della Grazia* 2,25: "the things of the Lord come from themselves" (on this still unpublished text and its parallels with similar passages in Isaac's writings, see my book on Simon of Taibuteh, *Violenza e grazia—La coltura del cuore* (Rome, 1992), 152 note 16.

[48] See *Capitoli della conoscenza*, 1,2, in *Discorsi spirituali*, 51.

[49] Rilke, *Das Stunden-Buch* 3,17, in *Samtliche Werke. Erster Band*, 356. For the ancients, see Simon of Taibuteh on the "light of thought" or of "the inner man," "of which the fathers speak;" this is none else than "the light of humility and meekness that our Lord has shown in himself" (*Libro della grazia* 3,21, on which see Simon, *Violenza e grazia*, 82 note 5).

Adam's Paradise in the Koran and in the Muslim Exegetical Tradition

Ida Zilio-Grandi

Numerous passages in the Koran recount the creation of Adam, his time in the Garden, his temptation and fall, and his final forgiveness by God. However, the most substantial description, the one which contains all the elements concerning Adam, and consequently the one most closely commented upon, is to be found in verses 29–37 of the second *sūra*, "of the cow" (*sūrat al-baqra*). I shall therefore pay particular attention to this passage, presenting it in the words of the Koran following the exegesis of certain orthodox authors, whose authority is such that they virtually comprise a canon.[1]

In the passage in question, the story of Adam is preceded by a long description of characters that recur often in Koranic preaching: in brief, the unbelievers and the hypocrites, those who question the truth of the Prophet Muhammad, the revelation contained in the Koran and indeed the entire prophetic structure found in the Holy Book, that structure, that is, which gathers all of history around the divine word of Revelation through a prophet. According to the Koran, God has a pattern, which is both history and natural law, which repeats from the era of the progenitors—i.e., the prophetic cycle of Adam, who, we will see, is the first man but also the first prophet—to the time of Muhammad, i.e., the cycle of Islam. The history of the created world is a continual

[1] The exegetical works are: Ṭabarī (d. 310 of the hegira/923 A.D.), *Ǧāmi' al-bayān*, ed. Šākir, Dār al-ma'ārif, Cairo n.d. (henceforth T); Zamaḫšarī (d. 538/1144), *al-Kaššāf 'an ḥaqā'iq ğaw āmid al-tanzīl*, Dār al-kitāb al-'arabī, Beirut n.d. (henceforth Z); Rāzī (d. 606/1209), *Mafā tīḥ al-ġayb*, Dār al-fikr, Beirut 3rd edition 1405/1985 (henceforth R); Qurtubī (d. 671/1271), *al-Ǧāmi'li-aḥkām al-Qur'ān*, Dār al-maktaba al-'ilmiyya, Beirut 1413/1993 (henceforth Q); Bayḍāwī (d. 691/1291), *Anwār al-tanzīl*, ed. Fleischer (Beidhawii, *Commentarius in Coranum*, 1846–1848), Osnabruck 1968 (henceforth B); Suyūṭī (d. 911/1505), *al-Durr al-manṯūur*, Beirut 1411/1990 (henceforth S); Alūsī (d. 1270/1854), *Rūḥ al-ma'ānī*, Dār al-turāṯ al-'arabī, Beirut n.d. (henceforth A).

succession of repetitions: revelation to a chosen community through a prophet; fall into error; punishment and then forgiveness of the merciful and compassionate God giving rise to new revelation; and so on down to Islam, which is considered the ultimate and definitive divine teaching.

Having repeated this point, the passage from the Koran then calls on all the impious to observe the clear proof that is represented by the Koran itself, and challenges them to produce something of equal beauty and wisdom. They will be unable to do this as the Word of God[2] is inimitable; it is the evidence of the Koranic miracle.

At this point, the text introduces the image of the eschatological Paradise: for believers there will be gardens in whose shade rivers flow, gardens full of fruit inhabited by pure spouses, where the elect will remain in eternity. Damnation, on the other hand, awaits those who *"break the covenant*[3] *of Allah after having affirmed it, and cut asunder that which Allah has bidden to be joined, and create disorder in the land; it is these that are the losers."*[4] In a solemn hymn to divine power and goodness, Islam's Holy Book then asks: *"How can you disbelieve in Allah? You were without life and He gave you life, then He will cause you to die, then He will restore you to life and then to Him you will be made to return"* (Koran 2:29). The song to the wisdom of creation now takes the form of the story of the origins:

> *He it is Who has created for your benefit all that is in the earth; then He turned towards the heavens and perfected them seven heavens. He has full knowledge of all things. 30) Call to mind, when thy Lord announced to the Angels: I am about to place a viceregent in the earth. They said: Wilt Thou then place there also such as will create disorder therein and shed blood, while we glorify thee*

---

[2] The Koran is the Word of God also in its formal expression.

[3] The covenant God stipulated with Adam and that Adam made on behalf of all his issue (see Koran 7:172). Adam's issue were called to the Covenant in a primeval call to life. According to the Tradition, his issue were then made to return into Adam's loins; the Covenant is therefore also the first death of entire humanity. Is it thus to be considered that Adam contains not only the life but also the death of every person?

[4] The translation here and henceforth is from *The Quran*, trans. Muhammad Zafrulla Khan (London and Dublin: Curzon Press, 1971).

> *with Thy praise and extol Thy Holiness? Whereupon He admonished them: I know that which you know not. 31) He taught Adam the names of all His attributes, then He presented the manifestations of those attributes to the Angels and asked them: Tell Me the names of these, if you are right. 32) They answered: Holy art Thou! No knowledge have we save that which Thou hast taught us. Thou alone art the All-Knowing, the Possessor of Wisdom. 33) He turned to Adam and commanded him: Adam, do thou inform them of the names of these. When Adam had told him the names, Allah said to the Angels: Did I not say to you: I know the secrets of the heavens and of the earth, and I know all that you disclose and all that you conceal? 34) Call to mind, when We commanded the Angels: Submit to Adam; they all submitted, but Iblis did not; he refused and was arrogant, being already one of the disbelievers. 35) We commanded Adam: Dwell thou and thy wife in the garden, and eat plentifully therefrom wherever you will, but approach not this one tree, lest you be of the wrongdoers. 36) But Satan caused them both to slip from their stand of obedience by means of that tree, and thus drove them out of the state in which they were. Whereupon We decreed: Go forth, some of you are enemies of others, and for you there is in the earth a place of abode and provision for a time 37) Thereafter Adam learnt certain words of prayer from his Lord, and began to pray as he was taught. So He turned towards him with mercy; surely he is Oft-returning with compassion towards His creatures and is Ever Merciful.*

Among the many elements of interest in this passage, let us first examine that of place. A first observation, which is also the most evident difference from Genesis 2, is the absence of any geographical-spatial elements, indeed a total absence of any description. This is true not only of this passage: throughout the Koran, the description of the place in which the scene of the origins takes place is always extremely brief. In particular, reference to the garden in which Adam finds himself is always extremely poor in detail: all interest is concentrated on Adam, the Angels and God. Any discussion of the original harmony of man with the cosmos, nature, the animal world and even with woman is therefore impossible, simply because, when the origins are examined, these elements either do not appear or are of no importance.

In other words, when the Koran speaks of the beginning, what begins is not the world, or even man in his relation to the world, but only Man in his relation to God. As is evident in the passage quoted above, the original scene is a dialogue, a scene composed of words in which God speaks and questions, Man and the Angels listen and reply. They are words spoken in a *non-place*: the reference to the earth and to all that it contains, from the seven heavens to the garden where Adam is placed with his wife, could not be more fleeting. It is significant that the garden is not even named: it is "*the* garden" (in Arabic *al-ǧanna*). Neither in this nor in any other passage dedicated to Adam is there any mention of the Garden of Eden,[5] or of the Hereafter (*al-dār al-Āl*ḫ*ira*), or of the Garden of Eternity (*ǧannat al-*ḫ*uld*), or of any of the names which the Koran uses for Paradise and which were the object of such debate between the exegetes on the various degrees or sub-divisions of Paradise itself.

The lack of a specific name for Adam's garden leads most exegetes to one conclusion: quoting as an example the commentary of Faḫr al-Dīn al-Rāzī, the great representative of the Sunnite Aš'arite[6] school:

> The wise ones do not agree on what the Paradise was that is mentioned in this verse: was it in heaven or on earth? And if it was in heaven, was it the Hereafter, in other words the Eternal Paradise?

In short, was it the eschatological Paradise or another Paradise? The scholar continues:

> Some claim that it was an earthly garden, relying on the following arguments: first of all, if it was the Abode of Reward, that is the Eternal Paradise,[7] Adam, who was already immortal, would not have been tempted by the promise of immortality given by the fruit of the tree of eternity.[8] Moreover, they claim, he who enters the Eternal Paradise does not leave it pre-

---

[5] *Ǧannat al-'Adn*. It is interesting to note that in the Koran this expression never refers to the Paradise of our progenitors but only to the eschatological Paradise; see L. Gardet, *Djanna*, in *Encyclopédie de l'Islam*, 2nd edition (Leiden-Paris: Brill, 1971), 459 ff. The question is closely examined by J. Van Ess, "Das begrenzte Paradies," in *Mélanges d'Islamologie, Volume dédié à la mémoire de Armand Abel...*, ed. P. Salmon (Leiden: Brill, 1974), 108–127.

[6] I, 3–4.

[7] See, for example, Koran 9:72: *"Allah has promised the believers, men and women, Gardens beneath which rivers flow, wherein they will abide, and delightful dwelling places in Gardens of Eternity...."*

[8] In Arabic, *šaǧarat al-*ḫ*uld*. The commentators do not agree on the nature of the tree: is it wheat, a grapevine or a fig tree? Here we simply recall Ṭabarī's conclusions (I, 179): in the Koran, God gives no indications as to the identity of the tree,

> cisely because he stays there in eternity, and yet Iblīs, the disobedient angel, and Adam both left it... Other learned men[9] claim that Adam's Paradise is in the seventh heaven because God said:
>
> *But Satan caused them both to slip from there, and thus drove them out of the state in which they were. [...] Whereupon We decreed: Go forth, and hate each other as enemies; on earth you will have a place of abode and provision for an hour.*[10]
>
> The first fall was from the seventh heaven to the first, the second fall from the first heaven to the earth. There is then the opinion held by most of us—that is the Aš'arite Sunnites, and therefore the most agreed-upon opinion—that this is the same garden as the Garden of Eternity because the verse reads '*the* garden,' and therefore speaks of it as something already mentioned, and the garden that every Muslim knows because the Holy Book has already spoken of it, is the Garden of Eternity...

With comment by the Andalusian Qurtubī[11] who asks, "Which Paradise is it? Mu'tazilites and Qadarites,[12] basing themselves on other verses of the Book of God,[13] claim that it is a different garden from that of Eternity and that it is an earthly Paradise, i.e. Eden; ...however, God said *the* garden and therefore it is a Paradise already known to those who listened; ...as for the fact that no-one leaves the Eternal Paradise, this is not true: the Angels come and go continually and even the Prophet leaves it to return to earth after the Ascension."[14] Qurtubī concludes by stating a general agreement among the wise on the identification of Adam's Paradise as the eschatological Paradise.

---

but speaks only of the prohibition of one of the trees in Paradise. The believer must therefore assume that Adam disobeyed the prohibition, but must not ask which tree it was: that is one of the things that God alone knows.

[9] Reference here is made to the famous Mu'tazilite thinker Abū 'Alī al-Ǧubbā'ī (d. 303 of the hegira/915 A.D.).

[10] Koran 2:36–38.

[11] I, 207–208.

[12] In general, Qadarites are those who do not believe in the absolute divine voluntarism proposed by the Aš'arite theological school, but tend towards a greater freedom of man.

[13] Koran 52:23, 78:35, 56:25, 15:48.

[14] The famous *mi'rāǧ*, the journey to the Hereafter quoted in the Koran and widely referred to in the tradition.

Even the much later comment by Alūsī[15] claims that Adam's garden is the eschatological garden, even though he cites opinions supporting the idea of an earthly Paradise situated between Fars and Kirman, or at Aden—i.e. 'Adn, in the Arabian peninsula—or in Palestine,[16] in any case in a high place given that Adam fell or slipped from it. In favor of an earthly Paradise, Alūsī recalls that the Koran described the creation of Adam on earth (the above-mentioned verse 2:30 *"when thy Lord announced to the Angels: I am about to place a viceregent in the earth"*) without ever later claiming that he was raised to heaven, thus implying an earthly Paradise. He recalls other arguments, such as the absurdity of the forbidden tree[17] in the eschatological Paradise where prohibition makes no sense. His long comment on these verses is indeed indicative of the embarassment created among the exegetes regarding the location of Adam's Paradise, and he concludes by citing the *epochè* of many scholars who ended the discussion with the formula *"al-kullu mumkin wa Allāhu 'alā mā yasā' qadīr"* ("All is possible and God is Powerful over all He wishes").

The exegetes' insistence in attempting to identify Adam's Paradise as the eschatological Paradise should not seem excessive; the idea of a single place corresponds perfectly to the central idea of Koranic Islam, which is the absolute unity of all that concerns the divine, and which is—another essential element—unity *in transcendence*. It is hard for Orthodox Islam to conceive a Paradise on earth, for all that is related to God transcends the earthly dimension. The issue is loaded with consequences: if Adam's garden and the eschatological garden are the same place, then it follows that Adam's Paradise is by no means a lost Paradise. It is instead that which the pious Muslim will find after his death. Rather than a lost Paradise it is a promised Paradise, something that lies

---

[15] I, 233.

[16] Like B, I, 52, who also does not agree; according to the words of the Prophet found in T, I, 153, it is Mecca.

[17] Besides 2:35, see, for example, 7:19: *"Dwell thou and thy wife in the garden and eat and drink therefrom wherever you wish, but approach not this one tree lest you become wrongdoers...."*

ahead and not only—or so much—behind. It means completely erasing nostalgia for an original Paradise.

This is most evident in the works of Ṭabarī, Bayḍāwī and Sūyūṭī, where the question of the identification of Adam's Paradise as the eschatological Paradise is not treated dialectically but takes the form of a tale. Commenting verse 37—*"Thereafter Adam learnt certain words of prayer from his Lord* [and began to pray as he was taught]. *So He turned towards him with mercy; surely he is Oft-returning with compassion towards His creatures and is Ever Merciful"*—the three authors specify what these Words were and thus integrate the silence of the Koran according to the Tradition.[18]

> Adam said: "O Lord, did you not create me with Your own hands?" "Yes, surely," He replied. "And is not Your mercy greater than Your ire?" "Yes, surely," He replied. "And, O Lord, did You not see that I have repented and have become virtuous? Will You allow me to return to the garden?" "Yes, surely," He replied. These are the words Adam received from his Lord.

Thanks to God's infinite mercy, humanity will return to the place from which it came, the original garden perfectly identical to the eschatological one.[19] This identity is not only spatial, as it may also be extended to the category of time. According to another story, again cited by Ṭabarī, God completed the creation of the heavens and the earth at the last hour of Friday; this is the hour of the creation of Adam, as well as of the resurrection of the dead.[20]

This view, which considers the human experience to be centered on return, is much better adapted to the prophetic structure of Islam, to

---

[18] There are no substantial differences in the story as it appears in the three commentaries cited (and indeed it is attributed to the same source, Ibn 'Abbās). This is the version in T, I, 187; see B, I, 53 and S, 116–117. The question of the distinction between the eschatological Paradise and the earthly Paradise does not interest the Mu'tazilite Zamaḫšarī; see I, 127.

[19] Here it must be noted that the ideas of repentance and forgiveness are connected—both words translate the same Arabic term—and assimilate the idea of return. As B in particular stresses, "Return is the foundation of repentance: if it refers to a servant, it means a return from disobedience [to the straight and narrow]; if it refers to the Creator, it means that the Highest One returns from punishment to forgiveness."

[20] I, 150.

the idea of divine pattern and the cyclical nature of history. Adam, the first prophet, is no more than the beginning of a concluded and abrogated (*mansūḫ*) prophetic cycle, later replaced by others. Nostalgia for Adam and for his world makes no sense, just as nostalgia for the figure, the life and times of Moses, or Jesus, or the other prophets makes no sense. Islam has superimposed itself on the whole past, it has recommenced history within the dictates of a new and definitive Law. The only nostalgia that makes any sense to the Muslim is for Muhammad and his world, for the first community of Islam, for the Followers of the Prophet, for the "Well-Directed" Caliphs (*al-Rāšidūn*), who knew him: it is no accident that modern and contemporary fundamentalisms use the reign of the first four caliphs as a point of reference.

A final comment to conclude this discussion on Adam's place and on the absence of a specific location of his Paradise/garden: just as its name is not defined, nor is its structure or composition. When it is described in the Koran, it is in a negative, apophatic manner, with no reference to the recollection of material and tangible joys: the green cushions, the golden armlets, or the rivers and streams that characterise the abode of the blessed souls. The first Man simply exists in a place where he does not suffer. In Koran 20:118–19, when God speaks to him, the text reads: *"It is ordained for you that you shall not be hungry in the garden nor shall you be naked, and that you shall not thirst therein not shall you be exposed to the sun."* Looking closely, not even quantity is defined. It is undoubtedly a place of plenty—God orders Adam to *"eat plentifully"* in verse 2:35—but plenty means "innumerable," "without needing to count."[21]

Let us now turn to Adam's condition and his function, the reason why he was created and placed in the universe: God created Adam to be a viceregent (*ḫalīfa*). On this question the Koran states at verse 2:30 *"...thy Lord announced to the Angels: I am about to place a viceregent in the earth."* The Arabic word translated as "viceregent" (*ḫalīfa*) also translates the term "caliph," "head of the community of believers," and is derived from the verb *ḫalafa*, to follow, to succeed, to be successor or heir to someone. The exegetes' reflections start precisely from the lexi-

[21] For example, S, I, 106: "*lā ḥisāb 'alaykim.*"

cographical definition of *ḫalīfa* as "he who succeeds to someone and takes his place."[22] Although it would have been possible to perceive in the use of the term *ḫalīfa* a reference to man's mortality (the son who succeeds to his father at his death), or an allusion to the continuation of evil in the world (man *"will create disorder therein and shed blood"* as verse 2:30 states, generation after generation[23]), or even to the fact that the creation of man succeeded that of the Angels and devils, the most commonly-accepted interpretation is that Adam is here called *ḫalīfa* because he took the place of God in bringing the Decree to the people, just as the Caliphs, the successors to the Prophet Muhammad, took his place in the Muslim community according to the same interpretation. This, naturally, does not imply God's need for help; on the contrary, given Man's weakness in bearing the weight of the revelation, God uses the angel as an intermediary.[24]

Rāzī[25] cites some passages from the Koran that point to the role as viceregent of Man in general, and of the prophets in particular: *"He it is Who made you viceregents in the earth"* (35:39); *"We made you their successors in the earth..."* (10:14); regarding Noah, *"We delivered him and those who were with him in the Ark, and made them successors of those who had passed away"* (10:73); *"He it is Who has made you take the place of others on the earth..."* (6:165). It is the nineteenth-century Alūsī who is the most exact and exhaustive:

> The meaning of the word *ḫalīfa* here referred to Adam is: successor to God on His earth, just as every prophet is caliph of God on the earth, in so far as he takes the place of God in maintaining (*'imāra*) the earth, in governing (*siyāsa*) men and perfecting their souls, transmitting the Decree of the Most High... The prophets are caliphs/successors in that they succeed all who were before them—in the case of Adam, to the *Ǧinn* and the Angels—or they succeed one another. Adam is the caliph of God and father of all the caliphs, Adam was the first prophet, the first to whom revelation was given...[26]

---

[22] T, I, 153; Z, I, 124; R, II, 180; B, I, 47.

[23] Both interpretations are cited by Ṭabarī.

[24] In particular, the Angel Gabriel; the observation that God requires no help appears in S, I, 48.

[25] II, 180.

[26] I, 120.

It is clear how the Muslim concept of the first man widens to include that of *ḫalīfa*, being granted power over people and things, and at the same time to that of prophet, instrument of the enunciation of the divine Decree. In the Koranic view, power is therefore closely linked to prophecy: the prophet, he who receives Revelation, is the caliph, the head, the prince.

Let us turn now to another question: Why is the prophet a caliph? Or, in other words, why is Adam, the first prophet, he to whom God delegated power over the world? What exactly raises him above other creatures, especially above the Angels, forced to bow down before him?[27] Continuing to read the Koran in the light of the commentary tradition, it emerges that Adam stands out because he has knowledge. As we can read in verses 2: 31–32, God

> *taught Adam the names of all His attributes, then He presented the manifestations of these attributes to the Angels and asked them: Tell Me the names of these if you are right. They answered: Holy art Thou! No knowledge have we save that which Thou hast taught us. Thou alone art the All-Knowing, the Possessor of Wisdom.*

This is another of the passages in the Koran that differs from the Biblical Genesis.[28] While in the Bible God lets Adam choose the names of things, in the Koran it is God who teaches—who reveals therefore—the names to Adam; it is God who thus expresses his inscrutable will to elect man. This passage stresses the divine prerogative of knowledge; only God is the "All-Knowing," and reveals knowledge to whomever he chooses. *"Innaka anta al-'alīm al-ḥakīm,"* reply the Angels questioned by God on the names of things, and God himself had told them "*Innī a'lamu mā lā ta'lamūna*" ("I know that which you know not"). Rāzī observes that God is the Master (*al-mu'allim*), recalling how he taught "seven things to seven people": the names to Adam, physiognomy to al-Ḫidr, the interpretation of dreams to Joseph, the fashioning of coats of mail to David, the language of the birds to Solomon, the Torah and the

---

[27] Adam is an elect (Koran 3:33). He is the one before whom the Angels prostrate themselves (Koran 15:29, 17:61, 38:72).

[28] See Genesis 2:19.

Gospel to Jesus, and lastly the Law and the oneness of God to Muhammad.[29]

When explaining the names taught to Adam, Ṭabarī's comment proposes a minimal solution; they are the words people use to communicate: man, animal, earth, plain, sea, mountain, etc. Suyūṭī adds the names of the Angels and all Adam's issue.[30] Reflecting on the fact that the name may not be separated from the thing it names, the Mu'tazilite Zamaḫšarī concludes that God first taught the things and then the names of each thing: how would it be possible to teach anything without using its name?[31] Bayḍāwī's explanation is more complex and openly reflects Hellenistic influence: the meaning of the verse, he writes, is that God created an Adam made up of different parts, with specific abilities, each suitable for grasping either intelligible things, or sensible things, or imaginable things, or debatable things, and these things inspired wisdom (*ma'rifa*).[32] Thanks to the fact that it is a compilation, and of later date, Alūsī's text[33] provides us with a fairly exhaustive view of what the commentary tradition sees behind the Koranic expression "all the names" (*al-asmā' kulluhā*) revealed to Adam. The most common opinion (recalls the scholar) is that the names are the languages spoken by humanity; in particular, the names are the etymologies, the roots of the words.[34] According to al-Aš'arī, the founder of the great Sunnite school of the Aš'arites, God, through Adam, was the initiator

[29] R, II, 200. See 226–227: "God is *al-Mu'allim*, for that is the name of he who makes knowledge arise in another and no one can do it as does God, to whom alone is given the knowledge of the mysteries."

[30] T, I, 155. See S, I, 101. Earlier (96, from Hasan) the latter text describes an interesting dialogue between God and the Angels, surprised by Adam's large number of children. "They said: 'O Lord, the earth is not big enough for them!' He replied: 'I will establish death.' They said: 'Then they will love not life.' He replied: 'I will establish hope [in the Hereafter].'" See also Q, I, 194 ff. "The names ...are perhaps names for all his issue" (the author here cites Koran 7:172 *'When thy Lord brought forth offspring from the loins of the sons of Adam...'*).

[31] Z, I, 125–126.

[32] B, I, 49.

[33] A, I, 224–227.

[34] In Arabic, a Semitic language, nearly all words derive from mainly three-letter roots.

of all the languages in the world, and men received a part of the teaching, just as a father teaches his son. The rationalist school of the Mu'tazila also interpreted the words as the languages, with the difference that they consider Adam the initiator, together with the men who followed him. Others claim that God created certain languages while men added others. Yet another opinion, recalls Alūsī, is that the teaching God gave to Adam was rather a natural disposition to knowledge, a kind of natural wisdom, an inspiration (*ilhām*) of the essence of things, and also the bases of the sciences, laws, arts, etc. The names were perhaps the names of all the things that were, and that will be until the Judgement Day, or the names of God, or the names of the Angels, or of the stars (according to a certain exegesis, the Angels are the stars). He continues that, for some, the knowledge of the names signifies knowledge through tradition, and for others, it signifies analogical, rational knowledge. Others believe that the names of the things are the named things themselves, in so far as the names are the essence of the things (*al-asmā' 'ayn al-musammiyāt*).

Alūsī's own opinion derives from a notable effert to synthesize all these opinions. Stressing the close link between knowledge through revelation (thus rank of prophet) and rank of *ḫalīfa* (therefore power over people and things), he believes that what God taught Adam was at the same time the words in the various languages and the exercise of power; in other words, the conditions of His viceregency. In his opinion, this is the same as saying *all the names of the earthly and celestial things, both interior and exterior,* and is, in the end, like saying *the names of God,* for power concerns God Himself in His ruling of the world.[35] The caliphate, which is possession and direction of things, and the establishment of justice, he continues, is exercised according to natural disposition and to the degree of knowledge reached. Indeed, how can he exercise power who does not know and, especially, who does not know the words to express it?

---

[35] Note, however, that it is not the knowledge of God but the only the knowledge of what concerns Him, of what points to Him; it is only one of His aspects, one of His names, i.e. *the name of the things*. God, in fact, conceals Himself in His Holiness.

God called the Angels to say the names, but did not allow them to reply; He had not taught them the words:

> *He taught Adam the names of all His attributes, then He presented the manifestations of those attributes to the Angels and asked them: Tell Me the names of these, if you are right. They answered: Holy art Thou! No knowledge have we save that which Thou hast taught us. Thou alone art the All-Knowing, the Possessor of Wisdom. (2:31–32)*

The sequence is that of the miracle/proof of the prophet, the *mu'ǧiza*, sent by God to complete an action that others cannot imitate, and their incapacity is the proof of the miracle itself. Alūsī[36] reflects on this point and sees in the Angels' inability a prefiguration of the inability of the unbelievers at the time of Muhammad.[37] Challenged to imitate the Koran, they could not do it and were forced to recognize the truthfulness of the Word of God. Alūsī concludes that the Angels' inability shows their scant natural disposition for the exercise of power on earth as God's caliphs. At the same time, their incapacity to speak the names shows their inability to be prophets. In an equally explicit manner, Bayḍāwī too observed that the words of God, *"Tell Me the names of these, if you are right,"* are a rejection (*tabkīt*) of the Angels, and show their inability to act as caliphs, for the command, the direction and the establishment of justice cannot be separated from wisdom (*ma'rifa*).[38]

Extremely high value is attributed to knowledge and—which is rather surprising in a culture that seems to be dominated by the observance of laws—far more than to obedience. Indeed, it is not by obedience that the ability to represent God in the governance of the world is measured, but by knowledge. And it is precisely this that the Angels did not understand: why God could grant the governing of the world to such a disobedient, corrupt and bloodthirsty being as Man. They did not understand that

> knowledge (*'ilm*) is the primary condition of power, it is even the pillar on which it rests... because the teaching of science (*ta'līm*) grounds its healthy

[36] I, 227 ff.
[37] In particular he stresses the formula: "If you are right," "*In kuntum ṣādiqīn,*" which appears in the many passages of the Koran concerning Muhammad's challenge.
[38] B, I, 49.

> roots in God, the first link in the chain (*isnād*)... Adam was better than those Angels because he had more knowledge, and he who has more knowledge is better; in fact, God said, *"Can those who know be like those who know not?"* (39:9).[39]

The similarity between the story of Adam and the Angels and that of Muhammad and the unbelievers leads to an observation: Adam's knowledge is the knowledge of names, and thus a knowledge of words, a linguistic knowledge. The miracle of Muhammad, the Koran, is a literary miracle; Muhammad's knowledge is again linguistic, and moreover stylistic, rhetorical. This correspondence between the first and last prophet is indeed worthy of attention and attests to the formidable unity and compactness of the prophetic system of Islam. It is also worth noting that power over people and things is considered to be closely linked to power over letters, which necessarily derives from the idea of God as Word, and from the consequent central idea of revelation.

At this point a new question arises for the commentators: Are knowledge and the enunciation of names the miracle of Adam, the proof of the veracity of his prophetic mission? Rāzī's comment[40] is particularly clear when he recalls that this is the opinion of the Mu'tazilites. They claim that the knowledge of names—which contradicts the ordinary, and therefore responds to one of the requisites of the miracle/proof of prophet—is the *mu'ğiza* which proves Adam's mission of prophet, since he was sent to Eve, or to the Angels. On the other hand, Rāzī, following the Aš'arite position, claims instead that, while he was in the garden, Adam had not yet had the rank of prophet conferred upon him. This would take place after the fall, as the verse recalls:

> *Adam learnt certain words of prayer from his Lord, and began to pray as he was taught. So He turned towards him with mercy; surely He is Oft-returning with compassion towards His creatures and is Ever Merciful.*

---

[39] B, I, 49.

[40] I, 193, ff.

Indeed, he observes, prophets do not sin or at least do not commit sins as serious as Adam's; moreover, they are sent to someone, and Adam was alone.[41]

We may now attempt a summary before concluding. The story of the Koran holds no nostalgia for the specific figure of Adam and for the Paradise in which he lived; rather the story of the first Man displays general nostalgia for the election of God, an election made concrete in every prophetic figure. The desire for return is therefore directed, rather than to the beginning of the world, to the beginning of every cycle of Revelation and, in particular, naturally, to the beginning of Islam. The election of God, which alone confers power over the world, takes form as knowledge, which in its highest form takes on the features of linguistic, rhetorical and literary knowledge.

Looked at closely, the passage of the Koran examined is simply a hymn to knowledge. The entire passage is constructed around the verb *'alima*, to know, the active noun of which is *'ilm*, science or knowledge; the second form yields *'allama*, to teach (see Koran 2:30–32: *"Anā a'lamu mā lā ta'lamūna... wa 'allama Ādam al-asmā' kulluhā... lā 'ilm lanā illā mā 'allamtanā"*). It is to Rāzī that we owe the clearest and most passionate interpretation of the entire passage in a gnoseological key:

> These verses prove that there is nothing better than knowledge (*faḍīilat al-'ilm*).[42] Indeed God shows the Angels the goodness of his creature by stressing his knowledge. If any other thing were better than knowledge, God would certainly have shown this other thing.[43]

He adds:

> Knowledge is the highest good of Man; while the beautiful things in the world are limited in degree, quantity and quality, knowledge is limitless (*al-'ilm lā nihāya lahu*): herein lies the excellence of knowledge.[44]

---

[41] Rāzī's argument is in actual fact much more complex: Adam was not sent to the Angels because they are higher than man with regard to obedience to God; he was not sent to Eve, who knew about the prohibition herself; nor was he sent to the men who did not yet exist, nor to the *Ǧinn* who are not in heaven but on earth. To this it must be added that prophets are sent to their own communities, to their fellow men.

[42] Qurtubī adds "and of men of science."

[43] R, I, 194.

[44] R, I, 196–197, 205, 207, 208 and 216.

The author goes on to cite numerous verses of the Koran to prove the excellence of knowledge, and also many of the Prophet's speeches—like the ones that follow—stressing the link already examined between knowledge, prophecy and the caliphate: "He who is surprised by death while he is seeking knowledge with which to vivify Islam, will enter Paradise, and only one step will separate him from the prophets;" "He who prays behind a wise man is as if he prays behind a prophet;" "One day the Prophet said: 'May the mercy of God descend on my caliphs.' They asked him: 'And who are your caliphs?' 'They are those who vivify my Tradition and teach it to the servants of God;'" "The wise men are the keys to Paradise, and they are the caliphs of the prophets;" and

> They asked the Prophet what were the best actions for the community of Believers. He replied: "The search for knowledge." "And after this?" they asked. "Looking at a wise man," he replied. "And then?" "Visiting a wise man."

Finally, "A wise man, unless he lives alone, becomes the head of all those who have lesser knowledge." The Muslim reflection on the correspondence between Paradise and knowledge leads to the conclusion that it is the correspondence of reciprocals. As the Prophet stated: "The darkness of ignorance is like the darkness of Hell."[45]

—Translated by G. Ludbrook

---

[45] R, I, 218.

Paradise and Nature in Johannes Scotus Erigena

Marta Cristiani

The *Periphyseon* or *De divisione naturae* of Johannes Scotus Erigena is of course the first systematic treatise, the first form that the reconquest of totality took after the *De consolatione* of Boethius. Even if it belongs chronologically to the second half of the ninth century, to the age of Charles the Bald, its cultural horizon tends to coincide with that of a Platonic-Christian imperial philosophy. The work can therefore easily be read from a perspective of late antiquity, more easily in fact than the works of Gregory the Great and Isidore of Seville, which were written much earlier.

In the fourth book of the *Periphyseon* the theme of paradise is placed within what is really a commentary *in Hexaemeron* which begins from the previous book and follows a basic exegetical principle: that of detemporalizing the biblical narration down to the smallest detail, and returning the succession of events to a descriptive procedure, conditioned by a language which cannot in itself express *semel et simul*, the simultaneous totality of the eternal structures of creation. It is therefore entirely in keeping that the treatment starts off from the problem of the possible duration of our progenitors' stay in paradise:

> When we talk of before and after sin, we are showing the changeability of our thinking, while we are still subject to temporality: to God, the foreknowledge of sin and its consequence were present simultaneously. So for man, not for God, sin was future, and the consequence of sin preceded sin in man, since sin itself has preceded itself in man himself. Ill-will, indeed, which is hidden sin, preceded the taste of the forbidden fruit, which is open sin.[1]

[1] *Periphyseon*, IV,14, PL, 122, 808AB: "Nam cum dicimus ante et post peccatum, cogitationum nostrarum mutabilitatem monstramus, dum adhuc temporibus subdimur: Deo autem simul erant et peccati praescientia ejusque consequentia. Homini siquidem, non Deo, futurum erat peccatum, et consequentia peccati praecessit peccatum in homine, quoniam et ipsum peccatum praecessit seipsum in eodem homine. Mala quippe voluntas, quod est peccatum occultum, praecessit vetiti fructus gustum, quod est peccatum apertum."

An Augustinian imperfect, *vivebat*, is interpreted with a procedure which is recurrent in John Scotus, as an inchoative form, which does not describe a segment of a length of time which has taken place, such as a *vixit* or a *vixerat* would describe, but rather describes the wish for something (human nature), which is still a long way from arriving at its stage of perfection.[2]

Though there are no arguments which demonstrate the length of time of a possible stay, according to Scotus there are some which allow us to deduce the temporal irrelevance of the stay itself:

> Of the orders themselves, which were given man before sin, we are unable to read whether he needed them, for example: *grow and multiply and fill the land* (Gen. 1:28), that is, the land of paradise. For what reason would man not have generated without interruption some happy offspring, if he had lived for a certain space of time in paradise before guilt, and if he had tasted of the tree of life, since his body did not show itself to be in any way corruptible? Why did not the virtue of the divine and spiritual medicine not prevail in his body so as to stop him from falling into corruption even in the act of sinning?[3]

---

[2] *Periphyseon*, IV, 14, 808–809: "Non enim ait (scil. Augustinus), vixit homo in paradiso, vel vixerat.... Nam si talibus verbis praeteriti uteretur, fortassis non incongrue intelligeretur docere voluisse, hominem in paradiso perfectam beatitudinem sine ullo peccato per spatia quaedam temporis habuisse. Sed: 'Vivebat,' inquit, 'homo in paradiso, vivebat fruens Deo, vivebat sine ulla egestate' (*De Civ. Dei*, XIV, 26). Ac si aperte diceret: inchoabat vivere homo in paradiso.... Haec enim species praeteriti temporis ab his, qui verborum significationes acute perspiciunt, inchoativa vocatur. Inchoationem quippe et auspicium cujuspiam rei significat, quae jam ad perfectionem nullo modo pervenit."

[3] *Periphyseon*, IV, 15, 810CD; "Ex his enim, quae ei jussa sunt, ante peccatum nihil legitur egisse, verbi gratia: 'Crescite et multiplicamini et implete terram,' videlicet paradisi. Qua ratione non continuo felicem prolem gigneret, si in paradiso quodam temporis spatio ante delictum habitaret, et si de ligno vitae gustaret, ne quid corruptibile corpus ejus pateretur? Quare divini ac spiritualis medicaminis virtus in corpore ejus non praevaluit, ne etiam peccando in corruptionem caderet?"

The Johannine theme of the devil, that *homicida erat ab initio* (John 8:44), a theme evoked several times in Augustine's *De Genesi ad litteram*,[4] is interwoven with the theme of the Good Samaritan (Luke 10:30), of the man who abandons Jerusalem, or paradise, the original innocence of his own nature; he becomes a prey to thieves, to diabolic perversion, precisely because he has already left his own self, the order of his divine destiny:

> A man went down from Jerusalem to Jericho, and fell among thieves.[5] He didn't say in effect, a man was in Jerusalem and fell among thieves. Because if human nature had remained in Jerusalem, or paradise, it would certainly not have come up against thieves, or the devil and his satellites. So he first descended from paradise, through the irrational movement of the impulse of his will, and fell as far as Jericho, into the imperfection and instability of temporal things; in falling he hurt himself, and was stripped of all the natural benefits with which he had been created. From which we are given to understand, that it was man himself that fell, before he was tempted by the devil. And not only that: it must also be realized that it was not in paradise, but in descending from it, and separating himself through his own free will from the happiness of paradise, which is what Jerusalem, the vision of peace, means; and in Jericho, by which is meant the fall into this world, he was contaminated by the devil and stripped of his happiness. It is quite unbelievable that the same man was at the same time contemplating eternal peace, and indulged himself in corruption allowing himself to be convinced by the woman corrupted by the serpent's poison; nor is it possible to believe that the serpent, the devil, having fallen from paradise, or the dignity of his angelic nature, could have prevailed over man who had not yet sinned, and had not yet fallen from the heights of his divine image.[6]

---

[4] See *De Gen. ad litt.* XI,16,21, CSEL 28/1, 349; XI,19,26, 352; XI,23,30, 355.

[5] See the theme in *De Gen. ad litt.* VIII,7,13,241, where however it is far from assuming the importance Scotus gives to it, because the parable is used as an example of the coincidence between real localities and localities of an instructive story.

[6] *Periphyseon*, IV,15, 811BD: "'Homo quidam descendebat ab Jerusalem in Jericho, et incidit in latrones.' Non enim ait, homo quidem erat in Jerusalem et incidit in latrones. Nam si in Jerusalem, hoc est, in paradiso humana natura permaneret, profecto in latrones, diabolum videlicet satellitesque ejus, non incurreret. Prius ergo descendebat de paradiso, suae voluntatis irrationabili motu impulsus, et in Jericho precipitabatur, hoc est, in defectum instabilitatemque rerum temporalium; et cadendo vulneratus est, omnibusque naturalibus bonis, in quibus condibus erat, spoliatus; Ubi datur

This unusual reading of the parable of the Good Samaritan, that seems to me entirely Scotus' own (he would surely have mentioned his source, especially if the author had been Greek), has the merit of radically demystifying the mechanism of the devil's temptation, of the irresistible persuasive powers of the serpent, whether acting directly or indirectly through the seduction of the fragile Eve. Human nature has abandoned Jerusalem, its divine destination, above the entire hierarchy of creatures, even above the angels, of its own impulse. These angels themselves, in their original perfection, would have had no power over original man, because angelic nature is inferior to man's in point of intellect and knowledge. Scotus argues this in a text justly famous, in complete opposition to Dionysius, the author for whom normally he feels such affinity:

> And this is why man is not inappropriately called the workshop of all creatures since in him the universal creature is contained. [For] he has intellect like an angel, reason like a man, sense like an [irrational] animal, life like a plant, and subsists in body and soul: [there is no creature that he is without].[For] outside these you (will) find no creature.
>
> But perhaps someone will say that all these are also contained in the angel. To him I reply that sense, which is distributed among animals, cannot subsist except in a body constituted of the four elements.... But the bodies of angels are simple and spiritual and lack every exterior sense.... So you will find many things in man which the angelic nature totally rejects, whereas there is nothing in the angel nor in any other creature which is not naturally present in man.[7]

---

intelligi, quod homo prius in seipso lapsus est, quam diabolo tentaretur; nec hoc solum, verum etiam, quod non in paradiso, sed descendente eo, propriaque voluntate a paradisi felicitate, quae Jerusalem vocabulo, hoc est visionis pacis intelligitur, deserente, et in Jericho, hoc est, in hunc mundum labente a diabolo sauciatus sit, et beatitudine spoliatus. Non enim credibile est, eundem hominem et in contemplatione aeternae pacis stetisse, et suadente femina serpentis veneno corrupta corruisse, au ipsum serpentem, diabolum dico, jam de paradiso, dignitate videlicet angelicae naturae, lapsum, in homine adhuc non peccante, neque celsitudine divinae imaginis corruente praevaluisse."

[7] *Periphyseon*, III,37, PL 122, 733BC; ed. I. P. Sheldon-Williams (for this edition, in three volumes, which stops at the third book, we shall use the abbreviation S. W.)(Dublin: Scriptores Latini Hiberniae XI, 1981), 286: "Ac per hoc non immerito

In this perspective of the superiority of the human over the angelic, it is quite unimaginable that a degraded and corrupt angel could exercise any persuasive or seductive power over a creature gifted with a much greater potential for knowledge. The Gnostic "angelism" and "spiritualism" that Scotus seems to abandon, boldly affirming the value of the knowledge of the senses mediated by a body made up of the four elements, regains its traditional pride of place when the question is raised of how original man should have reproduced while in Jerusalem; when the ideal animal component of the human being should practice some problematic form of sexuality. Starting from chapter 18 of Gregory of Nyssa's *De hominis opificio*,[8] in which sexual reproduction is considered a sort of expedient thought out by the creator to maintain the planned number of human souls, since the abandonment of angelic life would have eliminated the possibility of reproducing like the angels, similar to a purely numeric progression, John Scotus gets back to the theme of the eventual duration of the time in paradise to argue that there wasn't really a time, because otherwise man would have had the time to reproduce in a way which better matched his dignity, in other words without sex. But of these generations no trace has remained:

---

dicitur homo creaturarum omnium officina quoniam in ipso universa[lis] creatura continetur. Intelligit [quidem] ut angelus, ratiocinatur ut homo, sentit ut animal [irrationale], uiuit ut germen, corpore animaque subsistit [nullius creaturae expers]. Extra haec [enim] nullam creaturam inuensis. Sed fortassis quis dixerit haec omnia in angelo quoque contineri. Cui respondeo sensum animalibus distributum non posse subsistere nisi in corpore ex quattuor elimentis constituto.... Corpora uero angelica simplicia spiritualiaque sunt omnique exteriori sensu carentia.... Proinde multa reperies in homine quae nequaquam natura recipit angelica, non autem subsistit in angelo seu in alia creatura quod naturaliter homini non insit."

[8] See, for Erigena's translation of the text (amply quoted in *Periphyseon*), "Le 'De imagine' de Grégoire de Nysse traduit par Jean Scot Erigène," edited by M. Cappuyns, *Recherches de Théologie Ancienne et Médiévale 32* (1965), 205–262 (for 18, see 237). John Scotus confuses the Gregories of Nyssa and Nazianzus, the latter well-known for the discussions his text provided for Maximus the Confessor in the *Ambigua*. For these subjects see E. Jeauneau, *La division des sexes chez Grégoire de Nysse et chez Jean Scot Erigène*, in *Eriugena. Studien zu seinen Quellen*, ed. W. Beierwaltes (Heidelberg, 1980), 33–54 (now in E. Jeauneau, *Etudes érigèniennes* [Paris, 1987], 342–364).

> So if these words of the holy Theologian (Gregory) are to be believed, which I myself have no hesitation in believing, what else can be believed, if not that human nature remained in paradise, in which naturally it was created, without temporal intervals, without the taking place of effects on the senses; but which deviated immediately from the way of truth, and deserved, due to the impulse of a perverse free will, the division of nature into two sexes, through which to multiply like the beasts? It is for this, if it had remained in that happiness in which it had been created, it would not have needed sexual coupling to multiply; in the same way, in which the angels multiply, it would have multiplied without the intervention of sex.[9]

Jeauneau's research has clearly shown the different perspectives of Gregory of Nyssa and John Scotus on the subject of the division of the sexes. The former tends to deal with the mystery of man by saving the design of divine providence, while carefully avoiding, as an expert anti-manichean, the risk of attributing to divine responsibility every possible cause of evil. Genesis 1:27 is in this way split into two elements of creation: *ad imaginem*, and sexual creation. The latter cannot reflect the divine image, but remains in any case providential, because it guarantees the multiplication of souls. Scotus' objective throughout Book IV of the *Periphyseon*, exclusively devoted to the subject of paradise as described in Genesis, is to deny any spatial-temporal character to it, any material and empirical reality to the original Jerusalem; this is properly speaking the founding place, to which all things return, via the itinerary described in Book V. The basic obstacle in this process of demythification is the massive Augustinian exegesis in *De Genesi ad litteram*, which is of course constantly under discussion: according to Jeauneau, Gregory of Nyssa's treatise is for Scotus a vehicle leading directly to Origen, passing via Ambrose's *De paradiso*.

---

[9] *Periphyseon*, IV,15, 812BC: "Si itaque haec verba sancti Theologi veracia sunt, quod non temere crediderim: quid aliud datur intelligi, quam, ut humana natura, nullis temporum morulis, nullis rerum sensibilium effectibus, in paradiso, in quo naturaliter conditus est [grammatically this should be *condita*], stetisse, sed vox de via veritatis deviasse, et divisionem naturae in duplicem sexum, per quem jumentorum similitudine multiplcaretur, perversae voluntatis motu meruisse? Ac per hoc si in ea beatitudine, in qua creata est, permaneret, utriusque sexus copula ad multiplicationem suam non indigeret: eo enim modo, quo angeli multiplicati sunt, sine ullo sexu multiplicaretur."

A detailed discussion of the complex interrelationship of sources in Book IV of the *Periphyseon*, which involves the entire Erigenian hermeneutic of the *Hexaemeron*, has not yet been done, and this is not the place to undertake it. Since in this interrelationship the theory of the double creation and of the "later" division into sexes, not part of the original design, becomes especially important, it is impossible not to ask oneself the meaning of a doctrine which explicitly includes animality in the ontological structure of the human being, which considers animality a sign of completeness, the seal of the total and universal creatural being, but excludes from this ontological plan the division into sexes.

John Scotus does not fail to anticipate possible moralistic interpretations of his doctrine, explicitly affirming that he has no intention of condemning the *conjugia legitima*, that he does not intend to place on a pedestal a so-called empirical chastity; but on these subjects the Platonic can take on an even more dramatic tone than the Christian:

> But perhaps it may be said that we are condemning the matrimonial bond and the procreation of children, when we affirm that the division of human nature into male and female, thanks to whose joining the conjugal bond, the multiplication of children and the increase of nature takes place, happens by reason of sin. To which we answer: we do not condemn the matrimonial bond, if they are legitimate, consummated not because of desire, but to have children, maintaining both sexes chaste and reciprocally faithful; on the contrary we praise them.... However, we affirm without hesitation that carnal bonds, even if legitimate and practised by religious people, cannot be without their illicit impulse of desire and of the carnal itch. From no other origin, indeed, if not from this one, do the children who are born in the flesh derive in themselves the crime of eternal death, from which only baptism in the Catholic church can free them.[10]

[10] *Periphyseon*, IV, 23, 846–47: "Sed fortassis quis dicat, quod nos conjugium prolisque procreationem reprehendimus, dum divisionem naturae humanae in masculum et feminam, quorum copula et conjugium et filiorum propagatio naturaeque augmentatio perficitur, merito peccati fuisse affirmamus. Cui respondebimus: Conjugia non reprehendimus, si legitima sint, prolisque procreandae, non libidinis perpetrandae appetitu copulata, utriusque sexus fide castaque pudicitia servata: imo etiam laudamus.... Carnalia vero conjugia, etsi legitima sint et religiosis hominibus conjuncta, libidinoso tamen illicitoque motu carnalis pruritus carere non posse incunctanter affirmamus. Non enim aliunde nascentes in carne parvuli, nisi inde, aeternae mortis reatum attrahunt, quos solum catholicae Ecclesiae baptisma ab ipso reatu liberat."

This problematic defense of matrimonial bonds expresses a profound ontological pessimism towards a form of life generated by duality and splitting; the Platonic vocation for chastity tends to follow the mirage of the purity of being. The exegesis of Genesis 2:18 (*Non est bonum esse hominem solum*), immediately beforehand, is then an ultimate example of "rational" hermeneutics, conditioned by a speculative internal coherence. It ends up reducing the letter of the divine word to arbitrary sarcasm, addressed to the wretchedness of man, who was incapable of persisting in his original unity:

> As if he said openly: it does not seem good to man, whom we have made in our own image, to be alone, i.e. simple and perfect, nor to persist free from bonds (*absolutum*) in his universality, without the division of his nature into two sexes, like the nature of angels, but he prefers to roll about in earthly coupling just like beasts, and therefore multiply the unity of nature through the seed in carnal and sexual generation, having contempt for the dignity of the multiplication of celestial numbers.[11]

Scotus has the undoubted merit of explicitly rejecting the devilish figure of the serpent and sending it back into the realms of myth, as well as of affirming the principle of full ethical responsibility, when he recognizes that the birth of the serpent takes place inside human nature itself, in that fragility that leads him towards the senses, traditionally and obviously signified by the person of Eve:

> And you, woman, why do you remove your crime and place it in the serpent, while you yourself are the author of your guilt? That serpent, in which you place your guilt, creeps inside yourself; your serpent is your carnal lust and your pleasure, which is generated in your bodily senses by the movement of irrational spirit.[12]

---

[11] *Periphyseon*, IV, 23, 846BC: "ac si aperte diceret: non videtur homini, quem ad imaginem et similitudinem nostram fecimus, bonum esse solum, hoc est semplicem atque perfectum, universaliterque sine divisione naturae in sexus ad similitudine angelicae naturae absolutum permanere, sed pronum proclivumque ad terrenos coitus pariter cum bestiis ruere, ad sic unitatem naturae per carnalem generationem sexusque corporeos seminaliter multiplicare, caelestium numerorum multiplicationis dignitate contempta."

[12] *Periphyseon*, IV, 23, 847BC: "Et tu mulier, quare removes crimen tuum in serpentem, cum tu ipsa sis tuae culpae creatrix? Serpens ipse, in quem culpam refundis, in te ipsa repit: serpens tuus tua carnalis concupiscentia est atque delectatio, quae ex irrationabilis animae motu in sensu corporeo gignitur."

A *superba praesumptio*, in opposition to the humility which leads to salvation, to the *Christi humilitas*, led the naturally hegemonous spirit, the intellect, the masculine element of the soul, created in the divine image, to invert the rational order of values,[13] thereby transforming the material reality of things, that should be solely an instrument of knowledge, into an object of love and source of pleasure. The latter's origin does not lie in the perfection of nature, but in the imperfection of the irrational, in the necessarily imperfect nature of that which does not identify wholly with the absolute divine:

> The illicit pleasure in material things does not derive from nature, but from the imperfect and irrational movements of the sinning soul, which falls with mortal appetite, through the bodily senses, in the love of the things of the senses. Our old enemy would not have access to the man of the spirit, to the spirit made in the image of God, unless beforehand he had not seduced the bodily senses, like the work of a serpent, thanks to the pleasure principle in the soul, intrinsic to the bodily senses, which are in some way female. In the same way neither would the soul have allowed itself to be so degraded in the pernicious pleasure in material things and in the entirely secret enjoyment of the bodily senses, if beforehand a proud presumption had not been generated. So pride in the soul and illicit pleasure in the carnal senses, joined together reciprocally, consigned human nature to the damnation of death, from which only the humility of Christ, and the pleasure in spiritual things in the souls of the faithful, could recall it and free it.[14]

---

[13] See *Periphyseon,* IV, 22, 843C: "Ordo itaque divinae legis erat, primum Creatorem cognoscere ejusque ineffabilem pulchritudinem, deinde creaturam rationabili sensu mentis nutibus obtemperante considerare, totamque ipsius pulchritudinem, sive interius in rationibus, sive exterius in formis sensilibus, ad laudem Creatoris referre. Hunc autem divinae legis ordinem homo superbiendo spernens, Creatoris sui amorem et cognitionem materialis creaturae exteriori pulchritudini postposuit."

[14] *Periphyseon,* IV, 22, 847–848: "Non enim materialium rerum illicita delectatio ortum duxit ex natura, sed ex peccatricis animae imperfectis irrationabilibusque motibus, per corporeos sensus in amorem sensibilium rerum mortifero appetitu irrumpentis. Neque antiquus hostis ad virum animae,animum dico ad imaginem Dei factum, accessum haberet, nisi prius per insitam corporeo sensui, qui est veluti quaedam mulier, animi delectationem, quasi per quendam colubrum ipsum corporeum sensum seduceret: quemadmodum neque animus in rerum materialium perniciosa delectatione et perabusiva fruitione corporeo sensui consentiret, si prius in ipso superba praesumptio non praecederet. Superbia itaque animi, carnalisque sensus illicita delectatio, sibi

So irrationality consists in seeking some *fruitio*, some happiness and disinterested pleasure, in the Augustinian sense of the term, in that world of the senses that should be entirely functional to the values of the intellect. This would not happen were it not the intellect (*animus*) itself that generated the presumption and pride by which the senses, the fragile Eve, are seduced. In this case she is clearly revealed to be the victim not of the serpent but of an ancient metaphor, certainly more insidious than the serpent: the metaphor of the masculine nature of the intellect.

---

invicem copulatae, naturam humanam mortis damnationi tradiderunt: de qua sola Christi humilitas, et spiritualim rerum in animabus fidelium delectatio, eandem revocat liberatque naturam."

The Sexual Body in Dante and the Medieval Context

F. Regina Psaki

"Or do you so love lust that you force it
upon risen bodies, as you also
place it in paradise before sin?"
(Augustine, *Contra Julianum*, 3.9.54)

The May 1996 symposium on the earthly paradise which generated the essays in this volume, prompted me to consider a new dimension of a complex and sprawling work in progress on Dante. In it I examine the paradisal relationships that the poet sets up between the pilgrim and Beatrice, and among the pilgrim, Beatrice, all the blessed, and God. When I first undertook this research I had momentarily bracketed the *Comedy* as something of a closed system; my analysis focussed on evidence internal to the poem, and to some extent on such cultural intertexts as the alba, the pastourelle, the erotic lyric, and the language of mystical love. In this essay I will suggest that the ideal relationship posited between Beatrice and Dante derives in part from how the poet construes the ideal condition of man in Paradise, before the Fall. Dante's earthly and divine paradises, as I understand them, may depart substantially from exegesis (orthodox and heterodox) of Genesis 2–3, but they do have discernible roots in it. The patristic and medieval background offers an indirect genealogy for what I call Dante's redemptive erotics.

New analytical categories of the past two decades have taught us to be attentive, in some cases daring, in examining the ethical freight of the body in the textual production of canonical authors. Feminist, materialist, somatic and other kinds of (sometimes overlapping) criticism have had the effect of focussing analysis on conceptual categories inherited (in some cases) from the nineteenth century and long taken for granted. They have enabled a radical rethinking of accepted paradigms of desire, sexuality, and redemption in some of our founding texts.[1] In

[1] Prominent examples include Peter Brown, *The Body and Society: Men, Women, and*

this essay I look at the sexual body in Dante, with its significant ethical as well as esthetic freight, to argue that Dante hypothesizes a redeemed or even redemptive eroticism which makes a place for sexuality not only in earthly life but in beatitude.[2]

To make a claim for a redemptive erotics I will do four things. I will briefly discuss critics' reluctance to entertain the notion of a sexualized paradise, and propose a reading that takes Dante more at his word. I will refer briefly to some portrayals of heaven contemporary to Dante, to show that the sexualized heaven I argue for is a notion available in his cultural repertory. I will show how Dante construes human nature and sexuality in the earthly paradise, and recall some authoritative writings which established in the exegesis of Genesis an ideal and fully sexualized human nature. Finally, I will sketch the connection between the Garden and the post-resurrection paradise. I hope to show that Dante's vision of an individualized and eroticized experience of the sacred does not spring without precedent from one idiosyncratic and heterodox brain; rather it has cultural antecedents which, whether he consulted them directly or not, underlie a theological discussion about paradise which had gone on for centuries.[3]

Sexual Renunciation in Early Christianity (New York: Columbia University Press, 1988) and Caroline Walker Bynum, *Fragmentation and Redemption: Essays on Gender and the Human Body in Medieval Religion* (New York: Zone Books, 1991) and *The Resurrection of the Body in Western Christianity, 200–1336* (New York: Columbia University Press, 1995).

[2] At the outset I must bracket, as too large a topic for this forum, the danger of equating—automatically and unreflectively—modern with other historical constructions of the body, sexuality and gender. In this essay I try to work within a historical understanding of body and sexuality operative in Dante's time; but a full treatment of this methodological issue must await a more extensive version of this project.

[3] For successive periods it was rather less trouble to imagine a sexualized paradise; see, for example, "The Pleasures of Renaissance Paradise", Ch. 5 of *Heaven: A History*, eds. Colleen McDannell and Bernard Lang (New Haven and London: Yale University Press, 1988); James Grantham Turner, *One Flesh: Paradisal Marriage and Sexual Relations in the Age of Milton* (Oxford: The Clarendon Press, 1987), 53–4 and passim; and Clive Hart and Kay Gilliland Stevenson, *Heaven and the Flesh: Imagery of Desire from the Renaissance to the Rococo* (Cambridge: Cambridge University Press, 1995).

To say that Dante criticism has never been unanimous is an obvious understatement; still, I think it fair to say that mainstream Dante scholars axiomatically assume that the pilgrim's love for Beatrice, from *Purgatorio* 27 on, has been fundamentally transformed from the love the poet describes in the *rime* and the *Vita Nuova*. In other words, the pilgrim and his proleptic incarnation the poet pass beyond fleshly desire in *Purg.* 27, to an intimate but disembodied love for Beatrice, who never loses her specificity as the pilgrim's salvific muse but who does lose her specifically erotic attraction for the pilgrim. What had been the pilgrim's erotic desire for Beatrice is thought to have been transmuted into a non-physical, or post-physical, desire for beatitude. The distracting desire for the lesser good, in this scenario, is swept away by the proper desire for the greater good.

The erotic language of *Paradiso* is ubiquitous and well documented, and I will refer to it only in shorthand.[4] Dante deploys a register strongly marked for erotic love, both in innumerable single phrases (*amoroso drudo*) and in implied poetic contexts (the alba in *Paradiso* 10). Allegorical scenarios such as the marriage of Francis and Poverty, of Dominic and Faith, invoke the mystical conflation of erotic and spiritual love. The famed neologisms of this *cantica* include powerfully interpenetrative linguistic inventions ("s'io m'intuassi, come tu t'inmii" [*Par.* 9.81].[5] The language Dante uses to describe the love which we cannot begin to understand, the underlying machine which powers the pilgrim's ascent and the entire universe's motion, is the language of bodily, sexual love, the love which absorbs mind, body, eyes, heart, soul, skin and genitals.

---

[4] I explore the rhetorical means by which Dante aligns eroticism and the celestial paradise in a recent essay: "The Sexual Body in Dante's Celestial Paradise," in *Imagining Heaven in the Middle Ages: A Book of Essays*, eds. Jan Swango Emerson and Hugh Feiss, O.S.B. Afterword by Jeffrey Burton Russell (New York and London: Garland Publishing, Inc., 2000), 47–61.

[5] Teodolinda Barolini identifies a "transcendent linguistic eroticism" in such constructions, in *Dante's Poets: Textuality and Truth in the Comedy* (Princeton, NJ: Princeton University Press, 1984), 116. Folco of Marseilles, according to Patrick Boyde, "make[s] a bold and universal statement about the goodness of the sexual appetite in human beings" (*Perception and Passion in Dante's 'Comedy'* [Cambridge: Cambridge University Press, 1993], 287).

In a short article[6] I survey some recent and somatically-inflected interpretations by Marguerite Waller,[7] Madison Sowell,[8] Jeffrey Schnapp,[9] Patricia Zupan[10] and Rachel Jacoff.[11] I cannot do justice

---

[6] "Dante's Redeemed Eroticism", *Lectura Dantis*, 22 (1996), 12–20.

[7] In "Seduction and Salvation: Sexual Difference in Dante's *Commedia* and the Difference It Makes" (In *Donna: Woman in Italian Culture*, ed. Ada Testaferri [Toronto: Dovehouse, 1989], 225–245), Marguerite Waller acknowledges the pilgrim's "playful erotic 'intercourse' with Beatrice in Paradiso" (242). However, she relegates desire to the status of starting point in a higher undertaking: "It is sexual desire that initiates the long struggle toward a reordering of desire itself, desire that can be broken up into intellectual and erotic categories only in terms of a blocked, unredeemed human perspective" (232).

[8] Madison Sowell, in "Dante's Poetics of Sexuality" (*Exemplaria*, 5 [1993], 435–469), explores the range of meanings with which Dante invests his amatory language in *Paradiso*. Ultimately, however, he posits a purified, deliteralized, use of amatory language: "...the poet essentially desexes Beatrice in order to preclude or remove the possibility of sexual love or union. Dante defuses his lady's sexuality so that the language of sexual ardor can be glossed differently in the culminating canticle" (450).

[9] Jeffrey Schnapp's "Dante's Sexual Solecisms: Gender and Genre in the *Commedia*" (In *The New Medievalism*, eds. Brownlee, Brownlee and Nichols [Baltimore: Johns Hopkins University Press, 1991], 201–225), examines Dante's use of sexual ambivalence and instability in the *Comedy* to inaugurate a new, hybrid literary genre, the Christian epic. For Schnapp Beatrice is irreconcilably double in nature, owning a "dual identity as the historical flesh and blood Beatrice Portinari...and as the Christ-event in his spiritual biography" (210). In *Par.* 21–23, Schnapp explains, Dante assimilates Beatrice to the "power of the father" for a fundamental reason: to extricate Beatrice from a too 'lyrical' or overtly erotic relation to the poet-pilgrim..." to "sublimate or, at least, displace the erotic" (217).

[10] Patricia Zupan's "The New Dantean Alba" (*Lectura Dantis*, 6 [1990], 92–99), posits a "spiritually transformed yet ineluctably erotic poetics" (98), "transfigured but undeniably erotic" (97). She opts for the notion of an "achieved equilibrium of the language of eros and that of caritas" (94) rather than a full, coextensive, and deliberate overlay in which both literal and figurative meanings resound at once.

[11] Rachel Jacoff defines the entire poem as "a progress toward the congruence of legitimacy and desire" ("Transgression and Transcendence: Figures of Female Desire in Dante's *Commedia*," in *The New Medievalism*, cit., 183–200; p. 183). Her analysis is the most useful for my own, as she links binary oppositions to the contradictory verities of Christian theology: "The virgin mother, like the squared circle, forces us to the limits of language in order to communicate that which is beyond the human: 'Trasumanar significar *per verba* / non si poria...' [...] Dante reveals and revels in the potential intersection of transgression and transcendence... displays, compresses, and masters the paradoxes at the heart of language and theology" (193).

here to the variety and subtlety of their several interpretations, and can only summarize the tendencies their articles share. All emphasize the blatantly amorous language in which the poet frames the *Paradiso*, but all resist seeing the pilgrim's communion with Beatrice in Paradise as what he says it is, the exquisitely, even intolerably, pleasurable contacts between lovers. Although these critics openly ask what place human sexuality holds in the salvific itinerary, they seem to end up reinstating an impenetrable barrier between the erotic vocabulary of salvation and erotic vocabulary *tout court*. Dante uses this language, they say, deliberately, self-consciously, and audaciously, but he uses it to mean everything except what it says: he adopts and adapts the preexisting language of love to a new and sanitized kind of love. This insistent qualification of amatory language as a *redeemed* vocabulary, rather than as a whole, deliberate, and coextensive figure for what happens between the soul and God, or the soul and all other souls and God, invites the question: what happens if we allow the two registers to fully inhabit one another, rather than keeping them safely distinct? How would our reading of the *Comedy* change if we were to take the poet at his word, and reinstall the eroticism in his redemption?

Dante criticism has consistently discounted the bodily component of the pilgrim's love for Beatrice, or rather the role of that bodily component in the mutual inhabiting of God and the pilgrim, a role which is both parallel and causal. By this I mean that love between humans is *both* a figure for that between soul and God, *and*, in this case at least, an agent in it. This is not to say that any human love is inherently so; the *Comedy's* carefully ordered sequence of ethical instruction on love clearly tells us otherwise. But I would argue that this love of Dante for Beatrice is salvific, and simultaneously erotic, as so many have noted regarding so many single textual loci. Not all sexual loves are salvific, but this exemplary salvific love between a man and a woman remains sexual, even in heaven.

This claim seems excessive in the current critical climate, but there is solid evidence that in Dante's time heaven was often conceived in sexual terms. First, an early substratum of Christian thought (e.g., Irenaeus) offers a quite naively terrestrial idea of beatitude, strands of which could have reached down to Dante's time.[12] Second, popular medieval visions of heaven as a *locus amoenus* invoke a garden-of-delights in which eros is quite conceivable.[13] Third, the Koranic heaven as it is described in texts accessible to Dante is a famously corporeal construct.[14] Fourth, the *grand chant courtois* in Provençal, Old French, and Italian makes available a blurring of bodily and spiritual gratification. Fifth, the mystical writings in the Song of Songs tradition and the emergence of affective piety offer another frankly sexual version of beatitude, if only metaphorically.[15]

All these cultural parallels juxtapose, even superimpose, the two registers which scholars have been so eager to keep distinct, but they are still insufficient to explain Dante's position as I read it. That position is

---

[12] *Heaven: A History*, 48–53.

[13] Giacomino da Verona, *De Ierusalem celesti*; Bonvesin da la Riva, *Il Libro delle Tre Scritture: De scriptura aurea*; and the *Vision of Tundalus* are examples of paradise imagined in physical terms. Alison Morgan, *Dante and the Medieval Other World* (Cambridge: Cambridge University Press, 1990) examines such descriptions in relation to Dante (166–195).

[14] *Le Livre de l'échelle de Mahomet*, tr. Gisèle Besson and Michèle Brossard-Dandré (Paris: Livre de Poche, 1991), chapters 35 and 36; Franz Rosenthal, "Reflections on Love in Paradise," in Marks and Good, *Love and Death in the Ancient Near East* (Guildford, Conn.: Four Quarters, 1987), 247–54; Miguel Asín Palacios, *Islam and the Divine Comedy*, tr. H. Sunderland (London: Murray, 1926), 121–170; Enrico Cerulli, *Il 'Libro della Scala' e la questione delle fonti arabo-spagnole della 'Divina Commedia'* (Città del Vaticano: Biblioteca Apostolica Vaticana, 1949). Maria Corti, "La *Commedia* di Dante e l'oltretomba islamico," *Belfagor*, 50,3 (1995), 301–14, demonstrates Dante's possible access to a Latin translation of the *Libro della Scala*, and clear textual borrowings. However, her reading of the *Commedia* leads her to conclude that Dante borrowed much for his hell but little for his paradise: "La motivazione è palese: l'aspetto per così dire godereccio del Paradiso coranico...gli è del tutto estraneo" (312).

[15] *Heaven: A History*, 94–107; E. Ann Matter, *The Voice of My Beloved: The Song of Songs in Western Medieval Christianity* (Philadelphia: University of Pennsylvania Press, 1990). Matter notes, however, that "there is no 'non-allegorical' Latin tradition of Song of Songs commentary" (4). Bynum's *Resurrection* (ch. 7 and 8) offers a supremely sensual view of Dante's celestial paradise, but it is a love which binds souls and God; I claim that the poet preserves the specificity of the Dante–Beatrice relation, even in beatitude.

infinitely more intricate, due to the poet's sophisticated sense of its theological implications, and it has no real precedent in theological writings authoritative in his time. Indeed, my search for an "orthodox" sexualized paradise has been nothing if not unproductive; the one constant in the celestial paradise seems to be, in patristic writings at least, its asexuality. But there is another mental construct from which Dante could have extrapolated the sexual content which strikes me so forcibly in his celestial paradise. It is to his understanding of the ideal human body in the *earthly* paradise that I believe we can attribute his hypothesis of its role in the post-resurrection paradise. Although the conception of post-resurrection paradise is widely understood to have shifted from garden to city, from sensual to intellectual satisfaction,[16] I contend that Dante's portrayal of it carried an Edenic sexual charge precisely because he carried forward the ideal of the garden in his profound and well-known attention to the body and its claims, both in this world and in the next.[17] Sexuality is still and always, first, part of the divinely designed human bodily nature, and second, subject—like all components of human nature—to perfection, entailing a proper and perfected version that I do not *think* could be, for Dante, bodies without sexuality.

The last six cantos of *Purgatorio* portray the natural, ideal, sinless state of humanity as God created it; Matelda's identification and description of the Garden include the assurance that "'qui fu innocente l'umana radice'" (*Purg.* 28.142). Virgil had told the pilgrim, upon his entry into the Garden, that

"libero, dritto e sano è tuo arbitrio,
e fallo fora non fare a suo senno:
per ch'io te sovra te corono e mitrio." (*Purg.* 27.140–142)

Virgil is of course not infallible, and by his own admission we have reached the limits of his comprehension ("`dov'io per me piú oltre non discerno'", *Purg.* 27.129); still, we are invited to see the idyllic place as sinless, and the pilgrim's many desires there as innocent. He desires

---

[16] See, for example, Morgan (172–186) and *Heaven: A History* (70–88).

[17] *De Monarchia*, Bk. 3, ch. 16.

Matelda as Leander desired Hero;[18] he revels in the garden's pleasures, and desires more:

> Mentr'io m'andava tra tante primizie
> de l'etterno piacer tutto sospeso,
> e disïoso ancora a piú letizie... (*Purg.* 29.31–33)

Most clamorously, of course, he is reignited with desire for Beatrice as soon as he sees her: "d'antico amor sentì la gran potenza" (*Purg.* 30.39). We are to understand that desire here may be sexual without being sinful, immoderate, or base.[19] The fact that we may not understand *how* this can be, that it is incommensurate with our terrestrial experience,[20] does not suspend the poem's imperative to uphold the literal meaning simultaneously with the figurative one. Mankind in the Garden is innocent: "'Lo sommo Ben.../fé l'uom buono e a bene'" (*Purg.* 28.91–92), and so are all our desires there.

Now, ascetic readings of Genesis 2 by Jerome and Ambrose make even a sexualized Earthly Paradise an impossibility; nonetheless, there is a solid vein of precedent for such a reading in Augustine's authoritative and influential depiction of human sexuality before the Fall. As Peter Brown explains, Augustine distanced himself from the "high ascetic"

---

[18] Singleton, massively influential in English-language Dante studies, is so certain that the poet cannot mean what he says here, that he reads it as a clarion call to allegorical interpretation: "This love, which the sight of Matelda has at once inspired in Dante, as the simile is saying, is as Leander's was for his beloved. But was Leander's not a most sensual love? And is not the comparison saying that Dante...would be with Matelda, as her lover, if he could? But how can such love, how can any such desire, be now in Dante? [...] If the name of Leander here is prompting such reflections in the reader's mind, it may be doing its calculated work, which is to bring the reader to a special awareness: namely, that what seems to be, *cannot be*; that is, that since the literal import of the simile *cannot hold*, he must look beyond the literal for the meaning". *Dante Studies, 2: Journey to Beatrice* (Cambridge: Harvard University Press, 1958), 213 (emphasis added).

[19] Bernard Stambler, *Dante's Other World* (New York: New York University Press, 1957), 246.

[20] Dante's Christianity yields numerous contradictory verities, and he has Virgil note that "'Matto è chi spera che nostra ragione / possa trascorrer la infinita via, / che tiene una sustanza in tre persone. / State contenti, umana gente, al *quia*..." (*Purg.* 3.34–37).

views of Ambrose and Jerome, to conclude that in the Garden "will and sexual delight had run together in perfect concord".[21] Book 14 of the *City of God* describes what sex would have been in Eden:

> The seed of offspring then would have been sown by the man and received by the woman at such time and in such amount as was needed, their genital organs being directed by the will and not excited by lust.[22]

The controlled fashion of procreation does not, for Augustine, preclude love; sex and love were potentially neutral, and depended upon their "centering" or direction to become *caritas* or *libido*.[23] Like death, then, it is only spontaneous and rebellious sexual desire that is an unsanctifiable, because postlapsarian, dimension of human nature.

St. Thomas Aquinas builds on Augustine's speculations about Edenic sexuality:

> Augustine's words [in *City of God* 14] do not exclude intensity of pleasure from the state of innocence, but impetuous lust and disturbance of mind.[24]

Indeed, Aquinas makes an even more explicit case for physical delight than Augustine had:

> the pleasurable sensation would not have been any the less intense, as some say, for the pleasure of sense would have been all the greater, given the greater purity of man's nature and sensibility of his body. But the pleasure urge would not have squandered itself in so disorderly a fashion on this sort of

---

[21] Brown, 407. "In Adam and Eve's first state, sexual desire... coincided perfectly with the conscious will: it would have introduced no disruptive element into the clear serenity of their marriage" (Brown, 402–3).

[22] "Seminaret igitur prolem vir, susciperet femina genitalibus membris quando id opus esset et quantum opus esset, voluntate motis, non libidine concitatis". *City of God*, Vol. 4 (Books 12–15), tr. Philip Levine. The Loeb Classical Library (Cambridge: Harvard University Press, 1966), p. 386–87.

[23] Turner, *One Flesh*, 50–51. Turner explores the versions of Edenic sexuality prior to Milton (1–71).

[24] *Summa Theologiae*, Ia. quot. 98. In the Blackfriars edition: "Et hoc sonant verba Augustini, quae a statu innocentiae non excludunt magnitudinem delectationis, sed ardorem libidinis et inquietudinem animi" (New York: McGraw Hill, 1964–), 158.

> pleasure when it was ruled by reason. It is not demanded by this empire of reason that the pleasurable sensation should be any the less, but that the pleasure-urge should not clutch at the pleasure in an immoderate fashion...[25]

Augustine and Thomas Aquinas blend daring and caution in positing an ideal and sexual human nature which, because of man's fall, was never able to fully flower.[26] If many in Dante's time tend to posit both the earthly and the celestial paradises as ascetic and sexless, his more lushly corporeal inventions are not without theological grounding.

Elaine Pagels, in describing how Augustine's (in her view) somatophobic theology came to prevail, describes his views as "radical" and "idiosyncratic".[27] Indeed, an earlier tradition, whose echoes could still be heard centuries later, more fully accepted the sexual body as God created it—a divinely planned part of human nature. The various writings which argued in favor of a divinely-created sexual body have not come down to us intact. The text of Jovinian, who claimed that conjugal sexuality was no less sanctified than virginity, was destroyed entirely, except for the phrases Jerome quotes in refuting him.[28] From such snippets we cannot fully extrapolate Jovinian's premises, claims, assumptions, evidence or argument.

Augustine's long-standing quarrel with Julian of Eclanum, on the other hand, is slightly more revealing of what his opponent's opinions

---

[25] *Summa* Ia, Quot. 98. "...non quia esset minor delectatio secundum sensum, et quidam dicunt; fuisset enim tanto major delectatio sensibilis quanto esset purior natura et corpus magis sensibile; sed quia vis concupiscibilis non ita inordinate sed effudisset super hujusmodi delectatione, regulata per rationem ad quam non pertinet ut sit minor delectatio in sensu, sed ut vis concupiscibilis non immoderate delectationi inhaerat...."

[26] Indeed, some nearly-contemporary voices which valorize human procreation include the *Cosmographia* of Bernardus Silvestris, which elevates propagation itself into a consecrated act (as does the *De planctu Naturae* of Alain de Lille) and the 12th-century French *Ordo Ade* (*Jeu d'Adam*). Still, the dominant position is undoubtedly crude and contemptuous asperity toward generative functions (as in Giordano da Pisa's *Sul Terzo Capitolo del 'Genesi'* and Innocent III's *De contemptu mundi*).

[27] *Adam, Eve and the Serpent* (New York: Vintage, 1988), 99 and 117. Peter Brown also calls them idiosyncratic (399).

[28] *Adversus Jovinianum*, PL 23.221–352.

actually were regarding sex.[29] In two immensely important yet still insufficiently studied works — the *Opus Imperfectum* and *Contra Julianum* — Augustine quotes Julian's claims incessantly in order to grapple with them. He quotes Julian on sexual desire:

> You say, "The guilt of such appetite is not in its genus or its species or its mode, but in its excess, because the genus and species are the work of its Maker, and its mode pertains to honest decision, but its excess comes from fault of the will".[30]

Julian also defended sexual pleasure, thought to be a physical prerequisite for conception:

> "If the reproductive heat, the minister of conjugal honor, is withheld from immoderate acts by the effort of the faithful as well as by the power of the gift, and if it is not extinguished, but restrained through grace, it is acceptable in its own kind and its own mode, and is censurable only in its excesses".[31]

I would never claim that Dante knew Julian, still less that discredited Julian was authoritative; I merely note that before Christian doctrine had fallen into step behind Augustine, a learned and thoughtful Christian had mounted an energetic defense of sexuality and pleasure in the face of Augustine's unequivocal devaluation of them.

I mentioned earlier that sexuality is, like all components of human nature, subject to perfection, i.e., entailing a proper and perfected version which Dante had no Scriptural reason to suppose would be asexual. In my view, the Dante figure's love for Beatrice retains its powerful physi-

---

[29] On Julian, see Brown (408–415); Pagels (131–145); and F. Refoulé, "Julien d'Eclanum, théologien et philosophe", in *Recherches de Science Religieuse*, 52 (1964), 42–74.

[30] *Contra Julianum Pelagianum*, 3,13,27. Translated by Matthew A. Schumacher, C.S.C., *Saint Augustine Against Julian* (New York: Fathers of the Church, Inc., 1957), 130. "...dicis: 'Hujus itaque appetitus non in genere suo, non in specie, non in modo culpa est, sed in excessu: quia genus ejus et species ad conditoris operam pertinent, modus ejus ad arbitrium honestatis, excessus ad vitium voluptatis'" (PL 44.746).

[31] *Contra Julianum*, 171 (Bk. 4, ch. 2, par. 7). "'Si calor genitalis conjugalis honestatis minister ab immoderatis procursibus tam studio fidelium, quam doni virtute retinetur, nec exstinguitur per gratiam, sed frenatur; probabilis est in genere suo et in modo suo, et solis accusatur excessibus'" (PL 44.739).

cal dimension in part because the human body and human individuality retain a powerful dignity in the poet's eschatology. While the gospels tell us that in heaven there will be neither marrying nor giving in marriage,[32] we are also told that our bodies will rise again perfected. The recovery of the physical body which God created in His own image and likeness[33] is a constant preoccupation in the *Comedy*.[34] The additional bliss or pain which the separated souls will feel upon regaining their bodies is of course an object of extensive theological debate after Dante's death,[35] but it does not seem a particularly ambiguous point in the Comedy. The suicides, deprived of their bodies forever; the souls in the Ante-Purgatory, who valorize their lost bodies by the tenderness and nostalgia they show for them; and the blessed, "che ben mostrar disio d'i corpi morti" (*Par.* 14.63), make it clear that

> ...the author of the *Divine Comedy* prolonged yearning until the resurrection—perhaps even into eternity—and projected the motion of desire onto heaven itself.[36]

If we can see in Dante's cosmology, eschatology, and poetics that beatitude is not repose but desire, love,[37] can we not accept the permanence of the unique love between the pilgrim and Beatrice, "the Christ-event in his spiritual biography"?[38] If the glorified body is to rise with all its members intact, can we not accept that those members participate, in some way, in "l'amor che move 'l sole e l'altre stelle"? Or rather,

---

[32] Luke 20:35–36; Matthew 22:30.

[33] In *De Genesi ad Litteram* Augustine states that the "image and likeness" of God belongs only in man's principle part, the mind, not the body. Still, he admits that perhaps man's upright stature, thought to be a sign that he was created to gaze at the heavens, might be an argument for the body's also being made to the likeness of God.

[34] Patrick Boyde in *Perception and Passion* insists on the necessary physicality of the resurrected bodies, and hints distantly that there might be some parallel between human eroticism and beatitude, but leaves the implication unexplored (275–291, 141–169).

[35] Bynum, *Resurrection*, 279–298.

[36] Bynum, *Resurrection*, 305; see also 304.

[37] "The physicality and particularity we associate with body becomes an expression of self. Love is desire, not stasis" (Bynum, 299).

[38] Schnapp, 210.

should we not believe that Dante could have posited this in the way he construed paradise? If asked what conceivable importance the sexual body and the woman he loved might have had for Dante, I would answer that this specificity is one with the individuality which the poet so clearly valorized in the otherworld as in this one.[39]

In protecting Dante's heaven from sexual taint Dante commentators may be underrating the complexity of the poet's vision of humankind. If they perceive in Dante's paradisal language an interpenetration of erotic and spiritual language so incongruous as to constitute a mutual contamination of two wholly distinct registers, this rigid distinction might in fact post-date Dante altogether, and be of dubious value in deciphering the values he assigns to his Beatrice. On the other hand, a case could be made that a modern reader might not respond as vividly as a medieval Christian to the interpenetration of erotic and spiritual language; in that case, by trying to protect the two registers from each other, Dante scholarship is softening the theological implications that such overlap would have had in his time. The colonization of the language of courtship, caress, intercourse, and orgasm as components of divine bliss, would have struck a contemporary reader with considerable force – not because it was unprecedented, but precisely because it is not deployed in familiar fashion as simply a figure for the love which joins risen mankind and God. Instead, it serves to solidify and legitimize the human relationship which frames and generates the entire poem: the unique and permanent pairing of Dante and Beatrice. The erotic language of the *Paradiso*, in other words, is meant to have startling implications as we read it, even though a long and careful lesson may be seen to have divested it, in advance, of its sinful connotations.

An inescapable dilemma in Dante studies can be phrased as follows: If we argue for a radical originality in some aspect of Dante's thought, we risk being thought ahistorical and aberrant in our conclusions; if we try to show that every element in our understanding of his achievement

---

[39] "'They saw the body as the carrier of particularity, including gender and race', Bynum says. 'Choosing for the body was choosing for individual identity for all eternity'". Quoted in *Newsweek*, April 8, 1996.

has its roots in an earlier tradition (poetic, exegetical, or philosophical), we risk reducing his work to a collage or mosaic of predigested cultural commonplaces. The only interest in such a collage, it seems to me, is the cleverness of the arrangement, the beauty of the form, the elegance of the expression. I have argued elsewhere that what is even conceivable, let alone plausible, in Dante studies is strongly contingent upon the critic's cultural context and the persuasiveness of his or her evidence and argument; it is not, in other words, on the basis of their (ultimately undeterminable) truth-value that readings are or are not persuasive.[40] I have begun here to argue an unusual reading of the *Comedy*, one which both traces its cultural antecedents before and since Dante's time, and claims a portrayal of the sexualized body specific to this unique and difficult author. Much remains to be considered, that cannot be presented here.

I believe then that Dante posits in Beatrice a figure no less sexual than blessed, no less erotic than salvific. Rather than concluding that for Dante erotic love is desexualized, purged of the corporeal, superseded by the unimaginable experience of a purely mental communion, I believe that Dante's paradigm of bliss includes the specific, corporeal bliss of love in all the dimensions we now know, and others of which we can only dream. Dante's innovation is not, in other words, that divine love has corrected or replaced erotic desire; it is that finally, in that world beyond earth and beyond time, the two no longer conflict.[41]

---

[40] "La critica dantesca ortodossa e gli allegoristi", in Maria Pia Pozzato, ed., *L'idea deforme: interpretazioni esoteriche di Dante* (Milan: Bompiani, 1989), 263–279.

[41] Several readers of this essay made invaluable suggestions for which I thank them: Thomas C. Stillinger, Clare A. Lees, Barbara K. Altmann, and Alessandro Riccioni, as well as the participants of the Bertinoro symposium. The heterodoxy of my thesis is of course not to be laid at their door.

Therapy in the Garden: The Purgatorial Eden of Boccaccio's *Decameron*

Massimo Riva, Brown University

It is easy to concur with the general statement that "the Garden of Eden narrative (Genesis 2–3) has shaped the Western consciousness by its continual re-interpretation."[1] Not only is the continual re-interpretation of "sacred" texts an essential part of our secular heritage, but our own secularized critical practice (to which this essay belongs) is crucially influenced by what we might call a meta-exegetic perspective. It is clearly a paradox to consider the author of the *Decameron* a *scriptor religiosus*, or to look for the "sacred" in such a "profane" text.[2] Yet, as a literary work the *Decameron* occupies a strategic position in the exegesis (and secularization) of the Eden narrative. Indeed, the *Decameron*'s narrative strategy seems to consist of a re-creation of paradise on Earth, in order to retell (or disguise) in many ways, within its many stories, the Ur-story of the Fall.

I. Retreat to Eden

In his *Western Canon*, Harold Bloom recently acknowledged the crucial position of Boccaccio's *Decameron*: "Ironic storytelling whose *subject is storytelling* is pretty much Boccaccio's invention, and the purpose of this breakthrough was to free stories from didacticism and moralism, so that the listener or reader, not the storyteller, became responsible for their use, for good or for ill."[3] Such a secularizing move is perfectly synthesized in the *Decameron*'s Epilogue, when the Author makes clear

---

[1] Paul Morris, introduction to: *A Walk in the Garden: Biblical, Iconographical and Literary Images of Eden*, edited by Paul Morris and Deborah Sawyer (Sheffield: Sheffield Academic Press, 1992), 32.

[2] For a suggestive treatment of this paradox, see Paolo Valesio, "Sacro," *Lessico critico decameroniano* (Turin: Bollati Boringhieri, 1995), 372–418.

[3] Harold Bloom, *The Western Canon: The Books and School of the Ages* (New York: Riverhead Books, 1994), 102–103 (italics in the original).

for his readers that "these stories were told neither in a church...nor in the schools of philosophers." Instead:

> They were told in gardens, in a place designed for pleasure, among people who, though young in years, were none the less fully mature and not to be led astray by stories, at a time when even the most respectable people saw nothing unseemly in wearing their breeches over their heads if they thought their lives might thereby be preserved.[4]

According to a prominent critical view, Boccaccio's strategic "retreat to the garden" is the essential premise to a theory and practice of literature (storytelling) as a *marginal* and *secular* activity.[5] The Author's

---

[4] I use G. H. McWilliam's translation (London: Penguin, 1972–95), 799. The implicit reference made by the Author is to the second novella of Day IX (the novella of the Abbess who, rising hurriedly from her bed in the dark to scold one of her nuns surprised in bed with a man, being herself with a priest at the time, claps his breaches on her head mistaking them for her veil). The novella is introduced by its narrator, Elissa, with the following remarks: "As you all know a great many people are foolish enough to instruct and condemn their fellow creatures, but from time to time, as you will observe from this story of mine, Fortune deservedly puts them to shame..." (655).

[5] See Giuseppe Mazzotta, *The World at Play in Boccaccio's Decameron* (Princeton: Princeton University Press, 1986), 49–50: "Far from being an evasion into frivolity, the retreat to the garden is a dramatic strategy that enables Boccaccio to reflect on history and to find, in this condition of marginality, of provisional separation from the historical structures, a place for secular literature...Undoubtedly, the pastoral mode constitutes the primary strategy of Boccaccio's fiction." Fabio Coccetti has recently reaffirmed that the ideological framework of Boccaccio's "retreat to the garden" must be understood as the substitution of a transcendental and eschatological "labyrinth–literature" (best exemplified by Dante's *Comedy*) with a "garden–literature": along with Boccaccio's invention of ironic storytelling goes also the "invention" of a secularized textual space fundamentally structured according to the classical opposition *otium–negotium*, eminently coherent with the *urban* ideology of which the *Decameron* is undoubtedly one of the earliest modern embodiments. This urban ideology dissimulates itself precisely by producing one of the most effective and lasting figurative utopias, the project of a landscape totally uncontaminated by the opposite culture of the Rustic. F. Coccetti, "Dal labirinto al giardino: la topografia testuale del *Decameron*," RLI (1992), 82 . See also Mirko Bevilacqua, *Il Giardino del Piacere. Saggi sul Decameron* (Rome: Semar, 1995), 7: "La concezione sensistico-borghese fa da guida alla ricognizione del 'giardino terrestre' e alla fondazione di un nuovo gusto letterario e mondano del fatto artistico..."

ironic invitation (or instruction) to his reader to enjoy what can be defined (given the example provided) as the *carnivalesque* (Bakhtin) dimension of the book seems unequivocal: the enjoyment, or "pleasure," that storytelling in the garden provides is first of all based on parody.

> Boccaccio's novella...is first of all the re-writing, always tendentially a parody, of the most diverse literary genres: classical and medieval, oral and written, in prose or verse...as though [Boccaccio] sought a sort of multiple parody in which all the genres of medieval narrative [from fabliaux and lais to exempla etc.] converged.[6]

And yet, apparently suspending, ironically downplaying or openly parodying any eschatological idea of salvation — this remains, for a modern reader, the book's strongest if not entirely unambiguous statement in the shadow of the Black Death — the *Decameron* seems nevertheless to aim at its readers' "*recreatio* in the fullest medieval sense: attainment of physical, psychological, and perhaps ultimately spiritual well-being."[7]

A subtle ambiguity, if not a true ambivalence, is thus detectable within the text's very fabric, between an ironic/parodic and a therapeutic or morally and spiritually recreative *intentio operis*. And the burden of interpretation lies with the reader: "Like all other things in this world, stories, whatever their nature, may be harmful or useful, depending upon the listener" (799). This ambiguity is not confined to reading as a secularized practice but involves also the exegesis of "sacred texts." Thus, in the Epilogue, Boccaccio makes the following comparison between

[6] See Carlo Delcorno, "Ironia/parodia," *Lessico*, 174–175 and ff.: ("La novella boccacciana... in primo luogo la riscrittura [Sklovskij], sempre tendenzialmente parodistica, dei pi diversi generi letterari: antichi e medievali, orali e scritti, in prosa e in versi...quasi [il Boccaccio] ricercasse una sorta di parodia multipla nella quale convergessero tutti i generi della narrativa medievale [dal fabliau al lai alla letteratura religiosa, agiografia, exempla ecc....]."

[7] See Glending Olson, *Literature as Recreation in the Later Middle Ages* (Ithaca: Cornell University Press, 1982), 215. Another prominent critical view supports reading the *Decameron* in a moral and allegorical manner, reminiscent of (or heavily indebted to) Dante's *Comedy*. For such a "moral" reading of the *Decameron* as a whole, see Victoria Kirkham, "Morale," *Lessico*, 267: "In una lettura dinamica che tenga conto dell'intera composizione, possibile sovrapporre alle svariate trame dei singoli racconti linee narrative pi estese con un coerente significato morale."

his stories, the Scriptures and their continuous misreadings by tendentious interpreters:

> What other books, what other words, what other letters, are more sacred, more reputable, more worthy of reverence than those of the Holy Scriptures? And yet, there have been many who, by perversely construing them, have led themselves and others to perdition....and the same applies to my stories. (800)

Every text (the Scriptures, perhaps, in particular) implies its own "ideal reader." The hundred novellas cannot

> ever be thought of or described as anything but useful and seemly, if they are read at the proper time by the people for whom they were written... (800)

The Author's remarks in the Epilogue, quoted above, must be completed by those in the Prologue, where he dedicates his stories to the "melancholy ladies," his *ideal readers*:

> In reading them, the aforesaid ladies will be able to derive, not only pleasure from the entertaining matters therein set forth, but also some useful advice. For they will learn to recognize what should be avoided and likewise what should be pursued, and these things can only lead, in my opinion, to the removal of their affliction. (3)

But who is really the ideal reader for such an ambiguous, secular text as the *Decameron*, based on an open parody of competing narrative discourses, particularly those based on the Holy Scriptures? The ideal reader of the *Decameron* is certainly not the bigoted lady, "who is forever saying her prayers, or baking pies and cakes for her father confessor" (800). And it is not unambiguously embodied by the "melancholy ladies" of the Prologue. We are obviously closer to the truth if we assume that the *Decameron*'s "ideal readers" are its own protagonists, the merchants engaged in earthly enterprises. And yet, if read within its "ironic" framework, Boccaccio's allusion to the Scriptures does not entirely dispel the doubts (and self-doubts) of a (suspicious) reader who insists in adopting what we have called a meta-exegetical perspective.

Not the Holy Scriptures as such, we might hypothetically infer, but their "aberrant" interpretations are the target of the *Decameron*'s biting parody. Ironic storytelling is in direct competition with other kinds of "exemplary" narratives. Here too lies a possible key to Boccaccio's own complex treatment of what is perhaps the ultimate story set (and told) in a garden. By parodying "aberrant" interpretations or misuses of the narrative of Eden, the *Decameron* might claim to serve not only its internal "ideal readers," but any reader. And yet, the burden of exegesis ultimately rests in the readers' hands. This very ambivalence can be traced all the way back to the two fundamental components of the Eden narrative itself—the earthly Paradise and the story of the Fall. Perhaps in order to fully capture the complex, ironic *and* re-creative (not simply recreational or escapist) thrust that governs the *Decameron*'s "retreat to Eden," we have to recognize not only this meta-exegetical component (clearly linked to the book's "anti-ascetic" position) but also another crucial aspect of its rhetorical strategy: the therapy in the garden, the therapy of storytelling, ironically alluding to both physical well being and spiritual "salvation," is first of all a therapy for melancholy, to be considered, obviously, in its allegorical connections with the Black Death.

As explained in the book's Prologue (and reiterated in its Epilogue) this therapy is two-faced: a cure for the "love-sickness" suffered by the book's internal ideal readers (young women), storytelling is also the result of a literary practice conceived as a self-therapeutic exercise, a "restitution" (or repetition) of the cure effected by the Author's persona on himself. Compassion ("To take pity on people in distress is a human quality which every man and woman should possess..."[1]) and laughter (or *levitas*) are its two fundamental (and somewhat conflicting) rhetorical tenets, the basic ingredients of the *Decameron*'s ambivalent remedy (or *viaticum*) for an incurable post-lapsarian condition of which the Black Death is the ominous and devastating memento.[8]

---

[8] G. Mazzotta has already indicated how the remedies for love melancholy to which Boccaccio refers in his Proem and Introduction (rewriting Ovid's *Remedia Amoris* in the light of a long-standing medical tradition) echo "the remedies that Tommaso del Garbo and Giovanni Dondoli recommend against the plague...flee the place where the pestilence is rampant...take shelter in a spot where...thoughts can be delightful and pleasant...indulge in songs and entertainment," etc. "It is plain how the two medical opinions are thoroughly subsumed in the texture of the *Decameron*..." (32–33). On the topos of love sickness in the *Decameron*, see also Massimo Ciavolella, *La malattia d'amore nel Medio Evo* (1976), 117–123. About the connection with Ovid's *Remedia*

II. Frame and novella gardens: the architectural topography of paradise on Earth

A great variety of different sources (biblical, classical and medieval) are detectable in the design of the *Decameron*'s gardens. It is not within the limited scope of this essay to perform a complete topographical and textual survey. We will limit ourselves to a brief outline, to better appreciate the *Decameron*'s original and truly *encyclopedic* recreation. We begin with the Bible. The Septuagint and Vulgate (St. Jerome's) translation "*paradisus voluptatis*" (retraceable to Xenophon's Greek *paradeisos truphes*, which in turn translated the Persian *pairidaeza*, literally "enclosure") already conflates a complex textual tradition which, ambivalently indicating the nature of the garden as a fertile spot and an implicit geographical location, includes at least three Hebrew terms: *ha-adamah* (the ground where God creates man), *Eden* (the Eastern plain where the garden is located) and *gan* (the walled garden, or *hortus conclusus*, worth of Kings, planted by God in order to house Adam and to be tilled by him). The *Hexateuch* already synthesizes this varied topography into an individual place, called "garden *Eden* " (as an adjective, "Eden" in Hebrew means "delightful") or simply Eden, hence the Vulgata's translation of *paradisus voluptatis*.[9] Boccaccio's own primary source for this definition is most likely Isidore of Seville's *Etymologiae*, XIV 3, 2: "Paradisus est locus in orientis partibus constitutus, cuius vocabulum ex Graeco in Latinum vertitur *hortus*: porro Hebraice Eden dicitur, quod in nostra lingua deliciae interpretatur."

Amoris, see Hollander 1977 (102-106) and 1997 (89–107), where the complex intertextuality of the *Decameron*'s Proem – with its cross-references to Dante's *Inferno* V and Ovid's *Remedia* and *Heroides* – in the treatment of love melancholy, is only part of a broader argument on the satirical nature of Boccaccio's book. For a suggestive treatment of "love-sickness" in Medieval culture, with specific references to the *locus amoenus*, see also Giorgio Agamben, *Stanze. La parola e il fantasma nella cultura occidentale* (Torino: Einaudi, 1977), esp. 134–35. More recently: Mary Wack, *Lovesickness in the Middle Ages: The Viaticum and its Commentaries* (Philadelphia: U. of Penn. Press, 1990). On "laughter" in the *Decameron* see Giulio Savelli, "Riso," *Lessico*, 344–371 (Savelli's essay, although suggestive, does not particularly explore the therapeutic meaning of laughter).

[9] Gianni Venturi, "Eden e giardini nella *Divina Commedia*," 1992, 9–11.

The Oriental (Persian) "paradise" consisted in a complex system of gardens and parks surrounding the King's palace and embodying a precise cosmic symbolism, a true microcosmic "reproduction" of the Universe.[10] Two water canals perpendicularly disposed met at its center in a fishing pond or irrigation basin which divided the whole complex into four parts or areas. From this archetype can be derived not only the monumental Roman *horti* of the Imperial age, or the Byzantine and Arab gardens (like those in Granada, for example) but also, as already mentioned, the Bible's own textual tradition. We find three gardens in the Scriptures: Eden, the delightful place guarded by an Angel with a flaming sword; the *hortus conclusus* of Solomon's *Song of Songs*; and finally, the Garden of Joseph of Arimathea, near Calvary, the garden where the resurrected Christ appears to Mary Magdalen as the "hortulanus" and Lord of Creation, overturns the original sin with his *Noli me tangere*, and, as the New Adam, redeems humankind from the consequences of the Fall.[11]

In the medieval monastic tradition, the utilitarian function of the cloister's *hortus* (the *herbarium*) is thus coupled with its mystical meanings: it is a *hortus conclusus*, with a well at its center, or, more rarely, a large tree, symbols of Christ (*fons salutis*) and reminder of both Eden's Tree of Knowledge and of the *Arbor Crucis* (in Christian iconography the symbols often intertwine).[12] In the courtly and chivalric tradition,

---

[10] In recent exegetical studies, this cosmological and mythical dimension has been reemphasized. See for example Gary A. Anderson, "The Cosmic Mountain. Eden and its Early Interpreters in Syriac Christianity," *Genesis 1–3 in the History of Exegesis: Intrigue in the Garden*, ed. by G. A. Robbins (Lewiston, N.Y.: The Edwin Mellen Press, 1988), 187–224.

[11] Franco Cardini, "Appunti sul giardino medievale," in *Minima Mediaevalia* (Florence: Arnaud, 1987), 371–72.

[12] On medieval iconography of the baptismal *fons vitae*, Fountain of Life, which, although developed separately from that of the *lignum vitae/lignum scientiae*, the tree of Life and the tree of Knowledge, is strictly related to and entertwined with it, see Jennifer O'Reilly ("The Trees of Eden in Medieval Iconography," in *A Walk in the Garden*, 167–204), who stresses the transformation of this iconography in thirteenth-century Franciscan spirituality (a trace that could be worth following also in relation to Boccaccio).

the garden acquires instead a clearly erotic connotation, where classical and biblical sources (paramount, among the latter, the *Song of Songs*) again coalesce.[13] In religious poetry, the Virgin Mary is the *hortus conclusus*, the *hortus aromatum*, the *hortus deliciarum*, the *hortus nucum*, "and since Mary reverses Eve's action ('death by Eve, life by Mary'—Jerome, *Epistle* 22), she can be presented as an earthly garden transformed, Eden restored."[14] At the center of what is to many readers "the archetypal medieval love-garden," the *Roman de la Rose*, a Rose replaces the Tree of Life. "However idealistically it is portrayed, the rose represents the lady's sexual favours."[15] The garden or "verziere" is thus in medieval culture the place of ambivalence par excellence, where religious and secular, mystical and parodic motifs intertwine (as for example in the fabliau tradition). It is the seat of an explicit or implicit confrontation (and intertwining) of earthly and heavenly love.[16]

A free, ironic reassembling of these textual traditions and their sources constitutes the comprehensive framework for the *Decameron*'s secular recreation of paradise on Earth. Scholars widely agree that the garden imagery seems consistently linked in Boccaccio's work to the promotion of a civilizing myth of aesthetic temperance: a clear reminiscence of the Golden Age motif superimposing itself on (and mixing with) the

---

[13] See D'Arco Silvio Avalle, "Hortus Deliciarum," in: *Ai luoghi di delizia pieni* (Milano/Napoli: Ricciardi, 1977), pp. 107–129. And Helen Phillips, "Gardens of Love and the Garden of the Fall," in *Walk in the Garden*, 205–228. On the allegorical aspects: Dietrich Schmidtke, *Studien zur dingallegorischen Erbauungsliteratur des Spaetmittelalters: Am Beispiel der Gartenallegorie*. Germanistische Forschungen 43 (Niemeyer: Tubingen, 1982).

[14] Phillips, 207.

[15] Phillips, 210.

[16] Cardini, 374. Architecturally, the feudal garden, contiguous or internal to the Castle, repeated the model of the cloister; only later (through the Crusades and the *Reconquista*) did the Oriental models start spreading throughout Europe. A typical motif whose variations we also find treated with importance in the *Decameron* is that of the "magic garden."

narrative of Eden.[17] In the *Comedia delle Ninfe fiorentine*, for example, the garden of Pomona (the goddess of horticulture) contains many of the features which also characterize the many gardens of the *Decameron*: architecturally designed, this *locus amoenus* is the "herbarium of myth," a "Garten der Gesundheit" where the plants' medicinal properties are coupled with copious literary reminiscences, a *hortus deliciarum* which embodies a subtle balance between the natural and the artificial, the urban and the rural, a privileged setting for the encounter between man and nature.[18] As such it is the perfect stage for storytelling, reminiscent of the courtly stage epitomized in Book IV of the *Filocolo*, often cited as a direct *incunabulum* of the *centonovelle*.[19] In the *Comedia* this composite *locus* provides a setting for the allegorical tale told for the benefit of Ameto by the nymph Adiona (the "Non-Venereal," allegorically representing Temperance). Her story is itself a variation on the narrative of Eden, reset in the garden of Venus: she tells Ameto how in the garden she was tempted by Venus with the love of a dissolute young man, Dioneo, an attraction of opposites (Adiona-Dioneo) which eventually leads to the compromise solution of "tilling the garden" and sharing the moral benefits of this activity. The prize is a "mortal immortality" for

---

[17] See Jonathan Usher, "Frame and Novella Gardens in the *Decameron*," *Medium Aevum* LVIII, 2 (1989): "Garden sequences appear in the *Caccia di Diana*, II, 11 ff.; *Filocolo*, III, 11 ff., IV, 30 ff.; *Teseida*, IV, 65 ff.; *Comedia delle Ninfe fiorentine*, XXXVI passim; *Amorosa Visione*, XXXIX, 49 ff. and XLIX, 4 ff. The underlying role of all these gardens is constant: they are places where a life of virtuous activity is challenged or tempted by sensuality" (284, footnote 2). For Boccaccio's treatment of the myth of the Golden Age, see Gustavo Costa, *La leggenda dei secoli d'oro nella letteratura italiana* (Bari: Laterza, 1972), 20–25: "Per la prima volta nella storia della letteratura italiana, il mito dei 'Saturnia regna' appare associato ad un'opera che, indipendentemente dalla macchinosa allegoria etico-religiosa, è la celebrazione di un paradiso terrestre sensuale e pagano."

[18] Cardini, 377.

[19] Usher, 274–79: "The garden itself is first mapped out architecturally, with its walls in cardinal alignment, its pergola-decked avenues and its cunningly positioned stone benches..." On the Garden of Health as a metaphor for medieval medical discourse see Heinrich Schipperges, *Der Garten der Gesundheit. Medizin im Mittelalter* (Munich and Zurich: Artemis Verlag, 1985).

Dioneo while Adiona, after her flirt in the garden, will return to her legitimate husband Pacifico. Yet, as J. Usher rightly underlines:

> despite its moral purpose, the garden remains essentially an ambivalent symbol...In narrative terms, temperance is perhaps displayed to best advantage where temptation is strongest...the allegorical garden of virtue can quickly give way to a sensual garden of delight. (276)

A structural dualism informs the representation of the many gardens contained in the *Decameron*. On the one hand we have the "meta-diegetic" (or diegetic in the first degree) gardens of the so-called "frame story," the edenic retreats where the *brigata* of the seven young women and three young men takes refuge from the plague ravaging Florence and where the game of storytelling is allegorically set. On the other, we have the "infra-diegetic" (or diegetic in the second degree) gardens of a number of novellas, the stage of human comedy, the *narrated*, carnivalesque world that the ten storytellers bring to life. Any attempt at reconsidering the *Decameron*'s search for (or re-creation of) a paradise on Earth needs to take this structural dualism into account. As Jonathan Usher has written: "If the frame gardens [are] a secure, dignified auditorium for chaste narration, the story gardens are frequently grotesque, sometimes tragic, misuses of the *locus amoenus*."[20] This textual architecture is indeed crucial to my argument and allows me to formulate an initial hypothesis. In short, frame gardens seem to contain and exemplify one side of the Eden narrative: the myth of original innocence, recreated through (or contaminated by) the pagan tradition of the Golden Age, according to Dante's teaching ("Quelli che anticamente poetaro/ l'et dell'oro e suo stato felice,/ forse in Parnaso esto loco sognaro," *Purg.* XXVIII, 139–141); in other words, a Parnassian dream. Novella gardens instead seem to reenact or retell in various guises (in the form of parody, tragedy or comedy) the other side of the dream, or the awakening: the story of the Fall.

---

[20] Usher, 274 and 280, has shown "how both sets of gardens form part of a system of mutual commentary whose message is central to the purpose of the *Decameron* as a whole." Though my analysis develops in a different direction, I take Usher's perspective as my point of departure.

There are three *loci amoeni* where the act of storytelling is performed by the members of the *brigata*: the garden-extension of the first palace (Intro. 90–91),[21] the walled garden of the second palace (III, Intro., 1–10) and the Valley of the Ladies (VI, Concl. 18–32; VII, Intro. 1–6). As Franco Fido recently observed, summing up previous critical excavations, the move from one garden to the other seems to coincide with a progression into "the edenic character of nature, ever more welcoming, sheltering and vivifying," parallel to the *brigata*'s "deeper and deeper penetration into the garden of Venus."[22] And yet another pattern must be recognized, seemingly in contradiction with this simple "regressive progression" into a thoroughly natural, uncontaminated landscape: as Fido himself underlines, only the first move (from the first to the second palace-garden, at the beginning of Day III) is a true "resettlement" of the whole *brigata*, while the second move (from the second garden to the Valley of the Ladies, at the beginning of Day VII) is a simple "excursion" that lasts only a few hours (the time necessary to telling the Day's stories), followed by the *brigata*'s return to the "order" of the second garden. "Thus – Fido concludes – nine times out of ten, the ten young people tell their stories in the garden of the palace where they reside and seven out of ten in the garden of the second palace" (23). Only one day (and not the entire day) do they spend in the Valley of the Ladies' natural enclave.

A comprehensive reconnaissance of the "infra-diegetic" gardens which appear within the various novellas, reveals what seems to be an additional macro-textual pattern. Four Days (out of the ten which compose the book) register a more significant frequency of "garden-settings"

---

[21] All references are to the paragraph division in the Italian text edited by Vittore Branca (Turin: Einaudi, 1980).

[22] Fido, "Architettura," *Lessico critico*, 23. Usher thus describes this progression: "The first *Decameron* garden represents the passive appreciation of order; the second represents the strenuous, active pursuit of man-made imitations of natural order, whereas the third shows the brigata beginning, through their apprenticeship, to appreciate the underlying order of Nature herself" (278).

in their novellas:[23] Day III, aptly the day inaugurated by the fundamental move to the second, more sheltered and reclusive palace-garden where seven days of storytelling will be set, provides a threefold parody of the Fall; Day IV reverses with its tragic mode the "happy" parody of the previous day; Day VII, the day when storytelling moves to the Valley, provides perhaps the sharpest parodic exegesis of narrative of the Fall (itself an archetypal adultery); and finally Day X seems to perform both a (delayed) reversal of Day VII and a general synthesis of the topos in all its various nuances. A double reversal seems thus to constitute the fundamental structural tension behind the *Decameron*'s "retreat to Eden": a double architectural space (a palace garden on top of a hill and a walled garden, or *hortus conclusus*, within the boundaries of a second palace) and a more secluded *locus amoenus* (the Valley) concur (in problematic progression) to frame the *Decameron*'s multifarious representations of paradise on Earth. These three frame gardens and the many novella gardens, in their labyrinthine textual architecture, both contain and re-draw the map of Eden.

The architectural metaphor is not to be understood as an extrinsic one: rather, it characterizes Boccaccio's own original contribution to the

---

[23] As a curiosity, yet I believe not an entirely idle one for our attempt to recognize a pattern or series of patterns within the *Decameron's* numerological structure (if we take these lexical frequencies as a first, superficial indicator of the *topos*' frequency), at a rapid calculation the word "giardino" recurs 72 times in the *Decameron* (10 each the words "giardin" and "giardini"), with the following overall progression or distribution: 3–Day I; 5–Day II; 22–Day III; 20–Day IV; 9–Day V; 1–Day VI; 10–Day VII; 1–Day VIII; 0–Day IX; 20–Day X and 1 in the Author's Epilogue. If we subtract the number of times these three terms occur within the "frame story," we obtain the following results: 0–Day I; 4–Day II (1 in nov. 4; 3 in nov. 7); 12–Day III (4 in nov. 1; 4 in nov. 3; 4 in nov. 5); 17–Day IV (3 in nov. 1; 7 in nov. 6; 7 in nov. 7); 7–Day V (2 in nov. 4; 2 in nov. 6; 2 in nov. 9; 1 in nov. 10); 10–Day VII (1 in nov. 1; 7 in nov. 7; 2 in nov. 9); 19–Day X (7 in nov. 5; 8 in nov. 6; 2 in nov. 7; 2 in nov. 9). If we now look at the frequency of the word "paradiso" (as an ambiguous synonym of "garden," according to its etymology), it occurs 15 times (mostly with a double meaning), according to the following distribution: 2–Day I (both in nov. 1); 0–Day II; 5–Day III (1 in the intro.; 3 in nov. 4 ; 1 in nov. 8); 4–Day IV (all in nov. 2); 1–Day V (in nov. 7); 0–Day VI; 0–Day VII; 2–Day VIII (1 in nov. 9; 1 in nov. 10); 0–Day IX; 1–Day X (in nov. 7).

(re)-building of a literary space with the materials of different traditions. Multiple meanings coalesce in the redesigning of this secular space, ideally located a short stroll from the city. As a representation of paradise on Earth, the frame gardens clearly represent an alternative model to both the cloister garden and the feudal garden. In their architectural and allegorical nature, the frame gardens translate the archetype of the King's garden(s) into the idealized context of "bourgeois" and mercantile culture. They represent a true re-founding of a lay civil society on the ruins caused by the plague, since the hundred novellas (including the many which contain a variation on the story of the Fall) can be read as secular *exempla* meant to provoke a reader who is "fully mature and not to be led astray by stories" into adopting a rational attitude and code of social behavior, emancipated from the false constructs of religious asceticism (unmasked as hypocrisy), courtly desire (denounced as irrational) and instinctual anarchy (distanced as the expression of a world upside down). Storytelling in the garden thus itself reproduces an ambivalently edenic situation, where the *word* (of the storytellers) is restored to a prelapsarian innocence in order for the new Adam and Eve to be tested again and learn how to cope.[24]

What we have called the therapeutic virtue of the *Decameron*'s "retreat to Eden" seems thus primarily embodied in the frame gardens – although the novella gardens, as a repetition of the narrative of the Fall, are an essential, although ambivalent, component of the "remedy." The *Decameron*'s gardens directly oppose themselves to, indeed provide a direct parody of, the monastic garden, with its ascetic and mystical meanings (paramount in this sense are the gardens of Day III). The novellas of Masetto, Dom Felice and Rustico, recounted by the three male narrators Filostrato, Panfilo and Dioneo respectively, together perform this parodic treatment in an inverted progression: from the *hortus conclusus* of Eden (the nunnery, the garden "tilled" by the *hortulanus* Masetto, "cuckolding" Christ himself), through the mock Purgatory of frate Puccio ("many are those who, whilst they are busy making strenuous efforts to get to Paradise, unwittingly send some other person in their

[24] Cardini, 402.

stead...”), back to the *Ninferno* of Alibech and Rustico, which (literally) satirizes the virtues of ascetic abstinence and ironically teaches the Ladies that “the most agreeable way of serving God [is] to put the devil back in Hell.”[25] An altogether different kind of cure is represented by the tragic gardens of Day IV, where death rules. These gardens seem to directly oppose the typology of the feudal garden. In addition to the gardens which provide the setting for the “folk tales” of Andreuola and Gabriotto (IV, 6) and Simona and Pasquino (IV, 7, a tragic reversal of the medieval *herbarium*), we may also point to the grotto near the Castle, “almost entirely covered over by weeds and brambles,” that leads to Ghismonda’s room, in novella 1. This cavern, where Ghismonda lowers herself to meet Guiscardo, is the symbolic place of her fall. Moreover, it is Ghismonda’s stroll in the palace garden, one day, that leads to Tancredi’s discovery of her secret meetings with Guiscardo. Lisabetta’s pot of basil is also a symbolic garden, which conflates the folkmotif, a mercantile setting and an anti-feudal attitude. It is also fraught with additional symbolism: inundated by her tears and “because [its] soil was enriched by the decomposing head inside the pot, [the basil] grew very thick and exceedingly fragrant,” while she instead withers away, a macabre reversal of the motifs of the *fons vitae* (or *salutis*) and the tree of life.

In Day VII, instead, when stories are told in the Valley, it is the parody of the narrative of the Fall that reaches its climax, first with the novella of Madonna Beatrice, Egano and Anichino (VII, 7): here the meeting in the garden, under the pine-tree, turns into a “cure” for the husband and the “proof” of his wife’s innocence (crowned by Beatrice’s ironic remarks, well worthy of a new Eve: “Thanks be to God that he tested me with words, and saved his deeds for you,” 523.) Then with the novella of Lydia, Nicostratus and Pyrrus: here the “magic garden” and the pear tree at its center again are the tools of a cunning reversal of the story of the Fall, a mockery of the legitimate husband, forced to impotently witness his

---

[25] See III, 1, 4, 10 (and 3 can also be seen as part of this progression). For an alternative, suggestive (yet in my view problematic) reading of III, 10, detecting in the nudity of Rustico and Alibech an “edenic innocence” and a possible allusion to Franciscan spirituality, see Valesio, who also detects an “elegiac motive” in Boccaccio’s parody (*Lessico*, 385).

wife's betrayal, and a parodic vindication of Lydia's (Eve's) honor:

> "This pear-tree will certainly never bring shame upon me or any other woman again if I can help it...For however much your eyes may have borne what you were saying, Nicostratos, you should never have allowed your mind to accept it, or even to entertain the idea for a moment." (543)

The parodic motif of the "magic garden," conceived as a woman's (Eve's) cunning, will find its therapeutic "sublimation" in Day X, 5, the novella of Madonna Dianora, Messer Ansaldo and the magician. Also in Day X, the sixth novella (wherein King Charles the Old falls in love with a young girl in a garden whose fishpond reminds us of the Valley of the Ladies) provides a therapeutic solution to the other, potentially tragic motif of the courtly (feudal) garden as the place of melancholy fascination.

III. Eden revisited: parody and allegory

The recurring presence of the Eden narrative as a subtext (a blueprint) of practically all variations on the garden topos seems thus obvious in Boccaccio—as in many other medieval and modern authors. Yet, it must be carefully considered in light of the parodic contamination of heterogeneous sources programmatically performed by the *Decameron* as a whole. We must start, clearly, with the two fundamental model works of the religious tradition (in Latin and Italian, respectively), the reference to which is announced by the *Decameron*'s "name" and "surname" (*Galeotto*): the *Hexameron* of Saint Ambrose (d. 396)—itself a variation on the homiletic genre inaugurated by St. Basil of Cesarea—and, of course, Dante's *Comedy*. The title of Boccaccio's book (as well as its revised numerology, directly inspired by Dante's textual cosmology) thus alludes to a double (anti)-model: the *Decameron* presents itself as a sort of secular Genesis, the re-creation of the world in storytelling, and as a backward journey *nell'aldiqua*, opposed to Dante's *aldilà*; its sub-title contains instead a polymorphous set of allusions to the episode of Francesca da Rimini, punished among the lustful in *Inf.* V (137, "Galeotto fu il libro e chi lo scrisse...").[26]

---

[26] This reference, implicit in the *Decameron's* subtitle (*Galeotto*), is to be understood, according to recent interpretations, within the framework of the other intertextual

It is tempting to see in the *Decameron* not only the ironic repetition of a medieval genre (the *Hexamera*) but also a direct parody of Ambrose's writings, a parody following a precise anti-ascetic strategy.[27] In his exposition of Genesis, Ambrose takes a strong position against adultery (*Hexam.* V.7.19) and, in the *De Institutione Virginis*, the "explication of the Genesis text...forms the backdrop for [him] to champion the perpetual virginity of Mary." Elsewhere "he reminds his readers that Adam did not 'know' [in the Biblical sense] his wife until *after* they had been ejected from Paradise" and he "holds that marriage is for weak men, who like Paul's vegetable-eaters, cannot aspire to higher perfection."[28] For an experienced reader of the *Decameron* it is easy to see how to all these points, and to the topic of religious asceticism in general, Boccaccio applies his most biting satire. We should further note that the "virginity" of women about to marry is questioned precisely in Day VI, in the scene involving the dispute between Licisca and Sicofante, temporarily settled by Dioneo in a way that will then give the cue to the narrative theme of Day VII (set in the Valley of the Ladies).

A more complex ironic dimension, in this parodic reversal of the ascetic tradition, is clearly detectable if we look carefully at the frame story: sexual abstinence (abstinence from the forbidden fruit, the "bib-

---

references contained in the book's proem (in addition to the obvious one to Dante's *Comedy*), in particular those to Ovid's *Heroides* and *Remedia Amoris.* See Delcorno 171–72 and, for Ovid's strategic "double" presence in the *Decameron*'s proem, Hollander (1997) 99–100 who writes: "A working hypothesis might hold that, while the apparent compassionate atmosphere of the *Heroides* would not seem inappropriate as a source for the apparently compassionate Boccaccio, the reader who resorts to this text would not be as happy to consider the likelihood that Boccaccio was in fact more interested in the evidently ironic and distanced formulations of the *Remedia*...[yet] Boccaccio's view of himself as a remedial Ovid includes the awareness that Ovid himself was writing ironically and that the persona he knows he has apparently assumed is that of Dante, whose fifth canto is resolute in putting even the most sympathetic of carnal sinners into the pit."

[27] On the *Decameron* as a lay Genesis see F. Cardini, "Il *Decameron*: un Genesi laico?" in *Quaderni Medievali*, 12 (1981), 105–120.

[28] See Elizabeth A. Clark, "Heresy, Asceticism, Adam, and Eve: Interpretations of Genesis 1-3 in the Later Latin Fathers," *Intrigue in the Garden*, 102–104.

lical knowledge") is strictly observed by the members of the *brigata* (until, perhaps, *after* their "return" from Eden?). And yet, that very knowledge is also the *very premise* (and often the *very subject*) of their storytelling. In other words, the recreation of a prelapsarian condition, the brigata's "retreat to Eden," is the ironic *premise* for the parody of the Eden narrative of the Fall, multifariously performed, as we have seen, in the novella gardens. Unmasking the hypocrisy of the clergy is a fundamental tool of *ironic storytelling*. At the same time, this relentless parody is framed (and crowned) by a sort of self-purifying, allegorical and therapeutic filter. Here the reference to Dante's *Comedy* as *the* anti-model for Boccaccio's book becomes crucial.

In both the title and sub-title of his "remake" of Genesis, Boccaccio openly or surreptitiously replaces Dante as *Auctor*. If the title alludes to a parody of the ascetic tradition, the subtitle (Libro Galeotto), raises the stakes even higher with an additional, double allusion to the chivalric and courtly (feudal) traditions, through the reference to Dante's Francesca da Rimini. An epitome of the melancholy lover, she stands at the threshold of the book as both a figure of *pietas* or authorial compassion (as in Dante, where her story provokes the author into a faint, out of overwhelming compassion); and a warning to the *Decameron/Galeotto*'s "ideal" readers (melancholy women), an allusion to the book's own self-prescription as an ambivalent *pharmakos* (both antidote and *venenum*) for the victims of love-sickness. The book *itself* is thus implicitly presented – coherent with its comprehensive Edenic strategy – as a forbidden fruit of erotic knowledge "harmful or useful, depending upon the [reader]."[29] Francesca (as a woman reader and adulteress) is thus also recognizably a *figura Evae*, tempted by the serpentine *knowledge* of Love (a literal misreading of the "wrong" book, a narrative work, a ro-

[29] Interesting to quote by contrast this passage from Boccaccio's *Esposizioni sopra la Commedia*, which directly involves the author's responsibility. Explaining the words "Galeotto fu il libro... " Boccaccio writes: "E così vuol questa donna dire che quello libro, il quale leggevano Polo ed ella, quello officio adoperasse tra lor due che adoperò Galeotto tra Lancialotto e la reina Ginevra; e quel medesimo dice essere stato colui che lo scrisse, per ciò che se scritto non l'avesse, non ne potrebbe esser seguito quel che ne seguì..." (ed. G. Padoan [Milan: Mondadori, 1994], I, 324).

mance). This ironic (antiphrastic) allusion to Francesca as a *figura Evae* (and the "ideal (mis)reader" of the *Decameron*) is then supposedly (and, again, ironically) redeemed/reversed, at the book's end, by the cathartic compassion elicited in its readers by the figure of Griselda: a figure symmetrically (if not entirely unambiguously) readable (think of the motif of nudity) as the overturning of a *figura Evae*, the "perfect" bride's *purgatorial* "martyrdom."[30]

One passage is clearly crucial in defining the strategic position (and the irreducible ambiguity) of the narrative of the Fall in the *Decameron*'s structure (and message) as a whole, more specifically in relation to Dante's *Comedy*. In the Introduction, Pampinea proposes to leave the city and retreat to what turns out to be a simulation of paradise on Earth:

> "We could go and stay together on one of our various country estates, shunning at all costs the lewd practices of our fellow citizens and feasting and merrymaking as best we may without in any way overstepping the bounds of what is reasonable." (16)

---

[30] One could object that the tale of Griselda concludes the book with an exemplary figure of asceticism and *pietas*: a majority of critics indeed maintain that marriage is the regulatory ideal and the social pillar of the *Decameron*'s ideology of order, and what is Griselda if not an example of (female) "asceticism" in marriage, a sort of martyr of marriage? After all, also "Ambrose's interest in explaining the Eden tale revolves around social commentary: God's creation of a woman for the man shows the divine intent that humans live in a society" (Clark, 123). This would be in line with the *Decameron*'s celebration of marriage as a fundamental social institution, without weakening the sense of Boccaccio's "parodic" attack on the ascetic tradition (complicated by possible internal references to Franciscan spirituality, as suggested by Valesio, 384–87). Griselda's plight could thus easily be read as a redemption of Eve's (and all her followers') error, a *figura Virginis* more than a *figura Cristi*, although not without further ambivalence (one should always remember that it is Dioneo who tells her story): as a silent "martyr"—a rhetorical inversion of the Job narrative, as it has also been suggested—she is symmetrically opposed, at the opposite margins of the book, to Ciappelletto's eloquent and "serpentine" self-promotion to sainthood (whose story of inversion is told, as a *negative exemplum*, to be eventually reversed, by Panfilo, the King of Day X). A thorough interpretation of the figure of Griselda—since Petrarch one of the most passionately discussed characters of the *Decameron*—requires more space. For a recent review of Griselda's tale within the context of Day Ten, see Hollander, 1997, 144ff. who rejects most allegorical readings of the novella.

"Senza trapassare in alcuno atto il segno della ragione": as several commentators have noticed, this phrase is a direct quotation from Dante's *Paradise* XXVI, 115–117, where Adam himself speaks these words to Dante: "Or, figliuol mio, non il gustar del legno/ fu per sè la cagion di tanto essilio,/ ma solamente il trapassar del segno" [Now, my child, not the tasting of the tree, but the trespassing of the mark was the cause of such an exile]. Two influential interpretations emphasize respectively the scholastic background of Pampinea's quotation of Dante and the ironic use Boccaccio makes of it. According to V. Kirkham,

> the Adamic phrase, so poetically fraught for the *Divine Comedy*, filters into the *Decameron* not just as another nugget panned from an earlier poet's word flow, but as a cameo mounted to display renewed and serious meaning...Boccaccio restores to the surface of his master book the Thomistic concept of *ratio*...The *Summa theologica*, founded on Aristotle, spells it out logically: prideful trespassing opposes reason; whatever opposes reason is sin...the *Decameron* is a microcosm founded on the principle of reason.[31]

According to G. Mazzotta, instead,

> The passage, which in its original context describes Adam's experience of the fall from the Garden of Eden, discloses Boccaccio's irony: as the youngsters move into the idyllic space, halfway between reality and a fantasy world, they seem to reverse Adam's experience of the fall; at the same time, there is an intimation of precariousness, a hint that the safe bounds of the garden are just as illusory for them as they were for Adam.[32]

The ludic nature of the *Decameron*'s garden is thus obviously to be distinguished, according to Mazzotta, from the philosopher's pastime in the *scholae* (remember the Epilogue) and indeed opens the door to a parodic play with theological (or allegorical) exegesis.[33]

---

[31] V. Kirkham, *The Sign of Reason in Boccaccio's Fiction* (Florence: Olschki, 1993), 7–13.

[32] Mazzotta, 42. Reason is here "to be understood as restraint, rather than an abstract rationality which would conform either to the order of nature, which in reality is sheer chaos, or the order of the garden to which they move, for the garden is an artifice of nature."

[33] Mazzotta, 269: "In the *Decameron* the theology is absent or it is presented as the object of laughter, but play is the category through which Boccaccio enjoins us to look at the world and at its suspected but also elusive secrets."

Now, both interpretations seem compatible, in light of what we have characterized as the ambivalent strategy of the *Decameron*, aimed as it is at re-creating an anti-model of paradise on Earth. The *Decameron*'s complex parodic *and* ironic strategy (a duplicity embodied in particular by Dioneo) structurally implies a re-framing of the Eden narrative according to a comprehensive plan which undoubtedly has Dante's *Comedy* as its fundamental, antiphrastic model: from this point of view it is necessary to keep in mind that Boccaccio's own "return to Eden" immediately (and inevitably) follows in the footsteps of Dante's "canonization" of Purgatory.[34] I would like to suggest that a self-reflexive *purgatorial* strategy might be hiding behind the systematic parody and contamination of all the *Decameron*'s various sources. Purgatory, after all, is also a ground of direct contention between a religious and a secular *economy* of narrative discourse.[35]

IV. A purgatorial Eden?

As the ideal setting for a ludic experiment, the paradise on Earth architecturally composed by the *Decameron*'s frame gardens is first of all a place of waiting, not otherworldly but in direct proximity to the Earthly Jerusalem. Thus, Boccaccio's Parnassian dream is not a radical departure from the theological tradition. As Jean Delumeau has written:

> The Jewish tradition long maintained the belief in an intermediate paradise in which the souls of the elect await resurrection and entry into the kingdom of heaven.[36]

---

[34] On this it is canonical to recall Chapter Ten of Jacques Le Goff's *Birth of Purgatory* (1981).

[35] I intend to further develop this side of my argument in another essay currently in progress.

[36] Jean Delumeau, *History of Paradise. The Garden of Eden in Myth and Tradition* (New York: Continuum, 1995) (1992), 25–26. The *Zohar*, for example, composed between 1270 and 1300, says that "when the souls of the just leave this world, they enter into a palace located in the lower Eden and they remain there for as along as is necessary to prepare them for the ascent to the higher Eden."

And

> ... the only three occurrences of the word *paradeisos* in the New Testament were understood in the light of this belief in an intermediate place of happiness, a place that served as an antechamber for souls before the general resurrection...[37]

This tradition is clearly behind Dante's re-positioning of Eden on the top of the mountain of Purgatory (a place of waiting itself, as a whole) in his cosmological rearrangements.[38] Boccaccio's secularization of this "place of waiting," where storytelling is performed as a game while waiting, not for resurrection, but for the moment of return to the earthly Jerusalem, must be appreciated against the backdrop of Dante's otherworldly topography.

When exploring the *Decameron*'s textual topography in relation to Dante's *Comedy*, we inevitably begin with that passage contained in the Author's Introduction, where, addressing his lady readers, he compares the labors and rewards of reading his book to walking into a symbolic landscape:

> You will be affected no differently by this grim beginning than walkers confronted by a steep and rugged hill, beyond which there lies a beautiful and delectable plain. The degree of pleasure they derive from the latter will cor-

---

[37] Delumeau, 28. The three occurrences are Luke 23:43, 2 Cor. 12:4 and the Apocalypse of John (Rev 2:7).

[38] The idea of a place where souls are waiting was particularly alive, during the Middle Ages, "in monastic writings that follow the model of the 'apocalypses' of Peter and Paul and report the visions given to some privileged individuals who were able to journey into the next world..." Closer to the times of Dante and Boccaccio, in 1240 "the University of Paris had condemned as heretical the teaching about the place in which the just waited. Not until the 14th century, however, did the Catholic Church officially and categorically reject the idea of the *refrigerium*." Both pope John XXII (in 1331–2) and Benedict XII (in 1336) held this view, repeated by the Council of Florence in 1439: "The place of waiting had contracted to a purgatory in which the just suffer while also hoping. The verdant meadow around the heavenly Jerusalem had disappeared" (Delumeau, 37–38).

respond directly to the difficulty of the climb and the descent. And just as the end of mirth is heaviness, so sorrows are dispersed by the advent of joy. (4)[39]

Commentators (see for all V. Branca) have suggested how inescapable is the reminder here of Dante's itinerant topography, and more specifically of the allegorical polarity "selva aspra/dilettoso monte" in Canto I of the *Comedy* (prefiguring the ascension to the mount of Pur-

---

[39] The implicit quotation of *Proverbia* XIV, 13 (Risus dolore miscebitur| Et extrema gaudii luctus occupat) in this passage acquires an even more suggestive relevance for our reading, reinforced by an additional, Platonic reference (*Phaedo*), also noted by Branca. In *Phaedo* (also a dialogue in the presence of Death) we find abundant references to the fundamental ambivalence of sorrow and joy, pain and pleasure and their problematic aesthetic and moral "synthesis." "Socrates...: How singular is the thing called pleasure, and how curiously related to pain, which might be thought to be the opposite of it; for they are never present to a man in the same instant, and yet he who pursues either is generally compelled to take the other; their bodies are two but they are joined by a single head..." *Phaedo*, III. (I quote the Benjamin Jowett translation). Following this Platonic lead, we might recall yet another platonic subtext particularly relevant for the textual mapping of the *Decameron*'s earthly paradise (and its purgatorial therapy of lovesickness): the reader might in fact be reminded here of the *Symposium*, where Diotima of Mantineia, Socrates' "instructress in the art of love," tells his disciple the fable of Love's mythical birth from Poros (Plenty) and Pena (Poverty) on the same day of Venus' birth, in the garden of Zeus. Diotima is notably introduced as "a woman wise in this and in many other kinds of knowledge, who in the days of old, when the Athenians offered sacrifice before the coming of the plague, *delayed the disease ten years*." It is tempting to recognize here a possible connection to the numerological structure of the Decameron (obviously assuming that Boccaccio knew of Plato's dialogue): the ten days of storytelling, although spread over two weeks, are perhaps a way of *delaying* rather than *eradicating* the disease, a humanly impossible task—and this refers to both the Plague and "lovesickness," (black Death and black bile)—since both can be deemed a divine punishment for and an unequivocal "symptomatic" consequence of the "original" sin. Viktor Sklovski already pointed out how the *Decameron* structurally belongs to the genre of narratives in proximity of and meant to delay Death (like the Scheherazade cycle in the *Arabian Nights*). Interestingly enough, storytelling as a delaying tactic might be read within the Platonic framework of a therapy of Love (see further, footnote 49).

gatory, via the necessary "detour" into Inferno).[40] Yet, as C. Delcorno has observed, the direct allusion to the ascending purgatorial itinerary of the *Comedy* is, in the passage just quoted,

> sagaciously predisposed in order to suggest a precise reversal of meaning: the *Comedy* describes the vertical journey from Inferno to Paradise, the *Decameron* the horizontal move from the city ravaged by the plague to the *locus amoenus*, the *buen retiro* of the storytellers.[41]

Like the *Comedy's viator* at this mid-point of his vertical itinerary, the *Decameron's* narrators in their horizontal itinerary, *have already gone* through hell (the city ravaged by the Plague, described in the Introduction), taken refuge in the Church (the Dominican Santa Maria Novella), and then proceeded further in their decision to leave behind both the church and the city of sorrows for a place of delight which is also a place of waiting, symbolizing an intermediate, suspended condition.

In the *City of God*, XXII, 30, St. Augustine distinguishes between the Edenic and the resurrected states: the first is defined by the formula *posse non mori* (or the ability not to die), the second by the modified

---

[40] This has led a number of interpreters to underscore the symmetries between the two works (both written "nel mezzo del cammin...") and their reciprocal rhetorical strategies: the "divine" versus "human" comedy that they respectively perform in the face of an extreme physical and spiritual challenge (a journey of the body into the Other World and the threat – both real and allegorical – of the Plague). For two examples of this tendency, see Kirkham and Cottino-Jones, 1982. Both critics, coherently with their premises, see in Day Tenth of the *Decameron* a triumph of "reason" and "order" over the chaotic, transgressive forces evoked in previous days. Thus Kirkham can write: "Mentre Boccaccio conduce la sua brigata nell'ascesa dalla città infernale (I, Intr.) verso una campagna edenica (III, Intr.) e il Paradiso terrestre (VII, Intr.), noi lo seguiamo attraversando paesaggi spirituali e allegorici. L'itinerario conduce verso un ordine e una virtù sempre più elevati, a gradi progressivamente più sublimi" (269). Coccetti instead openly opposes the idea of a symbolic journey in the *Decameron*: city and garden coexist in the same time and the same narrative level, expressing simply two opposite polarities, so that the short walk that separates and links them does not possess the characteristics of a super-temporal journey, singular and inimitable, but rather those of a familiar road to be traveled again back and forth endless times in the secular space of bourgeois life.

[41] Delcorno, 173–74. Equally antiphrastic is the substitution of the Muses (*Purg.* I, 8) with the women as the "inspirers" of the *Decameron* (IV, Intro., 35).

formula *non posse mori* (the impossibility of dying). In a suspended, *purgatorial* condition between (eternal) life and death, a paradise on Earth reinterpreted as a secularized waiting place where the "ability not to die" is inextricably linked to the procrastinating game of storytelling, the members of the *Decameron*'s *brigata* playfully and parodically re-interpret, in a variety of ways, the story of Genesis. One might conclude that the *Decameron*'s parodic and carnivalesque retreat to Eden is a direct reversal of the apocalyptic and eschatological journey of the *Comedy*. Yet this textual retreat also implies what we might call a self-ironic therapy of desire: in Dante's itinerary, the therapy coincides with the progressive purgation of Love (perverted, defective, excessive) to reach the original state of innocence that will allow the pilgrim to undertake (and then retell) his final journey to the Celestial Rose; in the *Decameron* (as we have already suggested) the therapy for love-sickness and the purification of desire seem to remain irreducibly ambiguous (ambivalently physical and moral), often a direct parody of the "divine" (the definition is not by chance attributed to Boccaccio himself) sublimation of the *Comedy*.[42]

If we now look at the beginning of Day III, where the move to the second, walled garden is described ("On the following Sunday, when already the dawn was beginning to change from vermilion to orange with the approach of the sun..."), the clear reference to *Purg.*, II. 7–9

[42] According to its Platonic exegesis in the *Symposium*, Love, neither mortal nor immortal, but a mean between the two, is neither the source of simple pleasure nor simply the source of its opposite, sorrow (*luctus*), but of both joy and sorrow at the same time (and the simultaneous presence of sorrow and joy is also, we might recall, the most common definition of melancholy). In Dante's *Purgatory* , this ambivalent Eros is coherent with the sorrowful joy or joyful sorrow of the penitent souls, filled with longing and anticipation of their future journey upwards. Yet, rather than being a simple reversal of the *Comedy*'s "purgatorial mood," particularly detectable in the frame story's introduction and conclusion to each Day of storytelling, the *Decameron*'s own "edenic" mood itself becomes an allegory of secularization. The comedic laughter exploding in some of the *Decameron*'s novellas seems thus to reinscribe, as its *double* epigraph or epitaph, the old satiric chiasmus: *in Hilaritate Tristis/in Tristitia Hilaris* (and Juvenal as well as Horace). The most assertive proponent of a satirical dimension in the *Decameron* is Hollander, 1997, 159–163.

seems to confirm the purpose of a "parodic dissacration"[43] ("sì che le bianche e le vermiglie guance,/ là dov'i era, della bella Aurora/ per troppa etate divenivan rance..." Dante sets out, also on a Sunday, at dawn, on the difficult climb up the Purgatory mount toward the garden of Eden on the summit). The ten storytellers in the *Decameron*, instead, stroll *westward* "at a leisurely pace along a little-used path carpeted with grass and flowers..." directly into Eden or a simulation of it, geographically in direct contradiction with the traditional setting of Eden to the East.[44] The medieval cosmological topography of Eden is thus ironically re-drawn, at the periphery of the earthly Jerusalem (Florence, the City of Man): ."..they were shown into a walled garden alongside the palace, and since it seemed at first glance to be a thing of wondrous beauty, they began to explore it in detail...." After such pleasurable exploration, copiously thickened with literary reminiscences,

> they all began to maintain that if Paradise were constructed on earth [*se Paradiso si potesse in terra fare*], it was inconceivable that it could take any other form, nor could they imagine any way in which the garden's beauty could possibly be enhanced. (189-91)

The key word here is "*fare*" (which McWilliam translates as "constructed," emphasizing the artificial, architectural dimension of the place) in a subjunctive clause which stresses both impossibility and its opposite, the fact that this is an aesthetically perfect *representation* of Paradise ("*se Paradiso si potesse in terra fare*"): not a true Eden—paradise on Earth is only an approximation (or manmade imitation).[45] The description we are commenting on is unmistakably pervaded by an "anxiety of influence." Yet, the

---

[43] Delcorno, 174. See also Hollander, 1997, 58–59, where a summary of passages in the *Decameron* retraceable to Dante's *Comedy* show a clear majority of purgatorial references. See also A. Bettinzoli, "Per una definizione delle presenze dantesche nel *Decameron*. II. Ironizzazione e espressivismo antifrastico-deformatorio," *Studi sul Boccaccio*, XIV, pp. 209–240.

[44] On the earthly paradise and medieval geography, see Delumeau, chapter III.

[45] This brings us back to the order or "progression" of edenic sites in the *Decameron*'s architecture, with a hypothesis: Boccaccio doesn't *openly* and *directly* take on Dante, because it would be impossible to challenge him, so to speak, on his own turf (Boccaccio had done this already, with decidedly mixed results, in the platonic *Amorosa Visione*). See V. Kirkham, "Amorous Vision, Scholastic Vistas," in *The Sign of Reason*, 55ff.

architectural motif is even more subtle. With the second palace-garden of Boccaccio's *Decameron*, in Day III, we are introduced, in fact, into a traditional *hortus conclusus* which, *as a self-reflexive aesthetic ideal*, is *twofold*: natural and artificial at the same time, this garden is another exquisitely architectural place at whose center, as the Narrator informs us, in place of the tree of life or the tree of knowledge "stood a fountain of pure white marble, covered with marvelous bas-reliefs;" from "a figure standing on a column in the center of the fountain, a jet of water, whether natural or artificial I know not, but sufficiently powerful to drive a mill with ease, gushed high into the sky before cascading downwards and falling with a delectable plash into the crystal-clear pool below...;" from there "the water passed through a hidden culvert and then emerged into finely constructed artificial channels surrounding the lawn on all sides," then flowing "along similar channels through almost the whole of the beautiful garden, eventually gathering at a single place from which it issued forth from the garden and descended towards the plain as a pure clear stream, furnishing ample power to two separate mills on its downward course, to the no small advantage of the owner of the place" (190–91).[46]

Such a description (which recalls, almost literally, a number of sources, including Boccaccio's own *Amorosa Visione*) seems to confirm the secular, earthly orientation of the suburban ideology which, according to Coccetti and other interpreters, historically frames Boccaccio's work (hence a long tradition of topographic reconnaissance of the *Decameron*'s "paradise on earth" usually identified with Villa Schifanoia or Palmieri, on the Poggio di Camerata).[47] Yet, its symbolic, self-reflexive

---

[46] Cfr. *Amorosa Visione*, XXXIX, 49, ff. and XLIX, 4, ff.

[47] See Branca, 324, footnote 1. Broadening this perspective, it seems only reasonable to situate the *Decameron*'s repetition of the garden imagery (and the Eden narrative) within the trajectory of Western culture thus synthesized by W. A. McClung: "The history of Paradise is the history of the loss of belief in the possibility of pastoral, that is of unelaborated nature benign without reservation, limitation or threat. The uncertain status of the garden in history reflects the failure of an arcadian or pastoral model of beatific existence within the context of a purged and renewed heaven and earth; the survival of Eden depends, therefore, upon whatever accommodation can be reached with the city. To survive, in fact, Eden must become a garden-city." W. A. McClung, *The Architecture of Paradise* (Berkeley: The University of California Press, 1983), 19.

quality is undeniable. Although the *Decameron's paradisus voluptatis* could be viewed in its entirety as an *earthly* mirror-image of its most influential archetype—which Dante "suspends" between Heaven and Earth, as a hanging garden of sort, on top of the mountain of Purgatory—it is also reminiscent of other strategically *prefiguring* sites in Dante's own complex repetition of the Eden *narrative* in the *Comedy*: the "noble castle" of the pagan sages (encompassing "a green meadow blooming round" of *Inferno*, IV, 106 ff.) and the *valletta dei Principi* (Purg. VII).[48] Both these sites are, again, *pre-figurative* of Eden; they are *not* Eden (the first is technically an eternal *limbo*, the second a true waiting place, in the Ante-Purgatory). The Valley of the Princes (where the souls sing the *Salve Regina*) also reminds us directly (ironically?) of the Valley of the Ladies, where women rule (but under the Kingdom of Dioneo, the Venereal), in a sort of temporarily reconstituted prelapsarian condition (might it be just a coincidence that the Valley of the Princes is set in Canto VII of *Purgatory* as the Valley of the Ladies provides the setting for Day VII in the *Decameron*?).

V. Therapy in the Garden

Notwithstanding its position, roughly two thirds through the book, the Valley of the Ladies has been repeatedly described as the true "omphalos" of the *Decameron*'s architectural and intertextual labyrinth – the narrative core where the book's strategic and symbolic return to Eden reaches its climax (and reveals its most intimate ambivalence).[49] The

---

[48] Venturi, 12 ff. On Dante's "nobile castello," with the following, crucial memento of the second fundamental component of the Eden narrative, the narrative of the Fall – the appearance of the serpent, see Lino Pertile, "Il nobile castello, il Paradiso Terrestre e l'umanesimo dantesco," *Filologia e critica*, V (1980), I, 1–26.

[49] Lucia Marino, in *The Decameron Cornice: Allusion, Allegory and Iconology* (Ravenna: Longo, 1979) rightly describes the Valley as "a metonym for art itself" (87). Thomas C. Stillinger ("The Language of Gardens: Boccaccio's Valle delle Donne," *Traditio* 39 [1983]), underscoring that in the description "the narrative viewpoint is that of the absent onlooker," and that Boccaccio "recalls the whole tradition of the *locus amoenus*," focuses on three main textual sources (Dante's *Commedia*, the *Roman de la Rose* and Ovid's *Metamorphoses*) but mentions also Andreas Capellanus' Paradise of Love and

temporary "secession" of the seven ladies, who abandon their three male companions to venture alone into the Valley at the end of Day VI, is quickly transformed into the book's most daring narrative move: a scouting reconnaissance of idyllic (and perilous) lapsarian grounds, since Day VII, under the rule of Dioneo (the Venereal), is devoted to the

> "tricks which, either in the cause of love or for motives of self-preservation, women have played upon their husbands, irrespective of whether or not they were found out." (478)

Thus, as a clear contamination of the biblical garden of Eden with the literary garden of Venus, the Valley of the Ladies is the ideal setting for a parodic "repetition" of the Eden narrative: a garden of delights where mortal men are admitted at their own risk, a prelapsarian garden, where Eve—and the Snake—still rule unfettered. This hidden *locus amoenus*, with its complex meta-diegetic topography and intricate intertextual references, where the members of the brigata dwell for only one day before returning to the order of a self-contained *hortus conclusus*, is more than just a "garden"—in fact, it is not even defined as such—and is also, as we have seen, ambiguously positioned within the *Decameron*'s comprehensive architecture.[50] Yet, although the word "garden" is never used at the end of Day VI or the beginning of Day VII to characterize the Valley, the word appears ten times in the stories of Day VII, most frequently (seven times) in novella seven, which, among the novella gardens, represents, as already said, a climax of the Edenic parody.[51] Moreover, the Valley literally mirrors (as in a reversed angle) the previous architectural set-

---

"certain idyllic scenes in Boccaccio's own earlier writings" (305–306). Edith G. Kern ("The Gardens in the *Decameron* Cornice," *PMLA* 66 [1951] has argued that the *Decameron* repeats the narrative progression from garden to garden (the Garden of Deduit and Genius' Park) that characterizes the *quête* in the *Roman de la Rose.*

[50] Too general and unsatisfactory is the assessment of the Valley in Coccetti, 81. Within his perspective, the Valley of the Ladies is seen as the attempt to explore how the countryside (*contado*)—not the tamed nature of the garden but the open, wider horizon of the fields—would also establish itself as a convenient backdrop for urban [and civic] behavior.

[51] See Usher, 281–82.

tings, their ambivalent connotation, both natural *and* artificial:

> And according to the description I was given later...the floor of the valley was perfectly circular in shape, for all the world as if it had been made with compasses, though it seemed the work of Nature rather than of man. (480)

The Valley is graciously surrounded and almost walled in by "half-a-dozen hills, all comparatively low-lying, on each of whose summits one could discern a palace, built more or less in the form of a pretty little castle." The hills range "downwards in a regular series of terraces, concentrically arranged like the tiers of an amphitheatre, their circles gradually diminishing in size from the topmost terrace to the lowest," their slopes lined with fruit trees, facing south, and thickly wooded, facing north. The plain lying at the bottom, to which there is no other access than the very narrow path, bounded by "a beautifully clear stream," by which the ladies have entered, is also filled with trees "so neatly arranged and symmetrically disposed that they looked *as if they had been planted by the finest practitioner of the forest's craft*" (again an allusion to an absent Master of the place or *hortulanus*). A natural pool, a tiny lake, lies at the center of the Valley, fed by another "stream cascading down over the living rock of a gorge separating two of the surrounding hills" and flowing "swiftly along a neat little channel to the center of the plain." This lake resembles "one of those fishponds that prosperous townspeople occasionally construct in their gardens." In this pool the ladies bathe, in crystal clear water "which concealed their chaste white bodies no better than a thin sheet of glass would conceal a vermilion rose," swimming "in pursuit of the fishes, which had nowhere to hide, and [trying] to seize hold of them with their hands"(480–481).

Many commentators have suggested that this scene represents a sort of ritual purification (preparing the storytellers to innocently recount the daring stories of Day VII). And many are the implicit quotations from Dante's *Comedy* which, framed within this representation, can be construed either allegorically or parodically: the water "senza...mistura alcuna" of the Valley's fishpond is directly reminiscent of the water of the river Lethe ("Tutte l'acque che son di qua più monde,/ parrieno avere in sè mistura alcuna/ verso di quella, che nulla nasconde," *Purg.* XXVIII, 28-30). And the seven ladies, it has been suggested, are reminiscent of the "ninfe" to whom Matelda is compared as she guides Dante, the pilgrim, from the other side of the stream to the "foresta spessa e viva" (*Purg.* XXIX, 4–5).[52] In the Valley, Boccaccio not only "seems to naturalize" the representation of paradise on Earth (mirroring also the vision of the Celestial Rose, in *Paradiso* XXX),[53] parodically inverting the ascending order of the *Comedy* (from the garden of Eden deeper into the garden of Venus); he seems also to complicate and contaminate its narrative with a parody of the *Roman de la Rose* – itself, according to the influential twentieth-century interpreter D. W. Robertson, nothing but "a humorous and witty retelling of the story of the Fall."[54]

---

[52] The reference is noted by Stillinger, 306.

[53] Stillinger, 307: "The earthly image which is created [by Dante, in *Paradiso* XXX] is that of a natural amphitheater surrounding a pool, the very topography of the Valle delle Donne; the next tercet compares this breathtaking landscape to a single rose." The whole description appears to intentionally combine and re-write several sources, most prominent among them the Garden of Deduit, in the *Roman de la Rose*: "...in both texts [the *Decameron* and the *Roman*] the rose is first of all an image: in Guillaume's Garden of Deduit it is the vision of a rose reflected as if in glass; in Boccaccio's Valley it is the metaphor of a rose seen under glass." Thus, the Valley alludes not only to both Dante's Garden of Purgatory and its heavenly transfiguration, but also "to both gardens from the *Roman de la Rose* simultaneously [the Garden of Deduit and Genius' Park], juxtaposing distinctive traits from both." "These four gardens...form a symmetrical pattern. Two great questing narratives provide two gardens each..." (Stillinger, 308–09). Stillinger's reconstruction of the literary blueprint of the Valley of the Ladies also underscores the "artificial" character or, to use another expression, the conscious self-reflexivity of Boccaccio's authorial *tour de force*, describing it as "a fragmentary, combinatorial, deflating epic," thoroughly oriented to "literary immanence" (316). See also Kern, 512–13 and Mazzotta, 55–56.

[54] In *The World at Play* Mazzotta has analyzed the textual and rhetorical fabric of the double parody involved in its double set of references: "Boccaccio's mockery, actually, is twofold. He spoofs Dante's allegory of the spiritual pilgrimage, his ascent to Eden, and, in so doing, he follows Guillaume's [in the *Roman de la Rose*] own parody of the Earthly Paradise. But Boccaccio also mocks the naturalistic thrust of Guillaume's poem. Far from being Amant's erotic quest, the brigata's journey aims at a gratuitous, purely esthetic evasion into the artifice of nature...His garden is neither Dante's allegory of Eden nor is it Amant's garden of literal, fleshly delights. It is the imaginative domain where the allegory and the letter are alluded to and equally superseded, where the young people of the brigata indulge in esthetic pastimes and are drawn into the artifice: they dance, play, read romances, tell stories..." (110)

We should recall how the *Roman* was attacked on theological grounds by Jean Gerson (1362–1428) precisely as a *profane* repetition of the narrative of the fall: the Lover's (rebaptized by Gerson Fol *amoureaux*) preference for Amor over Reason is a dangerous "trapassar del segno," a "delusion which overturns God's order...a version of the primal sin"– exactly, also according to Augustine (*De Trinitate*, XXII, ch. 12), what happened in Eden.[55] Interestingly enough, as Helen Phillips reminds us, already in the thirteenth century the second author of the *Roman de la Rose*, Jean de Meun, had condemned the first garden (the Garden of Deduit), calling it a fable, a trifle, compared with the truth of the eternal park of the Lamb. The most interesting aspect for us of this re-writing is perhaps Jean de Meun's "anti-ascetic" attitude: "those who apply themselves assiduously to reproduction will win places in heaven (ll. 19497–868, 20607–664)." Drawing on Alain de Lille's writings, "Jean's utilitarian justification of sex, though it shocked some contemporaries [such as Cristine de Pizan] with its bawdy language and disregard for marriage, fits with his orthodox theological grounds for condemning the delights of the rose garden as transient and delusory..." As an instrument of reproduction, sex for Jean "is a weapon against Atropos" and "obediently serves the divine plan" (Phillips, 212). Boccaccio's own anti-ascetic parody of a parody seems also meant to "avoid the rebellious hubris of Amor" and yet it seems also to follow an opposite path in order to save the civilizing role of love, within the social framework of marriage.[56]

Another set of intertextual references, hidden in the description of the Valley of the Ladies as an anti-Purgatorial version of paradise on Earth, refers us again (as in the *Decameron*'s Prologue) to Ovid, this

---

[55] Phillips, 211.

[56] Other critics (C.S. Lewis, for example) have maintained that "the garden does celebrate a genuine idealization and civilizing of sexual passion," since "Reason represents an ultimately higher authority, but her voice does not entirely demolish the claims of the vision of human love." The terms of the discussion are not too distant from those applied by critics to Boccaccio's own ambivalently parodic and/or therapeutic recreation of paradise on Earth.

time to the *Metamorphoses*.[57] Topographically, there are four spots in the *Metamorphoses* which the description of the Valley alludes to glancingly, in the episodes of Acteon, Narcissus, Arethusa and Salmacis: all "these four scenes resemble each other and the valley; each is a clear pool or stream with grassy banks, tree-shaded and quite secluded" and each "is the setting for a brief Ovidian narrative, in which a hunter or wanderer seeks shelter from the midday heat."[58] It is the setting for the revelation of the ambivalently divine and demonic nature of Love, a setting, we may add, that also reminds us of a different tradition, the medieval monastic tradition of the "demon of noontide." It has been suggested that Ovid might well be Boccaccio's own Virgil, in the *Decameron*, with its complex strategic references to the *Heroides*, the *Remedia Amoris* (in the Prologue) and the *Metamorphoses*. This is clearly visible in the Valley and the inspiration that Boccaccio seems to draw from Ovid is crucially linked to the recreation of an Edenic setting which is also the setting for an ambiguous therapeutic exercise: "Ovid prefigures the notion of the absent onlooker...the voyeuristic author and the complicitous reader [who] see the women without being there, without being anywhere."[59] The ideal center (the *omphalos*) of the Decameron's labyrinth is in fact a *trompe l'oeil*, with all the irreducible ambiguity of a *natural artifice* ("simulaverat artem/ingenio natura suo," *Met*. 3.158–59).

The *Decameron*'s complex, multi-layered parody of the *Comedy* and the *Roman*, its double "anti-ascetic" and "purgatorial" re-presentation of a paradise on Earth, thus brings us back, one last time, to the therapy for "lovesickness," the malady of the Fall. At the very center of the Garden (in both the artificially natural walled garden of Day III and the naturally artificial Valley of the Ladies of Day VI–VII) we find a fountain, a pool (*whether natural or artificial I know not*): this *locus solus* or *locus amoenus par exellence*, in medieval culture, is both the place of

---

[57] "Boccaccio looks at the rose of Amant and Dante through Ovid's glass." Stillinger, 318.

[58] Stillinger, 313.

[59] Stillinger, 317.

purification and the dangerous and deceptive mirror, the *miroërs perilleus*, of a voyeuristic act. The self-reflexive fountain of Narcissus, a secularized *fons vitae*, "a reminder of the double face of carnal love,"[60] sums up all the ambivalences, all the ambiguities of the *Decameron*'s complex aesthetic reconstruction of Eden. The therapy in the garden, the therapy of desire, the therapy for both its readers' and its author's melancholy, has found its perfect setting.

Giorgio Agamben has retraced the myth of Narcissus to the medieval reelaboration of the poetic (imaginative) process, linking it directly to the medical tradition of lovesickness, as a disease of the imagination. To a medieval reader Narcissus' sin (or error) is not *amor sui*, but rather love of an *image*, a form of idolatry based on the replacement of the creature with its image.[61] Agamben thus provides a reading of the fountain episode in the *Roman de la Rose* entirely based on these premises and in particular on the idea of the imagination as a mirror, or, following the imagery of the fountain scene, a double crystal which, when lit by the sun, reflects now one side, now the other of the garden, yet never the whole thing—never both sides together. To Agamben, the fountain of Love (a *fons vitae*) and the mirror of Narcissus are both representations of the imaginative process, according to Averroes' commentary (Dante's "gran comento") on Aristotle.[62] This interpretation in turn allows him to interpret the figure of Oiseuse (the woman with a mirror who, in the *Roman*, introduces Amant into the garden) as a personification of imagination, coherently (and paradoxically) linked in medieval iconography either to Lust or to Prudence.

---

[60] Phillips, 210.

[61] Hence Dante's own reversed use of Narcissus in *Paradise* III, 17–18, where he says that in looking at the blessed souls he fell into an error opposite to Narcissus', mistaking the souls for images reflected in a mirror: "perch'io dentro a l'error contrario corsi/ a quel ch'accese amor tra l'omo e 'l fonte."Agamben, 1977, part III, chapter 2, 96–98. For Andreas Capellanus, whose treatise *De Amore* is considered a sort of theoretical manifesto of the new conception of love, the latter is describable as the *immoderata cogitatio* of a "mental" image ("ex eo, quod vidit, passio illa procedit").

[62] Agamben 98–99.

This ambivalent visualization is of a piece with the ambivalence of imagination, linked to both the *fin'amors* and the *fol amour* of the poets.[63] I would like to propose here an analogy with the *Decameron* and its complex, parodic and ironic, therapeutic revisitation of Paradise on Earth. Francesca, the "screen lady" of the *Decameron*'s subtitle, the woman with a book, Dante's fallen heroine, the "uncritical" reader of romances and Boccaccio's own ironic "ideal (mis)reader," a *figura Evae*, represents (*per contrappasso*) all the charming ladies who "out of fear or shame, conceal the flames of passion within their fragile breasts," and "cooped up within the narrow confines of their rooms, where they sit in apparent idleness, wishing one thing and at the same time its opposite" (2) are inevitably the victims of melancholy: for them the book itself is supposed to represent a "cure." As such, Francesca reminds us of Oiseuse (an allegory of idleness leading to love). Like Oiseuse, Francesca holds the mirror (the book) in which its onlookers (its readers) can find salvation or damnation. In the Prologue, the Author also tells us that he has already visited the garden (several times, as a matter of fact, in his previous works) and benefited from the therapy that he now in turn offers to idle and melancholic women—using Francesca, the adulteress, a compassionate personification of Lust, as a warning, and Pampinea, who, according to an allegorical reading, personifies Prudence, as Guide. Both stand at the double threshold of the *Decameron*'s paradise on Earth as gatekeepers, in order to lead Amant, its Ideal Reader, to an appropriately imaginative, therapeutic use of the book as both an ambivalent antidote to and a "preventive remedy" for the inescapable narrative of the Fall.[64]

---

[63] Agamben 100. I am here only highlighting the very rich and complex argument of this seminal book.

[64] Kirkham, 129.

The State of Innocence and Private Property in the Polemic on Evangelical Poverty at the Beginning of the Fourteenth Century

Gian Luca Potestà

What is true for the story of Eden may be true for any other part of the Bible, however short: the study of its interpretations can be carried out either within the well-defined field of the history of exegesis, or else in reference to broader theological debates, in which the appeal to a pre-lapsarian condition has fostered the development of new ideas. In this essay I shall be examining the debate in the High Middle Ages concerning the relationship between man and property in the state of nature before original sin. This was a juridical and theological, rather than exegetical, argument, through which a significant redefinition and modernization of the ecclesiastical outlook on property was carried out. The polemic on Evangelical and Franciscan poverty, which culminated in the 1320's in the open conflict between the leadership of the Order of Friars Minor and Pope John XXII, marks a decisive point in this long, drawn-out doctrinal debate. In the divergence of positions concerning the condition of Adam (and Eve) in Eden, very clearly opposing viewpoints on the original legitimacy of private property were established.

*

The problem of the natural condition of man in relation to property is clearly thematized in theological and exegetical thinking from the earliest centuries of Christianity; however, only after the *Decretum*, the massive work composed around 1140 by the Bolognese jurist and monk Gratian, did it take on a juridical and institutional dimension. A passage in the Causa XII of the second part of the *Decretum* will assume great importance in the later canon law and theological discussion:

> Bishop Clement to his beloved brethren and co-disciples, living in Jerusalem together with our dearest James, brother in the bishopric. To share this life in common, brothers, is necessary for everyone, and above all for those who

> wish to be irreproachable militants for God and wish to imitate the life of the Apostles and their disciples. In fact the use of all the things of this world was intended to be common to all men. But through iniquity, one says that this was his, another that that was his, and in this way the divisions between mortals were born. In the end the wisest of the Greeks, realizing that this was the way things stood, declared that all the possessions of friends should be held in common. Women were among these things, without any doubt. And since—he said—neither air nor sunlight can be divided up, nor should other things. They were given to everyone in common, and should be held in common.... Faithful to such a custom, the apostles too and their disciples, as was said before, led with us and with you a shared life in common.[1]

The text purports to be the first part of a letter by Clement, Bishop of Rome, to James, Bishop of Jerusalem. In fact it is a fraud, originating in the pseudo-clementine *Recognitiones* inserted in the pseudo-Isidorian *Decretales*: it is thus a fraudulent pontifical letter which Gratian draws out of the famous canon law collection produced around the middle of the ninth century.

As the complete text of the letter demonstrates, its aim is to propose to the clergy a model of life in common, whose founding justification would lie in the original condition of mankind. This condition is referred to in very vague terms; there is no reference to Eden, but rather to the Platonic idea of the original holding of things and women in common. The vocabulary too is indeterminate, with general talk of "usus communis" which completely disregards the distinction between *usus*, *proprietas*, and *dominium* established in Roman law:[2] in the beginning the use of everything was in common; after original sin this original unity fractured, yielding the appropriation of goods by individuals. Not existing in a natural condition, appropriation is then the fruit of an act of iniquity.

The *Decretum* achieved immediate authoritative status vis à vis previous canon law productions, and was therefore subject to the repeated

---

[1] Causa XII, q. 1, c. 2, in *Corpus Iuris canonici*, ed. A. Friedberg, I (Leipzig: Ex Officina Bernhardi Tauchnitz, 1922), 676.

[2] D. Willoweit has a clear summary of this in "Dominium und Proprietas. Zur Entwicklung des Eigentumsbegriff in der mittelalterlichen und neuzeitlichen Rechtswissenschaft," *Historisches Jahrbuch* 94 (1974), 131–156.

scrutiny of the schools, with the aim of clearing up difficulties in the doctrine and giving it more precision. Giovanni Tarello, Rudolf Weigand and more recently Bernhard Töpfer have collected and discussed the main interpretations of this section of the Causa XII provided by the canonists of the second half of the twelfth century.[3] Although they vary, they do have one basic concern in common: to weaken the conception of an original "communism" regarding the goods of the world and thereby reduce the gap between the condition desired by God and that which followed original sin, in which the Church finds itself. Thus in the *Summa decretorum* (1156–1159) Rufinus distinguishes, within the principles of natural right, between commands, prohibitions and simple indications (*demonstrationes*). The latter show what is good, but they are not absolutely binding. The principles concerning power and private property are also to be included in the *demonstrationes*. Power made its appearance in the world with Nimrod, the grandson of Ham (see Gen. 10:8). His was an act of iniquity; later, however, the long customary usage of law meant that power was not always synonymous with injustice. The same can be said of the appropriation of goods; introduced through the greed of some, it can now no longer be condemned, by virtue of its long tradition and the laws created for it.[4] This is a line that, through the glosses of the Bolognese canonist Gandolfo, emerges in the Anglo-Norman juridical school, as is demonstrated by the *Summa*

---

[3] G. Tarello, "Profili giuridici della questione della povertà nel francescanesimo prima di Ockham," in *Studi in memoria di Antonio Falchi. Annali della facoltà di Giurisprudenza dell'Università di Genova*, Vol. III (Milan: Giuffré, 1964), in particular 29–42 of the extract. R. Weigand, *Die Naturrechtslehre der Legisten und Dekretisten von Irnerius bis Accursius und von Gratian bis Johannes Teutonicus* (Munich: Hueber, 1967). B. Töpfer, "Vorstellungen von einem ursprünglichen und einem endzeitlichen Idealzustand als Ausdruck utopischen Denkens im Mittelalter (unter besonderer Berücksichtigung von Interpretationen des Kapitels Dilectissimis der Causa XII des Decretum Gratiani) bis zum frühen 14. Jahrhundert," in *Mittelalterforschung nach der Wende* 1989, ed. M. Borgolte, *Historische Zeitschrift. Beihefte* 20 (Munich: Oldenbourg, 1995), 387–406.

[4] H. Singer, *Die Summa decretorum des Magister Rufinus* (Paderborn: H. Schöning, 1902), 7.

Lipsiensis produced around 1186.[5] In that period, theoretical efforts to reduce the tension between natural norm and positive right multiplied. In this way the possibility of criticizing the Roman Church in the name of a different order, nearer to the will of God, was eliminated at the root. Further working-out of the theme was offered in the *Summa* of Uguccione of Pisa, written around 1190. Adding another possible explanation to that suggested by Gandolfo and by the *Summa Lipsensius*, Uguccione realizes that the *Decretum* does not exclude private property in principle: that all things are common to everyone only means that in time of necessity they should be shared with those who are in need of them; natural reason leads us all to keep what is necessary for ourselves, and to distribute any surplus to the poor.[6] Property relationships are therefore not subject to discussion, and Gratian's text is manipulated so that the authentic Christian and ecclesiastical vocation lies in its work of charity rather than in the giving up of goods.

Outside of the science of canon law, in the first decades of the thirteenth century, perspectives and solutions of this kind were widely shared in the more important theological productions. One example is that of William of Auxerre, a leading figure at the University of Paris. William was moderately open-minded about new doctrine and a trusted follower of Pope Gregory IX, who placed him at the head of the commission formed to examine and emend Aristotelian texts recently introduced into the West. Between 1215 and 1229 he wrote a *Summa Theologica*, better known as the *Summa Aurea*, the eighteenth treatise of which is devoted to natural right. The first chapter opens with the arguments of some unnamed "saints," according to whom "it was a precept of natural law that everything was held in common, and Adam and Eve in their original state had to keep to this precept."[7] And since the precept of

---

[5] See R. Weigand, *Naturrechtslehre*, 338 ff.

[6] See Tarello, *Profili*, 40 (with the relevant passages of the *Summa* of Uguccione, in n. 104). R. Weigand, *Naturrechtslehre*, 327 ff. and B. Töpfer, "Vorstellungen," 394.

[7] Magistri Giullelmi Altissiodorensis *Summa aurea*, ed. Jean Ribaillier, liber tercius, tomus I (Paris-Grottaferrata: Editions du Centre National de la Recherche Scientifique, Romae, Editiones Collegii S. Bonaventurae ad Claras Aquas, 1986), 369.

nature has not lost its validity, he who appropriates something commits a mortal sin, because he is doing something contrary to the law of nature. This is Gratian's thesis, enriched by the fleeting reference to Adam and Eve. William's reply makes use of the well-known distinction between precepts and prohibitions (endowed with absolute value) and *demonstrationes*, the latter meant to be binding only for a limited time and in certain circumstances. That everything has to be held in common is a simple *demonstratio*, valid as a precept in the state of innocence (i.e., in the state of nature prior to original sin), but no longer valid afterwards.

> In the state of covetousness or nature corrupted, [that all may be in common] is not a precept nor must it be so, given that if it were, the public institutions would be dissolved and men would destroy each other. It is however true that in times of extreme necessity everything must be shared, since natural reason obliges us to love the salvation of our neighbour more than these temporal goods.[8]

Having circumvented the statements of the *Decretum* in this way, William offers two different solutions to the question of whether appropriation means mortal sin: Nimrod certainly sinned mortally, because he appropriated power and possessions through greed; he is without sin, however, who appropriates something in the knowledge that in the state of corrupted nature the common possession of property is harmful.[9]

The interpretation which links the canonists to William of Auxerre can therefore be characterized by the following points:

1. the idea advanced by Gratian, that in an original state of nature (state of innocence) all property was held in common and there was no appropriation, is clearly upheld.

2. In our present historical situation (a state of corrupted nature), appropriation does not inherently mean mortal sin for the possessors of goods.

---

[8] *Summa aurea*, 371.

[9] *Summa aurea*, 374.

3. The tension between natural law and positive law is eased, so to speak, in favor of positive law. Nimrod's sin marks a watershed beyond which it is unthinkable to go. Juridical and theological thinking appears rather inclined to make what happened after original sin fit in with the previous situation, to legitimate the situation after the Fall, thus eliminating at the root any chance of questioning it.

*

In recent decades various studies have demonstrated the complexity of Minorite thinking in the thirteenth and fourteenth centuries on voluntary poverty. St. Francis of Assisi's evangelical style had been marked by "Imitation," lived through in extreme terms and proposed to the friars in all its radicality. The transformation of the primitive fraternity into a fast-growing *ordo*, rapidly charged with important ecclesiastical responsibilities, soon posed juridical and institutional problems for the Minorites, problems which the Rule of the Order had not foreseen. Without a doubt, the most delicate questions concerned the observance of poverty, since in the conscience of the friars and in the consideration of society this was the most characteristic feature of the order—a basic feature which it could not relinquish on any account. Thus it was necessary first of all to delve more deeply into the Rule, to furnish clearer definitions and enrich its rudimentary formulas, trying as far as possible not to contradict it. Therefore a series of papal letters, starting with Gregory IX's *Quo elongati* (1230), established that the friars could not have individual nor shared property in the goods they had at their disposal. The ownership of property had to remain with the benefactors, who gave it to the friars for their use.[10] Gregory IX and his successors, in collaboration with the Minorite leadership, aimed to preserve as far as possible the basic characteristics of the "genetic inheritance" of the Order, gradually introducing differentiations and more complex arguments capable of taking into account its change of profile and increasing importance within the Church and within Christianity. An important example of this was *Ordinem vestrum* (1245), the letter in

[10] H. Grundmann, "Die Bulle *Quo elongati* Papst Gregors IX," *Archivum Francescanum Historicum*, 54 (1961), esp. 22–23.

which Innocent IV put forward the Holy See as owner of the property of which the friars had use. With the letter *Quanto studiosius* (1247) the administration of the properties was given to proctors operating at a formal level in the name of the Pope, but in reality depending directly on the hierarchy of the Order; in this way, a juridical and institutional arrangement was reached which allowed the Minorites to keep their image of radical poverty, without intervention in their actual day-to-day regime.[11]

In actual fact, the Franciscan doctrines did not develop only because the problem of remaining faithful to Francis' *intentio* in a profoundly altered context was acutely felt within the order. From the 1250's on the Minorites had begun to suffer a series of attacks by rival institutions and ecclesiastical circles. The idea of voluntary poverty as a cornerstone of Christian perfection became the subject of bitter polemics, first by the lay teachers of Paris University and then by Dominican theologians. The Minorite doctrine of poverty and its language developed within powerful conflicts which pushed them to work out increasingly subtle solutions.[12]

According to the Minister General Bonaventure of Bagnoregio (*Apologia Pauperum*, 1269), there are two kinds of evangelical poverty: one for those who possess no private property and share all things in common, and one for those who have given up every form of ownership, whether private or in common.[13] The latter is the higher form of poverty, practiced by Jesus and the apostles and taken up by the Franciscans. All of Bonaventure's thinking subtly aims to show that Jesus and the

---

[11] For the juridical and historical significance of these papal indications see respectively G. Tarello, *Profili*, 22–29; M. D. Lambert, *Povertà francescana. La dottrina dell'assoluta povertà di cristo e degli apostoli nell'ordine francescano*, 1210–1323 (Milan: Edizioni Biblioteca Francescana, 1995), esp. 81–101. An English edition is being prepared by Franciscan Institute Publications.

[12] For an overall view of this set of problems see R. Lambertini, *Apologia e crescita dell'identità francescana (1255–1279)* (Rome: Istituto Storico Italiano per il Medio Evo, 1990).

[13] Sancti Bonaventurae "Apologia pauperorum," c. 7, in *Opera omnia*, VIII (Quaracchi: Ex Typographia Collegii S. Bonaventurae, 1898), 273.

disciples did not control the temporal goods they had at their disposal, and as such were the perfect predecessors of the Minorite Order. Petrus Johannis Olivi, a disciple of Bonaventure's who showed a great deal of independence from his master, went further, concluding that the *altissima paupertas* was the original pattern of the relationship between man and property, and that it was time to get back to it.

The conviction that the Minorites truly did try to practice a way of life similar to that of the state of innocence is already to be found in a reference in an anonymous *Comment on the Rule* traditionally attributed to Bonaventure, and now believed instead to be the work of Peckham.[14] At about the same time Olivi faces the question forcefully and from a new viewpoint in the eighth *Quaestio de perfectione evangelica*, devoted to *altissima paupertas*. The basic core of the issue is in the fifteen arguments in which he demonstrates the intimate relation between *altissima paupertas* and perfection. In the sixth argument, he shows that the choice of absolute poverty means the abandonment of all discord, division, contest, quarrel, and suspicion, which are the concerns of those who possess riches, even when held in common. Olivi takes up the pseudo-clementine text used by Gratian and comments on it extensively. On the expression, "the use of all the things of this world ought to have been in common for all men. But through iniquity one said that this was his, another that that was his, and in this way the divisions between mortals were born," he notes: "he does not say that the use should have been common to this college or to that, but in general to all men. This is how it was in the state of innocence."[15] Having recalled that this was the form of life that Plato had recommended, and that had been practiced by primitive Christian communities, Olivi concludes:

[14] Sancti Bonaventurae *Expositio super regulam Fratrum Minorum*, c. 4, in *Opera omnia*, 413a. B. Töpfer calls attention to this passage, "Vorstellungen," 399. On the authorship of the work see Lambertini, *Apologia*, 133–134.

[15] The question is edited by J. Schlageter, *Das Heil der Armen und das Verderben der Reichen. Petrus Johannis Olivi OFM. Die Frage nach der Höchsten Armut* (Werl/Westfalen: Dietrich-Coelde-Verlag, 1989). The passage in question is on 98.

> Yet it is certain that college fights college because they are striving for some right for themselves in the things held in common, and because that general community of all men does not exist. So what is of one college is not of another. Repeated experience teaches us how many lawsuits and how many quarrels, how much jealousy and competition among themselves there is for the prebends—those who have them and those who have yet to receive them; this would not happen, if there were no jurisdiction (*iurisdictio*) even in administration, and if there were no appropriation (*appropriatio*), even for our necessary sustenance. The prebend or the monk has the right to a living, or board, lodging and clothes. And to put it briefly, if the love of temporal power (*iurisdictio*) and of temporal things is not completely eliminated from the hearts of men, there can be no community without the aforesaid evils. The supreme profession of the highest poverty is not juridically connected to this land more than to that nor to this house more than to that. And he who observes it perfectly will be more concerned about looking after it for himself rather than for someone else. Thus every reason for division or for envy that may arise from whatever appropriation or jurisdiction (*iurisdictio*) or distribution of income, will necessarily cease.[16]

Olivi's doctrine breaks with theological tradition and with previous Franciscan thinking in several respects. In affirming that the state of innocence is characterized by the absence of any kind of jurisdiction and appropriation, he forcefully repeats pseudo-clementine teaching, ignoring the interpretative efforts carried out in canon law and theological circles to reduce its relevance and implications. On the contrary, where the canon lawyers tended to legitimate both power and property in the name of custom and law, Olivi rejects them both as the cause of social disorder. A few pages later, still with reference to the provisions of the *Decretum*'s Causa XII, Olivi states flatly,

> whoever wanted to say that in the state of innocence things or laws about things (*appropriarentur*) were given individually to a person or college would be judged to be insane by every right reasoning.[17]

Olivi states clearly that it is solely the renunciation of power and appropriation that creates the conditions for a human society in which tensions and conflicts disappear. The society he is looking for is a resto-

---

[16] *Das Heil der Armen*, 99. On the model of society which Olivi outlines see also 30–37.

[17] *Das Heil der Armen*, 126.

ration of the state of innocence on earth. The *altissima paupertas* propounded and practiced by the friars minor is an important step in this direction, in that it satisfies the pattern of relationship with property which is characteristic of that state of innocence. By now we have gone beyond the *Decretum* itself: the sin of appropriation is no longer felt to be an insuperable watershed; following the road of Minorite poverty, men will once again be able to give vitality to the peaceful sociality of our original condition.

Olivi's doctrines were not adopted by the Order, which looked on his theological production and his theses on poverty with some suspicion. Several times he had to defend himself from accusations, undergoing trials and censure. From the start of the fourteenth century his doctrinal influence was defended with difficulty by the Minorite tendency within the Spirituals, until John XXII placed his works under further inquiry (and condemnations followed), in the context of a much wider campaign carried out against the Spirituals.[18] At about the same time the Pope launched an attack on the Order of the Friars Minor overall, entering into bitter conflict with its leadership.[19] John XXII immediately focussed on the nature of evangelical poverty, and set up wide-ranging consultations on it between prelates and teachers.[20] Among

---

[18] For the difficulties met by Olivi in the Order and for his collocation on the margins of the Francisan "school" see my "Maestri e dottrine nel XIII secolo," in *Francesco d'Assisi e il primo secolo di storia francescana* (Turin: Einaudi, 1997), esp. 329–335. Fundamental for Olivi's positions on the subject of poverty is D. Burr, *Olivi and Franciscan Poverty. The Origins of the Usus Pauper Controversy* (Philadelphia: University of Pennsylvania Press, 1989).

[19] On the reasons for the Pope's anti-Minorite attitude see T. Turley, "John XXII and the Franciscans: A Reappraisal," in *Popes, Teachers, and Canon Law in the Middle Ages*, ed. J. R. Sweeney and S. Chodorow (Ithaca and London: Cornell University Press, 1989), 74–83; and my own *Angelo Clareno. Dai poveri eremiti ai fraticelli* (Rome: Istituto Storico Italiano per il Medio Evo, 1990), esp. 172–173.

[20] L. Duval-Arnould, "Les conseils remis à Jean XXII sur le problème de la pauvreté du Christ et des apôtres (Ms. Vat. lat. 3740)," in *Miscellanea Bibliothecae Vaticanae*, Vol. III (Vatican City: Biblioteca Apostolica Vaticana, 1989), 121–195. On the entire polemic more generally, see A. Tabarroni, *Paupertas Christi et apostolorum. L'ideale francescano in discussione, 1322–1324* (Rome: Istitutio Storico Italiano per il Medio Evo, 1990), and M. D. Lambert, *Povertà francescana*, 201–241.

the various writings produced in this period by the leadership of the Order in defense of the Bonaventure tradition, the most notable was without doubt the *Tractatus de paupertate Christi et apostolorum* (1322) of the Proctor General Bonagratia of Bergamo. A pre-eminent representative of the ruling group which had held to erase the memory of Olivi, Bonagratia approached the connection between Franciscan poverty and the state of innocence from a different perspective from that of the master of the Spirituals.

Among the objections to Minorite poverty raised most often by lay writers and Dominicans, and dearest to the Pope, was the one that stated the inseparability of dominion and use in the case of consumable goods. The purely fictitious character of Franciscan poverty could be demonstrated precisely by the existence of those goods which, like food, in the act of being consumed are used up; at least in the case of such goods, the distinction between property and use can be seen to be fictitious, since the use means the consumption of the property. One of Bonagratia's replies to this objection falls back on the Biblical story of Eden. God ordered our progenitors: "But of the tree of the knowledge of good and evil, thou shalt not eat of it..." (Gen. 2:17). The use of consumable goods—the fruits of the other trees of paradise—is therefore foreseen in natural law and sanctioned by the divine order of things. God remained the owner of the goods and conceded their use to Adam and Eve. For men, use in common is therefore the original pattern of relationship with these goods, preceding every form of property; property entered into the world following upon sin and was recognized only with the advent of positive law. It does not matter that the state of innocence lasted for such a short time; if the first man had not sinned, everything would have remained in common use for all men, at all times and everywhere, without property.[21]

The apologetic nature of Bonagratia's thinking on the state of innocence is evident; its representation is constructed to legitimate the

---

[21] See L. Oliger, "Fr. Bonagratia de Bergamo et ejus *Tractatus de Christi et apostolorum paupertate*," *Archivum Franciscanum Historicum*, 22 (1929), esp. 504 (with explicit reference to the pseudo-clementine letter).

Franciscan identity which is in danger. Its apologetic perspective should however be distinguished from that of Olivi. In Olivi, the reference to the state of innocence allows a radical criticism of power (*iurisdictio*) and appropriation (*appropriatio*) to emerge; the *altissima paupertas* of the Minorites opens up a means by which the whole of human society can ultimately overcome discord and conflict. Bonagratia's perspective does not contain this eschatological dimension, and is intended exclusively to safeguard the institutional space available to Minorite poverty, to which it offers a solid foundation. The state of innocence means the simple use of goods excluding every form of property or possession, whether private or shared. The Son of God, who was made man in order to restore the state of innocence, used goods without owning them or having dominion over them; as followers of Christ, the Minorites use goods without having property or possession, and in this way they reaffirm on earth the original state of innocence.[22] Where the language of Olivi was lacking in definition, Bonagratia avoids any sign of linguistic slippage, since what he wants is precisely to identify the edenic condition with the Minorite condition.

*

John XXII's attack on the Minorite leadership, on the identity and doctrinal memory of the Order, culminated in the two letters *Ad conditorem canonum* (1322) and *Cum inter nonnullos* (1323). In the former, the Pope gave up domain over the goods given in use to the Minorites, and conferred the property upon the Order; in the latter the idea, so dear to the Franciscans, that Jesus and the Apostles did not possess anything, either individually or in common, was declared heretical. The Friars Minor did not passively accept the Papal declaration. In 1328 the leadership fled Avignon and placed itself under imperial protection. A double *appellatio* against the Pope, issued by the Minister General Michael of Cesena but written by Bonagratia, polemically repeated the main arguments against the Pope, openly accusing him of

---

[22] L. Oliger, *Fr. Bonagrat de Bergamo*, esp. 496–497 and 489. J. Oakley aptly calls our attention to these passages in "John XXII and Franciscan Innocence," *Franciscan Studies* 24 (1986), 217–226, esp. 222.

heresy. The latter replied with the letter *Quia vir reprobus* (1329). In this extensive text John XXII refuted, among other things, the idea of the lack of property in the state of innocence, going back to the pseudo-clementine letter contained in the *Decretum* and offering an interpretation of it which was completely different from that of the Minorite leadership.[23]

Two important passages are relevant here. In the first, the Pope comments on the quotation attributed to his predecessor:

> Without any doubt this text imagines that if our progenitors had not sinned, everything relating to dominion or property would have been in common. This is clear from the statement that through iniquity, i.e., through the sin of our progenitors, one said that this was his, another that that was his, and in this way the divisions between mortals were born. These divisions related to what was previously held in common; so a dividing up of things occurred, and not simply a division of actual use, as is clear from one saying that this was his, the other that that was his; not saying that one said the use of this thing was his and the other the use of that thing was his, but the one said that one thing was his and the other that that other thing was his. It is clear that the division concerned the domain and not the use of things, and it therefore follows that before the division there was communion concerning the domain over things.[24]

John XXII is affirming that in Eden there was common property in goods; the sin of Adam and Eve marked the introduction of private property, well before Nimrod. Eden is thereby de-Franciscanized: the Pope takes over a vision of paradise which actually coincides (but it is no coincidence) with that of the Dominicans (who unlike the Franciscans held their goods in a regime of undivided property).[25]

The basic concern of the Pope however was certainly not to oppose common ownership and common use. His deepest intentions are re-

---

[23] The passage in question in Michael of Cesena's *Appellatio minor* is to be found in *Bullarium Franciscanum*, ed. C. Eubel, Vol. V (Rome: Typis Vaticanis, 1898), 412b (note); in reference to the pseudo-clementine text, the arguments of the *Tractatus* of Bonagratia, on the lack of property in the state of innocence, are more or less reprised.

[24] *Quia Vir Reprobus*, in *Bullarium Franciscanum*, ed. C. Eubel, Vol. 5, 417b–418a.

[25] See the authoritative reading that Hervaeus of Nédéllec, master general of the Order of Preachers, had offered some years before, of the state of innocence as a condition establishing property in common. Hervaeus Natalis, "De paupertate Christi et apostolorum," *Archives d'histoire doctrinale et littéraire du Moyen Age*, 12–13 (1937–1938), 272.

vealed a few pages later, where he rereads the first two chapters of Genesis from a perspective which greatly reduces the value of the passage of the *Decretum* just commented on:

> What [Michael of Cesena] affirms—that our progenitors in the state of innocence did not have domain over anything, but just simply the use—explicitly contradicts the Holy Scripture, at least after that blessing: "Grow and multiply," etc. In the first chapter of Genesis the Lord says to our progenitors: "Grow and multiply and fill the earth and subject it;[26] and he goes on: "and have domain over the fish of the sea and the birds of the sky and all the living beings that move on the earth." From this it is evident that our progenitors after that blessing had domain over the earth, the fish in the sea, the birds of the sky, and all the animals that move over the earth, in the state of innocence. And if it is asked if that domain was private or in common, it seems that it must be said that since at the time of that blessing only Adam had been created, and not Eve (as the order of the Holy Scripture clearly indicates, since the blessing was given to Adam who was outside paradise, while Eve was formed after Adam himself had been transferred to paradise, as the first two chapters of Genesis reveals), it seems that before the creation of Eve the domain of Adam over temporary things had been individual, not common. It could not have been shared, since he was alone at that time, and nothing can be said to be shared in relation to one person alone, who has never had others around him.[27]

The Edenic condition of common property in goods is therefore reduced to a simple interval between two conditions both marked by private property: Adam's pre-Edenic condition, prior to the creation of Eve (the real original condition!), and the historical condition following from original sin.

In this phase of the polemic on poverty Bernhard Töpfer has seen an important stage in the movement toward the modern. The first symptoms of a radically critical attitude towards private property may be recognized, and also the tendency to legitimate it; these two opposing attitudes are destined to emerge clearly in the following centuries.[28]

---

[26] Another version has "dominate it" in place of "subject it," and Augustine follows that version in *Super Genesis ad litteram* and in the *De Civitate Dei*, XIV, 21.

[27] *Quia vir reprobus*, 422ab.

[28] B. Töpfer, *Vorstellungen*, 389–390 and 405.

With the *Quia vir reprobus*, John XXII completely rehabilitates property, placing it back in a theological and exegetical context which makes it the basic pattern of the relationship between man and the world. Besides the language, John XXII's position reflects a profound change of mentality; the unease so often manifest in canon law and theological circles towards Gratian's most authoritative text is finally overcome, thanks to an exegetical expedient which sanctions the reconciliation between the Church and private property, elevated to the status of a prelapsarian condition. The conflict between natural right and positive law, on which the Franciscan tradition had insisted so strongly, is resolved with a clarity very different from the cautious attempts of the canonists. In terms of property, the pre-Edenic state of nature is placed on a par with the historical state following original sin. It is not a question of imagining a world without private property, but of fully accepting the worldly condition marked by relations of power and property.

The firm rejection of the cardinal points of the Minorite doctrine of poverty marked a severe crisis in the identity of the Order. In the same group of the old leadership which fled to Munich, William of Ockham began to profoundly rethink the notion of dominion in relation to the condition of Eden, and carried out a shrewd revaluation of private property for the state after original sin.[29] In the modern age supporters of the return of the state of innocence as a condition without property will not be lacking, but they will be found elsewhere, outside the Franciscan order.

---

[29] See the *Nachwort* of J. Miethke to William of Ockham, *Dialogus, Auszüge zur politischen Theorie* (Darmstadt: Wissenschaftliche Buchgesellschaft, 1992), esp. 219 ff. (with bibliography). On this point Ockham may have taken into account the doctrinal revision carried out before his own, in the same circle, by his fellow brother Francis of Ascoli. For the evolution of the latter see R. Lambertini, "La proprietà di Adamo. Stato d'innocenza ed origine del dominium nel Commento alle Sentenze e nell'Improbacio di Francesco d'Ascoli," *Bullettino dell'Istituto Storico Italiano per il Medio Evo e Archivio Muratoriano* 99.2 (1992), 201–252.

The Three Gardens in the Paradisal Scene of Pico della Mirandola's *De hominis dignitate*

Pier Cesare Bori

In 1496, two years after the death of Giovanni Pico, his fond nephew Gianfrancesco published among other works that "most elegant oration" later called "De hominis dignitate." It had originally been intended as an introduction to the "900 Theses," in that extraordinary year of 1486. This essay is devoted to a re-interpretation of the opening pages of the "Discourse on the Dignity of Man," perhaps the most renowned of all of Italian humanism, in order primarily to bring out the many-sided paradisal imagination that can be found there.

It is with the recognition of human dignity that Pico begins the *Discourse*, quoting the "magnum miraculum" of Asclepius, as well as "Abdala Saracena." From his own point of view, however, human dignity is founded not so much on ancient clichés (such as the primacy of man based on his central place in the universe), but on the fact that man, not having a fixed image and therefore being able to share freely in the essence of various creatures, will in the end be able to draw on his final identity with God.

Let us remember the words that God uses to address his creature:

> The excellent creator established in the end that to he to whom he could give nothing of his own be given all that appertains to individual creatures. So he took man, a creation of undefined image, and placing him at the centre of the world spoke to him thus: "To you, Adam, we have given neither a definite home, nor particular appearance, nor any specific function, so that you may obtain and possess according to your wishes and wisdom whatever home, appearance and function you choose for yourself. The fixed nature of others, is limited by laws prescribed by us. You, unconstrained by want, will define it according to that free will I have entrusted to you. I have placed you in the midst of the world, so that from there, on looking about you, you can better observe all that there is in the world. We haven't made you either of the heavens or the earth, neither mortal nor immortal, so that you may happily give yourself the form you prefer, as free and sovereign creator of yourself. You can degenerate down into the inferior beings, the

brutes; but if you wish, you can regenerate into superior things, divine."[1]

Ever since his premature death, Pico della Mirandola has retained his place in the popular imagination and continued to attract the attention of scholars. The five hundredth anniversary of his death gave rise to academic conferences, new translations, and studies of his sources. In all this ferment of activity, however, a gap has remained for decades between two basic interpretative attitudes towards Pico, and towards the page I have just quoted.

Resisting the prevailing interpretative trend that runs from Gentile through Garin, from Cassirer to Kristeller, through to the latest studies that insist on the connections between Pico and the culture of magic, astrology, and esoteric and cabalistic traditions, another trend sees in Pico continuity with theological tradition, from the Bible to the Fathers of the Church and to scholastic theology. Among the representatives of this tendency, Henri De Lubac springs to the fore with his *Pic de la Mirandole*,[2] both for its genuine pathos and the high quality of its erudition. Showing a different style and sensibility, H.Reinhardt in his *Freiheit zu Gott. Der Grundgedanke des systematikers Giovanni Pico della Mirandola*[3] similarly insists on the premodern character of Pico's "systematic" thought.

The pages that follow are inspired by the desire to make further progress in the understanding of the opening pages of the *Discourse*, starting from the sources, rather than from the desire to take sides vis à vis the two opposing schools of thought; nonetheless I must acknowledge my debt to those who have insisted on the importance of the theological perspective.

---

[1] This is translated from G. Tognon's edition of Pico della Mirandola, *Discorso sulla dignità dell'uomo* (Brescia: Editrice La Scuola, 1987). This edition along with other writings appears also in French in a useful volume: Jean Pic de la Mirandole, *Oeuvres philosophiques*, eds. O. Boulnois and G. Tognon (Paris: Presses Universitaires de France, 1993). See now *Progetto Pico / The Pico Project* at www.brown.edu/Departments/Italian_Studies/pico/

[2] Paris: Aubier Montaigne, 1974.

[3] *VCH, Acta humaniora* (Wenheim 1989); see also his "De illis Pici vestigiis quae in regno theologiae . . . supersunt," in *Vivens homo* 5/2 (1994), 269–298.

1. The Garden of Eden

In speaking of sources one must be discriminating. I refer here to what is basic to Pico's thought, in the *Discourse*, and not to the innumerable authorities from all kinds of traditions to which Pico refers with a mass of references, allusions, and rhetorical figures that modern commentators show only a limited capacity to decode.

We begin with Genesis 2, which is obviously essential despite the problems raised by its numerous revisions, some of them significant:

a) Biblical is Pico's sequence of creative acts that place Adam at the center of a creation already completed, even if the way the creation takes place is different from the Hexaemeron. Here the creation occurs in a movement downwards from on high: the area above the heavens, the animate heavenly bodies, the animals on the earth, and man.

b) The idea of God speaking to his new creature is also biblical, but the contents are quite different: instead of prohibiting access to the tree of knowledge, there is the invitation to direct desire, knowledge and one's whole being towards the highest possible aim. It is in this that the human vocation consists, and not respect for the prohibition. It is as if the divine discourse also takes into account Genesis 3:21: "Therefore man has become like one of us, through his knowledge of good and evil."

c) The theme of the image is biblical, although Pico's man has not been created in the image of God, but is "opus indiscretae imaginis;" he does not have a pre-defined image (cf. a little later, "non esse homini suam ullam et nativam imaginem").[4]

d) The idea of sovereignty over things, which in Genesis 2 is also expressed with the faculty of naming, is also biblical. Gentile saw in this idea, which is very important in Giannozzo Manetti's *De Dignitate et excellentia hominis* and in Marsilio Ficino,[5] the origins of the concept of "regnum hominis."[6] In Pico the idea of dominion exists in the sense

---

[4] Eugenio Garin's translation does not do justice to this important aspect.

[5] See Charles Trinkaus, "Marsilio Ficino and the Ideal of Human Autonomy," in *Marsilio Ficino e il ritorno di Platone* (Florence: Olschki, 1986).

[6] "Il concetto dell'uomo nel Rinascimento" (1916) in *Giordano Bruno e il pensiero del Rinascimento* (Florence, 1991), 66.

that the human creature dominates things with his gaze, and in fact can become the thing he wants to be, as a microcosm containing within himself the principles, the seminal causes of all things. But this is not his main end; his end is to transcend every principle (vegetable, animal, rational, and intellectual), until he arrives at mystical union with divinity, which he discovers at the center of his interior cosmos, through the spirit. And only *after* all this will he be really able to exercise dominion over creation:

> He who has *been placed above all things*, if, not content with the destiny of any creature, will gather himself to the center of his unity, made a single spirit with God, in the single darkness of the Father, *will be above everything* (132v).[7]

Human dignity does not consist primarily in a horizontal domination over the cosmos, but in a vertical tension towards a goal which is not creatural. This is why Pico goes beyond the content of letter 41,4f of Seneca, who exalts the superiority and the quasi-divinity of rational creatures. Pico is obviously thinking of the Stoic idea expressed so effectively in Seneca's letter (this as far as I know has never been pointed out), but wants to go beyond it.[8] He wants to give a tension to his creature which is not present in the static quality of the biblical paradisal condition, and to do this he changes the picture, and evokes another garden.

2. The Garden of Zeus

The dynamism intrinsic to the human creature in Pico's account derives its power and peculiar quality from the direct influence of a Platonic source, the *Symposium*. Curiously, while the presence of the myth of Epimeteus (*Protagora* 321c–d) has been noticed, the substantial influence of the *Symposium* (interpreted by Ficino in his *De Amore*, and by Pico himself in his *Comment*, also written in 1486) has been

---

[7] "...et si nulla creaturarum sorte contentus in unitatis centrum suae se receperit, unus cum Deo spiritus factus, in solitaria Patris caligine qui est super omnia constitutus omnibus antestabit."

[8] Seneca: "Si videris ... non subibit te veneratio eius?" Cf. Pico: "Si quem videris ... Si recta philosophum ratione omnia discernentem, hunc venereris." See also the use of "numen."

missed by every previous analysis, as far as I know. The account is well-known, according to which Eros was conceived by Poros (resource) and Penia (poverty) the day Aphrodite was born, in the garden of Zeus. Eros gets his imperfect nature from this intermediate position between ignorance and knowledge, and always seeking the latter (*Symposium*, 203d–204c).

At this point it is worth recalling that Origen saw in this story a reflection of the Genesis narrative. In *Against Celso* (IV, 39) he replied to Celso who "turns the story of the serpent into a play" and believes it to be "a legend like those that are told to old women." But, says Origen, even the Platonic myth of the *Symposium* could seem the same, and yet is of extreme interest, because it hints at the Genesis tale (Poros stands for Adam, Penia for the serpent, and the "Garden of Zeus" stands for the "Garden of God"), even if we do not know how Plato could have come to know it. The first Latin translation of Origen's work had appeared not many years before Pico's *Discourse*, in Rome in 1481, the work of Cristoforo Persona, who dedicated it to Sixtus IV. Pico had a copy.[9] We know that Pico defended Origen's memory: "It is more reasonable to believe that Origen is saved, than that he is damned," was one of his *Conclusiones*.[10]

In any case Pico had Ficino's comment on the Platonic *Banquet*, the *De Amore*, very much in mind at that time, and he criticized it more than once in his *Commento* on Benivieni's *canzone*. In *De Amore* the exegesis of the birth of Eros, the day of the birth of Venus, receives ample treatment, and the *Commento* also deals extensively with "the birth of love and what is meant by the gardens of Zeus and by Penia and by the birth of Venus."[11] Indeed, one of the 900 theses is about the "hortus Iovis."[12]

---

[9] P. Kibre, *The Library of Pico della Mirandola* (1936; New York: AMS Press, 1966), 185.

[10] Part IV, 29: *Conclusiones nongentae. Le novecento tesi dell'anno 1486*, ed. A. Biondi (Florence: Olschki, 1995), 93. E. Wind, "Porus consilii filius," in *L'opera e il pensiero di Giovanni Pico della Mirandola*, II (Florence 1965), 197ff.

[11] *De hominis dignitate, Heptaplus. De ente et uno e scritti vari*, ed. E. Garin (Florence: Vallecchi, 1942), 501–504.

[12] Part V, 21; *Conclusiones*, ed. Biondi, 96ff.

Now, in both the *Discorso* and the *Symposium*

a) we find praise of someone — Eros, and the human creature, respectively — not for his real dignity, based only on stereotypes and clichés, but for his potential capacity to reach the highest of ends;

b) we find someone who is in an intermediate condition, "neither mortal nor immortal, neither of the earth nor of the heavens";

c) we find someone placed "in the midst" ("medium," *metaxù* in the *Symposium*), capable of reaching, through the love of knowledge, the supreme reality;

d) we find the priority of love, of desire, of the will as the final essence of the human being, "cui datum est id habere quod optat, id esse quod velit" (and again: "Possumus si volumus... id simus quod esse volumus... Erimus illis, cum voluerimus, nihilo inferiores"), while the intellectual element is not *against*, but *inside* the spiritual development, supported by the dynamic of desire (and here there is again a parallel between the ascent described at the end of Diotima's intervention and the exit from the cave described in the *Republic*, VII).

Of course in Plotinus too, the above mentioned elements had already found a synthesis, of which Pico may perhaps be thinking;[13] but the influence of Plato's *Symposium* appears to be direct here, compared to the intellectualism with which Plato is generally read by humanistic neoplatonists (and by the more scholastic Pico himself in *Conclusiones* and in the *Commento*), and it is faithful to the original spirit of the text, in which Eros is a philosopher and seeks *Sophia*, before possessing her.

The son of Eros and Penia is therefore fused with the creature made of earth and spirit, and while in the biblical myth it is forbidden to desire knowledge, here the divine warning to the "creature of indefinite image" concerns instead the orientation of desire, that must push knowl-

[13] *Enneads* III,2,9: man "is not the best of living beings, but occupies that middle place that he has chosen..." (tr. G. Faggin). In Marsilio's paraphrase: "Ait genus humanum non summum animalium esse, sed medium inter bruta deosque, id est daemones," *In Plotinum*, *Opera omnia*, II,2 (Basil, 1576), 1691. Plotinus also has an exegesis of the "Garden of Zeus," which appears to be present in the passages quoted above in the *Conclusiones* II part V, 21; ed.Biondi, 96ff.

edge further, towards wisdom and a higher identity. The route indicated to the creature without an image lies through images, to go beyond all images, finding fulfilment only in the final identity with the One who lives in obscurity, over and beyond every image.

3. The Paradise of the Angels

At this point the Platonic source is inadequate for a metaphorical illustration of the vertical development of the vocation of the demon-creature. So Pico changes the setting, inviting us to go from Eden, the paradise of our origins, to the heavenly paradise. He uses the model of the mystical ascent in three phases (purification, illumination and perfection, borrowed explicitly from the pseudo-Dionysius the Areopagite, whose Platonism in its turn developed visionary experiences [2 Cor 12:2–4]), as well as formulas characteristic of the spiritual language of Paul (spiritual tension [Phil 3:13], the *epèktasis*) and "running" (I Cor 9:24).[14]

We disdain earthly things, we despise those of heaven, and at last abandoning all the things of the world we fly to the court beyond the heavens, next to the highest divinity. There, as the sacred mysteries relate, the Seraphim, the Cherubim and Thrones have first place; of these we too emulate the dignity and the glory, unable to bear the pains of anything less.

The end of humankind is precisely to emulate the angels: the Thrones furthest from God represent the disciplined active life; the Cherubim contemplation, or the intellectual life branching out into its various philosophical disciplines, to then unify them dialectically as in the "curriculum studiorum" of the *Republic* VII; the Seraphim, nearest to God, represent the mystical union in love. In this perspective, philosophy reaches its highest meaning: the *Discourse* is also its foundation as a necessary intermediate stage in the mystical process.[15]

---

[14] See G. Lettieri, "In spirito e/o verità. Da Origene e Tommaso d'Aquila," and also "Nicola da Cusa e l'ambiguità della rivelazione," in the volume *In spirito e verità*, ed. P.C. Bori (Bologna: Edizioni Dehoniane, 1996), 43–72 and 89–130.

[15] This is also the most immediate justification of the *Discourse*, Pico's justification for the bold enterprise of the 900 theses; but it is not the final substance of the *Discourse*, as some, including Kristeller, affirm.

As proof of the truth of his model of the initiate's route in three phases, Pico has recourse to a series of authoritative figures, belonging to various cultures:

1. St Paul, who in his vision (2 Cor 12:2–4), according to Dionysius the Areopagite, saw the triple chorus of angels, which stand for "purgatio," "illuminatio" and "perfectio;"

2. Jacob, who saw the ladder stretching from the earth up to heaven, with the angels going up and coming down;

3. Job's proverb: "he makes peace in the high places" (25, 2). Peace is pursued through the three stages;

4. The Mosaic and cabalistic doctrine of the triple structure of the temple at Jerusalem (Exodus 25);

5. As well as the "Mosaic and Christian mysteries," there is the "theology of the ancients," i.e. the "mysteries of the Greeks": the Socratic *manià*, the Delphic precepts (*medèn àgan* [nothing in excess], *gnòthi seautòn* [know yourself], and *ei* [you are]: the three stages), and Pythagorean doctrine;

6. And finally the Chaldean Oracles, that Pico attributed to Zoroaster.

Pico certainly wished to impress his readers with an erudition whose limits can easily be seen today. But besides the content, what strikes us is his desire to establish the universal character of a paradigm of mystical evolution in three stages. Concerning this universalism, I am confident that we are dealing with something more than a rhetorical ornament or apologetic expedient in the service of Christocentric universalism. Pico's Christianity cannot be doubted, from the beginning to the end of his short life; and yet there is a striking absence of Christological references in the *Discourse* (it can be seen that even Jesus' words are transformed and put into the mouth of "Theology").[16] Of course, no modern critical-historical reduction of the figure of Jesus lies at the bottom of this universalistic attitude, but on the contrary the limitless expansion

[16] "Come to me, you who are tired, and I will restore you; I will give you the peace that the world and nature cannot give."

of Christology, including its tendential identification with the anthropological theme. The perfection which the *Discourse* talks about, and which is its general trend, is that of the *aner teleios*, capable of embracing all reality through its knowledge, according to its "breadth, and length, and depth, and height" (Ephesians, 3:18). Every human being, for the fact of being human, is *already potentially* Adam.

The first part of the *Discourse* ends with an invocation to the angels Raphael, Gabriel, and Michael (who stand for morality, philosophy and theology). The second part will be rather a defense of his intellectual choices. Here too Platonic suggestions will be essential, but the figure emerging in the background, someone greater than Pico, will be a Socrates engaged in justifying himself, rather than Diotima.

4. "Tibi Silentium Laus"

From the earthly-spiritual creature, to the demon, to the angel; from Eden to the Garden of Zeus, to the court of heaven: this is the sequence of the metaphorical contexts Pico draws upon, in outlining the human vocation. We should also notice, however, that in the passage on which we have concentrated most attention, the angelic model itself is considered transitional.

> O highest liberality of God the Father, O highest and admirable happiness of the man who can have as much as he desires, or can be whatever he wishes! The brutes in the very moment of their birth bring with them from their mother's womb what they will possess. The higher spirits either from the beginning or shortly afterwards were what they are for ever afterwards. In man as he was being born God hid the seeds and germs of every kind of life. Depending on what he has cultivated, will they grow and bear fruit in him. If they are vegetable, they will be plants. If sensitive, brutes; if rational, a heavenly animal; *if intellectual, he will be an angel and Son of God. But if, not content with the fate of any creature,* he will gather himself at the center of his unity, made a single spirit with God, in the isolated obscurity of the Father, he who has been placed above everything will be the highest of all.[17]

---

[17] "O summam Dei patris liberalitatem, summam et admirandam hominis foelicitatem! Cui datum id habere quod optat, id esse quod velit. Bruta simul atque nascuntur id secum afferunt (ut ait Lucilius) e bulga matris quod possessura sunt. Supremi spiritus aut ab initio aut paulo post mox id fuerunt, quod sunt futuri in perpetuas aeternitates.

When Pico later (133r) presents his model of angelic paradise in three stages, indicating in the Seraphim the final stage, he contradicts this passage slightly. This is because there he is considering the condition of the Seraphim as supreme condition, whereas here he seems to be suggesting *epèktasis*, insufficiency and transitoriness, more in line with the theology of infinite transcendence. He thinks, in reality, that beyond the various seminal reasons to which the soul is host, and that enable humanity to take on any kind of image including that of angels, there is in it a center of unity in which the spirit of God itself dwells, a center to which we must return, to rediscover our unity with the Father who dwells in obscurity.

Unlike the Platonic source, the conclusion of the mystical path has nothing to do with light, but with the "solitary obscurity of the Father." Here the model is the experience of Moses on Sinai, according to theologians such as Philo, Gregory of Nyssa,[18] and above all Dionysius the Areopagite. Here the possible limits of receiving Plato into the Christian (and Hebrew) contexts are reached. Further on, arguing in favor of Aristotle in his *De ente et Uno* against Plato's idea that unity is above being, and allying himself with the Thomistic thesis of the primacy of "esse" over "essentia," he will again quote Dionysius' mystical theology, according to which it can certainly be said of God:

> Neque veritas, neque regnum neque sapientia neque unum neque unitas neque divinitas aut bonitas neque spiritus est ... neque filii neque patris est denominatio ... neque sermo ipsius est, neque nomen neque scientia neque tenebrae neque lux est, neque error neque veritas...[19]

Nascenti homini omnifaria semina et omnigenae vitae germina indidit Pater. Quae quisque excoluerit illa adolescent, et fructus suos ferent in illo. Si vegetalia planta fiet, si sensuali obrutescet, si rationalia caeleste evadet animal, si intellectualia angelus erit et Dei filius. Et si nulla creaturarum sorte contentus in unitatis centrum suae se receperit, unus cum Deo spiritus factus, in solitaria Patris caligine qui est super omnia constitutus omnibus antestabit."

[18] See Gregory's *The Life of Moses* II,182 with the comment by J. Daniélou (*La vie de Moïse* [Paris, 1955] 80 ff., *Sources Chrétiennes*).

[19] *Mystica theol.* 5 PG 3, 898-1046; *Corpus dionysiacum*, eds. G. Heil and A.M. Ritter, II (Berlin-New York: De Gruyter, 1991), 149ff.

"Tibi silentium laus"[20] [to you, silence is praise], is the conclusion of a path which begins with the absence of identity, passes through many possible identities, and arrives at the identity with what is beyond all identity, offering in this end result the final definition of Paradise, the one most radically bare of images and words.

5. A Third Garden?

My exposition could end here; I have evoked the Garden of Eden, the Garden of Zeus, and heavenly paradise; or Adam, Eros, and the angels. But at this point I should like to advance the hypothesis that the *Discourse* contains the evocation of a third garden.

We must first recall the beginning of the text:

> In the writings of venerable Arab fathers I have read that Abdallah the Saracen, when asked what seemed to him the most admirable thing on this world's stage, replied that nothing seemed to him more admirable than man. This agrees with the saying of Mercury: "a great miracle is mankind."[21]

The reference to Asclepius is quite clear, important for the entire argument of the *Discourse*, and easily verifiable.[22] The reference to "Abdallah the Saracen," on the other hand, remains a mystery which none of the explanations proposed so far has been able to solve.[23]

There is however, one "Abdallah" among the very many of that name, who did speak of the dignity of man, and who did like Pico give a

---

[20] *De ente et uno* 5, from his reading of Psalm 64:2. See De Lubac, 301.

[21] "Legi, Patres colendissimi, in Arabum monumentis, interrogatum Abdalam Sarracenum, quid in hac quasi mundana scena admirandum maxime spectaretur, nihil spectari homine mirabilius respondisse. Cui sententiae illud Mercuri adstipulatur: 'Magnum, o Asclepi, miraculum est homo'."

[22] "Propter haec, o Asclepi, magnum miraculum est homo, animal adorandum et honorandum. Hoc enim in naturam dei transit, quasi ipse sit deus ..." (*Corpus hermeticum*, ed. A.D. Nock - A.-J. Festugière [Paris: Les Belles Lettres, 1954], II, 301ff.).

[23] See also P. Zambelli, *L'apprendista stregone. Astrologia, cabala e arte lulliana in Pico dela Mirandola e seguaci* (Venice: Marsilio, 1995), 29. Tognon suggested that Pico was referring to "Abdallah Ibn al- Muqaffa," but added that we are dealing with a common name hard to contextualize.

theological foundation for it: 'Abdallah al-Tarjumân, alias Anselmo Turmeda.[24] A Franciscan friar born in Palma de Majorca in 1352, he studied at Bologna where, according to his autobiography, the *Tuhfa*,[25] he received from a pious cleric the idea of aligning himself with Islam. He moved to Tunis, where he was welcomed by the sovereign Abu-l-Abbas, and converted. Having married, he worked as a translator (hence his surname) at the customs in Tunis, but also composed in Catalan a *Libre de bons admonestaments*; this book was written from a Christian perspective, though heavily anticlerical in tone, and was written "at Tunis, by friar Anselmo Turmeda, otherwise known as 'Abdallah'." In 1417, after various other little works, he composed a *Dispute with an Ass*, which has survived only in a 1544 French version. In 1420 he wrote his apologetic biography, the *Tuhfa*, in which he defended his conversion. Several attempts to bring him back to Christian lands failed. "'Abdallah" died halfway through the 1420's in Tunis, and his tomb is to be found in the Suq of the saddlers there. Curiously enough, his memory was revered both by Islamic Arabs and by Catalan Christians, and he still receives respectful attention, as can be seen from the recently renovated epigraph on his tomb.

Whatever the reasons behind his choices, still shrouded in mystery and likely to remain so, we are here concerned only with those parts of the *Dispute with an Ass* which can be relevant to us. The frontispiece of the French version runs thus:

> Disputation de l'asne
> contre frère Anselme Turmeda
> sur la nature et la noblesse des animaulx
> faicte et ordonnée par ledict frère Anselme
> en la cité de Tunicz, l'an 1417
> En laquelle ledict frère Anselme preuve comme les enfants de
> notre père Adam sont de plus grande noblesse et dignité que

---

[24] My attention was called to this Abdallah by my good friend Mohammed Kerou at Tunis in November 1995.

[25] The *Tuhfa* is studied in depth by M. de Epalza, *Fray Anselm Turmeda ('Abdallah al-Taryumân) i su polémica islamo-christiana. Ediciòn, traductiòn y estudio de la Tuhfa* (Madrid: Hyperiòn, 1994).

ne le sont tous les aultres animaulx du monde, et par plusieurs
et vives preuves et raisons.
Traduite de vulgaire hespaignol en langue françoise.[26]

The story begins in a garden in Tunis. One summer morning, when the moon was still out, Brother Anselmo arrives at a very lovely garden:

Dedans lequel avoit infiny nombre
de toutes fleurs et fruits pour servir d'umbre.
Là découloit une claire fontaine
Qui doulcement murmuroit en la plaine,
Dessus laquelle le rossignol gentil
Chantoit ung chant fort plaisant et subtil.
Brief, je pensoys à contempler ceste estre
Que pour certain fust paradis terrestre
ou pour le moins le jardin sumptueux
Des Hésperides tant beau et fructueux.[27]

There are many animals in the garden to celebrate the new king, the red lion. The hidden Anselm falls asleep, but a rabbit reveals his whereabouts, saying that here is someone who believes "that the sons of Adam are nobler and more excellent, and of greater dignity than we animals are."[28] To put it briefly, Brother Anselm is forced to defend his position against the animals, and all his arguments in favor of the superiority of mankind are defeated (often with salacious comments on the corrupt practices of Christians, which are the parts for which the work

---

[26] *Dispute de l'âne. Texte établi, annoté et commenté par A. Llinares* (Paris: Vrin, 1984), 39. A previous version exists in Catalan: *Disputa de l'ase*, versìo per E.N.C., Eò nostres clàssics, Barcelona 1928. [Disputation of the Ass against brother Anselm Turmeda on the nature and nobility of the animals written and laid out by the above-named brother Anselm in the city of Tunis, A.D. 1417, in which the abovenamed Brother Anselm proves that the children of Adam our father are of greater nobility and dignity than all the other animals in the world, with many and compelling proofs and reasons. Translated from the Spanish into the French language.]

[27] *Dispute*, 45. [In which there were an infinite number of all flowers and fruits to give shade. There flowed a clear fountain that murmured sweetly in the meadow, above which the noble nightingale sang a song both pleasant and subtle. In short, I sat contemplating this place which was certainly the earthly paradise, or at least the lush garden of the Hesperides, so lovely and fruitful.]

[28] *Dispute*, 50.

was famous in its time). Anselm wins out only at the end, when he invokes the authority of writing.

> "Seigneur Asne, l'aultre raison pour prouver mon opinion estre vraye, c'est à sçavoyr que entre nous filz d'Adam somme de plus grande noblesse et dignité que vous aultres, si est que Dieu tout puissant a voulu prendre chair humaine, mettant sa haulte divinité avec nostre humanité, et n'a pas prinse vostre chair ne vostre semblance, mains en long temps s'est fait nostre frère, et s'est faict filz d'Adam, ainsi comme nous aultres de la part de la mère, tellement que nostre chair est aujourdhuy colloquée là hault, au ciel impérial. Et de ce, disoit sainct Jehan au premier chapitre de son Evangile: 'La parolle a esté faicte chair et a habité entre nous'." Et sur cela, disoit sainct Augustin: 'La parolle du Seigneur est le filz du Père', c'est a sçavoyr Jésus Christ, qui es le filz du Père éternellement, et filz de la mère temporellement. *Et ceste nostre dignité surmonte toute aultre dignité et honneur*. Parquoy c'est saincte et juste raison que nous soyons vos seigneur et vous nos vassaux et subjectz. Et pour ce disoit ce grand prophète le roy David: 'Tu, as, Seigneur, subjugué toutes choses soubz ses pieds', c'est à sçavoyr toutes aultres bestes et animaulx, les oyseaulz du ciel et les poissons de la mer; disant davantage ledict royal prophète en son 8e *Pseaulme*: 'Seigneur, tu l'as constitué un peu moindre que les anges, tu l'as couronné de gloire et honneur, et tu l'as constitué sur les oevres des tes mains'."[29]

There are objections, however, to identifying this Abdallah as Pico's referent. One objection concerns the fact that the *Dispute* is signed by Anselmo Turmeda, not by Abdallah. One reason for this could be that the double identity Turmeda-Abdallah had been well-known for some time, because the *Admonestaments* had been signed "in Tunis, by Friar Anselmo Turmeda, otherwise known as 'Abdallah," and the quotation could have been of use to Pico only if Abdallah was the author quoted.

---

[29] *Dispute*, 138. [Lord Ass, the other reason which proves my opinion to be true — that is, that we sons of Adam we are of greater nobility and dignity than you — is that God Almighty deigned to put on human flesh, blending his high divinity with our humanity, and did not take your flesh or your semblance, but for a long time became our brother, became a son of Adam, just as we are, on his mother's side, such that our flesh is now present on high, in the imperial heaven. And of this Saint John said in the first chapter of his Gospel, "The Word was made flesh and dwelt among us." And about this Saint Augustine said, "The World of the Lord is the son of the

Secondly, Pico states he has read in the "monumenta" that Abdallah the Saracen, when interrogated, answered etc. But in reality it is unlikely that Pico could have read long texts directly in the original Arabic, as is evident also from his correspondence.[30] The *Dispute* is not to be found among Pico's books, but news of the disputation by Abdallah-Turmeda, whether he knew it himself or whether it was mentioned to him by others, was ideal, in that it offered him an authority to place beside that of Asclepius at the beginning of the *Discourse*; an authority from the world of Islam, the great antagonist, to be treated therefore with respect in a *Dispute* whose purpose was to further peace.[31]

A third objection concerns the presence of another Abdallah in Pico's *Theses*. Among the *Conclusiones secundum Adelundum arabem*, number VIII, there is one about an Abdallah and his theory of dreams,[32] so far not traced to the works of Abdallah-Turmeda. This can be answered simply by recalling that Abdallah is a very common name, so this other reference may be to someone else yet to be identified, as is the case with "Adelando."

Father," that is, Jesus Christ, who is the son of the Father eternally, and son of the mother temporally. And this dignity of ours surpasses all other dignity and honor. For which it is holy and right reason that we be your masters and you our vassals and subjects. And about this the great prophet King David said, "You, Lord, have subjugated all things beneath his feet," that is, all other beasts and animals, birds of the sky and fishes of the sea; and the royal prophet says, moreover, in his eighth Psalm, "Lord, you have made him a little less than angels, you have crowned him with glory and honor, and you have made him with the work of your hands."]

[30] "Et ne credas nostrae industriae et laboris quicquam remissum scito me post multam assiduis indefessisque lucubrationibus navatam operam hebraicam linguam chaldaicamque *didicisse et ad arabicae evincendas difficultates nunc quoque manus applicuisse*: haec ego principis viri et existimavi semper et nunc existimo." This letter to A. Corneo of Oct. 15th, 1486, is exactly contemporary with the *Discourse*. This is the reading of the Bologna 1496 edition.

[31] A little later he quotes Mahomet: "... qui a lege divina recesserit, brutum evadere," probably from the Koran, sura 95, 4f: "In truth we created man in a harmonious form, to reduce him afterwards to the lowest of the low."

[32] "Quia, sicut dicit Abadala, videre somnia est fortitudo imaginationis, intelligere ea est fortitudo intellectus, ideo qui videt ea ut plurimum non intelligit ea," *Conclusiones*, ed. Biondi, 38ff.

A fourth objection has to do with the popular rather than humanistic character of the *Dispute*. In fact the *Dispute* derives largely from a heterodox Arab text of the tenth century, the fourth of the hegira: a fable contained in the twenty-first treatise of the fifty-one that make up the encyclopedia of the "Brothers of Purity," the Ikhwân as-safa', as Asín Palacios showed in 1914.[33] In structure and in content the fable bears an extraordinary resemblance to the *Dispute*, and indeed also in the conclusion, in which the superiority of man is based on theological and mystical arguments. What the learned, ultra-orthodox Asín Palacios required, in an anti-modernistic climate, to diminish the anticlerical, indeed apostate Turmeda, becomes an advantage if the high, theological genealogy of the *Dispute* is to be demonstrated. The latter's originality, compared to the ancient Arab model, remains intact not just because of its extensive narrative sections, but also because of its specific theological conclusions linked to the theme of incarnation.

In favor of this proposal is the fact, so important as to prevail over any reservation on our part, is that *here we have an Abdallah who writes of the dignity of man using theological arguments*.[34] That the "Humanist Manifesto" should begin with an encoded reference to Abdallah-Turmeda is a fascinating conjecture. In itself it is capable of provoking a good deal of reflection, confirming the justice of the saying of James Rendel Harris, learned and gifted discoverer among other things of the *Odes of Solomon*, according to whom "a good conjecture is better than evidence."

---

[33] "El original àrabe de la 'Disputa del asno contra f. Anselmo Turmeda'," in *Revista de filologia espanola* 1 (1914), 1–51.

[34] The fact that in the Palatine manuscript of the *Oratio*, published by E. Garin, Abdallah is defined as a "prophet," is consistent with the *Dispute*, which contains a "prophetic" section in verses.

Studium simplicitatis: The Letter of Grace in Luther's Commentary on Genesis 1–3

Stefano Leoni

Luther's great *Genesis Commentary* (1535–45)[1] retains its fascination for many reasons. First, it deals with a text of decisive importance,[2] one of the most extensively commented upon in the entire Christian tradition, and loaded with enormous implications, both philosophical and speculative, as well as theological. It is also Luther's exegetical enterprise on the largest scale, of what is in any case a monumental Lutheran corpus; it is the one he worked on the longest, despite various interruptions. Finally, it is also his last commentary, finished only three months before his death. All these factors would suggest that the *Genesis Commentary* can be read as a testament and *summa* of the entire work of the Reformer.

The commentary, however, also contains some extremely problematic features, not the least of which is the nature of the text; our text of

---

[1] *Vorlesungen über 1. Mose*, in *Luthers Werke. Kritische Gesamtausgabe*, Weimar 1883 ff. (WA), Vols. 42-44 (1911-1915); the translation is that of the American edition (Am): "Lectures on Genesis," translated by G. V. Schick and P. D. Pahl, in *Luther's Works*, eds. J. Pelikan and H. T. Lehmann (Saint Louis, 1958–), Vols. 1-8.

[2] Luther had already written on Genesis; there are the notes from a first course, probably held between 1519 and 1521 (WA 9, 329-415), and in particular a cycle of sermons from 1523-24, published in 1527 (WA 24, 1-710), with the listeners' notes (WA 14, 97-488). The presentation of *Genesis* in the *Preface to the Old Testament*, written for the first translation of the Pentateuch (1523) and still conserved in the edition of the German Bible of 1545, is important: "In his first book Moses teaches how all creatures were created, and (as the chief cause of his writing) whence sin and death came, namely by Adam's fall, through the devil's wickedness. But immediately thereafter, before the coming of the law of Moses, he teaches whence help have to come for the driving out of sin and death, namely, not by the law or men's own works (since there was no law as yet), but by 'the seed of the woman,' Christ, promised to Adam and Abraham, in order that throughout the Scriptures from the beginning faith may be praised above all works and laws and merits. Genesis, therefore, is made up almost entirely of illustrations of faith and unbelief, and of the fruits that faith and unbelief bear. It is an exceedingly evangelical book" (Am 35, 237/WA DB 8, 13,23).

the commentary is based on the notes of two listeners, and conspicuous editorial intervention. Because it is not first-hand, there is constant uncertainty about whether it corresponds exactly to what Luther said, obliging interpreters to use a good deal of caution.[3] Secondly, and most important, the commentary appears to be problematic purely for reasons of content, which emerge primarily when it is compared with Luther's other great exegetical and theological works. I limit my analysis to the commentary on chapters 1–3, which Luther himself indicated as the most controversial and difficult, and which is therefore methodologically and theologically programmatic; and yet an extensive analysis of Trinitarian and christological questions, of metaphysical, cosmological and anthropological problems linked to the subject of the creation, is lacking, as is conceptual and speculative development of questions such as the dialectic of sin and grace, and faith and justification, about which Luther felt so deeply. Indeed various questions, with which elsewhere he grapples strenuously, are here dismissed as unfathomable; the commentary, in addition to long-windedness that Luther

[3] On the complex editorial history of the commentary, see F. Cohrs, "Zur Chronologie und Entstehungsgeschichte von Luthers Genesisvorlesung und seiner Schrift 'Von den Konziliis und Kirchen,'" *Lutherstudien zur 4. Jahrhundertfeier der Reformation* (Weimar, 1917), 159–169, and above all E. Seeberg, *Studien zu Luthers Genesisvorlesung*, (Gütersloh, 1932). But the classic study is still P. Meinhold, *Die Genesisvorlesung Luthers und ihre Herausgeber* (Stuttgart, 1936). In summing up the conclusions of his research, Meinhold defines this work "an enormous work of compilation, the result of welding together many pieces of material both Lutheran and non" (*Die Genesisvorlesung*, 427), in which there are "relatively numerous traces of a Melanchthonizing theology that... influenced the theological content" (*Die Genesisvorlesung*, 427) and in which "the thoughts of Luther are not only clothed in expressions introduced by the editors, but are also misunderstood and distorted" (*Die Genesisvorlesung*, 428); according to Meinhold, therefore, "the only criterion for calculating its authenticity, as E. Seeberg has already argued, is to be found in the theology of the young Luther. If such a criterion cannot be applied—which often happens with the *Commentary on Genesis*—it cannot be drawn upon as a valid source for our knowledge of Luther" (*Die Genesisvorlesung*; in the quotations from Luther and from the secondary literature, the German translation, where an English edition is not used, is my own). For a brief synthesis see, for example, M. Brecht, *Martin Luther*. Bd. III: *Die Erhaltung der Kirche 1532–1546* (Stuttgart, 1987), 139–143.

himself recognizes, and despite the richness of so many of the analyses, appears overall to be a work of a man whose creative force was by now exhausted.[4] Luther himself seems to be aware of this: indeed in the preface to the first volume he confesses: "I have expressed myself in a popular and improvised fashion, with the first words that came into my head, often mixed up with German, and certainly much more long-windedly (*verbosius*) than I would have wished";[5] in two passages in *Table Talk* he describes the course as "hasty and imperfect" (*tumultuaria*

[4] It is difficult to explain the contrasting opinions of scholars on the overall relevance of this work only through the critical difficulties it presents (Meinhold gives a brief outline in *Die Genesisvorlesung*, 34 ff. and H.-U. Delius, *Die Quellen von Martin Luthers Genesisvorlesungen* [Munich, 1992], 7 ff.), and still more, however much Meinhold's discouraging opinion must have weighed, the surprising thinness of the bibliography devoted to it. After over twenty years, only recently have scholars begun to show a certain interest again: J. P. Boendermacher, "De roeping van Abraham in Luthers Genesis-uitleg," *Debharim. Opstellen aangeboden aan Frans Breukelman*, edited by N. T. Bakker (Kampen, 1986), 123–128; R. Kolb, "Sixteenth-Century Lutheran Commentary on Genesis and the Genesis Commentary of Martin Luther," *Théorie et pratique de l'exégèse. Actes du troisième colloque international sur l'histoire de l'exégèse biblique au XVIe siècle (Genève, 31 août–2 septembre 1988)*, eds. I. Backus and F. Higman (Geneva, 1990), 243-258, who argue significantly that Luther's commentary was often highly praised but not very closely followed already by his immediate successors; H. Schoubye, *The Church of Shem in Luther's Genesis Commentary: Luther's Position of the Unmediated Presence of God* (St. Paul, 1991); U. Asendorf, "Luthers Genesisvorlesung als Paradigma christlicher Weltverantwortung," *Christentum und Weltverantwortung* (Erlangen, 1992), 71–94; M. Lienhard, "Luther et sa conception de l'homme. Regards sur le Commentaire de la Genèse (1535 à 1545)," *Positions lutheriennes* 40 (1992), 105–120; M. Lienhard, "Luthers Menschen- und Weltbild im Genesiskommentar (1535–1545)," *Luther-Bulletin. Tijdschrift voor interconfessioneel Lutheronderzoek* 3 (1994), 22–39.

[5] WA 42, 1,27; the quotations from WA 42 will from here on be indicated, after the slash, only by the page and the first line; before the slash I shall indicate the pages according to Am 1 (which however leaves out the preface, corresponding to WA 42, 1–2). In the references without explicit quotation I shall provide the reference according to WA.

et imperfecta), but above all "too weak" (*zu schwach*),[6] even "far too weak" (*vil zu schwach*);[7] and we can easily imagine how painful such self-criticism would be for such a forceful thinker as Luther.

We cannot, however, stop here. First, with reference to the critical difficulties the text presents, Luther himself very likely checked over the first volume of the commentary before its publication, and added a preface and an afterword;[8] thus despite our philological reservations we can trace back to Luther, if not every individual word, certainly at least the general intentions behind the work and its key terms. Secondly, and most importantly, concerning the importance of the contents, these general intentions emerge clearly right from the preface and, as we shall see, were already put into practice in the early chapters in a systematic, persistent, and pedantic way even at the cost of sacrificing a great number of intriguing ideas. It is certainly worth asking whether, despite Luther's dissatisfaction with a work in other ways "weak," a strongly-formed theological perspective can nonetheless be traced in it, fully consistent with the main lines of his thinking.

1. *Sola historica sententia docet*

"I have been concerned about one thing above all others: to avoid any obscurity as much as possible, and to communicate, in the clearest way I was capable of, what I wanted to convey" (1, 30). The basic intention of the course, which Luther thus expresses in the preface, is to

---

[6] "The lectures are hastily thrown together and are imperfect (*tumultuaria et imperfecta*). In them I offer others a stimulus for further reflection. Accordingly it wouldn't be prudent to make them public. They are too weak (*zu schwach*). A single work like this demands the whole of a man. I'm too busy for it. I can't do justice to such a thing while I'm busy with many tasks" (Am 54, 289/WA Tr 3, 689,8, n. 3.888, recorded by Lauterbach, May 29, 1538).

[7] "...enough of this book!; it is far too weak (*vil zu schwach*). Moses is not a bad prophet; he needs however to be gone into very deeply, and this I have not done sufficiently" (WA Tr 4, 543, 3, n. 4.845, recorded by Khummer, July 1543).

[8] WA 42, 1-428, which arrives as far as Gen. 11:26, corresponds to the first volume, published in 1544; the rest of the commentary appeared posthumously in three volumes, published in 1550, 1552 and 1554, respectively.

explain Genesis in the simplest way possible. Clearly this premise does not depend on an immediate pastoral concern for an illiterate population; the intended audience of the (Latin) commentary were his students of theology and the pastors of the young evangelical church. Explaining Genesis in an absolutely simple way means applying a very precise exegetical criterion: Luther's interpretation of Genesis is indeed rigorously and programmatically literal, founded on the "historical and strict meaning" of the scriptural text, and forcefully excluding the allocation of any primacy or autonomy to allegorical interpretation: "It is the historical sense alone which supplies the true and sound doctrine" (*sola enim historica sententia est, quae recte et solide docet*) (233/173,32). At the end of his examination of the first three chapters, he confirms his intentions:

> At last we have passed over that expanse of text on which all expositors have toiled exceedingly—to some degree also we ourselves, although its entire content was rather clear to us because we did not concern ourselves with allegories but adhered to the historical and strict meaning (*relictis Allegoriis historicam et propriam sententiam secuti sumus*). Since the majority of the interpreters did not concern themselves with this but attached greater importance to Origen, Dionysius, and others than to Moses himself, it is no wonder that they went astray. The chapters which now follow are less subject to debate and are clearer. Moreover, they support our conviction; for nobody can fail to see that Moses does not intend to present allegories but simply to write the history of the primitive world (*primi mundi historiam*). (237/176,19)

This exegetical criterion leads Luther to set out and sum up the content of these first chapters in a purely historical way, faithfully following their very simple narrative events:

> In the course of these three chapters we have the story of the creation of all creatures. We have heard how heaven and earth were created, the sea and everything in them; how Paradise was established by God to be a palace for man, the lord of creation; how in Paradise God founded for man a temple intended for divine worship, namely, the tree of the knowledge of good and evil, in which he was to give evidence of his obedience to God. We have also heard of man's activity in Paradise, how he fell wretchedly and sinned against God, thereby losing all the glory of his innocence and immortality. According to our ability, we have treated all these facts in their historical meaning, which is their real and true one (*genuinus et verus*). In the interpretation of

> Holy Scripture the main task must be to derive from it some sure and plain meaning (*certam et simplicem sententiam*), especially because there is such a variety of interpreters—Latin, Greek, and Hebrew too. Almost all of these not only do not concern themselves with the story but bury it and confuse it with their nonsensical allegories. (231/172,32)

Luther's interpretation of Genesis, therefore, possesses "a sure basis in the words themselves or in the historical account" (*fundamentum certum in ipsa litera seu historia*). (234/174,39) Luther does not restrict himself to expressing this criterion in the preface and recapitulation; he applies it constantly throughout the commentary. From the outset he emphasizes, for example, that "the first chapter is written in the simplest language (*simplicissimis verbis*); yet it contains matters of the utmost importance and very difficult to understand (*res maximas et obscurissimas*)." (3/3,15) Leaving to God the profound understanding of the article of the creation, he is satisfied with drawing out of the text a very simple "general knowledge" (*generalis notitia*):

> God has reserved His exalted wisdom and the correct understanding of this chapter for Himself alone, although He has left with us this general knowledge that the world had a beginning and that it was created by God out of nothing. This general knowledge is clearly drawn from the text. As to particulars, however, there are differences of opinions about very many things. (3/3,24)[9]

On these grounds, and against Origen, Hilarius and Augustine, Luther rejects every allegorical interpretation both of the creation and of knowledge of the creation, which is founded on the distinction between the spiritual world and the material world, and of the six days it lasted:

> Although these subjects are debated with keen reasoning, the result is no real contribution. For what need is there of setting up a twofold knowledge? Nor does it serve any useful purpose to make Moses at the outset so mystical and allegorical. His purpose is to teach us, not about allegorical creatures and an allegorical world but about real creatures (*de creaturis essentialibus*) and a visible world apprehended by the senses... without allegory.... Therefore so far as this opinion of Augustine is concerned, we assert that Moses spoke in the literal sense, not allegorically or figuratively, i.e., that the world, with all

[9] This concept is reiterated also in 4,23. 6,24. 8,30. 15,7.

> its creatures, was created within six days, as the words read. If we do not comprehend the reason for this, let us remain pupils and leave the job of teacher to the Holy Spirit. (5/4,32)[10]

Similarly, Luther denounces all speculation about the nature of God founded on the text of Genesis. On the one hand he constantly interprets the passages which speak of God in the plural as a reference to the Trinity, according to which "in the divine nature, apart from the creation, there is a plurality of Persons."[11] On the other hand, he does see in these passages of Genesis simple allusions to the question that can only be fully revealed in the New Testament; he gives up not only the idea of working it out, but even of raising it at all. Thus for example he does not interpret the words "in the beginning" as "in the Son":[12] "I prefer what is simplest and can be understood by those with little education (*rudioribus*). So, then, I have the conviction that Moses wanted to indicate the beginning of time" (10/9,8).

Faithfulness to history and the rejection of allegory guide Luther in the reading of many other passages: he denies Augustine's interpretation of the moon as an allegory of the church (see 31,15); Origen's interpretation of paradise with its trees and rivers as allegories respectively of heaven, of the angels and wisdom;[13] of Adam and Eve as allegories of "the upper and the lower part of reason";[14] of the serpent as an allegory of Satan;[15] and the Dionysian speculations on the celestial hierarchies (see 174,41). Luther takes paradise literally as a "true and visible garden in a certain place of the earth,"[16] as well as taking literally the virtues of the tree of life (see 70,30), the creation of Eve from Adam's rib

---

[10] On the six days as the real duration of creation see also 5,15. 52,23. 91,22. 92,8.

[11] 12/10,31; see also 8,21. 10,11. 14,10.15. 15,19. 16,20. 17,1.24. 37,35. 43,24.38. 166,32.

[12] This is a classical interpretation; see Origen, *Sermons on Genesis*, 1,1 (PG 12, 145).

[13] "But, I ask you, is this not a desecration of the sacred writings? Origenes makes heaven out of Paradise and angels out of the trees. If this is correct, what will be left of the doctrine of creation?" (232/173,20). See also 68,13. 74,5. 75,37.

[14] See 119,29. 138,1. 139,2.

[15] See 138,36. 140,24. 141,4.

[16] 172,19; see also 66,30–69,32.

(see 97,13), the definition of the woman herself as "building" (see 98,30), the breeze that frightens Adam and Eve after sin (see 127,14), and the flaming sword of the guardian angel of the garden (see 172,20).

His literalism here is all the more reason why he rejects philosophical and philosophical-theological speculations—particularly those of Aristotle and the Scholastics—on metaphysical, cosmological and anthropological issues raised by Genesis: the concept of matter (see 5,30. 7,23), the nature of the stars (see 31,27), the beginning and the number of the worlds (see 92,39), the primal cause of the movement of the heavenly bodies (see 23,3), the creation of Eve,[17] the birth and the reproduction of mankind (see 93,14. 95,35), the nature of the trees of life and knowledge (see 168,40) and above all the natural faculties of humanity, especially free will and original justice,[18] and their presumed wholeness even after original sin.[19]

To all these questions, and in general when attempting to interpret a text so difficult and of such decisive importance, Luther replies with an obstinate, if not entirely mechanical, literalism. In some cases, especially with questions of cosmology, he holds firmly to the letter of the Scripture even when it seems to go against plain common sense, and he seems to prefer to mortify his intellect, considering any further enquiry futile (see 20,35. 22,1); sometimes underlining the evasiveness of the text, but considering it sufficient nonetheless (*satis est scire...*) and indeed functional to what mankind should know, and therefore to the revelation of the intentions of God in it.[20] Sometimes, in particular on the instability of the original condition of mankind and on the permission given for the Devil's temptation, Luther explicitly warns us not to scrutinize too closely the mysteries of divine counsel (see 85,6. 108,33). Sometimes, as in an important reference to the mystery of the real pres-

---

[17] See 92,27. 97,13. 98,7.

[18] See 107,27. 108,8. 123,35-127,5. 138,25.

[19] See 64,26. 86,1. 139,41.

[20] See 17,36. 18,30. 31,15. 33,27. 69,23. 97,13. See also the texts quoted in the reference to 3,24.

ence of Christ in the elements of the Supper, he orders us explicitly to stick to the Word of God: "This must be believed; it must not and cannot be understood."[21]

All this could lead us to believe that the literalism of Luther's interpretation has only a critical or negative function, aiming at eliminating from the exegetical horizon a whole series of questions which cannot be decided from the perspective of a strict textual analysis. But in many other cases Luther justifies his rigorous adherence to the historical sense of the Scriptural text, and in fact develops a literal interpretation of great insight, on the basis of quite precise theological premises, such as the nature and power of the Word of God, the condition of mankind after original sin, the New Testament as a revelation of the mysteries of the Old, and the content of the faith. These theological keys allow us to understand that the literalism of Luther's interpretation of Genesis does not depend solely on an exegetical premise, nor does it have a merely negative function; rather it is supported by profound theological reasons. Starting from these reasons, Luther can even rescue allegorical interpretation of the Scriptures, and point with precision to the conditions and limits of its correct use and theological legitimacy and utility.

2. *Grammatica divina*

The first theological assumption to guide Luther in his historical and literal interpretation of the scriptural text lies in his conception of the Word of God. The human word and our "rule of language" (*grammatica*) actually refer to things which already exist; human language in other words comes after being, and has to confine itself to naming it, so that we have to go beyond its literal meaning if we want to realize what it means and what it refers to:

---

[21] 157/118,39. Here Luther breaks off; but we cannot forget that in his great eucharistic treatise *Confession Concerning Christ's Supper* (1528) he had worked out a philosophical-linguistic explanation, quite extraordinary for its speculative commitment, precisely on this question. See my "Nicht Nachwort, sondern Machtwort. La grammatica dello Spirito in 'La cena di Cristo. Confessione' di Lutero," *In spirito e verità. Letture di Giovanni 4,23–24*, ed. P. C. Bori (Bologna, 1996), 131–148.

> We, too, speak, but only according to the rules of language (*grammatice*); that is, we assign names to objects which have already been created. But the divine rule of language (*Grammatica divina*) is different, namely: when He says: 'Sun, shine,' the sun is there at once and shines. Thus the words of God are realities (*res*), not bare words. (22/17,20)

When we are dealing with the Word of God, on the other hand, this relationship between being and language is turned upside down. The Word of God is not an "afterword" (*Nachwort*) but a "powerword" (*Machtwort*);[22] it does not follow the being of things but precedes and creates it:

> Here attention must also be called to this, that the words 'Let there be light' are the words of God, not of Moses; this means that they are realities. For God calls into existence the things which do not exist (Rom. 4:17). He does not speak grammatical words; He speaks true and existent realities. Thus sun, moon, heaven, earth, Peter, Paul, I, you, etc.—we are all words of God.... Thus God reveals Himself to us as the Speaker (*Dictor*) who has with Him the uncreated Word, through whom He created the world and all things with the greatest ease, namely, by speaking. Accordingly, there is no more effort for God in His creation than there is for us in the mention of it. (21 ff./17,15)[23]

God is therefore the creator in the sense that he is "Speaker": we must not go beyond the literal sense of his Word in the direction of a meaning which would be both beyond it and prior to it; on the contrary, it is precisely the letter of his Word in creation that gives it its meaning, which can be understood only by our submitting ourselves to it and remaining faithful to it. The letter of the Bible is the Word of God, and it is the Word that establishes at the same time the being of creation and our knowledge of it. Everything must be understood starting from this, to the exclusion both of purely rational speculation which excludes it from consideration, and of allegorizing interpretations which jump beyond it.

---

[22] Leoni, "Nicht Nachwort...," 139–145.

[23] See also 13,15.31.38. 14,6. 15,4.

> In many cases, as we have seen, we must hold firmly to the literal sense even when it cannot be understood: Although Aristotle makes the Prime Mover the cause of all these, while Averroes declares that forms which assist from without are the causes of the motions, we follow Moses and declare that all these phenomena are governed simply by the Word of God. He spoke, and it was done.... We Christians must, therefore, be different from the philosophers in the way we think about the causes of these things. And if some are beyond our comprehension (like those before us concerning the waters above the heavens), we must believe them and admit our lack of knowledge rather than either wickedly deny them or presumptuously interpret them in conformity with our understanding. We must pay attention to the expression of Holy Scripture and abide by the words of the Holy Spirit. (29 ff./23,3)

In actual fact, it is precisely taking the Word of God literally that allows us to arrive at certain fundamental truths, even among those concerning the natural order, which otherwise would remain entirely unknown or incomprehensible to the human intellect; thus fidelity to a "powerword," far from entailing our renunciation of a deeper knowledge, is the only condition of the knowledge of reality over which the natural reason of philosophers exhausts itself fruitlessly (see 92 ff.). So for example we know that the Word of God has made everything out of nothing (see 13,15. 15,4); that God did not make use of pre-existing matter but only used the power of his Word (see 13,31); that it is this power that keeps everything in being (see 23,32; see also 328,20); that it is owing to the lasting effectiveness of this Word that everything is conserved and reproduces itself through the seeds of its species (see 27,33. 40,32); and that it was due to this Word that Eve was drawn out of the rib of Adam:

> Our answer to all this is the statement: "God said." This statement puts an end to all such debates. Why is it necessary to discuss where God found the remaining material, God, who is able to do anything by a single word and who creates all things? These questions have their origin in philosophy and in the science of medicine, which discuss the works of God without the Word. Moreover, the result of this procedure is that the glory of Holy Scripture and the majesty of the Creator are lost. Therefore, passing over these discussions, we shall simply adhere to the account as it is presented by Moses: Eve was created from a rib of Adam, and part of his body was again clothed with flesh. Just as Adam was made from a clod, so I was made from a droplet of my father's blood. How my mother conceived me, how I was formed in

> the womb, and how my growth took place—all this I leave to the glory of the Creator. For it is truly unbelievable that a human being comes into existence from a drop of blood; and yet it is true. Therefore if there is that power of bringing a human being into existence from a drop of blood, why not also from a clod? Likewise, why not from a rib? (130/97,21)

The primacy of the Word of God over being and over the nature of things, and the resulting necessity of founding our knowledge of creation and its meaning on this, is further confirmed in Luther's discussion of the trees of life and knowledge. Here Luther disagrees even with Nicholas of Lyra, whose literalness he often praises elsewhere,[24] rejecting the interpretation that attributes to them—as a natural or intrinsic property—the capacity to breathe life into or kill a human being.

> I reject Lyra's opinion because he assigns the power of making alive directly to the nature of the tree, although it is certain that the tree did not have this power by its nature but only through the efficacy of the Word. In the same way also the tree of the knowledge of good and evil did not kill because its fruits were poisoned and destructive, but because a word or kind of label had been attached to it with the warning written on it: 'On whatever day you eat from this tree, you will surely die.' (226 ff./169,20)[25]

The trees of life and knowledge are therefore trees like any other, and the Word of God concerning them is not expressing a different kind of nature, but simply attributes to them a new function which is connected to God's intention; it is the Word that establishes the true nature and the theological meaning of these trees, which have to be understood on that basis, and not by speculating on their mysterious qualities. The same is true of Moses' serpent in the desert, that healed because of the Word of God that was attached to it (169,40); as well as (as Luther emphasizes in an important passage) for the water of baptism, the elements of the Supper, and Christ's human nature itself. These justify not because of their intrinsic nature, but because of the word of the Promise, the actual presence realized through the words of Christ, and the incarnation of the divine Word in the person of the man-God (see 170,8). But this is also true of the creation, which receives its meaning

---

[24] See for example 71,15. 377,14; but also 143,12. 166,32. 169,5. 172,15. 174,23.

[25] See also 70,30. 73,4.16.32. 168,40. 171,1.

in the Word through which God has it made subject to humanity, and which suffers the utterance of the curse together with mankind. And above all, it is true of mankind after sin, who is already dead "before God" (*coram Deo*) even before dying in the flesh, because of the threatening word attached to being ordered not to eat of the tree, and somehow already living again "before God," even before the justification worked by Christ, because of the word of the Promise:

> This is the true life, which is lived before God. Before we come to it, we are in the midst of death. We die and decay in the earth, just as other dead bodies do, as though there were no other life anywhere. Yet we who believe in Christ have the hope that on the Last Day we shall be revived for eternal life. Thus Adam was also revived by this address of the Lord—not perfectly indeed, for the life which he lost he did not yet recover; but he got the hope of that life when he heard that Satan's tyranny was to be crushed. (196/146,28)

It is therefore entirely incorrect to speak of a "nature" of the tree, of the serpent, or in general of mankind or of creation in themselves, abstracting them from the Word that establishes them in their being, and that at the same time reveals the meaning they have "before God." In a theological sense, indeed, the true being and the true nature of every thing consists in its being *coram Deo*, in the intention with which God created it and in the end assigned to it, and this being is realized fully only in the fulfilment of this meaning and in achieving this end.[26] The Word of God establishes the being of everything not only in a philosophical and "ontological" sense, as the word of creation, but also in the more strictly theological and spiritual sense, insofar as in creating it assigns to every thing its own meaning and its own "nature." Literal adherence to the Word is then for Luther the only condition of understanding creation and the Scriptures, not only in their being in themselves, but—and this is theologically decisive—in their being "before God."

[26] For a focusing of the theological understanding of being in Luther, which underlies these observations, see my "Fides creatrix divinitatis. La fede come esistenza di Dio in Lutero," *Archivio di filosofia* 59 (1991), 13–35, in particular 14–17; and "Motus essentia Dei, Deus essentia beatorum. Ontologia e teologia in una predica giovanile di Lutero," *Protestantesimo* 51 (1996), 219–246.

This primacy of being "before God," placed and revealed by the Word, in comparison to the being in itself as the presumed "natural" being of every thing, is the first, fundamental theological premise which sustains Luther's exegesis of Genesis; it is on this that the primacy of the literal and historical sense of Scripture is established, as well as the interpretation addressed to the Word of God and to the intention which it reveals, compared to that addressed to a being in itself independent of this Word and this intention, and understandable independently of them. But we shall see that such a primacy of the Word refers us to a further and more radical premise, in order to become operative not only in the outer creation but also in the intelligence which we have of it.

3. *Loquitur de re incognita*

The impossibility of arriving at an understanding of God and the creation that goes beyond the letter of the Bible, according to Luther, is based on a second fundamental theological premise; i.e. that the cognitive and moral faculties of humanity after original sin are radically corrupted, and human nature substantially altered. This makes human nature incapable of understanding the sense and the being of the words and works of God in general. This applies in a very particular way for the understanding of the first three chapters of Genesis, which narrate a reality and a human condition by now irredeemably lost; thus the Bible is the only way left open to mankind to arrive at an understanding of reality, which might have been understood in other ways only if there had been no original sin. But because of sin, these realities must now remain either completely hidden, or accessible only through the literal sense of the Word of God. This essentially theological theme, then, is another *Leitmotiv* of the early chapters of the Commentary. To justify his rejection of the allegorical interpretation of Genesis, Luther on the one hand sets out very fully the theme of the corruption introduced by original sin concerning the knowledge we can have of God, of creation and of ourselves. On the other, he further strengthens this rejection by emphasizing that not only has our original knowledge been lost, but that its objects also have now been lost. The allegorical interpretation of Genesis would perhaps be legitimate if our knowledge and its objects were still what they had been originally; but the garden of Eden and the whole of creation, the nature of humanity and even God Himself, at least in his being and operation towards ourselves, are now radically different from the original. Pretending to leave the Word of God out of consideration seems to Luther a negation of these consequences and their cause, and so is itself an effect and confirmation of original sin.

This is applicable in the first place to our knowledge of God and to his being for us: regarding this, in fact, Luther on the one hand denies categorically that the nature of God can in some way be penetrated by human intelligence:

> What will you assume to have been outside time or before time? Or what will you imagine that God was doing before there was any time? Let us, therefore, rid ourselves of such ideas and realize that God was incomprehensible in His essential rest (*in sua essentiali quiete*) before the creation of the world, but that now, after the creation, He is within, without, and above all creatures; that is, He is still incomprehensible. Nothing else can be said, because our mind cannot grasp what lies outside time. (11/9,25)

On the other hand, he emphasizes energetically that the limits of our faculty of understanding in general depend on sin; he even goes so far as to hypothesize that before sin Adam had been able to contemplate "the uncovered God":

> Perhaps God appeared to Adam without a covering (*nudus*), but after the fall into sin He appeared in a gentle breeze as though enveloped in a covering.... This nature of ours has become so misshapen through sin, that it cannot recognize God or comprehend His nature without a covering. It is for this reason that those coverings are necessary. It is folly to argue much about God outside and before time, because this is an effort to understand the Godhead without a covering (*nudam divinitatem*), or the uncovered divine essence (*nudam essentiam divinam*). Because this is impossible, God envelops Himself in His works in certain forms.... If you should depart from these, you will get into an area where there is no measure, no space, no time, and into the merest nothing (*merissimum nihil*). (11/9,34)

It is therefore because of sin that the absolute being of God is transformed for us into "the merest nothing," and because of sin that God cannot reveal himself as He is in Himself, but has to change his aspect and hide himself in the realities we can understand, i.e. his works and above all his Word. This is of course the reason that his outer revelation and especially his Word become our only source of theological knowledge:

> God also does not manifest Himself except through His works and the Word (*nisi in operibus et verbo*), because the meaning of these is understood in some measure (11/9,32). Therefore if we want to walk in safety, let us accept what the Word submits for our reflection and what God Himself wants us to know. Let us pass by other things—things not revealed in the Word. (14/12,1)[27]

Luther assumes this principle of theological knowledge so completely that he takes literally even the crudest anthropomorphisms of the Bible; he assumes unconditionally a "zeal for simplicity" (*studium simplicitatis*) as the first intention of the Holy Spirit in the Scriptures, and hence as the first criterion for its interpretation:

> A papal decree condemns the Anthropomorphites for speaking about God as if they were speaking about a human being, and for ascribing to Him eyes, ears, arms, etc. However, the condemnation is unjust. Indeed, how could men speak otherwise of God among men? ...give me the most learned doctor—how else will he teach and speak about God? And so a wrong was done to good men. Although they believed in the omnipotent God and their Savior, they were found guilty because they said that God has eyes, with which He beholds the poor; that He has ears, with which He hears whose who pray, etc. How can this nature of ours understand the spiritual essence of God? Scripture, too, here and there makes use of this very manner of speech. Therefore they were unjustly condemned. Their zeal for simplicity (*studium simplicitatis*) should rather be commended as something supremely necessary in doctrinal matters. (14 ff./12,8)

Because of sin God Himself became no longer just the creator, but he who orders all his work around the justification of sinners, revealing himself and working the faith in His Word in them. This Word, taken literally, appears to the sinner either too simple or too difficult, and he tends therefore to interpret it through speculations and allegories; only the Holy Spirit can really make us understand this Word according to the letter, that disguises or suppresses what there is no use for us to know about, or reveals in the easiest way what we must absolutely know:

---

[27] See also WA 43, 458,35, in reference to *The Bondage of the Will* (see WA 18, 685,3. 689,18).

that we are slaves of sin, and that God is the God who frees us of sin, precisely through His Word. Luther can thus defend even the anthropomorphisms of the Biblical text by recalling this concept of God and His Word, which is the heart of his theology and his faith:

> Therefore such figures of speech have the approval of the Holy Spirit, and the works of God are set before us so that we can grasp them. Such works are: that He created the heaven and the earth, that He sent His Son, that He speaks through His Son, that He baptizes, that He absolves from sin through the Word. He who does not apprehend these facts will never apprehend God. But I shall stop here, since I have often discussed these facts at great length. (15/12,37)

Not only is God no longer the same for us after sin: the entire creation, prepared for mankind who should have been its lord (see 35,22), although continuing to be good in itself (see 79,30), turns out to be totally corrupt and in vain because of the curse (see 48,6. 75,25). Similarly the plants, that should all originally have been the bearers of good fruit, become in part useless, and begin to produce thorns and evil fruits (see 29,1); harmful and irritating insects appear, and fierce beasts, sickness and calamities (see 40,25. 58,29). The creation deteriorates and degenerates, and the life of mankind grows harder with the passing of time:[28]

> ...the curse changes things so that the best becomes the worst.... If man had not sinned, all the beasts would have remained obedient until God finally transferred man from Paradise, or from the earth; but after sin all things underwent a change for the worse (78/59,26). After sin all these things were marred to the extent that all creatures and the things which were good at first later on became harmful on account of sin (90/68,31). Therefore after its corruption one must speak about all of nature as about a new face of things, which nature put on first because of sin, then because of the universal Flood. (99/75,25)

Still more radical is Luther's position on Paradise, which must be understood as a "true and visible garden in a certain place of the earth" (172,19). Luther keeps to Genesis, according to which Paradise was shut down after sin so that mankind was no longer able to re-enter it;

[28] See 152.29. 153,1. 154,12.35. 155,27. 161,30.

afterwards it was destroyed by the Flood, which devastated the entire surface of the earth. It no longer makes sense for us to ask ourselves where it is or how it is possible that the four great rivers all rise from the same source in it (74,13; 75,37). It makes even less sense to interpret it allegorically, as if the realities it stands for still existed:

> At this point people discuss where Paradise is located. The interpreters torture themselves in amazing ways.... The opinions are numberless. My answer is briefly this: It is an idle question about something no longer in existence. Moses is writing the history of the time before sin and the Deluge, but we are compelled to speak of conditions as they are after sin and after the Deluge.... Into this garden, that the Lord Himself had planted with so special care, He placed man. All this, I say, is historical. Therefore we ask in vain today, where or what that garden was.... It was a more excellent and better part of the earth. And I judge that this garden remained until the time of the Deluge; but before the Deluge it was guarded by God, as Moses says, by a watch of angels, so that the place was known to the descendants of Adam but inaccessible until later on it was disintegrated and obliterated by the Flood. Such is my opinion, and this is how I answer all questions inquisitive people raise about something that does not exist after sin and the Deluge. The distance between the rivers troubles Origen, for he has in mind a garden area of the size they are among us. Therefore he turns to allegory. Paradise he takes to be heaven; the trees he takes to be angels; the rivers he takes to be wisdom. Such twaddle is unworthy of theologians, though for a mirthful poet they might perhaps be appropriate. Origen does not take into consideration that Moses is writing a history and, what is more, one that deals with matters long since past. (88 ff./67,7; see also 76,3)

Luther's renewed polemical attack on Origen's allegorizing, and in general against attempts to go beyond the letter of the Scriptures concerning Paradise, can be easily explained: admitting a "natural" knowledge of Paradise means in fact to deny the consequences of original sin on Paradise itself, and in the last analysis deny the sin; but it is because of original sin that Paradise is now destroyed and unknown, and it is only the literal reading of the Bible that can restore some traces of it to those who humbly submit themselves to the letter of the text. Once again, it is theology which guides the exegesis.

According to Luther's theological premise, however, original sin naturally displays its consequences especially on mankind. On this point the interpretative policy of the first chapters of Genesis, the theological anthropology that he draws from it, is absolutely clear, and reiterated with a persistence that goes well beyond mere pedantry.[29] He absolutely refuses to interpret the *imago Dei* in mankind on the basis of the trinitarian analogies worked out by the Christian tradition beginning with Augustine, in the sense of attributing to mankind as natural powers memory, intellect and will, and as gifts of grace the relative perfections (see 45,1). If the *imago Dei* constituted the being of man in himself, mankind would still be the same even after original sin, free will could cooperate "as the preceding and efficient cause of salvation,"[30] and original sin itself would be denied:

> If these powers are the image of God, it will also follow that Satan was created according to the image of God, since he surely has these natural endowments... to a far higher degree than we have them (61/46,7). The scholastics argue that original righteousness was not a part of the human nature (*connaturalis*).... Therefore they maintain about man and about demons that although they have lost their original righteousness, their natural endowments have nevertheless remained pure, just as they were created in the beginning. But this idea must be shunned like poison, for it minimizes the original sin. (164 ff./123,38)

So on the one hand, as we have seen, Luther means by *imago Dei*, i.e., the *substantia*, the *natura*, the *essentia* of mankind and his original justice, not as an absolute reality in itself and an accidental quality of this substance. From the theological point of view substance and quality coincide, and consist in the relation of recognition between man and God, in that being and recognizing oneself *coram Deo* which implies the knowledge of everything, and the peace of conscience:

> Therefore my understanding of the image of God is this: that Adam had it in his being (*in sua substantia*) and that he not only knew God and believed that He was good, but that he also lived in a life that was wholly godly; that is, he was without the fear of death or of any other danger, and was content

[29] On the theological anthropology of the later Luther, our basic reference point must be the three tomes of G. Ebeling, *Lutherstudien*. Bd. II. *Disputatio de homine*, Tübingen 1977–1989; see also O. H. Pesch, "Luthers Verstandnis vom Menschen," *Martin Luther. 'Reformator und Vater im Glauben.' Referate aus der Vortragsreihe des Instituts für europäische Geschichte Mainz*, ed. P. Manns (Stuttgart, 1985), 238–261.

[30] 45,34 ff. See also 138,25.

> with God's favor (62 ff./47,8). But here [Gen. 2:17] a question arises about which the books of all the sophists make foolish statements and yet clear up nothing, namely: 'What is original righteousness?' Some make it a quality; others make it something else. If we follow Moses, we should take original righteousness to mean that man was righteous, truthful, and upright not only in body but especially in soul (113/86,1). Let us rather maintain that righteousness was not a gift which came from without, separate from man's nature, but that it was truly part of his nature (*vere naturalem*), so that it was Adam's nature to love God, to believe God, to know God etc. (165/124,4)

On the other hand Luther argues that the image of God in man was destroyed by original sin, which radically corrupted all his cognitive, moral and physical faculties, turning him into something wholly different (*qualitas mutata est, ratio tota in aliud mutata*)[31] from what he had originally been, and hence investing his nature and essence themselves:

> Our adversaries today maintain the foolish position that the image and similitude of God remain even in a wicked person. To me their statement would appear to be far more correct if they said that the image of God in man disappeared (*periisse*) after sin in the same way the original world and Paradise disappeared (90/68,3). After sin Adam is not the person he was (*non est, qui fuit*) before sin in the state of innocence (109/82,31). But see what follows if you maintain that original righteousness was not a part of nature (*non fuisse naturae*) but a sort of superfluous or superadded gift. When you declare that righteousness was not a part of the essence of man (*non fuisse de essentia hominis*), does it not also follow that sin, which took its place, is not part of the essence of man (*non esse de essentia hominis*) either? Then there was no purpose in sending Christ, the Redeemer, if the original righteousness, like something foreign to our nature, has been taken away and the natural endowments remain perfect. What can be said that is more unworthy of a theologian? (166/124,32)[32]

The theological premise behind Luther's reading could not be clearer; basing a "natural" and philosophical anthropology on the first chapters of Genesis means in reality denying original sin and its consequences:

---

[31] See 76,14. 124,31.

[32] See also 46,28. 49,39. 77,4.29. 78,3. 79,30. 82,15. 83,26.86,6. 87,23. 88,26. 89,14. 90,3. 93,14. 96,11. 98,7. 99,12. 102,16.32. 105,3. 129,16. 130,40. 132,9.16.32. 135,27.40.

> This should be emphasized, I say, for the reason that unless the severity of the disease is correctly recognized, the cure is also not known or desired. The more you minimize sin, the more will grace decline in value. (142/107,11)

"...yet this is in truth the same as denying the suffering and resurrection of Christ" (110/83,27), and this is "unworthy of a theologian." However, original sin means that in mankind and for mankind both the corruption of nature and corruption of knowledge coincide; and this means that mankind cannot have any direct experience or any natural knowledge of his original condition (see 124,39). Only the biblical text can provide humanity with some knowledge, and only then if taken literally without seeking elsewhere. If he does not hide a certain irritation over some of the repetitions and long-windedness, especially in Genesis 2, devoted to the second story of creation and mankind's original state,[33] Luther seizes the opportunity for a two-sided interpretative operation, both exegetical and theological. He makes use of the text to underline the excellence of humanity's original nature (see 42,10), his character of *imago Dei* (see 65,17), his spiritual and physical superiority over every other creature (see 46,16), his immortality[34] and his eventual destination—a divine, eternal and spiritual life.[35] In addition, he never misses an opportunity to exalt the perfection of the knowledge, purity and happiness of humanity's original state, that would have been preserved and developed if sin had not intervened.[36]

---

[33] Luther for example complains of what from time to time he defines *verba otiosa, repetitio, digressio, comoditas Mosi, prolixa descriptio*: see 62,23. 73,41. 90,7. 91,5. 105,3. 367,4.

[34] See 33,14. 34,22. 63,25.

[35] See 35,3. 60,35. 61,28. 65,25. 70,20. 84,15.

[36] See the following examples: 50,6.16.33. 56,5. 80,1. 84 ff. 90,39. 96,19. Particularly interesting is the use Luther makes of the classical Aristotelian doctrine of the four causes to point out the difference between the knowledge of fallen man and Adam's original knowledge; whereas the former is purely philosophical and limits itself to the material and formal cause of things, i.e. to their being in themselves, the latter is genuinely theological since it extends to the efficient and final cause, i.e. to the being of things in relation to God: "Therefore let us learn that true wisdom is in Holy Scripture and in the Word of God. This gives information not only about the matter (*de materia*) of the entire creation, not only about its form (*de forma*), but also

But Luther also constantly reiterates that, precisely because what Genesis tells us of Eden refers to a condition we have lost, the knowledge we can have of such a condition must always remain negative and "by way of contrast":

> But after the fall death crept like leprosy into all our perceptive powers, so that with our intellect we cannot even understand that image.... Therefore no one can picture in his thoughts how much better nature was then than it is now.... Therefore when we speak about that image, we are speaking about something unknown (*loquimur de re incognita*). Not only have we had no experience of it, but we continually experience the opposite (*perpetuo contraria experimur*); and so we hear nothing except bare words (62 ff./46,28). Therefore we retain the name and word 'dominion' as a bare title, but the substance itself has been almost entirely lost (67/50,33). Thus, as it always is with correlatives, original sin shows what original righteousness is, and vice versa (114/86,27). All these things we have lost through sin to such an extent that we can conceive of them only in a negative and not in a positive way (*privative et non positive*). From the evil which we have with us we are forced to infer how great the good is that we have lost (168/126,20). Moreover, this detriment also helps us to gain an insight into original righteousness on the basis of what we have lost, or by way of contrast (*privative seu a contrario*). (170/128,6)[37]

Genesis taken literally allows us to learn of our original nature, and our immediate experience leads us to realize our fallen nature. The meaning of Genesis, and the key to its literal and theologically correct interpretation, is to reveal the abyss of knowledge and happiness that separates these two conditions.

---

about the efficient and final cause (*de efficienti et finali causa*), about the beginning and about the end of all things, about who did the creating and for what purpose He created (*Quis creaverit, et ad quid creaverit*)" (125/94,1; see also 49,39. 86,6. 93,14. 96,11. 98,7. 102,16); on this key theme of Luther's thinking, see the splendid page in the *Commentary on the Epistle to the Romans* (1515-16) concerning the "*expectatio creature*" (WA 56, 371,1).

[37] See 106,4.

4. *Analogia fidei*

The corruption of knowledge by original sin obscures the knowledge of original sin itself, and hence also the distance between original and fallen nature; sin prevents man from understanding naturally this revelation in a literal sense, and leads him to deny it and interpret it. If the outward letter of the Word of God is perfectly clear, it becomes obscure because mankind, through sin, cannot accept what it makes clear, preferring to speculate and allegorize: "This is the beginning and the main part of every temptation, when reason tries to reach a decision about the Word and God on its own without the Word" (154/116,18). And here emerges the final and most radical premise sustaining Luther's interpretation of Genesis, a premise which on close inspection implies recognition of both the primacy of the Word of God and original sin: we are dealing with faith and its object, the mercy of God for sinners that is realized in Christ and in the Gospel, and the justification by faith without the workings of the Law. The article of justification, which is at the heart of Luther's theology, also constitutes the final key to the Scriptures and the principal criterion for its interpretation.

This premise, considered in a simply external way, displays a strictly exegetical character which is moreover entirely traditional: it consists in interpreting the Old Testament (and therefore also the history of our origins) in the light of the New, and in view of the perfect revelation and vision that will be realized at the end of time. When the letter of Genesis remains obscure, this does not mean we have the right to leap beyond it and interpret it, because the full understanding of its meaning is reserved to the clear light of the Gospel. This is true for example for the article of the Trinity,[38] for the presence of Satan in the serpent,[39] and above all for the words that God addresses to our first parents after sin, in which in a veiled way the promise of pardon for our sins, of the grace of Christ, and of eternal life, is already present:[40]

---

[38] See 44,26. 166,32.

[39] See 109,25. 112,40. 113,34. 139,33.

[40] See 135,3.17. 136,32. 137,14. 139,19. 141 ff. 145,9. 146 ff. 148,35. 164,18. 165,8. 171,7.

> When someone does not believe the revealed and plain Gospel, it serves him right if he does not understand these darker statements of Scripture and does not believe them. Nor is it our intention to confirm the Gospel or to throw light on it by means of this passage [Gen. 3:19]. But we make use of the Gospel as the clear light to illumine this darkness (217 ff./162,33). Therefore we must take into account the light of the Gospel, just as I said above; it makes clear the dark statements of the Old Testament. (223/166,40)

In the light of the Gospel, Luther is able not only to interpret the letter of Genesis, finding in it all that is essential, and only the essential, of Christian revelation, i.e. the doctrine of justification by faith; he can even go back and recover the allegorical interpretation, to the extent that an interpretation of this kind has a basis in the Scripture itself, and confirms the essential content of revelation. When allegory is characterized by *analogia fidei*, Luther not only does not reject it, but considers it useful and instructive, and makes use of it himself.

So for example he speaks of "the first state of this world as a type and figure of the future world" (39/30,4); he does not condemn attributing to the Persons of the Trinity the words "'God said,' 'He made,' 'He saw'... since they are in accordance with the faith (*analogae fidei*) and are suitable and useful for strengthening and teaching our faith" (49 ff./37,26); he accepts, conditionally, understanding Satan for the serpent.[41] He himself offers, with reference to Luke 23:43, an allegorical reading of the concept of Paradise (see 67,27); and even an anagogical reading of the creation of man in the image of God:

> ...here by a very beautiful allegory, or rather by an anagoge (*per pulcherrimam allegoriam, seu potius Anagogiam*), Moses wanted to intimate dimly that God was to become incarnate... that God was to reveal Himself to the world in the man Christ. (87/66,20)

He clearly establishes the criteria for the legitimate use of allegory:

> Ever since I began to adhere to the historical meaning, I myself have always had a strong dislike for allegories and did not make use of them unless the text itself indicated them or the interpretation could be drawn from the New Testament.... It is the historical sense alone which supplies the true and sound doctrine (*recte et solide docet*). After this has been treated and correctly understood, then one may also employ allegories as an adornment and flow-

---

[41] See 141,8. 142,39. 163,9.

> ers to embellish or illuminate the account.... Therefore let those who want to make use of allegories base them on the historical account itself. The historical account is like logic (*Dialectica*) in that it teaches what is certainly true; the allegory, on the other side, is like rhetoric (*Rhetorica*) in that it ought to illustrate the historical account but has no value at all for giving proof. (232 ff./173,26)

As examples of a use of this kind, Luther gives the New Testament reading of heaven and earth as Church and world, of Adam and Eve as Christ and Church, of Adam as "the first figure of Him that was to come" (*forma futuri*) (see also 163,32), and of Hagar and Sarah as the two Testaments. He adds the reading of faith as the door to Paradise, but draws back at once from this use of allegory, however legitimate:

> The tree of the death is the Law, and the tree of life is the Gospel, or Christ. Those who do not believe in Christ cannot draw near to these trees.... But for him who acknowledges his sin and believes in Christ, Paradise remains open. He brings with him not his own righteousness but Christ's, which the Gospel announces to all so that we all may place our reliance on it and be saved. There is no need at all for dwelling at greater length on this matter of allegory. Let this reminder suffice: that those who wish to make use of allegories, make use of those which the apostles point out and which have a sure basis in the words themselves or in the historical account. (234/174,31)[42]

---

[42] In confirmation of Luther's position here see also the *excursus* "Concerning Allegories" (*De allegoriis*), which he inserts in the course of the commentary on Gen. 9 (Am 2, 150-164/WA 42, 367,3-377,24); in particular: "Hence allegories either must be avoided entirely or must be attended with the utmost discrimination and brought into harmony with the rule in use by the apostles.... Yet these remarks must not be understood to mean that we condemn all allegories indiscriminately, for we observe that both Christ and the apostles occasionally employed them. But they are such as are 'conformable with the faith' (*'Analogae fidei'*), in accordance with the rule of Paul, who enjoins in Rom. 12:6 that prophecy or doctrine should be conformable to the faith. When we condemn allegories, we are speaking of those that are fabricated by one's own intellect and ingenuity (*proprio spiritu et ingenio*), without the authority of Scriptures. The others, which are made to agree with the analogy of the faith, not only embellish doctrine but also give comfort to consciences" (Am 2, 151/367,27); "I urge you with all possible earnestness to be careful to pay attention to the historical accounts. But wherever you want to make use of allegories, do this: follow closely the analogy of the faith, that is, adapt them to Christ, the church, faith, and the Ministry of the Word. In this way it will come to pass that even though the allegories may not to be altogether fitting (*minus sint propriae*), they nevertheless do not depart from the faith" (Am 2, 164/377,19).

5. *Fides et Verbum docent*

The Gospel, and faith, are the final key to Luther's exegesis. In the light of Christ, Luther can understand in a literal sense all the words of the biblical text as well as its silences, and can even arrive at a positive recovery of the abhorred allegorical sense; but as long as Christ and justification alone constitute the object and the content of the New Testament, their utilization for the explanation of the Old remains an extrinsic and theologically weak hermeneutic criterion. In the alternative between literal and allegorical interpretation, and in the use or otherwise of the New Testament as key to the Old, it is by no means simply a question of objective exegetical options, more or less adequate and "scientific." If the allegorical reading is the necessary and inevitable consequence of sin, then the natural reason of mankind, free only for the realities that are inferior to it,[43] is in no way free to choose between the various exegetical options, is unable to understand the Gospel, and cannot use it for the correct interpretation of the rest of the Bible.

Luther's ferocious polemic against allegory and his strenuous defense of the literal reading then send us back to the wholly theological alternative between faith and unbelief, between sin and grace, and between God and Satan. The Gospel as the final premise of Luther's exegesis must however be explored more deeply, so that it may reveal its essentially theological character: we are dealing with the claim that only faith worked in us by grace, only the Gospel intended not simply as an outward letter but as the effective word of the Holy Spirit in our hearts, can allow us in the last analysis to read the letter of the Bible according to its true meaning. The Gospel and the grace of God must operate on our inner selves and begin to restore in us the image of God constituted by faith, by the relation of recognition in which, if only in hope up to now, "we may live in God and with God, and be one with Him":

> But now the Gospel has brought about the restoration of that image. Intellect and will indeed have remained, but both very much impaired. And so the Gospel brings it about that we are formed once more according to that

[43] See 64,27. 107,27; also WA 18, 638,4.

familiar and indeed better image, because we are born again into eternal life or rather into the hope of the eternal life by faith, that we may live in God and with God, and be one with Him, as Christ says. (64/48,11)[44]

Only to the extent that grace operates in us, only in the light of faith and the effective word of the New Testament that reveals our liberation from sin, can humanity really recognize sin itself, and in it the infinite distance between our original condition and our fallen one, and can understand what the image of God, which Genesis speaks of, may be:

Until this is accomplished in us, we cannot have an adequate knowledge (*Antequam hoc in nobis compleatur, non possumus satis scire*) of what that image of God was which was lost through sin in Paradise. But what we are stating faith and the Word teach (*fides et Verbum docent*), which, as if from a distance, point out the glory of the divine image. (65/48,32)

In the same way, it is only through the intimate illumination of the Holy Spirit that Adam, already fallen and not yet fully aware of the dimension of his sin, receives this awareness, and then transmits it to us, together with the promise of eternal life which was revealed in the name of Eve, imposed on the woman:

Moreover, he adds the reason: 'Because she is the mother of all living.' It is clear from this passage that after Adam had received the Holy Spirit, he had become marvelously enlightened, and he believed and also understood the saying concerning the woman's Seed who would crush the head of the serpent.... By assigning this name to his wife he gives clear indication that the Holy Spirit had cheered his heart through his trust in the forgiveness of sins by the Seed of Eve. He calls her Eve to remind himself of the promise through which he himself also received new life, and to pass on the hope of eternal life to his descendants. (220/164,18)[45]

The claim that the allegorical interpretation is the fruit of sin, that only the letter of the Bible utters its nucleus—that is, the sin of mankind and the mercy of God—and that only by the guidance of the Holy Spirit can this nucleus be perceived, is the final key to Luther's exegesis;

---

[44] See 14,15; also in 518,4, for example, Luther refers to Paul (1 Thessalonians, 2:13) about the effective word of God in man.

[45] See also 109,30. 112,42.

and it is for this key that Luther claims his own theological originality. Taking up a traditional allegorical interpretation, that of Adam and Eve as respectively the superior and inferior parts of reason, Luther declares himself in terms that by now we can easily understand, and that sound definitive:

> This ridiculous interpretation is the source of the familiar secular discussions about free will and about reason's striving toward the supreme good, which finally turn the whole of theology into philosophy and into specious prattle (*Donec Theologia tota abiit in Philosophiam et sophisticas nugas*). Therefore we shall disregard such destructive and foolish absurdities and proceed by a new route, unconcerned if the footprints of our predecessors lead elsewhere. For we have the Holy Spirit as our Guide. Through Moses He does not give us foolish allegories; but He teaches us about most important events (*de rebus maximis*), which involve God, sinful man, and Satan, the originator of sin. (184/138,27)

The theological nucleus of Luther's interpretation of Scripture is by now perfectly clear. Because of mankind's sin the letter of the Bible, that in its simplicity reveals nothing other than sin itself and the mercy of God, and requires none other than adherence, with humility and confidence, to such revelation, becomes scandalous to reason. Reason finds this literal sense too obscure or too banal, and so tries to interpret it by hiding the scandal behind speculations that discard or dismiss it, and allegories that leap beyond it; only grace allows mankind to remain faithful to the letter of the Word of God, and only through the outward letter of the Word of God can inner grace operate and be effective.[46]

In this analysis I have tried to highlight the coherence, rigor and strength of the theological framework that sustains the exegesis of these

---

[46] "Scripture suggests this allegory also, since in several passages it compares olive oil to grace or mercy or the forgiveness of sins. This the dove brings in its mouth [see Gen. 8:11] to represent the outward ministry or the spoken Word. For the Holy Spirit does not—as the enthusiasts and the Anabaptists, truly fanatical teachers, dream—give His instruction through new revelations outside the ministry of the Word" (Am 2, 162/376,1).

first chapters of Genesis.[47] It is true that Luther's Commentary is often repetitive and sometimes problematic; leaving aside the occasionally indiscreet but certainly not overwhelming intervention of the editors, it seems reasonable to accept the confession of the aged author, who attributed the weaknesses mainly to overwork.[48] I would argue, however, that this does not compromise the solidity of the theological frame of the Commentary, nor create any doubt that it is fully consistent with Luther's previous thinking.

---

[47] I contend that it is this framework that must provide the basic content criteria, if we really wish to try to distinguish the interpolations from the body of Luther's text, using criteria that are not strictly philological. Meinhold presupposes as "content criterion" (*sachliche Kriterium*) to distinguish the interpolations, a clear distinction between the thought of the editors of the *Commentary* (and their main theological reference point, Melanchthon, who would seem to be Meinhold's main target, see *Die Genesisvorlesung*, 370), as if the latter was entirely independent of the Reformer, on the one hand, and that of the young Luther, considered normative for the whole of his theology, and at any rate perceived in a partial and restrictive way, on the other. Thus it happens, for example, that Meinhold, when he finally indicates in the *Commentary on Genesis* what "the traces of an extraneous theology" (370-428) and even "non-lutheran [theology]" (373) should be, begins by claiming as "the most astonishing divergence... the firm approval of the doctrine of inspiration" (the verbal inspiration of the Scripture through the Holy Spirit, 371 ff.), and goes on to declare a whole series of passages spurious. I note, however, that the statement that the Holy Spirit is the author of the Scripture, before becoming an axiom of Lutheranism, is not only a cliché of the entire Christian theological tradition, but is reiterated by Luther himself in the preface to the first volume: "it is with the Scripture—I mean the Scripture of the Holy Spirit—that we are dealing" (WA 42, 2,5). Such a "distraction" casts a murky light on the entire work of Meinhold, who seems to walk into a fatal error in his viewpoint: he considers spurious every element in the Commentary that will be picked up by Protestant Orthodoxy, however excessively and unilaterally, but that, if only in a marginal role, belongs legitimately to the genuine theological identity of the Reformer. At least as far as its results go, I prefer Seeberg's more balanced judgment: "The analysis of literary criticism has exhorted us to be careful towards the formal structure of the Commentary; critical research on these topics has increasingly restored confidence in its genuine theological content. If its critical foundations may seem to wobble on occasion, it can nevertheless be leant on happily" (*Studien...*, 105). J. Pelikan seems to agree with Seeberg: see his "Introduction" to Am 1 (1958), X-XII, and "Luther the Expositor. Introduction to the Reformer's Exegetical Writings," Am Companion Volume, 1959, 90 ff. 103.

[48] See above, note 6.

* * *

The exegetical primacy given to the letter of the text reveals itself to be a theological primacy of grace. The primacy of *grammatica* reveals itself to be a primacy of *res*; on the one hand Luther continues to repeat that one must on no account abandon the words of God and their plain sense: "Unless, however, you learn the subject matter (*ipsas res*) together with the language (*cum grammatica*), you will never become a good teacher."[49] On the other he emphasizes all the more strongly that these words are in any case the necessary vehicle and tool of the *res*, that is to say the Gospel: "To be sure, grammar is necessary. What it says is true. But grammar should not rule the subject matter; it should serve it (*Grammatica quidem necessaria est et vera, sed ea non debet regere res, sed servire rebus*);"[50]

> As for yourselves, see to it first that you are thoroughly familiar with the subject matter (*res*); after that it will be easy to learn the grammar.... Furthermore, I consider knowledge of the subject matter (*notitiam rerum*) nothing else than a knowledge of the New Testament (*notitiam novi testamenti*); for when this is understood well, the entire Scripture of the Old Testament is clear.[51]

Only as *notitia novi testamenti*, as *notitia Christi*, does the Scripture open up definitively and reveal itself as *sui ipsius interpres*, as capable itself of operating in us the right intelligence of itself; Luther's claim for the *claritas Scripturae* receives in the *Commentary on Genesis* its final and definitive testimony. It is well known of course that Luther distinguishes between *claritas externa* and *claritas interna*, between the absolute simplicity of the scriptural *grammatica* in revealing the *res* of Christianity, and the absolute necessity of the Spirit of God to understand this *res*, and he opposes them respectively to the *obscuritas externa*

---

[49] Am 3, 69/597,29 (from the comment on Genesis 16).
[50] Am 3, 70s/599,6; see also WA 5, 634,14.
[51] Am 3, 72s/600,23.

and to the *obscuritas interna*.[52] It has been observed that Luther does not develop this distinction in full;[53] however, this distinction did not have to be developed, but rather simplified, since the *claritas externa* is revealed only thanks to the *claritas interna*, and the *obscuritas externa* is the direct consequence of the *obscuritas interna*. And it is precisely this operation which Luther carries out in the *Commentary on Genesis*, in which this double distinction is powerfully contracted into the simple distinction between allegory as expression of sin and the letter as reference to the faith: where the *claritas interna* required by the letter is missing, the *obscuritas externa* which requires allegory necessarily substitutes for it.

The letter of the text requires grace, and grace requires the letter: the gracious letter or literal grace, in other words the Word that works faith, constitutes the final theological foundation of Luther's exegesis. Only the word of the Gospel, which is at the same time outward and inward, literal and effective, renders all the methodological and content-based instruments of Luther's interpretation of the Bible operative, in the living practice of exegesis: the sufficiency of the literal sense, the primacy of the Word, original sin and its effects, the New Testament, the analogy of the faith. The simplicity of the biblical text is the complex simplicity of a reality that is vivifying letter, letter-Spirit, word-faith, supported by the same *communicatio idiomatum* that unifies and

---

[52] The locus classicus is in *The Bondage of the Will*: "To put it briefly, there are two kinds of clarity (*duplex claritas*) in Scripture, just as there are two kinds of obscurity: one external and pertaining to the ministry of the Word, the other located in the understanding of the heart. If you speak of the internal clarity, no man perceives one iota of what is in the Scriptures unless he has the Spirit of God.... For the Spirit is required for the understanding of Scripture, both as a whole and in any part of it. If, on the other hand, you speak of the external clarity, nothing at all is left obscure or ambiguous, but everything there is in the Scriptures has been brought out by the Word into the most definite light, and published to all the world" (Am 33, 28/WA 18, 609,4); see also WA 18, 653,13. 663,12. 781,32.

[53] See G. Ebeling, "Word of God and Hermeneutic," *New Frontiers in Theology: Discussions Among Continental and American Theologians*, Volume II: *The New Hermeneutic*, ed. by J. M. Robinson and J. B. Cobb Jr. (New York-Evanston-London, 1964), 81.

simplifies the man-God in Christ and the bread-body in the Supper. Approaching this simplicity is not so much a condition of grace, as much as it is already the gift of grace itself.[54]

---

[54] Franz Rosenzweig, who also translated the Jewish Bible together with Martin Buber, in his 1926 essay "The Scripture and Luther" ("Die Schrift und Luther," now in F. Rosenzweig, *Der Mensch und sein Werk. Gesammelte Schriften.* Bd. III: *Zweistromland. Kleinere Schriften zu Glauben und Denken* [Dordrecht-Boston-Lancaster, 1984], 749-772, from which I quote, only partly translated in *Translation Literature. The German Tradition from Luther to Rosenzweig*, ed. A. Lefevere [Assen-Amsterdam, 1977], 110-111) very clearly realizes the theological premise that guides Luther the translator of the Bible (but that is valid for Luther the interpreter too): "According to Luther's way of seeing things, where did the necessity of 'leaving room for the Hebrew language' originate? Where what is said, in such a really decided way, is really said to us, to 'our conscience'; where the Bible for him, for the living Christian of today, is today Word of God that addresses him in a living way, a living teaching, and living consolation. In the 'analogy of the faith' he is in possession of the infallible rod of the diviner, that, at every passage of the Old Testament that 'signals Christ,' begins to vibrate. Where for him, i.e. for the Christian, there was the living Word of God, there and only there, there however absolutely, the text should be taken literally, and therefore also translated in the most 'rigidly' literal way. In every other passage... the translator 'lets the Hebrew words go and expresses the sense freely in the best German he's capable of.' Luther's faith determines down to the smallest detail how the great work of mediation takes place: ...Luther's faith and, since it cannot be an isolated faith, his concept of a content of faith able to be outlined because outlined" (752).

Rosenzweig does not do justice to Luther when he seems to overestimate the content-based pre-comprehension of the Scripture that he attributes to him, and that as we have seen is certainly important but not of ultimate importance; and in any case Rosenzweig himself insists on a "new literalism" (thus defined by G. Bonola in his introduction to F. Rosenzweig, *La Scrittura. Saggi dal 1914 al 1929* [Roma, 1991], 62) and of a new "concept of faith," setting out the image of a man who "is not a believer, but not even a non-believer. He believes and doubts. So he is nothing, but lives. More exactly, he has neither faith nor unbelief, but rather faith and unbelief happen to him. He is not held to anything except to not let what happens slip past, and when it happens, to obey it...for this man the days of his life enlighten Scripture and in their humanity they make him know, here today and there tomorrow—and today never gives any guarantee for the morrow—what is more than human. In the human itself: it is everywhere human....Not everything in the Scripture belongs to him—not today, nor ever. However, he knows he belongs to everything. This availability, and it alone, is, addressed to Scripture, his faith" (760 ff.).

Rosenzweig rejects every too human content-based prejudice in favor of this obedience to what, "more than human," can "happen" in Scripture: "that basis that led Luther to leave room, up to a certain point, to the Hebrew language, and to contort the German language so that it could adapt to the Hebrew, there where the text deals with 'doctrine' and the 'consolation of our conscience,' that basis must not perhaps bend us—we who do not know from which word the doctrine and the consolation may be set off, and who believe that the hidden sources of the doctrine and the consolation can one day burst out from every word of this book—to a new veneration for the word?" (761). With this faith "that the hidden sources of doctrine and of consolation can one day burst out from every word of this book" Rosenzweig gives weight, although in an entirely modern way, to the need for a "new veneration for the word," in my opinion not that far from the *studium simplicitatis* of the Reformer.

A Portrait of the Exegete as a Geographer: The Map of Paradise as a Hermeneutic Instrument in Calvin and his Contemporaries

Max Engammare

As if there were no longer any precise place left to be sought or found by the heirs of Columbus—myth having supplanted geography—the exact location of Paradise disappears from navigational maps in the mid-sixteenth century.[1] In the same period, as though biblical science raced to the rescue of the imaginary, an engraving of the region of paradise appears on an unexpected page: that of John Calvin's commentary on Genesis (fig. 1).

This insertion has been noted, principally by Jean Delumeau[2] and Jean–François Gilmont,[3] but unremarked by the specialists of Calvinian exegesis,[4] while its fortune in the bibles of the sixteenth century has

[1]See Jean Delumeau, *Histoire du paradis*, ch. 1. "Le Jardin des délices" (Paris, 1992), 81–97. In his *Histoire d'un voyage fait en la terre de Bresil* in 1556–1557, Jean de Léry never refers to a search for paradise (see the edition of the 1580 text by Jean–Claude Morisot, Classiques de la pensée politique, 9 [Geneva, 1975], esp. 1–21). See also Frank Lestringant, *L'expérience huguenote au Nouveau Monde (XVIe siècle)*, Travaux d'Humanisme et Renaissance, 300 (Geneva, 1996), 363–365.

[2] *Histoire du paradis*, 183 and 211–213.

[3] Rodolphe Peter and Jean–François Gilmont, *Bibliotheca Calviniana. Les oeuvres de Jean Calvin publiées au XVIe siècle.I. Ecrits théologiques, littéraires et juridiques*, 2 vols., 1532–1554 and 1555–1564, Travaux d'Humanisme et Renaissance, 255 and 281 (Geneva, 1991–1994), t. 1, no. 54/2, p. 498 and no. 54/8, p. 523. Gilmont explicitly adds: "Chose rare dans les publications de Calvin, ce commentaire contient une illustration: une gravure expliquant la localisation du paradis, avec légendes latines 98x96".

[4] Not a word in, among others, T.H.L. Parker, *Calvin's Old Testament Commentaries* (Edinburgh, 1986); David L. Puckett, *John Calvin's Exegesis of the Old Testament* (Louisville, 1995); or Colleen McDannell and Bernhard Lang, *Heaven: A History* (New Haven and London, 1988), 146–56, though the work is concerned more particularly with the celestial paradise.

been catalogued.[5] Those who *have* mentioned the map, however, have not noticed that its inclusion is utterly unique in sixteenth-century Genesis exegesis.[6] What can we make of this insertion? What place does it have in biblical interpretation and illustration in the sixteenth century? Finally, how should we understand the use of a map in Calvin's exegetical principles? I will base my discussion on the 1554 Genesis commentary, and a sermon on Gen. 2:7–15, preached in Geneva in September 1559.

Calvin's Map

It is in his commentary on Genesis, published in 1554, that Calvin inscribed a map of paradise. There is no doubt that it was the reformer (rather than an editor) who did so, and expressly, because he dwells on the point:

> I will here place before your eyes a figure, by which readers will be able to understand where I believe Moses places paradise.[7]

---

[5] See Catherine Delano-Smith and Elizabeth Morley Ingram, *Maps in Bibles 1500–1600: An Illustrated Catalogue*, Travaux d'Humanisme et Renaissance, 256 (Geneva, 1991) 3–24, esp. 4 ff. and figure 5, p. 16.

[6] The map is reproduced in the second edition of Calvin's commentary on the Pentateuch (1564), and in the commentary by Marlorat, a veritable compendium of the Christian Hebraists on Genesis: *Genesis cum catholica expositione ecclesiastica... sive Bibliotheca expositionum Geneseôs* (Geneva: Henri Estienne, 1562), 19. Marlorat gives a choice of commentaries by Sebastian Münster, Martin Luther, Wolfgang Musculus, John Calvin, Paul Fagius, Joannes Oecolampade, Petrus Artoepeus; to these Protestants he adds references to François Vatable, Sante Pagnini and Agostino Steuco, without forgetting his own commentaries. A detail, but in the 1671 Amsterdam edition of Calvin's *Opera omnia*, published by the widow of Johann Jacob Schipper, the map is no longer exactly the one that Calvin had wanted; the terrestrial isle no longer exists and "Eden paradisus" is clearly marked (t. 1, 1671, 12). It is plausible that the editor simply used a map already in his possession.

[7] "Nunc figuram oculis subjiciam, unde intelligant lectores ubi Paradisum locari sentiam a Mose". See *Commentarius in Genesis*, in *Calvini opera* 23, col. 40; *Commentaires de Jean Calvin sur l'Ancien Testament.* Vol. I, *Le livre de la Genèse*, text established by André Malet et al., reprint of the 1955 Geneva edition, Aix-en-Provence and Fontenay-sous-Bois, 51 (abbreviated, respectively, as Calvin, *Genesis*, and Calvin, *Genèse*).

The map is spare, without the tree of knowledge, or Adam or Eve, or even any precise inscription of "Paradise" or "Eden", the historical referents seeming unnecessary. This map is all the more remarkable in that it is the first geographical map of paradise to break with previous cosmological maps. Although we do not know the name of the engraver, we can at least be certain that Calvin virtually dictated to him the text that he wanted to see illustrated, and provided him with a map of Syria taken from Münster's *Cosmographia* as a model to complete and correct (fig. 2).[8] The commentary brings out, first, on the subject of Gen. 2:8, that

> Although we stated that the position of paradise was situated between the rising sun and Judea, we may yet inquire more precisely into the region. Those who claim that it is close to Mesopotamia do so on the basis of reasons which must not be scorned, for it is plausible that the sons of Eden lived close to the Tigris river.[9]

In the following century Pierre Daniel Huet, bishop of Avranches and member of the Académie Française, in his *Traitté de la situation du paradis terrestre à messieurs de l'Academie françoise*, upheld Calvin's explanation:

> Of all those who have engaged in this research [i.e., on the location of the terrestrial paradise] none has come closer to the solution that I propose than John Calvin in his Commentaries on Genesis. Joseph Scaliger followed him closely, and after him the theologians of Louvain and then an infinite number of others.

Here Huet offers the Reformer a handsome posthumous compliment, as did Samuel Bochart and many others, but not all had recourse

---

[8] See Sebastian Münster, *Cosmographiae universalis libri VI* (Basel: Henri Petri, 1550; *idem* in 1554), map of "Syria cum suis provinciis", book V, 1001.

[9] See Calvin, *Genesis*, col. 37 ("Quanquam autem diximus, locum paradisi inter ortum solis et Judaeam fuisse situm, certius tamen aliquid de regione quaeri potest. Qui Mesopotamiae fuisse vicinam contendunt, rationibus non contemnendis nituntur: quia filios Heden Tigri fluvio probabile est fuisse continguos"); Calvin, *Genèse*, 48.

to a map.[10] What interests me is less the placement of paradise—fixed in Mesopotamia after Agostino Steuco and before Sixtus of Siena,[11] Ieronimo Zanchi,[12] Huet and so many others—than the reason why the Genevan reformer had a map engraved in his edition of the Genesis commentary. We could settle for the hypothesis of a visual aid for a difficult biblical passage, or the general sixteenth-century relish for cartography,[13] but it strikes me that the use of this map deserves a fuller explanation.

---

[10] P.–D. Huet's *Traitté* has a map in the frontispiece that is very close to Calvin's, showing Adam and Eve, and a "Carte de la situation du paradis terrestre" attached to the end of the work (but not all editions of this *Traitté* possess a map; for example the seventh edition [Amsterdam: François Halma, 1701], lacks it.) Samuel Bochart, *Opera omnia*, third edition (Leiden, 1692), tome 1, has a map labeled "Edenis seu paradisi terrestris situs", between columns 7–8 and 9–10 (a map very close to Calvin's, with some modifications – such as the addition of an "Eden insula" – and the figures of Adam and Eve naked, to the east of the river, and the tower of Babel to the west). By contrast there is no map in Marin Mersenne, *Quaestiones celeberrimae in Genesim cum accurata textus explicatione* (Paris: Sébastian Cramoisy, 1623), columns 1135–1144. On this work, see Albano Biondi, "L'esegesi biblica di frate Marin Mersenne," *Annali di storia dell'esegesi*, 9/1 (1992), 35–52 (still on the question of paradise).

[11] See *Bibliotheca sancta a F. Sixto Senensi, ordinis Praedicatorum, ex praecipuis catholicae Ecclesiae auctoribus collecta, et in octo libros digesta* (Paris: Rolin Thierry, 1610; first edition, 1566), liber quintus, "De annotationibus et censuris in interpres et expositores divinorum vet. Testamenti voluminum", annotatio XXXIIII, 336.

[12] *De operibus Dei intra spacium sex dierum creatis*, in *Operum theologicorum D. Hieronymi Zanchi* (Geneva: Etienne Gamonet, 1613), vol. 3, col. 503: "Manifestum est Mesopotamiam, ab Euphrate et Tigri allui et irrigari".

[13] One thinks of the maps in the cosmographies of Münster, Thevet, Belleforest; of Postel's maps in his *Description et charte de la Terre Saincte, qui est la proprieté de Jesus Christ ... paincte et descripte par Guillaume Postel depuis l'havoir et par livres et par experience veuë* (n. p., n. d.), etc. See Marcel Destombes, "Guillaume Postel cartographe", in *Guillaume Postel 1581–1981*. Actes du colloque international d'Avranches (Paris, 1985), 361–371; Frank Lestringant, "Cosmologie et mirabilia à la Renaissance: l'exemple de Guillaume Postel", in *Ecrire le monde à la Renaissance. Quinze études sur Rabelais, Postel, Bodin, et la littérature géographique* (Caen, 1993), 225–251 (first published in *Journal of Medieval and Renaissance Studies*, 16 [1986]).

A Unique Decision

None of the Christian Hebraists of the sixteenth century who produced an edition of either the whole Bible or the Old Testament inserted a map of paradise, regardless of the book format adopted, from in–folio to in–octavo: Antonio Brucioli (1532), Sebastian Münster (1534–35), François Vatable (1540 and 1545), Isidoro da Chiari (1542), Leo Jud and the Zurcher (1543), Sebastian Châteillon (Castellio, 1551–1556), Benito Arias Montano (1572), Franciscus Junius and Immanuel Tremelius (1575–1579), down to Corneille Bertram for the *Bible genevoise des Pasteurs et Professeurs* (1588). Several among them presented maps of the world, of the land of Canaan or of Israel, but none had a map of paradise engraved in it.

It is not that these Christian Hebraists had any objection to using images. The Geneva edition of the Bible had thus introduced, from the 1550's and at the urging of Robert Estienne, engravings from the large–format Bibles of the time: Noah's Ark; a plan of the Tabernacle; the habits and accessories of the High Priest; the Temple of Solomon; the royal palace and even the throne of the wise king—images that I have called the learned archaeological representation of the Bible.[14] Images serve as a translation: they permit the visualization of a complex passage, or powerfully describe details and minutiae. It is thus not surprising that good Christian Hebraists advised the engravers: François Vatable before Benito Arias Montano or Corneille Bertram.[15] Nonetheless in these learned editions Paradise receives no visual aid.

---

[14] "Les représentations de l'Ecriture dans les Bibles illustrées du XVIe siècle. Pour une herméneutique de l'image imprimée dans le texte biblique," *Revue française d'histoire du livre*, 86–87 (1995), 118–189; here, 131–144. The qualifier "savant" [learned] refers to the use of philology in the archaeological search for certain biblical places and objects.

[15] François Vatable for the 1540 Latin Bible of Estienne; Benito Arias Montano for the volume of engravings (Vol. VIII: *Apparatus*) accompanying the 1572 Antwerp polyglot bible. See Corneille Bertram for the *Bible des Pasteurs et Professeurs genevois* of 1588. See my "Cinquante ans de révision de la traduction biblique d'Olivétan: les bibles reformées genevoises en français au XVIe siècle," *Bibliothèque d'Humanisme et Renaissance*, 53 (1991), 352–356.

It is by contrast undeniable that the introduction of the map of paradise in Calvin's commentary is responsible for the popularity of the theme in biblical editions of the second half of the sixteenth century. From the 1560's on, Latin Bibles and vernacular translations, particularly those published in Geneva and Lyons, inserted such a map; one example is Rustici's Italian Bible, published in Geneva in 1562 (fig. 3).[16] A margin around the map either includes a part of Calvin's commentary verbatim, or simply paraphrases a few lines of it.[17] The map serves as an annotation, just as a comment identifying a pronoun or interpreting a biblical passage might do.

Although related to the editorial practice of sixteenth–century Lyons and Geneva Bible publishers, then, the insertion of the Calvin map is distinctive. It constitutes a unique moment in that it obeys a theological design rather than any decorative plan; moreover, Calvin never inserted into a commentary any other engraving, whether of Noah's Ark, the tower of Babel, or a map detailing the forty years of wandering in the desert.

---

[16] See *La Bibia, che si chiama il vecchio Testamento, nuovamente tradutto in lingua volgare secondo la verita del testo Hebreo (*Geneva: Francesco Durone, 1562). See Edoardo Barbieri, *Le Bibbie italiane del Quattrocento e del Cinquecento* (Milan, 1992), n. 71, t. 1. Pp. 352-357 (with the only illustration being the title page, t. 2, plate A55).

[17] I have compared the maps and annotations of several bibles. *La Bible, qui est toute la saincte Escriture ...*, by François Perrin for Antoine Vincent (Geneva, 1567; no. 382 in Bettye Thomas Chambers, *Bibliography of French Bibles: Fifteenth- and Sixteenth- Century French-Language Editions of the Scriptures*, Travaux d'Humanisme et Renaissance, 192 [Geneva: Droz, 1983]), between folios 1 and 2, takes up verbatim the second part of Calvin's commentary in *Genèse*, 52 ff., but the map — very plausibly engraved by Pierre Eskrich — is not Calvin's! The following year, the *Biblia latinogallica. La Bible Françoiselatine* ... from the workshop of Jaques Bourgeois (Geneva, 1568; no. 395 in Chambers, *Bibliography*), f. 1 verso, gives a more succinct commentary, only three sentences of which are inspired by Calvin's text; the map however is Calvin's. Finally, in the Italian bible of 1562, the second part of the note is a near–faithful translation of the end of Calvin's commentary, and the map is his (see *La Bibia*, f. 2 recto, and Calvin, *Genèse*, 53). These differences signal various degrees of allegiance on the part of translators and editors to the "master's" words.

Calvin the Geographer

It is in commenting Gen. 2, verse 8 and then 10 and following, that Calvin clarifies the location of paradise. He understands, though he does not accept, the traditional recourse to allegory because of the difficulty of establishing the precise location of the Garden of Eden:

> It is possible that some, constrained by necessity, had recourse to allegory because they did not find this place such as it is described by Moses, in any part of the world.[18]

In his 1554 commentary, as in one of his sermons on Genesis of September 1559,[19] Calvin flatly condemns all such allegorizing readings. This condemnation is not unique to him; since St. John Chryostom in particular, many indicted such readings. But that condemnation never incited any of them to draw a map of paradise.

Because they did not resort to allegory, many of Calvin's contemporaries emphasized the difficulty of identifying the precise location of paradise, particularly while expounding on the courses and the names of the rivers. We recall in fact that two rivers, Pishôn and Gihôn, were unknown to early geographers, or at least of uncertain identification. Some even suspended judgment, regardless of which side of the sixteenth-century religious fault they stood on. The horizon of investigation was swallowed up in a "mare questionum,"[20] to use Luther's phrase, and "apud quos quanta est rei ignoratio atque obscuritas, tanta est varietas sententiarum,"[21] to quote Agostino Steuco on Gen. 2:8 ("plantaverat

---

[18] "Il se peut bien faire qu'aucuns, contraints par la nécessité, aient eu recours aux allegories, parce qu'ils ne trouvaient ce lieu tel qu'il est decrit par Moise en aucune partie du monde." Calvin, *Genèse*, 47.

[19] Sermon of Wednesday, 20 September 1559 (Oxford, Bodleian Library, Ms. Bodl. 740, ff. 22 recto – 29 recto), to appear in the *Supplementa Calviniana* IX/1 (Neukirchen, 1999).

[20] The expression is Luther's, in the beginning of his commentary on Genesis 2:8: "Hic mare questionum nascitur de Paradiso". Martin Luther, *In primum librum Mose*, in *Doktor Martin Luthers Werke* 42, 66.

[21] See Agostino Steuco, *Recognitio Veteris Testamenti ad Hebraicam veritatem* (1529), in *Opera omnia* (Venice: Dominicus Nicolinus, 1591), f. 93 verso – 94 recto.

autem Dominus Paradisum").[22] Cajetanus thus declares that he does not know where Paradise was situated: "As to where Eden is, that is uncertain."[23] Münster, the illustrious cosmographer to whom Calvin in translating and commenting the Bible makes constant reference—though he is one of Jean Delumeau's great oversights—is similarly circumspect:

> About the sources of the rivers of Paradise which remain, nothing certain can be said, except that, just as the entire face of the Earth was transformed by the Flood, just so were the rivers and their sources changed, certain sources having been completely blocked up, while others arose.[24]

Since the earthly paradise no longer exists, having been destroyed by the Flood, it is not surprising that Münster in his *Cosmographia* of 1545 (as in the 1550 and 1554 editions) gives no location for it, either in the initial maps or in the chapter he devotes to the topic.[25] François de Belleforest takes up and elaborates Münster's assertion several years later (1575), in decisive terms:

---

[22] "Quanquam multa ac varia ab Hebraeis, Arabibus, Chaldaeis, Graecis, et Latinis de paradiso referantur, nihil tamen eorum attingere decrevimus, cum nostro id refragetur instituto, qui circa simplices voces, nos versaturos sumus polliciti. Quod si quis ea de re accuratius cognoscere voluerit, ab his petat necesse est, quorum est munus copiosus haec explicare. Apud quos quanta est rei ignoratio atque obscuritas, tanta est varietas sententiarum." In Agostino Steuco, *Recognitio...*, f. 93v – 94r.

[23] "Verum non esse hoc impossibile quod Moses describit, ex aliis fluviis depraehenditur, qui sub terra absorpti post longa etiam marium spatia emergentes apparent. Ubi autem sit Heden, incertum est. Ex hoc tamen quod fluvius inde egredi dicitur, mons videtur esse, naturalis enim generatio fluminum in montibus apparet." Thomas de Vio, *Commentarii illustres planeque insignes in quinque Mosaicos libros Thomae de Vio, Cajetani quondam cardinalis sancti Xisti...* (Paris: Jean Yvernel, 1539), XXII.

[24] "De fontibus fluviorum è Paradiso manantium, nihil certi dici potest, nisi sicut in diluvio tota facies terrae mutata fuit, ita quoque fluvii et fluviorum fontes mutati sunt, quaedam scaturigines penitus obturatae, et quaedam novae excitatae." In Sebastian Münster, *Hebraica Biblia, latina planeque nova Sebastiani Munsteri tralatione* (Basel, 1546), 6, note f.

[25] *La cosmographie universelle de tout le monde... auteur en partie <Sebastian> Mu<e>nster, mais beaucoup plus augmentée, ornée et enrichie par François de Belle-Forest...* 2 tomes (Paris: Nicolas Chesneau, 1575), Book I, ch. 30, t. 1, col. 67–74; Sebastian Münster, *Cosmographiae universalis libri VI* (Basel: Henri Petri, 1550; *idem* in the 1554 edition), 35 ff., and maps I and II.

> Now, to desire to determine where this garden is, I think that there is no man so out of his senses as to presume to demonstrate it by probable reason, given that the sacred history of Genesis makes no mention of any particular place, from the creation of the world until Noah...[26]

Other commentators of Genesis, such as Paul Fagius, Sebastian Châteillon (Castellio) and Huldrych Zwingli, simply did not pronounce on the location of paradise, and Zwingli settled for evoking a "lustgarten," "deliciarum hortus."[27]

We see no such reserve in Calvin, who, far from remaining neutral before the proliferation of opinions, sets to with a will. Taking the tone of a geographer, the Reformer affirms at once that "le jardin a été situé sur la terre et non pas en l'air" [the garden was located on the earth and not in the air, 47] before describing the four-branched river. This, he explains, is the Tigris and the Euphrates and their two falls which have changed their name; the map is only there to better illustrate and confirm this claim.

Further along, explaining verses 10–14, Calvin adopts the Mesopotamian location. He nevertheless bases his demonstration on ancient geographical knowledge: Pliny, Pomponius Mela, Arianus citing Nearchus, Quintius Curtius, and especially Strabo are invoked in turn, a legion of witnesses whom Calvin is far from being in the habit of summoning in his other biblical or polemical works. His recourse to the geographical wisdom of the Ancients is confident and complete. In this case the Ancients, always *auctoritates*, offer Calvin indispensable support for his argument. When the Reformer adds to the biblical text a "joining or confluence which [he has] marked in the figure," and

---

[26] "Or de vouloir asseurer où est-ce que ce jardin se trouve, je pense qu'il n'y a homme si hors de son sens qui vueille presumer de le monstrer par raison probable, comme ainsi soit que la sacrée histoire du Genese ne fait mention de lieu particulier quelconque, dés la creation du monde jusqu'à Noé." *La cosmographie universelle*, Book I., Ch. 30, t. 1, col. 73. On Belleforest, see Michel Simonin, *Vivre de sa plume au XVIe siècle ou la carrière de François de Belleforest*, Travaux d'Humanisme et Renaissance, 268 (Geneva: Droz, 1992), esp. 171–186.

[27] See Uldreich Zwingli, *Exegetische Schriften... Erläuterungen zur Genesis*, eds. Oskar Farner and Edwin Künzli. Uldreich Zwinglis sämtliche Werke, 13 (Zurich, 1963), 18.

affirms that this confluence of the Tigris and the Euphrates was natural, not dug by men, he is relying on Strabo's claims.[28]

This heavy reliance on ancient geographers authorizes us to offer a criticism similar to the one Calvin so often raises of vain questions and the frivolous curiosity of men, recalling Augustine or, nearer to him, Thomas à Kempis.[29] In his commentary on the spiritual rapture of Paul into the third heaven, the very place to which Origen moves paradise (2 Cor 12:14), Calvin contested such useless and frivolous questions:

> We are by nature inclined to curiosity. Why, leaving aside the doctrine that serves to edify us, or at the most tasting it hastily and by rote, do we pursue frivolous and useless questions? From this follow audacity and temerity, so that we have no hesitation to conclude things that are unknown and hidden from us... And yet we must be all the more sober and modest, such that we do not crave to know anything other than that which the Lord chose to reveal to His Church. Let us establish there the bounds and limits of our knowledge.[30]

---

[28] "Assemblement ou confluent qu'[il a] marqué en figure." Calvin, *Genèse*, 52; Calvin, *Genesis*, col. 42 (relying on Strabo, *Geographia*, Book XI, ch. 12,3).

[29] "Dans la lecture de l'Ecriture sainte, souvent notre curiosité nous nuit, voulant examiner et comprendre lorsqu'il faudrait passer simplement" [In reading Holy Scripture, often our curiosity harms us, desiring to examine and understand when we should simply move on] (*Imitatio Christi*, ch. 5,2). Already in the Genevan ordinances on pastors of 1541, among the "vices qu'on peut supporter pourveu qu'on les avertisse" [vices that may be endured provided that they are signalled], the first two touched on the "façon estrange de traicte[r] l'escripture, laquelle tourne en scandalle" [the strange way of treating scripture, which turns into scandal] and the "curiosité de chercher questions vaines" [curiosity to pursue vain questions]. See the *Registres de la Compagnie des Pasteurs de Genève*, tome I, eds. Jean–François Bergier and Robert Kingdon, Travaux d'Humanisme et Renaissance, 55 (Geneva: Droz, 1964), 4. Du Bartas will also speak out against being curious on the subject of paradise (Delumeau, *Histoire du paradis*, 200 and 203).

[30] "Nous sommes de nature enclins à curiosité. Parquoy laissans là la doctrine qui sert à edification, ou pour le plus la goustans legerement et par acquit, nous nous transportons apres des questions frivoles et inutiles. Avec cela il y a puis apres de l'audace et temerité, en sorte que nous ne faisons point de difficulté de terminer des choses qui nous sont incognues et cachées... Et pourtant il faut que nous soyons d'autant plus sobres et modestes, en sorte que nous n'appetions point de sçavoir autre choses, sinon ce que le Seigneur a voulu reveler à son Eglise. Mettons–là les bornes et limites de nostre sçavoir." See the *Commentaire sur la seconde epistre de Paul aux Corinthiens*,

But the search for the exact location of the earthly paradise does not strike Calvin as a matter of vain curiosity, contrary to the allegations of Münster, Cajetanus or in particular Belleforest. Calvin claims that the Bible gives precise elements of an answer—elements that seem insufficient to the cosmographers of the sixteenth century, but not to Calvin. The Reformer invokes one of his favorite exegetical principles, that of accomodation. God, the Holy Spirit, Moses, all accomodated themselves to the ignorance, the intellectual incapacity, the infirmities of humanity:

> Add that Moses accomodated his description or figure of the country to the capacity of the people of his time... If one grants to me what is manifest to all, that Moses did not speak at all subtly or in the manner of the philosophers, but popularly, so that the most ignorant could understand him.[31]

The elements that Moses gave, although summary, are sufficient to place the earthly paradise. The Reformer however completes the elisions of the biblical text, as he only rarely does, by ancient wisdom as I

---

in *Commentaires de M. Jehan Calvin sur toutes les Epistres de l'Apostre S. Paul... Item sur les Epistres Canoniques*, 2 vols. (Geneva: Conrad Badius, 1556), t. 1, p. 411 (see *Calvini opera* 50, col. 138: "Natura proclives ad curiositatem sumus ... ad quaestiones frivolas abripimur... Sit hic scientiae nostrae terminus.") Similarly, in his *Brieve instruction pour armer tous bons fideles contre les erreurs de la secte commune des anabaptistes* (1544), Calvin took issue with an interpretation of Luke 23:43, "This day you will be with me in paradise", and wrote, "Par ce mot de 'paradis,' nous n'avons que faire d'imaginer qu'il [nostre Seigneur Jesus] ait voulu specifier un certain lieu, mais seulement la joye et felicité qu'ont ceux qui vivent en luy" [By this word 'paradise', we are not to imagine that He [our Lord Jesus] meant to specify a certain place, but only the joy and felicity that they have who live in Him] (*Calvini opera* 7, col. 117).

[31] "Ajoutez que Moïse a accommodé sa description ou figure du pays à la capacité des gens de son temps... Si on m'accorde ce qui est manifeste à tous, que Moïse n'a point parlé subtilement ni à la façon des philosophes, mais populairement, afin que le plus ignorant le pût entendre." *Genèse*, 50 ff. In the sermon, Calvin speaks again of "nostre tardiveté" [our slowness] and adds "Mais voicy Dieu qui use d'une façon grossiere de parler, afin de nous enseigner priveement. Quand donc il use d'une telle familiarité, malheur sur nous si nous ne venons à luy et que nous ne recevons l'instruction qu'il nous donne" [But here God uses a clumsy way of speaking, in order to teach us secretly. When thus he uses such common speech, woe to us if we do not come to him and receive the instruction that he gives us]. See the ninth sermon on Genesis 2:7–15, of 20 September 1559 (Bodleian Library, Ms. 740, f. 24 verso).

have said, and very little by the Bible, referring only to two Old Testament allusions to Eden (Es 37:12 and Ez. 27:23).[32] In doing so Calvin shows himself to be closer to the methods of Agostino Steuco than that of Peter Martyr Vermigli, his coreligionist, whose demonstration is founded exclusively on Scripture.[33] Martin Borrhaus writes equally prudently, since he bases himself only on the elements known from Moses' description.[34] Calvin, by contrast, uses secular geography to illuminate sacred geography.[35]

I mentioned a sermon that the Reformer delivered in Geneva in 1559 on the location of paradise. The few passages that I will quote from it will enable me to complete my explanation of Calvin's recourse to the map. In the pulpit Calvin did not provide himself with any planisphere to accompany his homily; he did, however, advance an argu-

---

[32] Musculus did the same. See Wolfgang Musculus, *In Mosis Genesim plenissimi commentarii* (Basel: Johann Herwagen, 1554), 57.

[33] "Illam vero regionem esse colligimus ex variis lociis: infra cap. 4, dicitur de Cain quo modo profugus habitarit in terra Nod ab oriente Heden. Et Ezechielis 27, mentio habetur filiorum Heden, qui cunjunguntur cum Chamne et Charam. Charam vero scimus esse regionem Mesopotamiae, in quam venit Abraham cum egrederetur e patria sua. Idem videmus in Esaia cap. 37. Quare non modo scitur regionem esse, sed ex Prophetarum lectione conjicimus tractum et situm in quo est. De horto praeterea Heden saepe fit mentio in sacris literis." See Peter Martyr Vermigli, *In primum librum Mosis, qui vulgo Genesis dicitur, commentarii* (Zurich: Christophorus Froschauer, 1579), f. 10 verso.

[34] "Proinde paradisi situm partim ex locis memoratis, ut sunt Havila et Chus, partim ex fluminibus, ut sunt Euphrates et Tigris, partim ex opibus quas refert Moses, ut sunt aurum, margaritae et gemmae preciosae, cognoscere licebit." Martin Borrhaus, *In Mosem, divinum legislatorem, paedagogum ad Messiam Servatorem mundi, Commentarii* (Basel: Joannes Oporin, 1555), col. 49.

[35] See the intriguing pages of François Laplanche on the links between philology and geography, in *La Bible en France entre mythe et critique XVIe–XIXe siècle* (Paris, 1994), 35–38, on the subject of Samuel Bochart.

ment very similar to that of the written text, contesting again any spiritualizing or allegorizing reading of paradise, though he does not seem to have been aiming at any specific enthusiasts or millenarians.[36] A "certain region" is marked on the earth, the biblical description being neither figure nor allegory.

With the prolix and repetitive pedagogy of the preacher, Calvin ridicules yet again any displacement of the *hortus amoenus* to heaven:

> Thus, since the place is marked for us on earth, what good is it to fantasize and say that that paradise is in the air or the circle of the moon,[37] or that it

---

[36] Thus in his *Contre la secte phantastique et furieuse des libertins qui se nomment spirituelz* (1545), Calvin quotes two passages from a work by Antoine Pocque (or Pocquet) who mentions the "jardin de volupté" [garden of delight] and associates it with the Apocalypse: "Mais si nous commettons encores l'offense et entrons au jardin de volupté, lequel nous est encore defendu, de vouloir rien faire, mais nous laisser mener selon le vouloir de Dieu..." [But if we commit the offense again and enter into the garden of delight which is still forbidden us, of wishing to do nothing, but let ourselves be led according to the will of God...] Calvin does not however return to this spiritualizing reading (see *Calvini opera*, 7, col. 236ff.).

[37] The idea that paradise was situated in the halo of the moon or touches the sphere of the moon goes back to Ephrem the Syriac and runs throughout the Middle Ages, as for example in Pierre d'Ailly (see Delumeau, *Histoire du paradis*, 60–78). The Glossa Ordinaria reports the interpretation, attributed to Strabo: "... in alto situm: pertingentem usque ad lunarem circulum." See *Biblie jampridem renovate pars prima, complectens pentateuchum. Una cum glosa ordinaria et litterali moralique expositione Nicolai de Lyra, necnon additionibus Burgensis ac replicis Thoringi* (Basel: Johannes Amerbach, Johannes Petri and Johannes Froben, 1502), t. 1, f. 36 verso (on Genesis 2:7); Peter Lombard, anonymously, but with the same words (*Sententiae in IV libris distinctae*, Book II, dis. xvii, ch. 5.4). Michael Psellos also offers a spiritual interpretation which Steuco reports (see *Recognitio*, f. 94 verso). Origen thought that paradise was in the third heaven (see *Peri archôn, Traité des principes*, Book IV, 3.1, eds. Henri Crouzel and Manlio Simonetti, Sources Chrétiennes, 269 (Paris, 1980), 342–345. Augustine also gave a very allegorizing reading of this passage in his *De Genesi contra Manichaeos*, II.ix. Among the moderns, Francisco Giorgio adopted Origen's interpretation, in his *De harmonia mundi totius cantica tria* (Paris: André Berthelin, 1545), "canticus primus, tomus septimus, capitus XXI," f. 146 recto – 147 verso; Sixtus of Siena, *Bibliotheca sancta*: annot. XXXIIII, 336. St. Thomas Aquinas already opposed this conception (see *Summa theologiae*, I, q. 102, art. 1, ad primum (ostensibly citing the Venerable Bede, but in fact referring to Strabo).

> was eternal life? But the intention of Moses, or rather of the Holy Spirit, was to specify in full the goodness and love of God toward humanity.[38]

Calvin defends the earthly reality of paradise, and refuses its spiritualization or allegorization: God, placing man in a place of delight, where even the labor of Adam was only a "labor of pleasure,"[39] took care of the first man—as He still does of us. Earlier in his sermon Calvin had come to the four rivers, whose names and courses are so contested. Relying at least putatively on his audience's powers of abstraction, Calvin describes the map of paradise from memory, without showing it:

> Now we must see where the four rivers are. If we take the source in the middle, that is at the conjunction and the confluence, as it is called, there we will have two rivers; and from the separation to where they come to meet, two others; we will have four rivers. For in moving upstream toward the sources, there are two rivers, and then in moving downstream to where they reach the sea, two others, so that we find the four headwaters of which Moses speaks here. In any case this land of Assiria, as it is called, that is between these two rivers, has always been the richest and most fertile, and the most delightful that has existed in the world. And God has desired that traces of it remain.[40]

---

[38] "Ainsi puis que le lieu nous est marqué en terre, que fait il maintenant phantastiquer pour dire que ce paradis là est en l'aer ou au cercle de la lune, ou que c'estoit la vie eternelle? Mais l'intention de Moïse, ou plus tost du saint Esprit, a esté de nous specifier en tout et par tout quelle a esté la bonté et l'amour de Dieu envers les hommes." The ninth sermon on Gen. 2:7–15, f. 25 recto.

[39] "Labeur de plaisir", Ninth sermon on Gen. 2:7–15, f. 25 verso and 27 recto. See also sermon 18, f. 97 verso.

[40] "Or maintenant il faut veoir où sont les quatre rivieres. Si nous prenons la source au milieu, c'est à dire en la conjonction et en la confluance qu'on appelle, là nous aurons deux rivieres; et depuis la separation jusques à ce qu'elles viennent à se rencontrer deux autres: nous aurons là quatre rivieres. Car en montant en haut vers les sources, voilà deux rivieres, et puis en descendant vers l'yssue de la mer, deux autres, en sorte que voilà les quatre testes dont parle icy Moise. Quoy qu'il en soit ce pais là d'Assirie, qu'on appelle, c'est à dire entre ses deux fleuves, a esté tousjours le plus riche et le plus fecond, et le plus voluptueux qui ait esté au monde. Et Dieu encores a voulu que les traces y demourassent." The ninth sermon on Genesis 2:7–15, f. 26 recto.

If this explanation allowed the listeners to visualize only with difficulty the double separation of the river, one phrase from the pulpit deserves emphasis: "traces of it." It is not the first time that Calvin makes such a reference; earlier in his sermon we read:

> Now it is true that to exercise ourselves unduly in searching for the true location of paradise does not belong to our Christianity. But yet one can judge from the words of Moses, that it was a country which we see still bears the traces of this largesse of God, which he mentions.[41]

Thus for Calvin the earth still bears traces of the *bonitas Dei originalis*, largesse, rich and fertile countries. By the same token, non-Christian man possesses traces of the *imago Dei*. The parallel is not arbitrary: it is precisely because the traces of God's love for His creature are discernible in the microcosm that is man as well as in the macrocosm that is the world, that Calvin insists so much on the earthly reality of paradise, offering an engraving of it unique in his time.

The introduction of a map is not only an aid to visualizing a place delectable but lost; rather it serves as a reminder of the importance of earthly life, dependent on the blessing of God *hic et nunc*. This place is essential because it is one of the first signs of God's love for and blessing upon humanity, signs upon which, according to Calvin, we still live.

Conclusion

"Exilé sur le sol au milieu des huées": not only the poet, but Calvin and all humankind, driven out of paradise under the flaming sarcasm of the cherubim, now silent, seek in the ancestral narrative of their wounded pride, the traces of unheard–of charms. Most of humankind neglect these traces or remand them to the end times; Calvin discovers them in a fertile and inexhaustible land bequeathed by God to all generations. There is thus no question of utterly spiritualizing this place, of

[41] "Or il est vray que de nous tourmenter beaucoup pour cercher [sic] la vraie situation de ce paradis, cela n'apartient point à nostre chrestienté. Mais encores on peut juger des motz de Moise, que ç'a esté un pais, lequel nous voions encores retenir les traces de ces largesses de Dieu, dont il est fait mention." The ninth sermon on Genesis 2:7–15, f. 25 verso.

removing it to the third heaven or toward the halo of the moon, of allegorizing it and transforming it into an image of eternal life; it is quite real, not destroyed by the Flood, but precisely localizable, as the map one may draw of it proves. The essential value of paradise thus lies in its earthly existence; the letter describing it carries within itself the spiritual dimension of God's love for humankind. Calvin inscribes paradise into the order of the world created by God, without calling into question the smallest piece of it, correcting in passing the maps of the most respected cosmographers of his time.

It is moreover remarkable that those who withhold judgment as to the exact location of paradise are precisely those who are curious about the New World, who travel the globe, who track the courses of the stars. Those who give an exact place to paradise defend an immutable order, a given for all eternity, binding themselves to the Bible as the essential source of knowledge, free to use profane wisdom to illustrate it. The relation between the curiosity applied to the Bible and the curiosity applied to the world is thus chiastic.

Calvin is guided by the idea that "c'est la mesme terre créée au commencement" [it is the same earth created at the beginning] and that it is "le mesme homme" [the same man] who inhabits it. The goodness of God still shines a little upon this earth and in humanity. A worthy reader of John Chrystostom, he shows the same knowledge in the face of the constant care of providence in man's regard.[42] Luther, on the contrary, had affirmed the destruction of the earthly paradise after the Flood, as the destruction of the *imago Dei* after the Fall:

> It seems to me that they would speak more correctly who propose that just as the image of God in man perished after sin, so did the original world and the paradise disappear.[43]

---

[42] See *Homeliae in Genesim*, homilies 13.3 and 14.2 (*Patrologiae graecae* 53, cols. 108 and 113).

[43] "Mihi multo rectius viderentur dicere, si dicerent: Imaginem Dei in homine ita post peccatum periisse, sicut originalis mundus et Paradisus perierunt." Martin Luther, *In primum librum Mose*, 68.

For the German reformer, only the grace of Christ restores the *imago Dei* in man. For Calvin, God's goodness still shines in every man and in nature, the map of paradise showing manifest signs of this benevolence.

Having taken on the mantle of geographer, the exegete creates the first explicit geographical map of paradise. He also succumbs, at least once, to the power of the image, summoned to confirm his long commentary. Christian Hebraists had already inaugurated the recourse of philology to the image; Calvin uses the same visual clarification. Bernard Palissy, in his *Recepte veritable* to construct "as beautiful a garden as there ever was under heaven, excepting the garden of the earthly Paradise,"[44] but especially an unconquerable city in the form of conch shell (murex), exposes himself to criticism. His edition (1563) in fact has no engraving to support his demonstration and he anticipates critics:

> Why then did you not put into your book the portrait and plan of the above-mentioned city? For in that way one could have judged whether your speech contains truth.[45]

Calvin for his part did add that "portrait and plan" whose fortune I have sketched here, and we have been able to judge to what extent his "speech contained truth."

—*trans. F. Regina Psaki*

---

[44] "Autant beau jardin, qu'il en fut jamais sous le ciel, hors–mis le jardin de Paradis terrestre." Bernard Palissy, *Recepte veritable, par laquelle tous les hommes de la France pourront apprendre à multiplier et augmenter leurs thresors* (La Rochelle: Barthelemy Berton, 1563). See the critical edition by Keith Cameron, Textes Littéraires Français, 359 (Geneva: Droz, 1988), 126.

[45] "Pourquoy est–ce donc que tu n'as mis en ce livre le pourtrait et plan de ladite ville? Car par là on eust peu juger si ton dire contient verité." *Recepte*, 221.

CHAPITRE II.

naiſſent, que les iſſues, par leſquelles ils ſe deſchargent en la mer. La autresfois a eſté Euphrates conioint auec le Tygre qui tōboit dedans luy: tellemēt qu'on pouuoit dire à bon droit, que c'eſtoit vn fleuue ſeparé en quatre chefs. Principalement ſi on m'accorde ce qui eſt manifeſte à tous, que Moyſe n'a point parlé ſubtilemēt ny à la façon des Philoſophes, mais populairemēt, afin que le plus rude qui y fuſt le peuſt entēdre. En ceſte façon il a appellé au premier chapitre le ſoleil & la lune Les deux grans luminaires, non pas que la lune ſurmonte les autres Planettes en grandeur, mais pource que cōmunement par le regard on l'eſtime plus grande. Ie mettray icy vne figure deuant les yeux, par laquelle on pourra entendre où i'eſtime que Moyſe met Paradis.

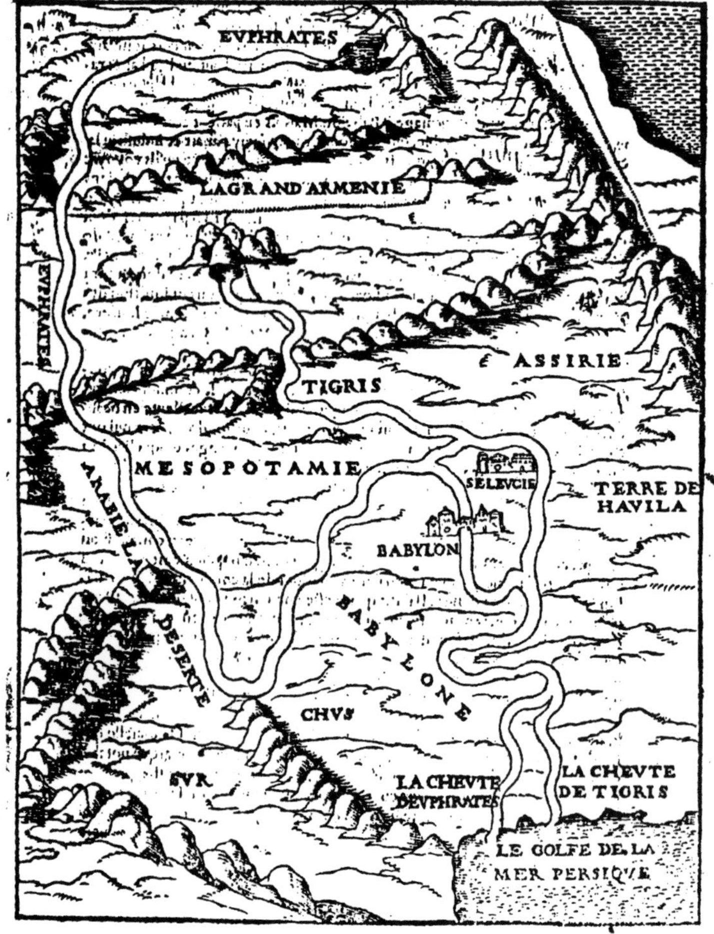

Illustration 1

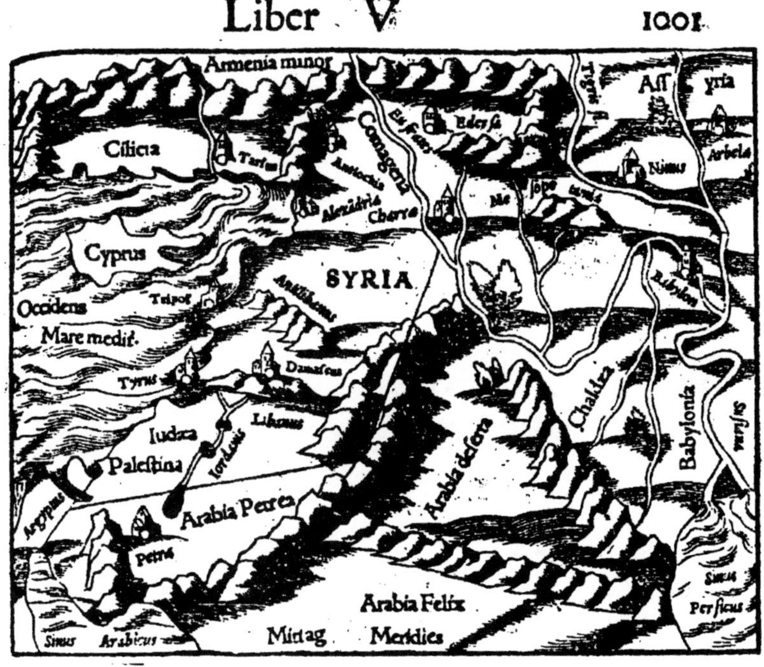

Illustration 2

Creatione de l'huomo. **Genesi.**

[illegible] la loro specie, e tutti i reptibili de
la terra secondo la loro specie: e vidde Dio
che *questo era* buono.
26 Disse inoltre Dio, Facciamo l'huomo a la nostra imagine, secondo la nostra somiglianza; e signoreggi a i pesci
del mare, & a i volatili del cielo, & a i giu
menti, & à tutta la terra, & à ogni reptibi
le, che si muoue sopra la terra.
27 Dio adunque creò l'huomo à la sua i-
magine: lo creò, *dico*, a la imagine di Dio;
maschio e femina gli creò.
28 E Dio gli benedisse, e disse loro, Cre-
scete, e moltiplicate, e riempiete la terra, e
sottoponetecela, e signoreggiate a i pesci del mare, & al volatile del cielo, & à
ogni bestia che si muoue sopra la terra.
29 E Dio disse, Ecco ch'io vi ho dato ogni
herba producente il seme, che *è* sopra tut
ta la terra, & ogni albero che *ha* in se frut
to di albero producente il seme: *asin che*
vi siano per cibo.
30 Ancora à tutti gli animali de la terra, &
à tutti gli vccelli del cielo, & à tutte le co
se che si mouono sopra la terra (lequali
hanno in se anima viuente) ogni verdura
d'herba *sarà* per cibo: e fu *fatto* così.
31 E Dio vidde tutto quello che haueua
fatto: & ecco *era* molto buono: e fu de la
sera e de la mattina il sesto giorno.

CAP. II.

Dio si riposa e santifica il settimo giorno: Mette l'huomo [illegible] *del male per segno de la ricognitione: Da i nomi à gli animali: Crea la donna, & ordina il matrimonio.*

1 Furono adunque finiti i cieli, e la ter
ra, e tutto l'essercito di quelli.
2 E Dio finì nel settimo giorno l'opera
sua, che haueua fatta: e si riposò nel set
timo giorno da tutta l'opera sua, che haueua fatta.
3 E Dio benedisse il settimo giorno, e lo
santificò: perche in esso s'era riposato da
tutta l'opera sua, che Dio haueua creata
per farla.
4 Queste *sono* le generationi del cielo e de
la terra, quando furono creati nel dì che'l
Signore Dio fece il cielo e la terra.
5 Et ogni arbuscello del campo, auanti
che fusse ne la terra: & ogni herba del cã-
po, auanti che germogliasse: perche il Si
gnore Dio non haueua ancora fatto pio-
uere sopra la terra; ne vi *era* huomo che la
uorasse la terra.
6 Ma vsciua vn vapore da la terra, e ba-
gnaua tutta la faccia de la terra.
7 Il Signore Dio adunque haueua formato l'huomo de la poluere de la terra, &
haueua soffiato ne la sua faccia respiratio
ne di vita: e fu *fatto* l'huomo in anima vi
uente.
8 Il Signore Dio haueua piantato ancora vn horto in Eden verso Oriente, e vi
messe l'huomo che haueua formato.

QVESTA FIGVRA RAPPRESENTA IL SITO DEL
iardino d'Eden.

E verisimile che questo giardino fusse in luogo a-moeno & dilettevole, abondante di frutti d'ogni sorte [illegible]. E secondo che si può raccogliere per le parole del 10. 11. & 12. vers. è in vna parte de la Mesopotamia. Imperoche sicome scriue Plinio, il Bdellio è vno albero che cresce non lungi dal seno Persico ne' confini de la Mesopotamia. Ancor che alcuni dicano, che il Bdellio nasca in Saraca città dell' Arabia Felice, il che non ferme è molto. In Eden dunque sorgeua vn fiume per adacquar il giardino, e di là si diuideua in quattro capi. Per iquali alcuni e forse meglio de gli altri, vogliono che siano significati tanto i principii e le scaturigini, da lequali nascono il fiume Eufrate, & il fiume Tigri, quanto le lor foci, per lequali sbocca no nel mare. Imperoche questi due fiumi si congiungono in vno appresso à Babilonia, come dice Strabone nel 2. libro: e di poi si separano, e ciascuno scorrendo per diuerse parti sbocca nel seno Persico. E ben che non siano che due fiumi, e qui nel testo ne siano nominati quattro, tuttauolta non [illegible]

Illustration 3

The Vision of Paradise in the *Journal* of George Fox

Pier Cesare Bori

What follows is an attempt to re-read some of the most significant pages of Fox's diary, concerning the earliest years of his mission.[1] I am aware there is a great deal of work still to be done, an awareness that grows the more I learn about the man and his age, and the more I think about Emerson's telling observation:

> But his true biography must be found in those revelations which in orchards, in lonesome places, and by the wayside, were made to him, and which are characterized by these two traits, 1. That they are of a liberal and philosophical tendency so as to agree well with the maxims of the schools of philosophy; 2. That they have a direct bearing on practical morals.[2]

1. In 1643, the nineteen-year-old George Fox left his home and his job,[3] and began a wandering existence through the countryside, towns and villages of the Midlands, clothed in a suit of skins he had made himself. A voice had led him to set out: "Thou seest how young people go together into vanity and old people into the earth; and thou must forsake all, both young and old, and keep out of all, and be a stranger unto all" (J 3). This is how he described himself in his diary in those years of seeking and suffering:

---

[1] This article appeared in *Annali di storia dell'esegesi* 10:1 (1993) 45–59, and was also used in a slightly shorter version as a preface for a short selection of Quaker texts edited by myself and Massimo Lollini: *La società degli amici* (Milano: Linea d'ombra, 1992).

[2] "George Fox," in *Early Lectures*, I, 165–182, 170. Emerson's discovery of Fox was very important; see F. B. Tolles, "Emerson and Quakerism," *American Literature* 10 (1938), 142–165, and, above, my "Emerson and Wisdom: Maternal Patterns of Knowledge in Emerson's Nature" in *Quaderni dei Nuovi Annali Università di Messina*, 31 (1993), 517–526.

[3] "I was put to a man, a shoemaker by trade, and that dealt in wool, and used grazing, and sold cattle" (J 2). I quote from *The Journal of George Fox. A Revised Edition by John L. Nickalls* (Cambridge University Press, 1952), abbreviated as "J." The diary was dictated by Fox thirty years after the events under discussion, probably from about 1674 on.

> I fasted much, and walked abroad in solitary places many days, and often took my Bible and went and sat in hollow trees and lonesome places till night came on; and frequently in the night walked mournfully about by myself, for I was a man of sorrows in the times of the first workings of the Lord in me. (J 9–10) I was about twenty years of age when these exercises came upon me, and some years I continued in that condition, in great trouble; and fain I would have put it from me. And I went to many a priest to look for comfort but found no comfort from them. (J 4)

In fact he got precious little help from the clergy. One priest told him "to take tobacco and sing psalms" and he replied that he did not smoke and was not in any condition to sing. As soon as he was out of earshot this same priest recounted all his secrets to the lads milking the cows. Another put him off by attacking him for accidentally treading on a flowerbed. Yet a third suggested he should get himself bled ("but they could not get one drop of blood from me"). "I thought them miserable comforters, and I saw they were all as nothing to me, for they could not reach my condition" (J 6).

In the meantime however he found himself accompanied and gradually guided by signs and "openings." At the beginning of 1646 he was led to an understanding of the sufferings of Christ; how those who called themselves Christians, whether Papists or Protestants, were really no such thing; and that having studied at Oxford or Cambridge and having many "notions" was not enough to be a true minister of Christ. To his family, who disapproved of his not going to church, choosing rather the fields and orchards, he replied that the Apostle taught that believers do not need teachers, because their anointed spirit teaches them (J 7). On another occasion he was shown that the All-High does not dwell in temples made by human hands (J 8). Fox's most profound formative experience takes place in 1647:

> But as I had forsaken all the priests, so I left the separate preachers also, and those called the most experienced people; for I saw there was none among them that could speak to my condition. And when all my hopes in them and in all men were gone, so that I had nothing outwardly to help me, nor could tell what to do, then, Oh then, I heard a voice which said: "There is one, even Jesus Christ, that can speak to thy condition," and when I heard it my heart did leap for joy. Then the Lord did let me see why there was none upon the earth that could speak to my condition, namely, that I might give him all

> the glory; for all are concluded under sin, and shut up in unbelief as I had been, that Jesus Christ might have the pre-eminence, who enlightens, and gives grace, and faith, and power. (J 11)

A desire for the pure knowledge of God and Christ thereby grows up in him "without the help of any man, book or writing. For though the Scriptures that spoke of Christ and of God, yet I knew him not but by revelation, and he who hath the key did open, and as the Father of life drew me to his son by his spirit" (J 11).

The visions continue:

> And one day when I had been walking solitarily abroad and was come home, I was taken up in the love of God, so that I could not but admire the greatness of his love. And while I was in that condition it was opened unto me by the eternal Light and power, and therein saw clearly that all was done and to be done in and by Christ. (J 14)

A pure fire appears to him, the fire of the discerning of spirits (J 14 ff.). He learns that he must nourish himself with the food others trample on, that is true life, the life of Christ (J 19 ff.). He sees the mountains come down, so that the glory of the Lord may come to pass (J 16). He sees Babylon, Sodom and Gomorra, and his own tomb:

> Then could I say I had been in spiritual Babylon, Sodom, Egypt, and the grave; but by the eternal power of God I was come out of it, and was brought over it and the power of it, into the power of Christ. And I saw the harvest white, and the seed of God lying thick in the ground, as ever did wheat that was sown outwardly, and none to gather it; and for this I mourned with tears. (J 21)

In 1648 he sees the earth crack open, so that the divine seed may be planted therein (J 22). He sees the blood of Christ, the blood of the new covenant (J 23). His preaching, strengthened by extraordinary signs, shows an ample correspondence between words and deeds.

2. But again we have a momentary return of darkness:

> And one morning, as I was sitting by the fire, a great cloud came over me, and a temptation beset me; but I sat still. And it was said: "All things come by nature;" and the elements and stars came over me so that I was in a manner quite clouded with it. But inasmuch as I sat, still and silent, the people of the house perceived nothing. And as I sat still under it, and let it alone, a living hope arose in me, and a true voice, which said: "There is a

> living God who made all things." And immediately the cloud and temptation vanished away, and life rose over it all, and my heart was glad, and I praised the living God. And after some time, I met with some people who had such a notion that there was no God but that all things came by nature. And I had a great dispute with them and overturned them and made some of them confess that there was a living God. Then I saw that it was good that I had gone through that exercise. (J 25)

3. The *Journal* relates various other episodes, all of them related to those first great preaching successes, but a little further along he has another vision. This new vision is apparently connected to the previous one, which represents the culminating point of this period of initiation, in which Fox's basic formative experiences take place. This vision defines the essential contents of his preaching:

> Now was I come up in spirit through the flaming sword into the paradise of God. All things were new, and all the creation gave another smell unto me than before, beyond what words can utter. I knew nothing but pureness, and innocency, and righteousness, being renewed up into the image of God by Christ Jesus, so that I say I was come up to the state of Adam which he was in before he fell. The creation was opened to me, and it was showed me how all things had their names according to their nature and virtue. And I was in a stand of mind whether I should practise physic for the good of mankind, seeing the nature and virtues of the creatures were so opened to me by the Lord. But I was immediately taken up in spirit, to see into another or more steadfast state than Adam's innocency, even into a state in Christ Jesus, that should never fall. And the Lord showed me that such as were faithful to him in the power and light of Christ, should come up into that state in which Adam was before he fell, in which the admirable works of the creation, and the virtues thereof, may be known, through the openings of that divine Word of wisdom and power by which they were made. Great things did the Lord lead me into, and wonderful depths were opened unto me, beyond what can by words be declared; but as people come into subjection to the spirit of God, and grow up in the image and power of the Almighty, they may receive the Word of wisdom, that opens all things, and come to know the hidden unity in the Eternal Being. (J 27–8)

The story of Fox's preaching is still at its very beginnings, but we have to stop at this page and the others immediately following, for the decisive nature of the statements they contain. Fox continues to wander about. Arriving at the Vale of Belvoir, he receives another "opening" connected to the one above:

> While I was there, the Lord opened to me three things relating to those three great professions in the world, physic, divinity (so called), and law. And he showed me that the physicians were out of the wisdom of God by which the creatures were made, and so knew not the virtues of the creatures, because they were out of the Word of wisdom by which they were made. And he showed me that the priests were out of the true faith which Christ is the author of, the faith which purifies and gives victory and brings people to have access to God, by which they please God, which mystery of faith is held in a pure conscience. He showed me also, that lawyers were out of the equity and out of the true justice, and out of the law of God, which went over the first transgression and over all sin, and answered the spirit of God that was grieved and transgressed in man. And that these three, the physicians, the priests, and the lawyers, ruled the world out of the wisdom, out of the faith and out of the equity and law of God, the one pretending the cure of the body, the other the cure of the soul, and the third the property of the people. But I saw they were all out, out of the wisdom, out of the faith, out of the equity and perfect law of God.
>
> And as the Lord opened these things unto me, I felt his power went forth over all, by which all might be reformed, if they would receive and bow unto it. The priests could be reformed and brought into the true faith which is the gift of God. The lawyers might be reformed and brought into the law of God which answers that of God (that is transgressed) in every one, and brings to love one's neighbour as himself. This lets man see if he wrongs his neighbour he wrongs himself; and this teaches him to do unto others as he would they should to unto him. The physicians might be reformed, and brought into the wisdom of God by which all things were made and created; that they might receive a right knowledge of the creature and understand the virtues of them, which the Word of wisdom, by which they were made and are upheld, hath given them. Abundance was opened concerning these things; how all lay out of the wisdom of God, and out of the righteousness and holiness that man at first was made in. But as all believe in the light and walk in the light, which Christ hath enlightened every man that cometh into the world withal, and so become children of the light, and of the day of Christ; in his day all things are seen, visible and invisible, by the divine light of Christ, the spiritual, heavenly man, by whom all things were made and created. (J 28 ff.)

This section of the *Journal* then undergoes an ample development concerning one of the three classes mentioned above, the priests, and ends with some important statements related to spiritual hermeneutics and its connection to the recovery of the prelapsarian condition:

But as a man comes through by the Spirit and power of God to Christ that fulfills the types, figures, shadows, promises, and prophecies that were of him, and is led by the Holy Ghost into the truth and substance of the Scriptures, sitting down in him who is the author and end of them, then they are read and understood with profit and great delight.

Moreover the Lord God let me see, when I was brought up into his image in righteousness and holiness, and into the paradise of God, the state how Adam was made a living soul, and also the stature of Christ, the mystery, that had been hid from ages and generations, which things are hard to be uttered and cannot be borne by many. For, of all the sects in Christendom (so called) that I discoursed withal, I found none that could bear to be told that any should come to Adam's perfection, into that image of God and righteousness and holiness that Adam was in before he fell, to be so clear and pure without sin, as he was. Therefore how should they be able to bear being told that any should grow up to the measure of the stature of the fullness of Christ, when they cannot bear to hear that any should come, whilst upon earth, into the same power and Spirit that the prophets and apostles were in? Though it be a certain truth, that none can understand their writings aright without the same spirit by which they where written. (J 32–3)

4. From these pages, in my view, the two basic positions of early Quakerism emerge. The first concerns spiritual interpretation: it is impossible to read the Scriptures properly without "being in that spirit which gave them forth."[4] This principle allows us to go over the whole of Biblical history, understanding it from the inside, "duly applying them to their own states" (J 31), i.e., reproducing in oneself the Baptist's state, and that of the Prophet, of Moses, and in the end, of Adam: recovering the beginnings through the end, through the new Adam.

Having once been articulated at this particular moment of Fox's spiritual evolution, this principle will be repeated over and over again:

For I saw in that Light and Spirit which was before Scripture was given forth, and which led the holy men of God to give them forth, that all must come to that Spirit, if they would know God, of Christ, or the Scriptures aright, which they that gave them forth were led and taught by. (J 33)

---

[4] In my afterword to R. W. Emerson, *Teologia e natura*, It. trans. M. Lollini (Genoa: Marietti, 1991), 187–208, I study this formula, used by Emerson in his essay "Nature."

> I was to direct people to the Spirit that gave forth the Scriptures, by which they might be led into all Truth, and so up to Christ and God, as they had been who gave them forth... These things I did not see by the help of man, nor by the letter, though they are written in the letter, but I saw them in the light of the Lord Jesus Christ, and by his immediate Spirit and power, as did the holy men of God, by whom the Holy Scriptures were written. Yet I had no slight esteem of the Holy Scriptures, but they were very precious to me, for I was in that spirit by which they were given forth, and what the Lord opened in me I afterwards found was agreeable to them. (J 34)

...so that spirit of God must be in them that come to know them again, by which spirit they might have fellowship with the Son and the Father and with the Scriptures and one with another, and without it they cannot know neither God, nor Christ, nor the Scriptures, nor have fellowship one with another. (J 136)

5. The second basic position of early Quakerism is of an anthropological character. If the first principle is that in order to read the Scriptures one can and must recapture the spirit in which they were written, the second is that one must (and can) reaffirm, through Christ, the model of innocence and of the lordship of Adam over creation, before the Fall. Between the two assertions there is the closest of connections: the one depends upon the other, and Fox is aware of this. Note the sequence of his argument: "Therefore how should they be able to bear being told that any should grow up to the measure of the stature of the fullness of Christ, when they cannot bear to hear that any should come, whilst upon earth, into the same power and Spirit that the prophets and apostles were in?"

Note too how aware he is that it is a question of specific propositions, showing the novelty of his movement by comparison with the rest: "of all the sects in Christendom (so called) that I discoursed withal, I found none that could bear to be told that any should come to Adam's perfection, into that image of God and righteousness and holiness that Adam was in before he fell, to be so clear and pure without sin, as he was. Therefore how should they be able to bear" (J 32).

This position marks a break with the Puritan beliefs with which Fox had grown up, precisely because it takes a different anthropological approach. There is no question of Fox denying the reality of evil and of sin; on the contrary, this is his starting point, as his first experience fully testifies. We need only refer to Robert Barclay's *Apology for the True Christian Divinity* (1676, the clearest theological text in a technical sense, organized around theses), to realize that the acceptance of the doctrine of the Fall is quite clear (including his opposition to the Socinians and the Pelagians). As a counterweight to it, however, stands the doctrine of the universality and interior nature of redemption, which is proposed to every one through the "light that enlightens every man" (John 1:9), and the Seed present in every man. Fox sets all this out vigorously in one polemical letter.

> The deceivers are not worth the setting foot after; and yet ask them for what end Christ came. They will say: "To destroy the Devil and his works." And then ask them if the body of sin and death be not the Devil's work and imperfection. They will say "yes." And so are in confusion. Christ came to destroy the Devil and his works, they say, and yet they must carry them to the grave. People are saved by Christ, they say, but while you are upon earth you must not be made free from sin. This is much as if one should be in Turkey a slave, chained to a boat, and one should come to redeem him to go into his own country; but say the Turks, "Thou art redeemed, but whilst thou art upon the earth thou must not go out of Turkey, nor have the chain off thee." So you are redeemed, but must carry a body of sin and death about you and cannot go to your father Adam's house before he fell, but you must live in your father Adam's house in the Fall while ye be upon the earth. (Ep. 222, in 1662)

6. Many aspects of Fox's personality can only be understood in the context of his Puritan background and education: above all his sense of evil, in ourselves, in the world and in Christianity; the need for purity and for reform; his courage and the absolute independence of his seeking; and the primacy of the Bible. It is not to be wondered at that strenuous attempts have been made to see in the Quaker movement no more than an extreme expression of Puritanism.[5] That same phrase so decisive for Fox—"There is one, even Jesus Christ, that can speak to thy condition"—can and in a certain sense must be read above all against a

---

[5] Above all in the work of Geoffrey Nuttall, *The Holy Spirit in Puritan Faith and Experience* (Oxford, 1946) and Hugh Barbour, *The Quakers in Puritan England* (New Haven, 1964), but cf. Douglas Gwyn, *Apocalypse of the Word* (Richmond, 1946), XVI ff.

Puritan (or rather Protestant) background; it is indeed a protest against every form of religious mediation: "there is *one*."

But as has been noted, the spiritual experience of early Quakerism goes beyond the boundaries of "only Scripture" that define the essential line of demarcation between evangelical and reformed positions—less in the individual statements than in the basic assertion that both the individual and the community can and must receive the inner expression of that light, of that spirit, that even if present in the Scriptures, would otherwise remain shut up, a dead letter. Douglas Gwyn correctly insists that the eschatological attitude is a defining aspect of the early Quaker movement, which awaits in silence the inner, direct manifestation of Christ the Master, the substance of the Scriptures. "*Even* Jesus Christ can speak." In other words, "Christ is come to teach his people himself by his Spirit" (J 149). This eschatological experience also explains the richly apocalyptic tone typical of Fox's early visions, manifestations and "openings." It can all be better understood if we bear in mind the role of the apocalypse in primitive Christianity, as Ernst Käsemann has so clearly pointed out.

7. This interpretation, which would place the experience of Fox and the Friends in the archaic framework of the post-crucifixion community gathered together to await the Risen Lord, is quite fascinating (even if offered within a militant perspective by no means foreign to Gwyn and in general to those interested in these questions). In any case, precisely those texts I have highlighted, and whose relevance appears to escape more recent interpreters, do not allow us to accept this hypothesis for long. Those texts, with the two assertions I have just recalled (or rather one assertion, of a two-sided nature, one anthropological and one hermeneutic), are not entirely to be assimilated to the early Christian eschatology. Let us return to them.

The idea of a mystical ascent, of the reappropriation of Paradise, is certainly present in St. Paul (who was personally "caught up into paradise," according to 1 Cor. 12:4); from Paul comes the idea that believers in Christ, the New Adam, can in a certain sense regain a paradisal condition (1 Cor. 15). And it true that Adam, the Lord of Creation, already in the Genesis account gives things their names. And anyway in Fox's vision the recovery of Adam's paradisal condition—certainly not immediate, but in Christ, and therefore in a more stable and decisive form—is presented in an extraordinarily concrete way:

> The creation was opened to me, and it was showed me how all things had their names according to their nature and virtue. And I was in a stand of mind whether I should practise physic for the good of mankind, seeing the nature and virtues of the creatures were so opened to me by the Lord.

A passage in the apocryphal *Wisdom of Solomon* could well be the inspiration behind it: Solomon was given "an unerring knowledge," among other things, also of "the *natures* of living creatures" and of "the *virtues* of the roots." But none of this belongs to Fox's Bible, and nor does the last part of the description:

> Great things did the Lord lead me into, and wonderful depths were opened unto me, beyond what can by words be declared; but as people come into subjection to the spirit of God, and grow up in the image and power of the Almighty, they may receive the Word of wisdom, that opens all things, and come to know the hidden unity in the Eternal Being (J 27–8).

We owe to the great liberal Quaker scholar Rufus Jones, in his fine book, *Spiritual Reformers in the 16th and 17th Centuries* (1914), the most convincing case for Fox's sources:[6] a writer whom Fox never quotes (he typically does not), but who was circulating in translation just at the time of his early experiences: the mystic Jacob Boehme. Around 1600 Boehme had gone through an analogous experience. In the introduction by translator John Sparrow to the *Forty Questions* (1647), one can read of the possibility of knowing the works of the Creator "in signatures, shapes, figures and qualities or properties." If we take into consideration texts a little later than Fox's vision (the *Journal* was written much later), Justice Hotham's *Life* of Boehme of 1653 may be compared (still following Rufus Jones). In addition, John Ellistone's 1649 introduction to the translation of Boehme's *Epistles* shows an even greater affinity: the knowledge drawn from divine light leads us to know the "different secret qualities and vertues" hidden in all visible things, which

[6] The classic study by W. C. Braithwaite, *The Beginnings of Quakerism* (1912; Cambridge, 1955) 38–41, notes the importance of Fox's vision of Paradise, and refers to Boehme already on the basis of R. Jones, *Studies in Mystical Religion* (1909).

can be "applied to their naturall use for the curing and healing of corrupt and decayed nature." Behmenist correspondences can be seen also in the passage through the sword of fire, and through the "perfume" of Paradise. Likewise the reference to Wisdom, to Sophia, which demonstrates the unity of the created with God, is a typical, constant theme of Boehme's. Even the idea that it is impossible to understand the Scriptures without the gift of the Spirit occurs frequently in Boehme and his English interpreters.[7]

8. R. M. Jones's historical work in now consigned to the usual oblivion of positivist historiography of a liberal theological bent. Yet his *Spiritual Reformers* is indispensable in placing the Quaker movement correctly in a context of reform, humanism and mysticism, and as such the work should be reconsidered.

There are however certain aspects of Fox's vision of Paradise that cannot be attributed to Boehme's influence, in particular the tendency to draw immediate, practical (rather than theological) conclusions from his mystical experience, which is a long way from Boehme's contemplative spirit. In the Vale of Belvoir Fox had understood that the members of the three professions, doctors, magistrates and clergy, were lacking in wisdom, judgment and faith. But he believed that the professions could be reformed, and be led back "into the wisdom of God by which all things were made and created" (J 29). Fox's concern was therefore to grasp at once the secular relevance of the paradisal vision; it meant the reappropriation of the basic professions—medicine and science in general, the magistrates and government activity, theology and the ministry—through a single reforming project. About this, in its three aspects, I offer some final observations.

9. Perhaps a classic like Christopher Hill's *The Intellectual Origins of the English Revolution* (1965) may be of use to evoke the atmosphere—in the century of Bacon and Pascal—in which to place that terrible doubt that assailed George Fox: "'All things come by nature'; and the elements and stars came over me so that I was in a manner quite clouded

[7] R. M. Jones, *Spiritual Reformers of the 16th and 17th Centuries* (1914; Boston, 1959) 221–227.

with them." Thus we may also remember with Hill, how the extraordinary developments in medical science in that age may explain why Fox, transported to Paradise, asks himself if it would not be best to become a doctor—"practise physic for the good of mankind." William Penn's Preface to the *Journal* may be relevant here:

> For in all things he acquitted himself like a man, yea, a strong man, a new and heavenly minded man, a divine and a naturalist, and all of God Almighty's making. I have been surprised at his questions and answers in natural things; that whilst he was ignorant of useless and sophistical science, he had in him the foundation of useful and commendable knowledge, and cherished it everywhere. (J XLVII)

This is a kind of idealization of Fox, to whom are attributed the features of the New Adam, so central to the Friends' way of thinking, all the more so for those who, like Penn, were moving forward into the new American experience.

10. In the England of Milton's *Paradise Lost* and *Paradise Regained*, and of Locke's *Two Treatises of Government*, the arguments concerning Adam's state were fundamental, and ideas of the state of nature and of natural law were decisive for modern political theory and practice. As far as Fox and the early Quaker movement is concerned, the anthropology implicit in the vision of paradise grows at once into a praxis in which politics and mysticism are perfectly in harmony.

The vision in which Fox explains why he must address everyone as "thou" and not take off his hat to anyone comes immediately afterwards (J 36). Fox is imprisoned in 1650 for holding to this vision:

> They put me in and out of the room from the first hour to the ninth hour at night in examinations, having me backward and forward, and said in a deriding manner that I was taken up in raptures, as they called it.
>
> At last they asked me whether I was sanctified.
>
> I said, "Sanctified? yes," for I was in the Paradise of God.
>
> They said, had I no sin?
>
> "Sin?" said I, "Christ my Saviour hath taken away my sin, and in him there is no sin."
>
> They asked how we knew that Christ did abide in us.
>
> I said, "By his Spirit that he has given us."

> They temptingly asked if any of us were Christ.
>
> I answered, "Nay, we are nothing, Christ is all."
>
> They said, "If a man steal is it no sin?"
>
> I answered, "All unrighteousness is sin."
>
> And many such like words they had with me. And so they committed me as a blasphemer and as a man that had no sin, and committed another me with me to the House of Correction in Derby for six months. (J 51 ff.)

Fox calls upon his vision once again in Derby prison when they want to make him an officer in the Commonwealth army, and he replies to their insistence and flattery, about his "virtue," "as they said," maintaining that he "lived in the virtue of that life and power that took away the occasion of all wars" (J 65 ff.). In the horrible prison at Derby he feels deeply concerned about the fact that the judges "put men to death for cattle and for money and small things." Spiritually oppressed by this, he has a vision that consoles him: "standing in the will of God, a heavenly breathing arose in my soul to the Lord. Then did I see the heavens opened and the glory of God shined over all" (J 65 ff.).

Out of faith in his vision, he will write to Cromwell in 1655: "Live in the wisdom of the life of God, that with it thou mayest be ordered to his glory, and order his creatures to his glory" (J 194); he writes similarly to Cromwell's sick daughter.

11. It is also out of faith in his vision, for the redemption of all marriages after the Fall, that Fox will much later, at the age of 45, marry Margaret Fell, widow of the magistrate Thomas Fell. I would like to end here by evoking the image of the first meeting between Fox and Margaret Fell, which took place in 1652. This vivid scene sums up the themes and methods of early Quaker preaching (here again there is no comparison with the contemplative Behmenist tradition). The words of Fox, his declarations and his questions, take as given what was described earlier as the two fundamental hermeneutic and anthropological positions of Quakerism. He translates all this however into two simple questions in which the ancient hermeneutic principles, of the early fathers still more than of the Behmenists, of reading the Scriptures in the same spirit in which they were written, becomes the productive prin-

ciple of a new relation between word and deed: "The Bible says: but what canst *thou* say?"

> And when they were singing before the sermon, he came in; and when they had done singing, he stood up upon a seat or form and desired that he might have liberty to speak. And he that was in the pulpit said he might. And the first words that he spoke were as followeth: "He is not a Jew that is one outward, neither is that circumcision which is outward; but he is a Jew that is one inward, and that is circumcision which is of the heart." And so he went on and said, How that Christ was the Light of the world and lighteth every man that cometh into the world; and that by this Light they might be gathered to God, etc. And I stood up in my pew, and I wondered at his doctrine, for I had never heard such before. And then he went on, and opened the Scriptures, and said, "The Scriptures were the prophets' words and Christ's and the Apostle's words, and what as they spoke they enjoyed and possessed and had from the Lord." And said, "Then what had any to do with the Scriptures, but as they came to the Spirit that gave them forth? You will say, Christ saith this, and the apostles say this; but what canst thou say? Art thou a child of Light and hast walked in the Light, and what thou speakest, is it inwardly from God?"
>
> This opened me so that it cut me to the heart; and then I saw clearly we were all wrong. So I sat me down in my pew again, and cried bitterly. And I cried in the spirit to the Lord, "We are all thieves, we are all thieves, we have taken the Scriptures in words and know nothing of them in ourselves."[8]

---

[8] From *Wait for the Light: The Spirituality of George Fox*, J. Lampen, ed. (London, 1981), 112 ff.

Love in Paradise: Milton's Pattern

Daniela Bianchi

1. The Desire of the Heart

Love is "the Son of *Lonelines*, begot in Paradise by that sociable and helpfull aptitude which God implanted between man and woman toward each other," and on love both Hebrew-Christian and classical culture are in agreement. Milton is mainly referring to Plato's *Symposium* and the book of Genesis. In the *Symposium* love is pictured as "the Sonne of *Penury*, begot of *Plenty* in the garden of *Jupiter*." Milton refers also to the myth of Antheros, who was the twin of Eros, to emphasize the necessity of mutual love. Without reciprocity "there can be left of wedlock nothing, but the empty husk of an outside matrimony," which God abhors as He abhors any other kind of hypocrisy.[1]

True love is only to be found in marriage—wedded love. It cannot "reign nor rejoice"

> "...in the bought smile
> Of harlots, loveless, joyless, unendeared,
> Casual fruition; nor in court amours,
> Mixed dance, or wanton masque, or midnight ball,
> Or serenate, which the starved lover sings
> To his proud fair, best quitted with disdain." (*Paradise Lost*, IV, 765–770)

Love is born of the need man has to overcome his loneliness; in fact, solitude tormented even the newly-created Adam:

> "...In solitude
> What happiness? Who can enjoy alone,
> Or all enjoying, what contentment find?" (VIII, 364–366)

He did not find in all the living beings with which God presented him "'what methought I wanted still'"; and when God showed him all the rich variety of living beings, he replied:

---

[1] John Milton, *The Doctrine and Discipline of Divorce*, in *Complete Prose Works of John Milton* (hereafter *CPW*), (New Haven–London, 1959), Vol. II, 252, 254 ff.

"Among unequals what society
Can sort, what harmony or true delight?
Which must be mutual, in proportion due
Giv'n and received; but in disparity,
The one intense, the other still remiss
Cannot well suit with either, but soon prove
Tedious alike. Of fellowship I speak
Such as I seek, fit to participate
All rational delight, wherein the brute
Cannot be human consort..." (VIII, 383–392)

God is perfect in himself, but man is not, and even in Eden longed to converse "'...with his like to help/Or solace his defects...'" (VIII, 418–419). When Adam asked God for a being like himself, he was showing his ability to choose and to express freedom of mind. So God, who was pleased to test and then satisfy Adam, gave him his "likeness," according to the desire of Adam's heart (VIII, 450–451).

In *Tetrachordon* Milton says that loneliness was the first and only thing which "God's eye nam'd not good." In this context, alone means without a woman:

> ...otherwise Adam had the company of God himself, and Angels to convers with; all creatures to delight him seriously, or to make him sport. God could have created him out of the same mould a thousand friends and brother Adams to have bin his consorts, yet for all this till Eve was giv'n him, God reckn'd him to be alone.[2]

Before the fall "not good" meant "not pleasing" and "not expedient." After the fall to be alone is not only "not expedient," but "plainly sinfull" for the man who has not received the supernatural gift of continence. God did not create a female for the male Adam, but a "meet help" for the lonely man: "God supplies the privation of not good, with the perfect gift of a reall and positive good."[3]

According to Milton, man's loneliness in Eden was often interpreted by the Christian tradition as absence of sexual intercourse. Augustine, for example, thought that male friendship would be "a more becoming

[2] Milton, *Tetrachordon: Expositions upon the foure chief places in Scripture, which treat of Mariage, or nullities in Mariage*, in *CPW* Vol. II, 595.

[3] *Tetrachordon*, 595.

solace for Adam, then to spend so many secret years in an empty world with one woman." Milton thinks this is a "crabbed opinion," since there is in the marital bed "a peculiar comfort" besides sexual intercourse which "no other society affords." It is possible to be alone even joined to another body. To be really joined means to be carnally united with "a fit conversing soul," with "an intimate and speaking help." The remedy for solitude is that "meet help" of Gen. 2:18. It means "effectuall conformity of disposition and affection," as if God, "not satisfy'd with the naming of a help," had gone beyond describing "another self, a second self, a very self it self," In this verse God had signified to man the first and most important end of marriage, mutual comfort and help, "a meet and happy conversation."[4]

2. Male and Female Created He Them

In *Paradise Lost* Milton introduces Adam and Eve together; they are creatures equal in many respects:

"Two of far nobler shape erect and tall,
God-like erect, with native honor clad
In naked majesty seemed lords of all,
And worthy seemed, for in their looks divine
The image of their glorious Maker shone,
Truth, wisdom, sanctitude severe and pure,
Severe but in true filial freedom placed." (IV, 288–294)

In *Tetrachordon* Milton says both were created after God's image (Gen. 1:26). In this context image means "wisdom, purity, justice, and rule over all creatures." In addition, the word image refers to the fact that God created both soul and body: man is God's image in the soul.[5]

The two creatures were not however wholly equal. Their gender diversity is soon revealed to be a diversity in their roles: on the male's side supremacy, on the female's side submission and obedience.

"'For contemplation he and valor formed,/For softness she and sweet attractive grace'" (IV, 297–298). Eve acknowledged Adam's supremacy, and this recognition made their conjugal relationship perfect:

---

[4] *Tetrachordon*, 596, 600; Milton, *The Doctrine*, 246, 251.

[5] *Tetrachordon*, 587. See also *A Treatise on Christian Doctrine*, in *CPW* Vol. VI, 316.

"...O thou for whom
And from whom I was formed flesh of thy flesh,
And without whom am to no end, my guide
And head, what thou hast said is just and right." (IV, 440–443)

And again:

"My author and disposer, what thou bidd'st
Unargued I obey; so God ordains.
God is thy law, thou mine; to know no more
Is woman's happiest knowledge and her praise." (IV, 635–638)

In fact, woman is not "primarily and immediately the image of God, but in reference to the man." In a much-quoted formulation, "He for God only, she for God in him" (IV, 299).[6]

Nevertheless Adam's "absolute dominion" does not turn into a crushing tyranny; Eve is not his servant. Man in fact

"receives her into a part of that empire which God proclaims him to, though not equally, yet largely, as his own image and glory: for it is no small glory to him, that a creature so like him, should be made subject to him."[7]

In Eden this "second self" plays many parts. Although Adam says that

"...nothing lovelier can be found
In woman, than to study household good,
And good works in her husband to promote," (IX, 232–234)

Eve is not confined to a mere domestic function. She shares all Adam's activities. Otherwise she could not have been his "intimate and speaking help," his "ready and reviving associate."[8] Both tend the garden, since God appointed them to daily work of body and mind:

---

[6] Referring to woman, Milton says that Genesis must be compared with I Cor 11:3, Col 3:18 and Eph 5:24. See *Tetrachordon*, 589. On the subjection of woman to man see *The Doctrine*, 324.

[7] *Tetrachordon*, 589.

[8] *The Doctrine*, 251. On Eve's role in *Paradise Lost* see B. K. Lewalski, "Milton on Women—Yet Once More," in *Milton Studies*, 6 (1974); 3–21; J. M. Evans, *Paradise Lost and the Genesis Tradition* (Oxford, 1968), 252 ff.; J. G. Halkett, *Milton and the Idea of Matrimony: A Study of the Divorce Tracts and Paradise Lost* (New York–London, 1970), 66 and passim. On women in the literature of Milton's time see P. S. Siegel, "Milton and the Humanist Attitude Toward Women," *Journal of the History of Ideas*,

"With first approach of light we must be ris'n,
And at our pleasant labor, to reform
Yon flow'ry arbors, yonder alleys green,
Our walk at noon, with branches overgrown,
That mock our scant manuring, and require
More hands than ours to lop their wanton growth." (IV, 624–629)

The garden is not perfect or unchanging. Since it is a part of nature, it becomes overgrown; left to itself, it would quickly turn into an image of excess and disorder. Milton significantly uses the word "reform" to indicate man's necessary intervention. Male and female share this fundamental task, happily in mutual help and mutual love (IV, 727–728).

Another activity which they perform together is conversation. In many cases their dialogue appears to be an instrument of education. Adam explains to Eve the succession of day and night, the function of the stars in the sky, the existence of millions of spiritual creatures, the relation between reason and lesser faculties, the nature of knowledge and imagination, and God's order to abstain from the tree of knowledge (IV,420ff; IV,660ff; V,100ff). It is indeed the man who knows, and then educates; his wisdom comes directly from God. But the course of Eve's education appears to be in no way different from her husband's.

In Eden maternity was not Eve's main or only role. God does define Eve's function as essentially a maternal one when he brings her, newly created, to Adam:

"...to him shalt bear
Multitudes like thyself, and thence be called
Mother of human race." (IV, 473–475)

Raphael too emphasizes Eve's maternal role when he says to Adam: "'Male he created thee, but thy consort/Female for race...'" (VII, 529–530). But the male Adam recognizes Eve prevalently as his "dear and inseparable comfort":

---

11 (1950); M. Todd, *Christian Humanism and the Puritan Social Order* (Cambridge, 1987), 105 ff. and passim; K. M. Davies, "The Sacred Condition of Equality: How Original Were Puritan Doctrines of Marriage?" *Social History*, 5 (1977).

"...Awake,
My fairest, my espoused, my latest found,
Heav'n's last best gift, my ever new delight..." (V, 17–18)

Adam and Eve together demand and seek personal identity: "...who himself beginning knew?" (VIII, 251) As soon as they are created, both wonder who they are; for both in their different ways love becomes an experience which builds their personal identity. When he sees Eve, Adam, "overjoyed," thanks God for the most beautiful gift he could make:

"...I now see
Bone of my bone, flesh of my flesh, my self
Before me. Woman is her name, of man
Extracted; for this cause he shall forgo
Father and mother, and to his wife adhere;
And they shall be one flesh, one heart, one soul." (VIII, 494–499)

Eve, on the other hand, did not recognize Adam at once. In the beginning she fell in love with her own image mirrored in "a liquid plain":

"...there I had fixed
Mine eyes till now, and pined with vain desire,
Had not a voice thus warned me: 'What thou seest,
What there thou seest, fair creature, is thyself....'" (IV, 465–468)

But the voice did warn Eve, and she was brought to Adam:

"...where no shadow stays
Thy coming, and thy soft embraces, he
Whose image thou art, him thou shalt enjoy
Inseparably thine...." (IV, 470– 473)

When Eve first saw Adam, she turned her back on him, thinking him far less attractive and seductive than the image mirrored. But Adam asked her to stay:

"...Return, fair Eve,
Whom fli'st thou? Whom thou fli'st, of him thou art,
His flesh, his bone; to give thee being I lent
Out of my side to thee, nearest my heart,
Substantial life, to have thee by my side
Henceforth an individual solace dear.
Part of my soul I seek thee, and thee claim
My other half...." (IV, 481–488)

So has Milton created in Eve a Narcissus? He seems to suggest that woman, if left to herself, does not turn spontaneously to man. Her feelings run the risk of taking the wrong direction. There is a similarity between woman's emotional growth and the natural growth of the garden. In order to be able to accept man, woman has to be able to choose; Eve chose because an alternative was laid before her. The free choice between different, even opposite options, allowed Eve to pass from the narcissistic phase to that of love object. Adam played an active role in Eve's search for identity and gender maturity. He asked her explicitly not to fly away from him; he recognized her as a woman, and Eve matured because of this recognition:

> "...With that thy gentle hand
> Seized mine, I yielded, and from that time see
> How beauty is excelled by manly grace
> And wisdom, which alone is truly fair." (IV, 488–91)

In the first phase of her creation, Eve did not know these things; she went to the liquid plain "with unexperienced thought."[9]

3. The Undefiled and Chaste Bed

In *Paradise Lost* the first representation of Adam and Eve is that of two human beings walking naked, hand in hand, making no attempt to avoid the sight of God and angels. They could not think evil. Even sexual pleasure was experienced innocently:

> Then was not guilty shame; dishonest shame
> Of Nature's works, honor dishonorable,
> Sin-bred, how have ye troubled all mankind
> With shows instead, mere shows of seeming pure,
> And banished from man's life his happiest life,
> Simplicity and spotless innocence. (IV, 313–318)

Naked they lay side by side:

> ...nor turned, I ween,
> Adam from his fair spouse, nor Eve the rites
> Mysterious of connubial love refused;

---

[9] On Eve's behavior see Lewalski, "Milton on Women"; Evans, *Paradise Lost*, 253; and James W. Earl, "Eve's Narcissism," *Milton Quarterly* 19 (1985), 13 ff.

> Whatever hypocrites austerely talk
> Of purity and place and innocence,
> Defaming as impure what God declares
> Pure, and commands to some, leaves free to all.
> Our Maker bids increase; who bids abstain
> But our destroyer, foe to God and Man? (IV, 741–749)

The embracing couple fell asleep "lulled by nightingales," while "...on their naked limbs the flow'ry roof/Show'red roses, which the morn repaired..." (IV, 771–773).

In Milton's Eden man is neither a self-sufficient hermaphrodite nor an angelic being devoid of passions or desires, doomed to remain virgin or to procreate in a spiritual way.[10] In Eden sexuality is an aspect of God's constant fertile creativity in an evolving world.[11] Milton breaks with an ancient Christian tradition, which legitimized sexuality only for procreation, and keeps sexuality and generation distinct. In the *Divorce Tracts* generation is presented as one of the ends of marriage (Gen. 1:28), mentioned by God "till afterwards, as being but a secondary end in dignity, though not in necessitie." The desire for children is "honest and pious, religious and prudent," but only if people know what is required "to breeding as to begetting."[12]

By itself sexuality "participates of nothing rational," and since in human actions the soul is the agent and the body acts "in a manner passive," sexuality has to be made active and different from "an animal excretion" by something inherent to the soul. What really makes procreation beneficial for humanity is the quality of the conjugal relationship. For this reason the sexual act has to be linked with love.

> When love findes it self utterly unmatcht, and justly vanishes, nay rather cannot but vanish, the fleshly act indeed may continue, but not holy, not pure, not beseeming the sacred bond of marriage; being at best but an animal excretion.[13]

---

[10] For an angelic anthropology see J. Delumeau, *Une histoire du Paradis* (Paris, 1992), 265 ff. See also B. K. Lewalski, "Innocence and Experience in Milton's Eden," in *New Essays on Paradise Lost*, ed. T. Kranidas (Berkeley, 1971), 96 ff. Milton, *Tetrachordon*, 589.

[11] See Lewalski, "Innocence," 107.

[12] Milton, *The Doctrine*, 235, and *Tetrachordon*, 593.

[13] *Tetrachordon*, 609.

The connection between sexuality and love is so fundamental that Milton, challenging a widespread opinion, dares to affirm that children born from "ill-twisted wedlock," without "any true love or contentment, or joy to their parents," may be called "the children of wrath and anguish." Begotten only out of "a bestiall necessitie," they are as unblessed as if they were bastards. They are the children of sin.[14]

4. In Loving Thou Dost Well, in Passion Not

In *Paradise Lost* Adam confesses to Raphael that he takes pleasure in every earthly thing; but they are "such/As used or not, works in the mind no change" (VIII, 525). This is a static pleasure, whereas in the conjugal bed

> "Far otherwise, transported I behold,
> Transported touch; here passion first I felt,
> Commotion strange, in all enjoyments else
> Superior and unmoved, here only weak
> Against the charm of beauty's powerful glance," (VIII, 528–533)

Eve's beauty is quite overwhelming for Adam:

> "...yet when I approach
> Her loveliness, so absolute she seems
> And in herself complete, so well to know
> Her own, that what she wills to do or say
> Seems wisest, virtuousest, discreetest, best;
> All higher knowledge in her presence falls
> Degraded, wisdom in discourse with her
> Loses discount'nanced, and like folly shows;
> Authority and reason on her wait,
> As one intended first, not after made
> Occasionally; and to consummate all,
> Greatness of mind and nobleness their seat
> Build in her loveliest, and create an awe
> About her, as a guard angelic placed." (VIII, 546–559)

Raphael, "with contracted brow," urges Adam not to overvalue things which have no value. Eve deserves Adam's tenderness, respect and love, but not his subjection: "'Weigh with her thyself;/Then value.'" The more Adam learns the art of self esteem, the more Eve will recognize

[14] *The Doctrine*, 259–260, and *Tetrachordon*, 608–609.

him as her head and guide. What seems to Adam the highest pleasure was given even to "cattle and each beast" (VIII, 560–585). "'What higher in her society thou find'st/Attractive, human, rational, love still.'" (VIII, 586–587) Passion is not true love, because love

"...refines
The thoughts, and heart enlarges, hath his seat
In reason, and is judicious, is the scale
By which to heav'nly love thou may'st ascend,
Not sunk in carnal pleasure, for which cause
Among the beasts no mate for thee was found." (VIII, 589–594)

A perfect correspondence between Raphael's words and Adam's is lacking, as with Raphael's traditional Christian approach to passions and Adam's new concern for them. Raphael praises rational love, but Adam speaks of a "transported touch," of a "commotion strange," of "the charm of beauty's powerful glance," which may transform wisdom into folly. The angel maintains that Adam must learn to control his passion for Eve. Adam seems to have understood, because he replies "half abashed" that he takes the highest pleasure not from bodily beauty, nor from sexual intercourse. What so much delights him are

"...those graceful acts,
Those thousand decencies that daily flow
From all her words and actions, mixed with love
And sweet compliance, which declare unfeigned
Union of mind, or in us both one soul;
Harmony to behold in wedded pair
More grateful than harmonious sound to the ear." (VIII, 600–606)

The idea of spontaneous self-control and discipline is alien to Eden. As with the perfection of the garden, the first human couple's perfection needs constant watchfulness to maintain the balance of forces which, being *natural* forces, are inclined to grow impulsively in various directions. At the same time, man cannot be free without continuous growth and constant watchfulness.[15] Raphael's exhortation to Adam to be strong and steadfast is not idle:

---

[15] See Evans, *Paradise Lost*, 269 ff. On Raphael's stance on Adam's passion for Eve see Lewalski, "Innocence," 113 ff., and P. Lindenbaum, "Lovemaking in Milton's Paradise," in *Milton Studies* 6 (1974), 299.

"...take heed lest passion sway
Thy judgement to do aught which else free will
Would not admit..." (VIII, 635–637)

In fact Adam does seem to love Eve too much, and her beauty is for him an all-embracing charm. Eve appears submissive, but at the same time she shows independence of judgment and sensitiveness to Satan's "overpraising."

In the *Divorce Tracts* the rational and spiritual aspects of love are exalted above the sexual. Inside and outside of Eden, sexuality as a mere carnal act is represented negatively, because it degrades man to the level of beasts. It becomes "human" when it is experienced in a conjugal relationship dominated by love, which alone is able to create harmony and peace. The biblical text "and they shall be one flesh" makes "legitimate and good the carnal act," which otherwise might seem to have "somthing of pollution in it." But without "correspondence of the minde," "unity of disposition," sexuality cannot generate that spirit of union and concord which is a true marriage. And without this harmony it will join a living soul to a dead body. The soul is not the servant of its vassal, the body, and the body without the soul is "a meer senseles trunck." All corporal delight will soon become "unsavoury and contemptible" without "a unity of disposition" and intellectual joy. Instead of being one flesh, they will be rather "two carkasses chain'd unnaturally together." The primacy of the soul in marriage has its roots in Eden: God responded first to the need for contentment and solace of the mind before "the sensitive pleasing of the body."[16]

The limits to love which Raphael describes concern Adam before the Fall and mankind afterwards. The difference lies in the difficulty fallen men meet in their experience of "unlibidinous love." Nevertheless there is no need for marriage as a remedy to carnal "burning"; the temperate man can keep "low and obedient" "the venom of a lusty and over-abounding concoction" by means of a strictly disciplined life, labor and a plain diet.[17]

---

[16] *The Doctrine*, 246, 326, 327; *Tetrachordon*, 598, 624.

[17] *The Doctrine*, 251.

5. Marriage and Divorce

The peculiar nature of edenic love and sexuality is fundamental to understanding Milton's ideas on both marriage and divorce because of incompatibility of character. In *Paradise Lost* the hymn to conjugal love is placed at the time of innocence, not at the Fall:

Hail, wedded Love, mysterious law, true source
Of human offspring, sole propriety
In Paradise of all things common else.
By thee adulterous lust was driv'n from men
Among the bestial herds to range; by thee
Founded in reason, loyal, just, and pure,
Relations dear, and all the charities
Of father, son, and brother first were known.
Far be it that I should write thee sin or blame,
Or think thee unbefitting holiest place,
Perpetual fountain of domestic sweets,
Whose bed is undefiled and chaste pronounced,
Present or past, as saints and patriarchs used. (IV, 750–762)

Marriage is a natural consequence of that deep and intimate relationship between Adam and Eve in the prelapsarian condition; it is the ordinance of "our solace and contentment," the remedy to our loneliness, "a mutuall help to piety, next to civill fellowship of love and amity," "an amiable knot."[18]

Genesis is far more important for Milton than the Pauline epistles, which had shaped the Christian marriage tradition. Milton did engage with Paul's ideas on the Fall and its consequences, interpreting the words "it is better to marry than to burn" (1Cor. 7:9), traditionally used to justify marriage as a remedy for concupiscence, from an "edenic" point of view. In this context to burn does not mean "the meer motion of carnall lust," nor "the meer goad of a sensitive desire." It is instead a special kind of desire that God put into Adam in paradise before he knew the sin of incontinence, that is the desire "to put off an unkindly solitarines by uniting another body, but not without a fit suole to his in the cheerfull society of wedlock." It is an original solitude of the soul.

[18] *A Treatise*, 355; *The Doctrine*, 229; *Tetrachordon*, 599.

> ...if it were so needfull before the fall, when man was much more perfect in himself, how much more is it needfull now against all the sorrows and casualties of this life to have an intimate and speaking help, a ready and reviving associate in marriage: whereof who misses by chancing on a mute and spiritless mate, remains more alone then before, and in a burning lesse to be contain'd then that which is fleshly and more to be consider'd; as being more deeply rooted even in the faultles innocence of nature.[19]

Marriage is the remedy for this rational and emotional burning. Its dignity lies in the mutual enjoyment of what the desiring soul seeks to satisfy a primal need. Paul's words must be interpreted by comparing them to God's declaration in Gen. 2:18: "It is not good that man should be alone." However, a marriage may become what it was in paradise,—"a serene and bliss condition"—only through an institution established after the fall, i.e., divorce (Deut. 24:1–2).[20]

Divorce gives us the possibility of choosing and then of choosing differently if the first choice was a mistaken one. Harmony can sometimes be best guaranteed only through division.

> While man and woman were both perfect each to other, there needed no divorce; but when they both degenerated to imperfection, and oft times grew to be an intolerable evil each to other, then law more justly did permitt the alienating of that evil which mistake made proper, then it did the appropriating of that good which Nature at first made common.[21]

In his comment on Gen. 2:23 Milton says that the strength and intimacy of the relationship between Adam and Eve was far greater than whatever held after the fall between husband and wife. No woman besides Eve was moulded out of man's rib, which is the place nearest the heart. Adam was given the gift of understanding perfectly whatever con-

---

[19] *The Doctrine*, 250 ff.

[20] Between 1643 and 1645 Milton published four tracts on marriage and divorce: *The Doctrine and Discipline of Divorce*; *The Judgment of Martin Bucer, concerning Divorce*; *Tetrachordon*; and *Colasterion*. Marriage and divorce are also discussed widely in *A Treatise on Christian Doctrine*, which was not published. The works are a passionate polemic against the Church of England doctrine which permitted divorce *a thoro et mensa*, but not *a vinculo*. In addition, Milton polemicizes with the Puritan reformers who admitted divorce only in cases of adultery and desertion.

[21] *Tetrachordon*, 665.

cerned him. He realized at first sight the fitness of the consort God had chosen for him.[22]

For the most part fallen men and women are strangers who come to have "that consanguinity which they have by wedlock." Outside of Eden the fitness of the partner is not immediately perceived. The choice may be difficult because "error, casualty, art or plot" happen to mislead the man who makes his first experience of love and marriage. What happens then to people who had been "but once handed in the Church, and have tasted in any sort of the nuptiall bed," and nevertheless find themselves mistaken because of their "different tempers, thoughts, and constitutions"? They cannot be mutually "a remedy against lonelines," neither live together "in any union or contentment all their dayes." They are obliged to cohabit "to their unspeakable wearisomnes and despaire of all sociable delight in the ordinance which God establisht to that very end."[23]

Man bears no responsibility for the peculiar qualities of character which may create incompatibilities in the actual experience of wedded life. Neither peace nor joy are possible in this case. Marriage then becomes a relation of the body, not of the mind, and the mind is "so disgrac'd and vilify'd below the bodies interest." This kind of marriage does not fulfill the ends prescribed by God at its first institution, and thus is not a marriage at all.[24]

Woman has a specific responsibility because she was given a special role in Eden. Man does not always remember that woman was created for him, and that he cannot attach himself to an inferior sex, becoming her slave. A woman unable or unwilling to become a wife frustrates the end for which she was created; it is lawful therefore for man to rid himself of her because of his "natural birthright" and the mark of preeminence which God had given him from the beginning. The sober man, who may by chance meet

---

[22] *Tetrachordon*, 601–602.

[23] *The Doctrine*, 235, 236, 249; *Tetrachordon*, 622.

[24] *Tetrachordon*, 598.

> if not with a body impenetrable, yet often with a minde to all other due conversation inaccessible, and to all the more estimable and superior purposes of matrimony uselesse and almost liveles,

does not overcome his solitude; the "mute and spiritless mate" he marries cannot be a wife at all.[25]

Milton is polemical towards those Protestant authorities who admit divorce only in case of adultery, because of the importance he ascribes to the institution of marriage in Eden. To consider adultery the weightiest violation of the conjugal bond means to transform the marriage bed into the most important end of marriage.

> What courts of concupiscence are these, wherein fleshly appetite is heard before right reason, lust before love or devotion?[26]

This is

> ... but to abuse the sacred and misterious bed of mariage to be the compulsive stie of an ingratefull and malignant lust, stirr'd up only from a carnall acrimony, without either love or peace, or regard to any other thing holy or human.[27]

There is a spiritual and rational burning rooted "in the faultless innocence of nature" which cannot be endangered by any supremacy given to corporal "burning."

The first couple represent the perfect state of conjugal love. Is it possible for fallen man to return to that happy condition? The Quaker George Fox says that it is.[28] But the kind of paradisal marriage which he refers to is probably a relationship without sexual intercourse.[29] Milton answers in the affirmative as well, but his answer is far more complex, first of all because of his doctrine of Christian liberty. Christ had dissolved the whole of law into charity:

---

[25] *Tetrachordon*, 589, 590; *The Doctrine*, 250, 309.

[26] *Tetrachordon*, 599.

[27] *Tetrachordon*, 600.

[28] See the essay by P. C. Bori in this volume.

[29] From early Quaker letters we know that some friends refused to have sexual relations with their wives as a sign of a newly achieved prelapsarian condition. See G. F. Nuttall, *Early Quaker Letters from the Swarthmoor Mss. to 1660* (London, 1952), 276–277.

> ...Christ having cancell'd the hand writing of ordinances which was against us, Col. 2:14. and interpreted the fulfilling of all through charity, hath in that respect set us over law, in the free custody of his love, and left us victorious under the guidance of his living Spirit, not under the dead letter; to follow that which most edifies, most aides and furders a religious life, makes us holiest and likest to his immortall Image...[30]

Christ had delivered us from "calamitous yokes" which endanger our souls, and had restored us to "a right in every good thing both of this life, and the other." Because of man's sin a merciful God had not made "such wast upon us, as to make utterly void to our use any temporall benefit," to "a peacefull and sanctify'd life" for "a a most incident error which no warines can certainly shun."[31]

Epistemologically the equivalent of Christian liberty is the liberation from custom, tradition, and from the bondage to serve "under the tyranny of usurpt opinions." It means free reasoning, to proceed by trial and error, to have an experience not grounded on the bondage of forms and traditions or the presumption of infallibility. Opinion is "but knowledge in the making."[32]

We must consider Milton's edenic anthropology as well. Between man before the Fall and man after the Fall there is no abyss; in both cases man learns through experience. By trial and error man walked and grew in the age of innocence. Both trial and error are features of the human condition in Paradise: "And what is faith, love, virtue, unassayed/ Alone, without exterior help sustained?" (IX, 335–336) In *Areopagitica* Milton says that "we bring not innocence into the world, we bring impurity much rather." But "which purifies us is triall, and triall is by what is contrary." "Blank vertue" is not a pure virtue.[33]

The first couple's perfection was conditioned by obedience; it involved growth and change through experience; it did not exclude errors, doubts, self deceit, dark zones, even tears. Eve was grossly mistaken about herself and her feelings when she "mirrored in the liquid plain."

---

[30] *Tetrachordon*, 587, 588.

[31] *Tetrachordon*, 601.

[32] *The Doctrine*, 222 ff., 343; *Areopagitica*, in *CPW*, Vol. II, 554.

[33] See Lewalski, 99 ff; *Areopagitica*, 515–516.

Adam had to correct himself after Raphael's lesson about the control of the passions.

> "God made thee perfect, not immutable;
> And good he made thee, but to persevere
> He left in thy power..." (V, 524–526)

Their conjugal harmony, moreover, was not a static one; before the fall they had slight disagreements, and even experienced different desires. An example is the dialogue between Adam and Even on that fatal morning just before Eve ate the forbidden fruit (IX, 205ff). Their harmony has to be conquered again and again.

Divorce is the admission of a mistake, but an error cannot destroy the life of the people who fell into it. God's ways are "equal, easy, and not burdensome." They do not "crosse the just and reasonable desires of men, nor involve this our portion of mortall life, into a necessity of sadnes and malecontent." They allow us "to remedy and shake off those evills into which human error hath led us through the middest of our best intentions." In fact, no heavenly or human ordinance can hold against the good of man.[34]

Divorce allows us to proceed through trial and error; in this sense it is a form of Christian liberty. The highway to edenic love is charity, which is "the bond of perfection." Marriage may become one of the "works of charity" only if grounded on love. Milton very often remarks that the inward knot of marriage is peace and love.[35]

Puritan reformers held that love was necessary for a happy marriage, but not essential to marriage itself. For Milton, on the contrary, love is the very soul of marriage, without which it can degenerate into hate.

> Then enters *Hate*, not that Hate that sins, but that which onely is naturall dissatisfaction and the turning aside from a mistaken object.[36]

Hate is "the mightiest divider, nay, is division it self."[37] Divorce is a break which can prevent a division of a far worse kind.

---

[34] *The Doctrine*, 342–343; *Tetrachordon*, 588.

[35] *The Doctrine*, 269, 331.

[36] *The Doctrine*, 253.

[37] *The Doctrine*, 345.

That marriage as an institution promoted peace is an idea expressed forcefully by Augustine, who thus justified the incest taboo. Thanks to this taboo most people were united by bonds of kinship. Social bonds intensified with the increase of kinship relations, and with them charity also spread.[38] Compared to the contemporary Protestant works on marriage which insisted a great deal on the incest taboo, Milton definitely prefers to connect charity and peace to the affection which married people feel for each other. Only in this sense is marriage a vehicle of social peace as well as of individual peace.

Milton has an individualistic concept of marriage as an institution which satisfies basic human needs, needs whose frustation is a sufficient condition for divorce. Like Raphael, he holds that without love there is no happiness (VIII, 621). On the other hand, acts of peace, the consequence of a happy conjugal relationship, irradiate into the society at large. Adam and Eve "reformed" the garden through the concord they found in work. Englishmen are called upon to reform the family, introducing divorce for incompatibility of character. The reform of the state begins from the foundations, that is to say from marriage and the family.[39]

True marriage is an expression of divine harmony, and divorce an act which resembles God's act of creation. The world rose out of Chaos through God's "divorcing command"; it cannot be renewed "out of confusion but by the separating of unmeet consorts."[40]

---

[38] *De Civitate Dei*, Book 15, ch. 16.

[39] Milton, *The Judgment of Martin Bucer, Concerning Divorce*, in *CPW* Vol. II, 431; *The Doctrine*, 226 ff.

[40] *The Doctrine*, 273.

Adamites Old and New in Seventeenth-Century French Morality

Lisa Ginzburg

1.

> Prodicus et ses disciples, nommées aussi adamites, prétendaient renouveler les joies du paradis terrestre par des pratiques fort eloignées de l'innocence primitive. Leur Eglise s'appelait le Paradis; ils la chauffaient et s'y tenaient nus. Avec cela, ils s'appelaient les continens et avaient la prétention de vivre dans une entière verginité. Au nom d'une sorte de droit naturel et divin [...] niaient la valeur des lois établies, qu'ils qualifiaient de règles arbitraires et de prétendus lois.

This was how Ernest Renan described the Adamite sect which emerged in Rome around 165 A.D., in his chapter on the decline of Gnosticism in *Marc-Aurèle.*[1] He was describing the very first example of an Adamite sect, the one which Epiphanius condemned so strongly;[2] it was a community united by its aversion to marriage, by its total chastity, and by its desire to relive the earthly paradise. They were convinced that if Adam had persevered in his innocence, he would never have married, and so therefore in order to return to the situation before the Fall it was necessary to live in the most absolute chastity. The only exceptions to this were the cult practices in which it was obligatory to strip completely naked.[3]

It has been suggested that the name "Adamite" refers to two distinct sects, the one Gnostic and immoral to which Renan is alluding, and the other, no less ascetic and bizarre, originating around the end of the

[1] *Marc-Aurèle et la fin du monde antique* (1882), *Histoire des origines du christianisme*, VII (*Oeuvres complètes de Ernest Renan*, V [Paris: Calman-Levy, 1952]), 819–820.

[2] *Adversus Octoginta Haereses*, l. II, haeres. XXXII sive LII.

[3] Bayle, *Dictionnaire historique-critique* (Rotterdam: R. Leers, 1697), entry on "Adamites." The Encratite heresy, emerging in a context analogous to that of the early Adamites, was different and in many ways more serious; it interpreted the rise of Christianity as a return to the asexuality of our original state, and in arguing for continence in marriage, meant to reproduce the sexual purity of Adam and Eve as children in the earthly paradise. See P. F. Beatrice, "Continenza e matrimonio nel cristianesimo primitivo," in *Etica sessuale e matrimonio nel cristianesimo delle origini* (Milan: Vita e pensiero, 1976), 3–68.

fourth century.[4] Many centuries afterwards there is further news of Adamite communities. In 1418 in Prague so-called Adamite "enthusiasts" arrived from Picardy; having retreated to the isle of Luschnitz, a few months later they began to scour the Bohemian countryside in search of money, before being defeated by the valiant Ziska. Theirs is a form of adamitism quite different from that of the early centuries of the Christian era: far from being chaste, they distinguished themselves by licentiousness and by completely immoral conduct. Their community included a large number of women, who would it was hoped have as many children as possible; when a member had chosen a partner he went to see the head of the sect, who blessed the couple with the formula from Genesis 1:28, "be fruitful and multiply." In this case also, as in ancient times, nakedness was considered a sign of perfection, above all during cult ceremonies. What these Adamites meant to imitate was the original nakedness prior to Adam's fall, because, they said, "whoever makes use of clothes cannot be free."[5] And this nakedness (intended in this particular sense, unlike another I shall examine) recurs constantly in a much wider heretical context. The Picardians[6] descended from Beghard heretics or followers of the Free Spirit, thrown out of Germany and Holland after persecution. As Rosanna Guarnieri has extensively demonstrated, nakedness was an important feature of the history of the movement of the Free Spirit.[7] The various episodes she collected together describe a kind of heresy that remained more or less unchanged for two centuries (with one substantial difference, which I shall consider later). There is a "Song of Nakedness" attributed (though

---

[4] "Adamites," *Encyclopédie des sciences religieuses* (Paris: Sandoz et Fischbacher, 1877), A. Jundt.

[5] "Adamites," *Encyclopédie des sciences religieuses* (A. Jundt).

[6] Bayle also devotes an entry to them in the *Dictionnaire historique-critique*, where he explains how their "aller toujours nus c'étoit demander plus que ne faisoient les adamites de saint Epiphane, qui se contentoient de se dépouiller dans leur Assemblées."

[7] R. Guarnieri, *Il movimento del Libero Spirito*, I: *Dalle origini al secolo XVI* (Archivio Italiano per la Storia della Pietà IV). Ed. di Storia e Letteratura (Rome, 1965), 351–708. For what follows I refer to the examples used in this important essay, which has the merit of tracing a hypothetical heretical development, even if the sources are sometimes used over-confidently.

undeservedly) to Tauler; in 1296 Boniface VIII condemned an (anonymous) sect which believed that only prayer when one was completely naked was authentic, and where the nude males exchanged women among themselves, so that they passed from one to another promiscuously. Like the Gnostic Adamites, the meetings of these brothers of the Free Spirit (really ritual orgies) were called "paradises," like those of the millenarian Beghards of Cologne, who around 1325, shut in catacombs, were incited by a preacher to strip before having a banquet which was to reproduce in each of the faithful the Adamitic state, and which ended in a sexual orgy. The Adam they meant to evoke was not the "old" Adam, as in the cases above, naked because he had been stripped after the Fall, but a new Adam, naked because whole and perfect, and fully aware of the dimensions of sin to such an extent as to be completely indifferent to it. (In 1342, in Nuremberg, a Beghard declared that Adam was perfect because he possessed "indifferentia;" similarly, but in a negatively inverse sense, Tertullian and Jerome had already spoken, in the case of Adamitism in the Gnostic sense, of "moral indifference.") Since indifference leads to a sort of acquired habit of sinning, this loses its negative meaning, or to put it more simply is not perceived as such (an English Ranter in the seventeenth century will put it concisely: "there was no man could be free'd from sin, till he had acted the so-called sin *as no sin*"). For the Turlupines (another heretical sect emerging around 1370, also in Bayle), according to a criterion which seems to reflect a polemical reading of Genesis 2:25, the greatest sign of perfection is to embrace "without emotion" (and not "without shame"!) a person of the other sex, naked. Insensitivity to vice is not even understood as a virtue, because even of this we must be stripped, given that according to the Beghards virtue appertains to imperfect spirits, while the perfect soul "licentiat a se virtute."[8]

Adamite heresy suffered the most violent of attacks. There is evidence concerning a small sect of Anabaptist tendency that in Amsterdam, in Feb-

[8] "(Faux) Abandon," *Dictionnaire de Spiritualité: ascétique et mystique, doctrine et histoire* (Paris: Beauchesne, 1937). There are very useful reflections on the connection between nudity and ascetic indifference in the excellent article by J. S. Smith, "The Garments of Shame," *History of Religions* 5/2 (1966), 217–238.

ruary 1535, was publicly urged by a prophet ("Dietrich le tailleur") to throw their clothes into a fire. To the citizens who had rushed up carrying new clothes with which to cover their ignominy, the heretics replied: "the truth must go naked." And some of them fled up some trees, where they waited in vain, and naked, for "the bread to fall from the heavens."[9]

2. Two different ideas of nakedness emerge from these examples. There is an innocent nakedness which precedes sin, and another, redeemed and aware, which is the consequence of sin. Both derive from the New Testament tradition in general, and Paul's letters in particular. Paul wrote to the Colossians (3:9–10): "...seeing that you have put off the old man with his deeds; And have put on the new man, which is renewed in knowledge after the image of him that created him." Being naked is the result of the wretchedness of the Fall; so it is necessary to put on new clothes (one must "be found clothed, not naked" [2 Cor. 5:3–4]) and clothe oneself in a new life in Christ (Gal. 3:27) with a garment which is Christ himself (Romans 13:14: "But put ye on the Lord Jesus Christ, and make not provision for the flesh, to fulfil the lusts thereof.")[10] On the one hand therefore the shame of nudity, on the other the clothing of purification. To the former corresponds the "old" Adam to whom the Adamites allude, and to the latter what they define as the "new" Adam. With this difference, and it is a fundamental one, that Paul meant the latter to be clothed of Christ and in Christ, while the heretics meant him to be naked, and naked in a perfect nakedness, because aware of the immorality of sin but indifferent to it. (This is a Pelagian idea: the indifference to sin is understood according to a scheme which is perfectly analogous to the indifference of free will.[11])

---

[9] Bayle, "Adamites," *Dictionnaire historique-critique*.

[10] To this flesh/spirit old man/new man dichotomy, correspond in Paul's theology the two symbolic figures of Adam and Christ; see C. K. Barrett, "The Significance of the Adam-Christ Typology for the Resurrection of the Dead," in *Résurrection du Christ et des chrétiens (1 Cor 15)* (Rome, 1985), 99–126.

[11] The indifference of Adam will be a recurring theme in Augustinian theology of the XVII century, when anti-Molinism will lead to a return to the anti-Pelagian ideas in Augustine's thought. Authors like Jansen and Malebranche have continuous recourse to Adam's "indifference to equilibrium" before sin (and in contrast to this the imbalance, his tendency to do evil after his guilt).

Bayle correctly observes that it is the scriptural principle of the coming of the new Adam that renders the Adamite heresy much more meaningfully and conspicuously present in Christianity than in paganism. He attributes the somewhat irregular behavior of the Turlupines, Picardians, Beghards and Anabaptists to the "infinite combinations" of "imagination, passions and animal spirits."[12] But there is more to it than this: there is the working out both of a conceptual framework useful to legitimize a deviation, and at the same time of a heresy that intends to oppose the Pauline hypothesis of redemption, leading it towards an excess that risks unhinging the very bases of Christian dogma.

In a similar way to the interpretation that we may (with reservations) define as "Gnostic," the clothing in Christ is read by the modern Adamites as a stage which is still impure, where the soul of the faithful is still bound to the materiality of the body. But unlike Paul, thinking of faith in Christ as necessary for salvation, as a new garment with which to cover oneself to avoid falling back into the sin of the flesh; and unlike Origen or Gregory of Nyssa, for whom the covering in flesh is an effect of the mercy intended to help us to return freely to God, because it is our animal condition alone that can lead us to hate sin and convert ourselves;[13] the Adamite heresy practices nakedness in the conviction that only by reaching total insensitivity to its ignominy, only through the most absolute immorality and consequent indifference to it, will it be possible to follow the true spiritual path and feel inside oneself the deepest faith—because naked.

3. In the entry in the *Dictionnaire* devoted to the Turlupines, Bayle brings out the connections to be made between the various forms of Adamitism (and more generally the sects of a libertine tendency), and their seventeenth-century expression. "Voilà l'écueil de toutes les Sectes qui se veulent distinguer par les Paradoxes de Morale," he writes:

---

[12] "Turlupines," *Dictionnaire.*

[13] See J. Daniélou, "*Les tuniques de peau chez Grégoire de Nysse,*" in *Glaube, Geist, Geschichte. Festschrift für Ernst Benz* (Leiden: E. J. Brill, 1967), 355–367.

> aprofondissez les visions des Illuminez et de Quiétistes &c., vous verrez que si quelque chose est capable de les démasquer, c'est la relation au plaisir vénérien; [...] c'est par là que l'ennemi donne l'assaut; c'est un ver qui ne meurt pas, et un feu qui ne s'éteint point.

His is a decidedly critical reading, influenced by the moralistic position of orthodoxy; in addition, it brings out the continuity between Adamite mysticism and its quietistic expression of the seventeenth century, according to a kind of interpretation typical of this period. I would like to demonstrate two things. First, that which links seventeenth-century heresy to the various forms of Adamitism occurring in previous centuries is a tradition established by the seventeenth-century interpreters themselves, representatives of the violent anti-mystical reaction which took place over the last decades (where anti-mysticism represents in reality a destabilizing factor of the main theological distinctions which run through the period). Second, this interpretation means that the Adamite conception of nakedness—which we have seen in opposition to that of Paul and also to Gnosticism—reaches, in the course of the seventeenth century, its most extreme conclusions.

4. In Cologne in 1640 a *Theologia mystica clavis* was published, a real dictionary of mystical spirituality.[14] The "clavis" offered a useful anthology of this spirituality—by and large still unknown, but in which elements of profound originality can already be discerned[15]—composed exclusively of the definitions given of each lemma by the main mystical authorities. For the entry *nuditas* the reader is referred to *fides nuda*; and here the author at once quotes—and quotes once only—a passage from the *Divine Institutions* attributed incorrectly to the German mystic, Tauler.[16] The eighth chapter of the *Institutions* explained:

---

[14] *Theologia mystica clavis, elucidarium onomasticon vocabulorum et loquutionum obscurarum, quibus Doctores Mystici, tum veteres, tum recentiores utuntur ad proprium suae Disciplinae sensum paucis manifestum*, ex Officina Gualteriana, Coloniae Agrippinae 1640.

[15] The author was a Jesuit, M. Saundt (Sandaeus), who in the brief preface recognizes the need for a more exact knowledge of mystical heresy's vocabulary, while naturally keeping his distance from it.

[16] See J. Beaude, *La mystique* (Paris: Les Editions du Cerf–Fides, 1990).

> Vere praeclara res est *Fides nuda. Nuda*, inquam, non quae bonis operibus destituta sit; sed quae nihil scire, nihil sensibilis consolationis experiri appetat. Gaudere deberent Deo militantes, quod saltem *Nudam* ac puram *Fidem* absque omni cognitione habere possent. Nam quo *Fides* purior, semplicior, nudior est eo vel centuplo laudabilior, nobilior, magisque meritoria est.

This idea of nakedness should now be compared to that of some mystical French texts of the seventeenth century:

a) in his *Entretiens spirituels*, François de Sales defines the "confiance" and "l'abandonnement" that the faithful must offer to God, explaining that to obtain the total abandon of oneself two virtues were needed, one of which was the aim or purpose of the other: "*se dépouiller pour s'abandonner.*" Further on, the "vrai dépouillement" is described in words that closely recall those attributed to Tauler.

b) the Jesuit Louis Lallemant writes a *Doctrine spirituelle* in which he affirms that we tend to remain bound to affections, projects, desires, and hopes of which we do not wish to be *stripped* so as not to find ourselves in that "détachement d'esprit" which is the only way to be totally possessed of God.

c) in 1644 Pierre de Bérulle, Oratorian, devotes a chapter of his *Oeuvres de piété* to the subject of "nudité intérieure," where he explains how only through "le dénuement et dépouillement ou apprauvissement de notre être" is it possible for us to participate in the infinite richness of God; God himself is naked, and his nakedness "tend à nous dénuer si profondement de nous mêmes et si intimement" to make our being naked a "pure ability" of being divine.[17]

d) in his comment on the *Song of Songs*, Jeanne-Marie Guyon several times alludes to the idea of "naked faith," and of a spiritual charity that must reach the stage of "ultimate nakedness."[18]

---

[17] *Oeuvres de piété* CL, in *Les oeuvres de l'éminentissime... Cardinal de Bérulle* (Paris: A. Estienne, 1644).

[18] "Foi nue" is also the title of one of the entries of the *Justifications* of Guyon, a mystical anthology very similar to that of Saundt (and the analogy between the two texts is an eloquent testimony to the non-univocal nature of the theological taking of sides which distinguishes this period).

5. These examples would seem to limit themselves to indicating a *spiritual* re-elaboration of the subject of Adamite nakedness, formulated in such terms as to avoid any kind of condemnation—because they are absolutely ascetic, without any immoral connotations whatsoever. And yet the idea of nakedness suggested by the mystics was seen as incredibly scandalous and heretical by their contemporaries. The scandal lay mainly in the continuity of the new mysticism with respect to the heresies of previous centuries, a continuity shown simply by starting from the idea of stripping, of nakedness.

In 1632 Archange Ripaut, a Capuchin friar, wrote a violent polemical work, the *Abomination des abominations*;[19] the targets of the invective are those heretics whom the author defines as the "*Illuminati* of France" and "new Adamites." The first part of the book is entirely devoted to illustrating the genealogy that has led to this latest and most serious form of deviation; the Adamites, so strongly opposed by Epiphanius and Augustine, succeeded to the Cainites and the Manicheans; then there were Waldensians, Picardians, Beghards, and Anabaptists. But the abomination represented by these various sects is as nothing compared to the "abomination of abominations," that of the Spanish "Illuminati," the followers of Molinos, now also settled in France. Ripaut writes that their fault is that through crafty dissimulation they manage to make abject actions appear virtuous:

> en faisant des attouchements lascifs, et actes deshonnêtes avec les femmes ou filles de leur secte, il n'y a point de peché, mais plutôt vertu et piété: promettant pour cela mérite et couronne, pour user de leur termes, et vous faire voir le centre et la fin dernière de toutes ces spiritualités sublimes et raffinées. Voilà les proposition autant impies qu'impudiques que l'esprit de ténèbres a mis au coeur et en la langue de ses prétendus Illuminéz.[20]

The result of such deviations, of this form of false and extremely dangerous spirituality, is that of a faith "de-raisonnable et de-naturée,"

---

[19] *Abomination des abominations des fausses dévotions de ce tems divisées en trois... ou se voit par antithèse du Ier livre... la diabolique naissance... de l'âme en la fausse dévotion... Seconde partie contenant les plus hauts point [sic] de la théologie mystique, avec un traité... de la présence de Dieu...* (Paris: C. Cramoisy, 1632).

[20] Ripaut, *Abomination*, 17 ff.

and of an "indulgence plenière à tout ce que désire le corps, sous prétexte d'une parfaite paix d'esprit."[21]

In England, a few years after Ripaut's polemical publication, pamphlets appeared which denounced the existence of a new sect of Adamites.[22] Ripaut seems not to know of them, and in fact the importance of his contribution lies in the continuity he establishes between the fanaticism of the "Illuminati" and the Adamite heresies of the previous centuries. This continuity will become a polemical topos of the antimystical literature of the last decade of the century, when after Pope Innocent XI condemns Molinos' doctrine, quietism is by now the main protagonist of theological debate, because unanimously recognized as the most evidently heretical religious expression of the age.[23]

---

[21] Ripaut, *Abomination*, 110 and 214.

[22] *The Adamite Sermon; containing their manner of preaching, expounding and prophesying... also a dialogue between an Adamite and a Brownist, concerning their religion &c.*, "printed from Francis Coules in the year 1641;" *A new sect of religion descried, called Adamites, deriving their religion from our father Adam, wherein they hold themselves to be blamelesse at the last day, though they sinne never so egregiously, for they challenge salvation, as their due, from the innocence of the second Adam...* by Samoth Yarb, "batchelor in Arts, printed anno 1643." I have not been able to consult *A nest of serpents discovered, or a knot of old heretiques revived, called the Adamites. Wherein their originall, increase and severall ridiculous tenets are plainly layd open*, published in London in 1641. No research has yet been done on the echoes in France of this form of English Adamitism.

[23] The papal condemnation dates from 1687; a great many antimystical publications date from this year, in which reference to the Adamite and Beghard origins of the Quietist heresy seems to be obligatory. See for example, P. Segneri, *Le quiétiste ou les illusions dela nouvelle oraison de quiétude* (Paris, 1687), 145 and 158. P. Nicole, *Réfutation des principales erreurs des Quiétistes* (Paris: G. Desprez, 1695), 4, 19, 23–24; J. B. Bossuet, *Instruction sur les état d'oraison* (Paris: J. Anisson, 1697), livre X; L. G. de Cordemoy, *Les désirs du ciel ou les témoignages de l'Ecriture Sainte contre le pur amour des nouveaux mystiques* (Paris: E. Couterot, 1698); J. Ameline, *Traité de l'amour du souverain bien, qui donne le véritable caractère de l'amour de Dieu, opposé aux fausses idées de ceux qui ne s'eloignent pas assez des erreurs de Molinos et de ces disciples* (Liège: H. Hoyoux, 1699). On Molinos and the Spanish "illuminati" see M. Menendèz y Pelayo, *Historia de los heterodosos espanoles* (Madrid: Libreria catòlica de San José, 1880–1881), Vol. II. 540–546. More generally, for the Jesuits' reaction to Molinos and the *alumbrados*, see H. Heppe, *Geschichte der Mystik in der katholischen Kirche* (Berlin: W. Hertz, 1875).

6. In the eyes of orthodoxy, the quietist idea of stripping and of spiritual nakedness before God thus ends up being considered "Adamite," and profoundly immoral. The association is more in evidence in the last years of the century, but it is preceded by invectives whose target is not just mystical Adamitism, as in the case of Ripaut, but also another enemy, less easily definable but just as dangerous: libertinism, whose licentious behavior presents the same features as the doctrine that defends nakedness, insofar as it purports to imitate the state of innocence (or of redemption) of the first man. This is presumably the case with the Jesuit René de Ceriziers; his *Le philosophe français* contains a section called *Contre les Apathiques ou Insensibles*,[24] within the context of a rehabilitation of the human passions, in opposition to the severe condemnation of them which the Stoic philosophers had formulated. Here the stoic error is analyzed for its modern repercussions, among which the most important are identified as the Adamite sects.[25] To whom is Ceriziers referring? He is of course aware of the Gnostic heresy and its following among the Bohemian heretics, and he may also have been aware of the Adamite meetings that were causing such a scandal in London at the time. It is however possible that, borrowing the term "Adamite" from this same tradition, but extending it to a generalized immorality, the Jesuit was referring to libertinism: it was characteristic not only of the sects of previous centuries, but also of the cultural movement that was so widespread in those years, and that was also based on the practice of a hedonistic liberation of the instincts, primarily sexual.[26] The target of Ceriziers' polemic may be Pierre Charron, who in *De la sagesse*

[24] *Le philosophe français* (Paris: A. de Sommaville/A. Courbé, 1644), 173 ff.

[25] Ceriziers will return to the subject of the Adamites in another work, *Les consolations de la philosophie et de la théologie* (Rouen: J. Viret/J. Bonsongne/C. Malassis, 1646), fifth edition (the first part consists in the translation of Boethius' *De Consolatione philosophiae*).

[26] On the "libertine" adamitism of Beghards and Turlupines see G. Schneider, *Der Libertin. Zur Geistes des Burgertums im 16, und 17 Jahrhundert* (Stuttgart: J. B. Metzeler, 1970). See also H. Busson, *Le rationalisme dans la littérature française de la Renaissance (1533–1601)* (Paris: Vrin, 1957), 296–317: J. C. Margolin, "Libertins, libertinisme et 'libertinage' au XVIe siècle," in *Aspects du libertinisme au XVIe siècle* (Paris: Vrin, 1974), 1–33, where the "lasting fortune" of the idea of libertinism in the sense of "a carnis libertate" (and therefore, of liberty for the carnal instincts also), is insisted upon.

(returning to a theme of Montaigne[27]) had demonstrated the affinity between men and beasts. He started with the remarkable natural defenses shown by those "qui n'ont encore su que c'est que vêtements," i.e. cannibals;[28] still more scandalously, he had gone out of his way to praise nakedness, in the sense that "nature ne nous a point appris y avoir des parties honteuses, c'est nous mêmes qui par notre faute nous nous les disons,"[29] and that "le vêtir n'est point originel ny naturel, ny nécessaire à l'homme, mais artificiel, inventé & usurpé par luy seul au monde."[30]

More than an invective directed implicitly at the immorality of the libertines, Ceriziers' intervention seems to me a demonstration of how the need to condemn the widespread licentiousness of the day leads seventeenth-century orthodoxy to conflate and confuse the various forms of transgression. Given the emphasis that both lay (scandalously) on nakedness, mystics and libertines are thrown together under the generic label of "Adamites."[31] In support of this association it is interesting to note how, restating the argument that had predominated among the earliest opponents of ancient Adamitism, to Ceriziers it is the eccessive religious and moral indifference consequent upon licentious behaviour that is the most serious philosophical implication of a defense of naked-

[27] *Essais* I, XXXVI.

[28] J. Elsevier, *De la sagesse*, Leiden n.d. (the edition follows "La vraye copie de Bordeaux"), I.I, ch. VIII.

[29] *De la sagesse*, ch. VXIV.

[30] *De la sagesse*, I, III, ch. XL. Against Charron's positions F. Garasse had already come out categorically (*La somme théologique* (Paris: S. Chappelet, 1624), I. II, sect. VI, 267–271). In this sense, Ceriziers' reference to the Adamites constitutes a confirmation of the connection that has been suggested between seventeenth-century libertinism and some of the heretical positions of the previous century: see A. Tenenti, "Libertinisme et hérésie milieu du 16e siècle, début du 17e siècle," in *Hérésies et sociétés dans l'Europe pré-industrielle 11e–18e siècles* (Paris and The Hague: Colloque de Royaumont, Mouton & Co, 1968), 303–321 (already in *Annales, Economies Sociétés Civilisation* 18 [1963], 1–19).

[31] The mystic Fénelon devotes a few pages to the "problem" of the libertines, using violent expressions of condemnation and crying out against the scandal (see "Sur le libertinage," in *Lettres et opuscules spirituels* [Paris: Pléiade-Gallimard, 1983], 739–744); this may be read as an attempt to wriggle out of accusations of quietistic immorality.

ness. Incidentally, the Jesuit associates this licentiousness with the error of Stoic apathy: with their attitude of indifference, the Adamites preached an apathy that was in reality only superficial, and behind which violence and furious passions raged.[32]

7. The superimposing of one enemy on another, and mistaking one for another, is a feature of an age torn by heated and complex debates. Above all in the last few decades of the century, these debates were witness to an orthodoxy in crisis, defined by ever weaker identities, in opposition to a heresy still firmly based in its mystical roots. What Henri Bremond defined as "conquête mystique" is at its peak in this period, and even in a rigorously antimystical environment such as that of the Jesuits there will be in the course of the seventeenth century surprising new forms of interest in the spirituality of the mystics.[33] So it is not surprising that in 1682, forty years after Ceriziers' invective, a booklet entitled *L'Adamite, ou le Jésuite insensible*[34] was published in Cologne. It

[32] The aversion to indifference is a recurring feature of seventeenth-century Jesuit treatises: Nicolas Caussin also devotes a short paragraph to the rejection of "philosophes indifférens" in the course of a description of "l'Empire de la raison sur les passions": see *La Cour sainte* (Rouen: J. et D. Berthelm, 1655) (Ist. ed. 1624), Vol. I/III: *De l'Empire de la raison sur les passions*. The paragraph "Contre les philosophes indifférens, qui disent qu'il ne faut rien aymer" is included in the dissection of the first passion, love (*De l'Empire*, 291–294). The implicit allusion would again seem to be to the libertines; this has been argued convincingly by L. Eymard d'Angers in "Sénèque et le stoicisme dans la *Cour sainte* du jésuite Nicolas Caussin (1583–1651)," *Revue des sciences religieuses* 28/3 (1954), 258–285 (in particular 263); see also V. Kapp, "La Théologie des realités terrestres dans la *Cour Sainte* de N. Caussin," in *Les Jésuites parmi les hommes aux XVIe et XVIIe siècles* (Actes du Colloque de Clermont–Ferrand, 1987.)

[33] In addition to vols. II–IV, VI–VII and IX of the *Histoire littéraire du sentiment religieux en France* by H. Bremond, see the fine article by Michel de Certeau, "Crises sociale et réformisme spirituel au début du XVIIe siècle: une 'Nouvelle spiritualité' chez les Jésuites français," *Revue d'ascétique et de mystique* 41/3 (1965), 339–386.

[34] *L'Adamite, ou le Jésuite insensible. Nouvelle doctrine*, chez Louis le Sincère (Cologne, 1682); the work was republished the following year. The publisher Sincère was quoted as "imprimeur imaginaire" (i.e. as a fictitious name, useful for the publication of scandalous books, potential candidates for banning) by G. Brunet, *Imprimeurs imaginaires et libraires supposés* (New York: Burt Franklin, 1964; a reprint of the Paris 1866 edition), 182.

tells of a very serious scandal that occurred in a convent in Rheims, where a Jesuit father (the anonymous writer refers to the religious order as "amphibious") corrupted a number of novices, making them strip naked and subjecting some of them to sexual abuse under the pretext that nakedness practiced without shame was the way to lead us back to the condition of innocence in which Adam lived before sin, and arguing that in this way he was professing Quietist doctrine. Of this doctrine—which consists of changing the name of every body part in order to become insensitive to the ideas that these names evoke—the differences are emphasized with respect to ancient forms of Adamitism (certainly not in order to dilute the heretical element in contemporary Adamitism, but rather if anything to exalt its own uniqueness). We read in fact that we are not dealing "de cette secte d'anabaptistes qui croyaient faire témoignage d'un degré élevé de perfection en imitant la nudité d'Adam," nor with the

> secte d'anciens hérétiques qui imitaient la nudité dans laquelle vécurent nos premiers parents pendant l'état d'innocence, et condamnaient le mariage par la raison qu'Adam ne connut Eve qu'après le péché et après sa sortie du Paradis.[35]

In spite of this, we are dealing with a doctrine that is, in many significant ways, comparable to that of the "true" Adamites. Indifference is one of the principal parallels: in the maxims by which the "insensitive Jesuit" outlines his new religious practice for the indoctrination of innocent young girls, the idea that modesty or shame about nakedness is merely the fruit of our first disobedience, recurs repeatedly; and indeed, the more we can free ourselves from this modesty the nearer we approach perfection, "la honte faisant toute l'imperfection que nous ayons à vaincre." And the state of perfection, i.e. the return to "primitive innocence," is reached not only when a person begins to forget he/she is naked and no longer bothers to notice if he/she who is in the vicinity blushes over the nakedness (a definition that indirectly evokes

---

[35] See the brief introduction to *L'Adamite* and that of the republication of the text in Cologne in 1712 by Pierre de Marteau (again a fictitious name, used by various publishers for pamphlets of anecdotes or erotic content).

Gen. 2:25); it is also reached when the subject attains an absolute indifference to surrounding people in general.

8. Wicked Father Roche had every right to be called an Adamite and Quietist by contemporaries: the state of indifference that he describes to the novices as the goal to aim at recalls the indifference of the Adamites, and also that of the "new Adamites," the "saincte indifférence" of François de Sales and of Fénelon. Of the former (that refers to the scandalous opinions on marriage of "quelques hérétiques de notre âge")[36] we have a definition of abandonment to God, of stripping within the exegesis of Col. 3:9–10: the act of reclothing here means a "petie réculement [...] qui ne se fait que pour mieux sauter et s'élancer en Dieu par un acte d'amour et de confiance," a temporary condition, while awaiting the definitive, abandoned spiritual nakedness. On the other hand between 1695 and 1697, in defense of Jeanne-Marie Guyon (who was on trial at the time), Fénelon produced an unpublished work *Le Gnostique de saint Clement d'Alexandrie*, where he explains, paraphrasing the seventh chapter of Clemente's *Stromata*, that "La gnose est un état d'impassibilité," that "cet état produit l'apathie," and that apathy in its turn is the condition "où il n'y a plus ni vertus à exercer, ni tentations à vaincre."[37] Since the one shows the fundamental importance attributed to the state of spiritual nakedness by modern mysticism, and the other the attention paid to the Gnostic tradition by the Quietists, these

---

[36] See François de Sales, *Introduction à la Vie dévote*, XXXIX (in *Oeuvres* [Paris: Pléiade/Gallimard, 1969], 242): the reflection (again probably to be read in an anti-libertine sense) is made in the margin to the marriage choice of Onan described in Gen 38:9.

[37] *Le Gnostique de Saint Clément d'Alexandrie*, introduction by P. Dudon (Paris: Beauchesne, 1930), 191 ff. The "saincte indifférence" of the mystics, who are going back to a few of the ideas of Augustine's anti-Pelagian polemic and of his theology of grace, imply the idea by which, since all the strength of the perfection of the will is directed towards God, such a will is held in suspense ("in equilibrium"), i.e. indifferent to everything while waiting to be determined by God, whose will constitutes the only *reason* for every choice or particular inclination (see the very effective description offered by Jean-Joseph Surin, *Questions importantes à la vie spirituelle sur l'amour de Dieu* (1630), cit. in M. Bergamo, *La Scienza dei santi. Studi sul misticismo del Seicento* [Firenze: Sansoni, 1984], 40).

two witnesses offer a useful tool for understanding in what sense in the seventeenth century Quietism can be interpreted as a continuation of the Adamite heresy.

9. What I have described so far is a reception history, one which consists in part in a term becoming the definition for various attitudes and issues. This is what happens in the course of the seventeenth century, when the physical nakedness of the Gnostic Adamites and of some modern heretical sects is understood as the equivalent to the spiritual nakedness of the Quietist mystics. What gives legitimacy to an association of this kind is a purely theoretical affinity, given that not unlike the Adamite heresy, Quietism understands the reclothing of the new Adam as a phase that only precedes authentic union with God (a "reculer pour mieux sauter," according to François de Sales, or a sort of regression that prepares the final, definitive progress). Nakedness is imagined as an authentic spiritual condition of the faithful, who have arrived at the state of perfection because they are now utterly convinced of the power of divine grace and of the need to abandon oneself to it entirely. But this theoretical affinity is a consequence of a similar hypothesis concerning redemption, understood not as a hope for a definitive work of salvation through the clothing of the shame of guilt, but as a lasting and definitive state of nakedness that will require no further assistance from grace.

If therefore in the seventeenth century there is a substantial overlapping of the "obscene" and "spiritual" meaning of nakedness, which results in the assimilation of the "western" (Christian) idea with the mystical one,[38] by which nakedness becomes the permanent and final condition of a process of ascesis; and if such a change of meaning can help us to a greater understanding of the history of quietism and that vitally important chapter of seventeenth theology which is antimysticism, it is also true that the different reception of the theme suggested by Gen 2:25—the different ways in which the category "Adamite" is used within it—indicates a specific exegetical line. Truth to tell, it is "specific" in an

[38] See the entry "Nudité" in both the *Dictionnaire de la Bible* (Paris: Letouzey et Ané, 1907) and the *Dictionnaire de spiritualité*, cited above.

extremely imprecise way, but revealing of a moment in which recourse to Scriptural themes is more instrumental than ever for the discussion of the urgent theological questions of the time—in this particular case, the problem of a spirituality which was spreading with a powerful new language, and that dangerously seemed to suggest that perfection is attainable in this life.

"Geographia Sacra": The Placing of Paradise in Late Seventeenth-Century French Theology

Franco Motta

> Tertullian argues correctly in the *Adversus Praxeam*, that everything that comes before is true, and everything that comes afterwards is false. It is indeed inevitable that truth precedes the lie, since of course the latter is the corruption of the truth. [...] In its turn, the antiquity of Christian doctrine cannot be better proved than by showing that all that is most ancient in the pagan peoples is borrowed—or a version taken—from our Scriptures.[1]

With these words Samuel Bochart, a Caen minister and important figure in the French reformed church, opens his *Phaleg, seu de dispersione gentium* (1646). Bochart was one of the most knowledgeable scholars of the *grand siècle*, repository of that philological culture taught in the Protestant schools of northern Europe that Richard Simon harshly criticized as *hébraisants*—excellent as far as the study of the grammar of Semitic languages went, but poor in their knowledge of Christian sources.[2]

---

[1] "Tertullianus adversus Praxeam recte asserit *id esse verum quodcunque primum, id esse adulterum quodcunque posterius*. Necesse enim est ut veritas sit prior mendacio, cum mendacium nihil alid sit quam corruptio veritatis. [...] Haec porro doctrinae antiquitas non aliunde melius potest adstrui, quam si doceamus in gentibus quicquid fuit antiquissimum, id ex Scripturis nostris aut petitum esse aut detortum." (Italics in the text) *Phaleg, seu de dispersione gentium*, column 2, here in the edition of 1707, *Samuelis Bocharti Geographia Sacra, seu Phaleg et Canaan, cui accedunt variae dissertationes philologicae, geographicae, theologicae, etc. antehac ineditae: ut et tabulae geographicae et indices, longe quam antea luculentiores et locupletiores. Editio quarta prioribus multo correctior, et splendidior*. Procuravit Petrus de Villemandy, Lugduni Batavorum, apud Cornelium Boutesteyn, et Jordanum Luchtmans; Trajecti ad Rhenum, apud Guillielmum vande Water (henceforth, GS).

[2] In the absence of recent biographies of Bochart (1599–1667), see the entry by H. Diez in A. Baudrillart (dir.), *Dictionnaire d'histoire et de géographie ecclesiastiques*, Paris-VI, Letouzey et Ané, IX, 1937, 313–14. More recently see F. Laplanche, *L'Écriture, le sacré et l'histoire. Érudits et politiques protestants devant la Bible en France au XVII siècle* (Amsterdam, Maarsen, APA: Holland University Press, 1986), 250–54. On Protestant Semitic studies, see S. Kessler-Merguich, *Les hébraïsants chrétiens*, in J.-R. Armogathe (dir.), *Le Grand siècle et la Bible* (Paris: Beauchesne, 1984), 83–95.

Simon was unsympathetic to Bochart's epistemology, despite its prodigious demonstration of erudition and subtlety, because in it the overlapping of conjectures risks overwhelming the overall framework:

> ...he has clarified a large number of biblical passages; but since he is too diffuse, and seems to assume the role of wise or judicious or erudite scholar, a compendium of these two works [the *Phaleg* and the 1663 *Hierozoicon*] is to be desired which retains what may be useful to the understanding of the Holy books.[3]

If in 1707 a late editor of the *Phaleg* finds himself having to extricate the author from the charge of being a *merus grammatista*,[4] Simon's authority evidently ends up seriously compromising the reception of the book in the decades following its publication. The point is that Bochart's probable goal is not to create an instrument for the consultation of the Scriptures, but rather an apology for Christianity on a grand scale, based on linguistics, ancient history and geography. The subject would become a classic in learned writing in the second half of the seventeenth century: the origins of man, the antiquity of the world, and the remote mythologies of the pagans. The problem was the struggle against libertinism which, after oriental chronologies spread throughout Europe, attacked the biblical foundations of biological and cultural monogenism.[5]

---

[3] *Historie critique du Vieux Testament, par le P. Richard Simon, prêtre de la Congregation de l'Oratoire,* V ed. (Rotterdam: Reinier Leers, 1685), 481: "Bochart a aussi composé deux grands ouvrages sous le nom de Phaleg, et De animalibus Scripturae Sacrae, où il a expliqué un grand nombre de passages de la Bible: mais comme cet auteur est beaucoup étendu, et qu'il semble avoir affecté de paroitre plutot sçavant et homme d'erudition, que judicieux, il seroit à desirer qu'on abregeat ces deux ouvrages, en retenant ce qui peut être utile pour l'intelligence des livres sacrés." A contextualizing, certainly limiting, discussion of Bochart's work in the context of the historical and geographical literature in support of the Bible is found in R. Fabris, "Strumenti e sussidi per lo studio della Bibbia nei secoli XV–XVII," in Fabris, ed., *La Bibbia nell'epoca moderna e contemporanea* (Bologna: EDB, 1992), 47–73, 64.

[4] GS, *Praefatio*, a4r.

[5] The standard reference work on this subject is of course P. Rossi, *The Dark Abyss of Time: History of the Earth and History of Nations from Hooke to Vico*, trans. Lydia G. Cochrane (Chicago: University of Chicago Press, 1984). On Bochart in particular, see 183 ff.

> Every time antiquity is spoken of at length, [the pagans] fall into ridiculous fables. Some say they were born of oaks or stones, others of mushrooms, cicadas, ants or the teeth of dragons. So how can information on the origins of other peoples, from those who spread such lies about themselves, be believed? The only thing to do is to fall back on Scripture, our anchor, that not only teaches that all men have been generated by one seed, i.e., Adam's at the time of the Creation and that of Noah and his three sons after the Flood, but also lists Noah's grandchildren, and which peoples go back to which one of them. And in this way, from a chapter of Moses properly interpreted, many more certain things can be understood on the origins of populations than from all that has survived of the most ancient pagans' teachings put together.[6]

Thus we are dealing with a genealogical reconstruction on a grand scale, leading a multiplicity of traditions back to the single genetic line of Adam. What goes first, then, is true, and everything that comes afterwards, where it differs, can only be a corruption of it. The truth, inasmuch as it is a primordial condition of being, is expressed in the corporeal realization, in the physical existence, of the characters in Genesis, and the only link between the contemporary and the first-born, the proof of that existence, is of a linguistic nature: the names are the connection between the Babel of races and cultures and its single root of divine origin. The problem lies in tracing the fragments and distortions of the names listed by Moses among the infinite number of names of the ancient peoples, an effort made all the more difficult, if possible,

---

[6] "Proinde quoties de rebus vetustis sermonem instituunt ad fabulas devolvuntur. Atque alii se ex quercubus aut lapidibus, alii ex fungis, alii ex cicadis, alii ex formicis, alii ex draconis dentibus se fabulantur ortos. Quis porro gentium aliarum incunabula et primordia edoceri posse se putet ab iis, qui de propria origine talia mentiuntur? Itaque hoc restat unicum, ut ad sacram anchoram, hoc est, ad Scripturam confugiamus. Quae non solum in genere docet omnes homines ex uno semine esse editos, nempe ex Adamo in Creatione et post Diluvium ex Noa et tribus filiis, sed et recenset nepotes Noae, et qui populi ex singulis ortum duxerint. Ita ex uno capite Mosis, si modo recte intelligatur, multo plura et certiora possint erui de populorum originibus, quam ex omnibus, quotquot supersunt, vetustissimarum gentium monimentis." GS, *in quatuor libros Phaleg praefatio*, 37.

by Greek historiography, through which most ethnographic knowledge had been transmitted. This historiography, believing Hebrew vocabulary to be crude, had deformed it to such an extent that it was not easily recognizable. Bochart wrote: "In this work we are trying to bring light to such darkness, keeping the true part of what the ancients said, and confirming it with new evidence, and in part rejecting what seems to us mistaken."[7]

The central point at issue clearly lies in the interpretative criteria: the decoding of a vast series of words, extraordinary both in quantity and variety, is the key to the progressive reduction of linguistic chaos, and therefore also of the ethnic chaos which is a substratum of it, to a clear and orderly biblical matrix. It is an achievement that the author carries out with the help of a specific methodology. First, a macro-analysis *ex sono vocis* is made possible by the assumption of the conservation of the names, however modified in the transition from one language to another, at the level of the root. The second and third stages of the research inquire into the *vocum origines*, the etymologies, and the *vocum significationes*, so that the Perizziti owe their surnames to the villages they live in, the Sinei to the muddy terrain on which they settled, the Gergesei to clay, and so forth. Further instruments are (in order) the resolution of synonyms, ethnographical summaries, naturalistic descriptions, the order the people are mentioned and their neighborhood, the territories Moses assigned to each of them, and the names of the cities, the mountains and the rivers.[8]

The first three stages of the method clearly determine the shape of the entire work, offering to the scholar the means to set up the linguistic links to lead the individual anomalies back to the common source:

---

[7] "Inde factum, ut Veteres in tam diversa abierint. Aliter enim haec nomina Josephus interpretatur, aliter Africanus, quos sequuntur plerique Patres, aliter Chaldaei paraphrastae, aliter Arabs interpres Lutetiae nuper editus, aliter denique Gorjonides et auctor libri Juchasim. [...] Nos in hoc opere conati sumus his tenebris lucem inferre, partim ea tuendo novaque argumentorum accessione firmando quae a veteribus recte dicta sunt, partim etiam ea oppugnando in quibus videntur errasse" (GS).

[8] GS, 38–42.

in the passage from the phonetic level (*vocis sonus*), to the etymological (*vocum origines*), to the semantic (*vocum significationes*), a progressive reification of the word seems to occur, thanks to which the exact and systematic attribution of meaning is made possible. Only later do the contributions of history, geography and ethnology come into play; their role is to support the linguistic analysis with its evidence, useful for the solution of such knotty problems as the presence of synonyms. Linguistics is therefore capable of "jumping over" history, of tracing the direct relation that, buried in the debris of the experience of human groups, still lives and speaks to us, capable of revealing the divine ancestry of the names to those who are able to decode them. Bochart was still operating within an analogical universe laden with meaning, in that "pre-classical" episteme explored by Foucault which survived until the second half of the seventeenth century, in which the link between signifying and signified was immediate, and the word and the thing both inserted in a continuous unit that guaranteed the correspondence of forms and concepts:

> Moses eloquently conveys [wrote Bochart's disciple and biographer, in his presentation of the massive treatise of biblical zoology, *Hierozoicon*], the way pack animals, beasts, reptiles, fish, enormous cetaceans, the birds and all living beings were created by God, and consequently [Bochart] was able to deal generically with all of them, and to explain their specific natures: above all the names, which are said to have been given by Adam, allowed him to carry out a careful examination of many of them, to check whether they conformed to [*convenientiam haberent*] the first primogenial original language, and the faculties assigned to them by nature; for example, the *camelus* of the Latini, and the *Kàmelos* of the Greeks, lead us spontaneously to the Hebrew *gamal* [...]; as far as the reason for the name is concerned, it is very obvious, since *gamal* means to give back, and it would seem that the camel has a better memory for offenses than any other animal, so much so that historians who have dealt with it call it *mnesíkakon*.[9]

---

[9] "Ex multiplici animalium mentione, quam fecit Moses, similiter coaluit, et longe plura etiam commemoranda fuerunt, quia nonnulla eorum nomina diversis fuerunt attributa speciebu, quas opus fuit attente considerare, ut ex earum proprietatibus agnoscerentur eae, quibus praecipue convenirent. Praeterea Moses disertis verbis declarat jumenta, feras, reptilia, pisces, immania cete, aveque et omnia viventia a Deo condita

Very much in evidence once again is the centrality of interpretation, understood as an act of removing the superficial strata of oral transmission (the differences in pronunciation) and written transmission (the adaptation of classical authors) that impede access to the expressive nucleus of the word. This expressive nucleus can be trusted to the extent that it fits into the probatory category of chronological precedence. The principle of *post quod, ergo propter quod* reigns unchallenged in Bochart's logical construction; he declares programmatically that he will not abandon the opinion of an ancient author unless he is contradicted by an author more ancient still. The historical-hermeneutic demonstration, in the context of late seventeenth-century apologetics, still enjoys a status of certainty equal to that of rational, Cartesian demonstration; this is the epistemological premise that justifies the massive labors on the ancestry of peoples, addressed to the production of a solid defense of religion against the attacks of the sceptics and followers of Spinoza. The equating of history with truth is among the first victims of the Enlightenment critique of Christianity, but its demonstrative force, and the fascination that emanates from it, evidently enjoy a good deal of credit until well after the middle of the century.[10] In Bochart's universe, a universe that makes sense, what follows descends necessarily from

---

fuisse, et consequenter de illis omnibus amplam de illis saltem generaliter agendi, et illorum peculiares dotes explicandi habuit occasionem: praesertim nomina, quae ipsis dicuntur fuisse ab Adamo imposita, fecerunt ut plurimorum nomina excuteret ad videndum an quamdam cum lingua primigenia, et inditis a natura facultatibus convenientiam haberent: verbi gratia, *camelus* Latinorum, et Graecorum Kàmelos ad *gamal* nos sponte deducit [...]: ad rationem nominis quod spectat, evidentissima est, *gamal* enim significat *rependere* [to give back], et *retribuere*, constat autem Camelum prae caeteris animalibus injuriarum memorem, et idcirco dicit ab historicis qui de illo agunt mnesíkakon." *De clarissimo Bocharto et ejus scriptis*, GS, 4. See the arguments in Claude Duret's *Trésor de l'histoire des langues* (1613) quoted in M. Foucault, *Les Mots et les Choses. Une Archéologie des Sciences Humaines* (Paris: Gallimard, 1990).

[10] On the distinction between hermeneutic demonstration and rational demonstration in rationalist apologetics, see A. McKenna, "Deus absconditus: quelques reflexions sur la crise du rationalisme chrétien entre 1670 et 1740," in M.-C. Pitassi (ed.), *Apologétique 1680–1740. Sauvetage ou naufrage de la théologie?*, Actes du Colloque de Genève, juin 1990 (Geneva: Labor et Fides, 1991), 13–28, 21 ff.

what preceded it: given the initial axiom of the chronological precedence of the Mosaic source over every other, this means that pagan cosmogonies are almost automatically reduced to millennial deformations of the crystal-clear narration of Genesis. The inhabitants of Hierapolis remember the Flood, only substituting Deucalion for Moses, while Abydene, Berosus, Polyhistor and Nicholas of Damascus expressly quote the arrival of the Ark on the mountains of Armenia; the Greeks consider themselves the descendants of Japheth, while the Africans' cult of Cham goes under the name of Amon and that of Noah, Saturn; likewise the *nebris*, the skin worn by Bacchus, goes back to Nimrod, or Nebrod, son of Cush, or Bar Chus, translated as Bacchus.[11]

From the comparative study of the languages, carried out against a background of the primordial nature of Hebrew which Bochart takes for granted, emerges the reconstruction of the descent of the whole of humanity from Adam: a bridge suspended over the emptiness of that grey zone distinguished by the absence of written testimony, going from the Flood to the first signs of classical historiography.[12] This reconstruction is developed in the follow-up to the *Phaleg*, the *Chanaan, seu de sermone Phoenicum*, also published in 1646, in Caen; it is presented by the publisher of the reprint as a passage through the dark corridor that extends from the world before the Flood to that already familiar to the Greeks. Although the *Hierozoicon*, Bochart's monumental catalogue of the animals to be found in the Bible, dates from twenty years later, with the *Chanaan* Bochart's great project achieves its first aim, touching the goal of a consistent theory of the spread of human groups according to God's design. In it we have the "sacred geography," the alliance between a literal exegesis of the Scriptures, of a faithfully Calvinist approach, and a complex historicization, carried out in the study of the evolution of the languages from the primordial act of *onomatesia*, the naming of the natural things with which mankind came into contact: the earth and the animals (the plan for a further treatise on botanical and miner-

---

[11] GS, *in quatuor libros Phaleg praefatio*, 43.

[12] On the question of the times of human history, see chs. 2 and 3 of P. Rossi, *The Dark Abyss of Time*.

alogical scriptural writing was never realized). It was an enterprise both profoundly religious and simultaneously rational. That immoderate demonstration of erudition and speculation, for which Simon criticizes the author of *Geographia Sacra*, is the distinctive figure of a tendency to join a deeply-felt biblical devotion with the decision to tackle the interpretation of the text in light of the complexity of the real, without conceding anything to the fondness for allegory or fideistic impasse. From this perspective, Bochart's entire activity can be structurally inserted into the context of the so-called school of Saumur, that network of reformed exegetes of northern France who made some of the most important contributions to the birth of testament criticism and of oriental studies.

The Academy of Saumur was founded in 1600 as the first Huguenot educational institution in the kingdom of France qualified to give degrees in philosophy and theology; it was suppressed in January 1685 on the eve of the Revocation of the Edict of Nantes. The Academy of Saumur paid for its "humanistic theology" with its conflict with reformed othodoxy, and incurred the constant hostility of the Catholic Church. If Moïse Amyraut, that moderate believer in predestination and a leading representative of the school, was condemned by the national synods of Alençon (1637), Charenton (1644–45) and Loudun (1659), interest in philology as a tool in resolving controversies able to demonstrate the uncertainty and contradictory nature of the Roman Catholic ecclesiastical institutions, resulted in repeated demands for closure sent by the French clergy to the Crown.[13] Moreover, even on the side of biblical exegesis, a territory in which the unusual and indeed undeclared pragmatic alliance between counter-reformation needs and libertine trends intended to emphasize the substantial uncertainty of

[13] On the Academy of Saumur see F. Laplanche, *L'Écriture,* which is entirely devoted to it, and J. P. Dray, "The Protestant Academy of Saumur and Its Relations with the Oratorians of Les Ardilliers," *History of European Ideas* 9/4 (1988), 465–78. Laplanche, recalling Troeltsch's distinction (*Die Bedeutung der Protestantismus für die Entstehung der Modernen Welt*, 1911) between forms of dissident protestantism in humanistic circles, sects, and individualistic mysticism, sees in Saumur "une résurgence humaniste à l'intérieur de l'orthodoxie réformée": Laplanche, *L'Écriture*, 17–18.

scriptural texts (with authoritative premises in one case, and skeptical ones in the other), fixed radical opposition is countered by Saumur philology with the vigorous affirmation of the *perspicuitas Scripturae,* the transparency of the Bible. This transparency is pursued through a work on the text which led the biblical scholars of northern France to point out a stratification in the Hebrew testament, work which culminated in Louis Cappel's *Arcanum punctationis* (1624), which contested the primitive nature of the Masoretic transcription.[14]

Samuel Bochart's work can clearly be understood within the framework of a vast project to revise biblical exegesis in a critical-historical sense, of a confessional kind, that towards the middle of the seventeenth century takes for granted the relevance of the Mosaic language to a varied Semitic branch. Nevertheless both *Phaleg* and *Chanaan* may have a more specific function in the cultural debate of the period.

The subjects of the ancientness or wisdom of the ancients, and of the selective activity of time, take various forms in the disputes of the seventeenth century. One of the most famous, which bears a notable resemblance to the *Geographia Sacra*, was launched by the pre-adamitic hypothesis of Isaac de La Peyrère, the disturbing attack on monogenism and hence on scriptural authority itself, against which the orthodox intelligentsia of Europe reacted violently. Bochart's proposal, that there was an occult coincidence between the figures of mythology and those of Genesis, was with reason considered to be an explanation, both flexible and constructive, for the multiplication of man's descendents, on the same level as the *Theologia gentilis et philosophia christiana* by Gerhard Voss (1642), and the later *Demonstratio evangelica* of Pierre-Daniel Huet (1679).[15] While accepting on the whole the conceptual validity of this interpretation, we must recall that la Peyrère's *Preadamitae* were published in Amsterdam in 1655, a decade after the *Phaleg* (though the first draft was complete in 1642), so that the latter should rather be placed in the context of already existing polemic against the skeptical tastes of

---

[14] Laplanche, 211 ff. By the same author, see also *Débats et combats autour de la Bible dans l'orthodoxie réformée*, in Armogathe (dir.), *Le Grand siècle et la Bible,* 117–40.
[15] Rossi, 183 ff.

humanists and classicists, of a clearly libertine matrix. The clash over the mythology of the gentiles recalls the figure of François de La Mothe le Vayer, the Dauphin's tutor and *esprit fort* who appealed greatly to the cultured circles of the kingdom, and whose *De la vertu de payens* was published in 1642 with a dedication to Richelieu.[16] Here the philosophical universe of Greek and Latin antiquity was described with stylish elegance, converging with the barely concealed theory of a skeptical relativism open to recognizing the possible coexistence of the various traditions. The most natural result was the blurring of the luminous clarity of the Christian example.[17] The second part of the volume is structured as a gallery of famous people to be praised, and includes Epicurus, Julian the Apostate and Confucius (typical of missionary literature); in it the provocations which damage the uniqueness of Christian morality play on the comparison between the religious *topoi* of the various cultures, unscrupulously matched on the basis of the criteria of analogy alone. Even the specificity of Christ's teaching and the story of Genesis are put to the test:

> According to Origen, Celsus was so impious as to argue that Jesus took his finest phrases from Plato, especially the one in which a camel, or rather a rope, would pass more easily through the eye of a needle, than a rich man enter into the Kingdom of Heaven. [...] Those who loved Plato and his work excessively found the birth of the world explained better in the *Timaeus* than in Genesis. That fine country that Socrates describes to Simmias in the *Phaedo* was far more full of grace than the earthly paradise. And the fable of the Androgyne was incomparably better devised than all that Moses had said about the extraction of Eve from one of Adam's ribs. [...] And instead of admitting that Homer and Plato in their fantastic stories counterfeited what

---

[16] The influence of le Vayer on La Peyrère is suggested by Giuliano Gliozzi in *Adamo e il nuovo mondo. La nascita dell'antropologia come ideologia coloniale: dalle genealogie bibliche alle teorie razziali* (Florence: La Nuova Italia, 1977), 533 ff.

[17] On the pyrrhonism of La Mothe le Vayer see L. Bianchi, *Alle fonti della ragione. Il pensiero libertino di fronte alla tradizione filosofica*, in G. Canziani–Y. C. Zarka (eds.), *L'interpretazione nei secoli XVI e XVII*, Atti del Convegno internazionale di studi (Milan: Franco Angeli, 1993), 127–53. The classic text on the author and his intellectual background is R. Pintard, *Le libertinage érudit dans la première moitié du XVII siècle* (Geneva-Paris: Slatkine Reprints, 1983; original edition, 1943).

> they learnt in Egypt from the books of Moses, more ancient by several centuries than any pagan, they had the audacity to argue the opposite, and pretend that Moses was the transcriber of the inventions of Homer and Hesiod.[18]

The heart of the *Geographia Sacra* lies in this coherent polemic against this kind of use of classical authorities—a polemic which aimed less to reject profane sources and knowledge indiscriminately, or to renounce the use of critical reason, but rather to reduce to zero their dignity as plausible alternatives to revealed history. If le Vayer sets out the moral and civil forms established by God and those established by the profanity of the gentiles horizontally, one next to the other, Bochart tries to bring out the existence of a hierarchical criterion which makes the latter descend from the former in every case. As we have already seen, the criterion is that of identifying antiquity and causality.

The crisis lasted for decades, as can be seen from Pierre de Villemandy's preface to the 1707 edition, which reiterates the work's total extraneity to the imaginative Genesis of Adam, to the Columns of Seth, to the prophecies of Enoch and to the rest of fabulous ancient repertory of the libertines.[19] But already in 1646, in introducing the original, Bochart prudently allows us to glimpse the nature of the adversary—who, we should recall, held a prestigious position at court:

---

[18] "Nous voions dans Origene que Celsus avoit eu assez d'impieté pour soustenir que Jesus Christ tenoit de Platon les plus belles sentences qu'il eust dites, et particulierement celle qui porte qu'un chameau, ou plutot un cable, passeroit plus aisément par le trou d'un aiguille, qu'un homme riche n'entreroit au Royaume des Cieux. [...] Ceux qui ont eu de ces passions indiscrettes pour luy, et pour ses ouvrages, trouvoient que la naissance du monde, estoit bien mieux couchée dans le Timée, que dans la Genese. Ce beau païs que Socrate décrit a Simmias dans le Phaedon, avoit beaucoup plus de grace que le Paradis terrestre. Et la fable de l'Androgyne estoit sans comparaison mieux inventée que tout ce que Moïse a dit de l'extraction d'Eve de l'un des costes d'Adam. [...] Et au lieu de reconnoistre qu'un Homère et Platon ont deguisé dans leurs contes fabuleux ce qu'ils avoient appris en Egypte des livres de Moïse, plus ancien de tant de siècles qu'aucun auteur profane; ils estoient si impertinens que de soustenir tout le contraire, et de vouloir que Moïse eust esté le Transcripteur des inventions d'Hesiode et d'Homere." *De la vertu des payens*, in *Oeuvres*, Vol. V(Paris: Louis Billaine, 1669), 93–95.

[19] GS, *Praefatio*, a2r–v.

> The year just past, having been asked by friends to express myself on the placing of the earthly paradise, I embarked on a new path, trodden by no one. When I realized that because of its novelty it irritated those who still clung on so stubbornly to the opinions of the ancients that they believed it to be illegitimate to deviate from them by as much as an inch, I felt I would be doing a service if, by eliminating this misconception, I had shown with a second example, itself very well-known, that Moses' words on geography are not well enough known. So I decided to add as an appendix to the treatise on paradise a short exposition of the tenth chapter of Genesis, on the descent of humanity from the descendents of Noah, from which it was clear the way not just the ancients, but also their present-day interpreters, have often deviated from the sacred writer through ignorance. And while I reflected on this many things came to mind, so that what I had hoped to finish in a chapter spread out into many books while I was writing it.[20]

At the origin of the work, then, is the wish to show how only a superficial knowledge of the historical and geographical context of Moses' narration can lead one to prefer, for reliability and completeness, the ancient sources. Bochart reaches his objective in his ambitious reconstruction, through the models of the genealogy of humanity (*Phaleg*) and the universal diffusion of the primeval language (*Chanaan*) of the centuries before the Flood; but he recalls the way that the original project, the "first example" that can be produced to support this thesis, depends on the localization of the earthly paradise. This is a subject that he did not manage to face in its entirety, devoting himself to the exegesis of the chapters following on from Genesis; to his heirs, frantically seeking that treatise on Paradise expected by the correspondents of the erudite scholar

---

[20] "Anno proxime praeterito rogatus ab amicis ut sententiam meam scriberem de loco Paradisi Terrestris, novam instititi viam, neque a quoquam tritam hactenus. Quod cum ipsa novitate illis displicere sensissem, qui decessorum sententiis haerent ita mordicus ut ne latum quidem unguem ab iis discedere fas putent; operae pretium me facturum putavi, si, ut ex hominum animis hunc errorem revellerem, altero exemplo docerem, eoque perillustri, geographica Mosis vocabula nondum fuisse satis cognita. Consilium igitur fuit Tractatui de Paradiso pro appendice subnectere brevem expositionem decimi capitis Geneseos de humani generis propagatione ex stirpe Noae. Ex qua non veteres modo, sed et novitios interpretes horum ignoratione a Sacri Scriptoris scopo saepe aberrasse pateret. Sed hoc meditanti mihi tam multa se obtulerunt, ut quod unius capitis angustiis concludi posse speraveram sub manum creverit in multos libros." GS, in *Phaleg praefatio*, 37.

after his death, only a few manuscript drafts remained, together with the text of a sermon.[21] In fact, the idea of studying the question more deeply never left Bochart, to the very last years of his life; in April 1665 he imputed the lack of time to dedicate to it to the tensions provoked by the Catholic party, who that year had formally requested Louis XIV to close the Protestant schools.[22] He did however manage to outline his opinion on two occasions; the first perhaps in 1645, on the occasion (mentioned above) that gave rise to the *Phaleg*, he wrote to Louis Cappel, the author of the *Critica Sacra*, that he essentially accepted Calvin's comment on Genesis. This proposal placed Paradise in Mesopotamia on the basis of his liking of the text of LXX, which translates the Hebrew terms *eden* and *mikkedem* using the spatial attributes Eden and orient, whereas in the Vulgate they stand for *garden of delights* and *in the beginning*. This proposal still prevails among Protestant theologians of the sixteenth and seventeenth centuries: the four rivers described by Moses would be none other than the Tigris and Euphrates, which meet near Apamea and then divide up again later.[23] Bochart restricts himself to inverting the position of the Havilah and Chus regions, the former to the west of the lower reaches of the Euphrates, Pishôn in the Bible, the latter to the west of the lower Tigris or Gihôn. There are just a few lines, with clear favor being given to that linguistic analysis so characteristic of this writer.[24] A second time, writing to Jacques Cappel (the son of Louis and also a Saumur orientalist), Bochart hints at the place of Paradise in the context of a dissertation on the nature of the tempting serpent: "in a word, I place it in the same place as Calvin," except for a correction of the major mistakes of the lands around the rivers;[25] the issue of the serpent, however, can be indicative of a more general hermeneutic, applicable also to the localization of Eden.

---

[21] GS, *De clarissimo Bocharto et ejus scriptis*, 5.

[22] GS, *De serpente tentatore, Paradiso terrestri, nonnullisque aliis*, 834.

[23] The question of its placing is fully dealt with in J. Delumeau, *Une histoire du Paradis, Le Jardin des délices* (Paris: Fayard, 1992), 209 ff.

[24] GS, *Paradisi terrestris situs juxta Sa. Bochartum*, 29–30.

[25] GS, *De serpente tentatore*, 833.

The polemic against the allegorists, with the firm position taken in favor of a literal exegesis, runs throughout the entire piece. The opinion of those—among them Moïse Amyraut—for whom the serpent is none other than a symbolic reference to Satan, tends toward that emptying of literal meaning carried out by the allegorists, who see in Paradise the delights of the spirit, and in the four rivers the moral virtues. This for Bochart is a very dangerous choice, in that it comes near to negating even what in the Bible is related in the clearest possible way, and to substituting it with fantasies, *phantasmata*. It is to be rejected on two levels: anthropologically, because it presupposes that man may be seduced by temptations even in the state of innocence; and figuratively, in that the description of the animal is too exact not to imply the concrete reality of the subject represented. The serpent's characteristics in Genesis exactly fit the zoological framework of the tradition of medieval bestiaries, to whose model Bochart was still faithful; it is the most cunning of animals, with the sharpest sight, with a sense of taste and smell similar to mankind's, greedy for fruit, vegetables, meat, milk, and wine, and able to penetrate everywhere thanks to its flexibility. It was chosen by Satan as his instrument of seduction because of these physical characteristics, and for others of a symbolic nature, which can be included in the discourse of analogy. The serpent and the devil are in this sense mirror images that reflect each other in the world, going beyond the limits of the material and the spiritual: just as one slides along the ground, the other attempts hidden ambush; just as one has a forked tongue, the other hypnotizes with words, and so forth.[26]

The problem remains of the absence of an actual key within the text which could explain the allegory: why did not Moses make any explicit reference to the Devil, narrating only the meeting between Eve and the serpent? The point is that

> ...in telling the story, Moses functions as a historiographer [*historiographus*] rather than as an interpreter, and for this reason he only recounts those things that were evident, rather than those which were hidden.[27]

[26] GS, 838 ff.

[27] "...in ea narratione Moses historiographi, minime vero interpretis, fungitur officio; eapropter ea tantum, quae apparebant, non autem quae latebant, commemorat...." GS 840.

If the Bible is a *historia*, an exposition of the facts as they happened, it should be read with the instruments that allow us to grasp its original meaning, which is that of a narration; once the evidence of that meaning has been reached, such a *historia* receives the confirmation of its own truth. It is quite natural that the instruments are those which are made available at various times by the natural and historical sciences, by geography, and by philology. A correct exegesis, for this reason, understood as a reappropriation of the original sense of the text in order to progressively overcome the different interpretations in approaching its nucleus of meaning, must be carried out with the help of an enormous accumulation of information; only the erudite scholar is capable of constructing informed hypotheses, and not *phantasmata*.[28] Bochart's correctives concerning the real latitude of the lands of Chus and Havilah, in the context of the localization of the site of Eden, are to be understood in the same way, as a manifestation of the race backwards towards the primitive sense of the Scriptures, in this case relating to the representation of space—as in Louis Cappel, the original lesson of the text.

This does not mean that Bochart wants to reduce the hermeneutic to a bare, literal sense. He was a minister at Caen, and the sermons on the second chapter of Genesis were the point of departure for his research. The question of the placing of Paradise, also for reasons beyond his control, was brought to an end for him in those few lines to the Cappels. It was still very much an open question, however, to his contemporaries, and destined to become still more so over the last decades of the sixteenth century and the first decades of the seventeenth; "sacred geography" was raised to the level of a subject in itself, studied by Bible scholars and orientalists (categories which still for the most part overlap) on the tracks of the hydrography of Eden, on the route

[28] Jean-Robert Massimi's analysis goes in the same direction, in reference to the *Traité de la situation du Paradis terrestre* by Pierre Daniel Huet, in *Montrer et demontrer: autour du Traité de la situation du Paradis terrestre de P. D. Huet (1691)*, in A. Desreumaux and F. Schmidt (eds.), *Moïse géographe. Recherches sur les représentations juives et chrétiennes de l'espace* (Paris: Libraire Philosophique J. Vrin, 1988), 203–25, 223.

Solomon's fleet took to Ophir, and of Mount Garizim.[29] There is probably no single reason for the popularity of this public debate. One important reason would seem to derive from the tastes of an educated public, in connection with the spread of interest in an exoticism of Asiatic matrix. A second reason is the specifically Protestant tendency to emphasize the centrality of the Hebrew text of the Bible (as opposed to the Latin text) and the ultimate clarity of the word of God. Some texts, from this point of view, were born with the needs of controversy obviously very much in mind: the *Dissertatio de Paradiso* of Joannes Vorst, the Lutheran theologian active in Brandenburg, rejects the placing in Armenia proposed by Robert Bellarmine in the book *De gratia primi hominis* of the *Controversiae*.[30] In fact, the tracing of the primordial sense of the Scriptures, carried out through a rigorous critical method, can only be damaging to the authority of the Roman Catholic institutions, founded on an interpretation of the text which can be determined historically.

The third reason for the proliferation of the genre, which with the onset of the eighteenth century involved Roman Catholic culture as well, is undoubtedly the spread of a scepticism which doubts the very bases of religion of the book—that cultural relativism which Bochart himself had already attacked. Sacred geography (as can be argued for chronology, history and the other sacred sciences) is not a subsidiary subject, an aid to, the reading of the Bible, despite the fact that the prefaces to the individual works boast of their practical usefulness for exegetes and theologians. It is essentially an apologetic genre, redacted by extremely competent scholars for a highly educated public dangerously vulnerable to the lure of rationalism, which required refined instruments rather than defensive reactions. The aim was to establish a solid relationship between two truths of a superficially different nature,

---

[29] An exemplary collection of this kind of literature is Vol. VII of the *Thesaurus antiquitatum sacrarum... in quibus, veterum hebraeorum mores leges, instituta, ritus sacri, et civiles illustrantur*, "ed. Biagio Ugolini, Venetiis, apud Johannem Gabrielem Herthz, 1747".

[30] *Dissertatio de Paradiso*, in Ugolini, 695–714.

to demonstrate that they were substantially identical: the truth of the text and that of the geographical place.[31] The earthly Paradise, in this sense, offered a very important testing ground for that truth. Insofar as it was the chronologically founding moment of the relation between man and the world, the very relation that presides over the birth of modern science in the seventeenth century, it could, if guaranteed by the concrete reality of geographical space, contribute to the foundation of a new relation between man and Christianity, this time based on reason. If what is most ancient is by virtue of its antiquity most true, Paradise, as the most ancient place of all, the primordial place, contains in itself the truth in its condition of purity.

In 1691 Pierre Daniel Huet, under the pretext of putting the chaos of topographies in order, dedicates to Eden a disquisition which is a brilliant example of this apologetic attitude. His *Traité de la situation du Paradis terrestre*—here *situer* is meant in its locative sense—opens with a detailed map of Mesopotamia, with the Garden in the middle. This is no longer Calvin's 1553 map, full of imprecisions and reproduced mainly as an aid to the Bibles of the Dutch, English and French Reformation, but an accurate geographical map of the whole region which sums up the sense of the written text itself, in other words the visible representation of the reality in Moses' narration.[32] Huet is not interested in anything in the second chapter of Genesis except the geographical determination of Paradise. He proceeds to analyze verse by verse, imposing a clear framework on the intricacies of the glosses with the criterion of biblical philology. The return to the original sense of the words is the leitmotif of the entire work. Huet is Roman Catholic, and very close to Bossuet, and will soon be appointed bishop of Avranches; but as a scholar of European fame and *politique* far from confessional conflicts, he does not hesitate to consider the *perspicuitas* of ancient Hebrew the most suitable instrument for the defense of the Bible. Moreover,

[31] On this see Massimi, 205 ff.

[32] On Calvin's map of Paradise, and more in general on the representation of geographical space in editions of the Bible, see C. Delano-Smith and E. Morley, *Maps in Bibles 1500–1600: An Illustrated Catalogue* (Geneva: Droz, 1991).

psychological reasons are not quite extraneous to the composition of the treatise; in taking on the question of Eden, a treatment of which was so eagerly awaited by Bochart's readers and never found among his papers, Huet is settling an intellectual debt. He had been a disciple of Bochart, and a friend and traveling companion at the court of Christina of Sweden, before the relation was broken off because of a controversial edition of Origen and the sudden death of the old theologian. Huet pays off the debt with interest, with the insinuation that he had copied Bochart's notes on the subject. Certainly Huet, their religious differences aside, shares with Bochart the flexible and innovative approach of the polemic against the libertines; in the *Demonstratio evangelica* (1679), for example, he replies to Spinoza in seeking the rational proof of Christianity, and finding in the pagan Gods the germ of revelation.[33] His use of reason in the dissertation on Paradise conforms entirely to the hermeneutic project of sacred geography; not a further interpretation of Genesis, but its clarification, achieved thanks to a comparison of the ancient sources so as to contextualize the speaking Moses as closely as possible in reality. He takes a circular route, starting with the Masoretic text, which he thinks is the nearest to the original, and going back to it, rendering it more objective through fields of knowledge extraneous to the religious dimension.[34] Huet maintains that the exposition is so clear that it is hard to believe that Eden could have been placed in places so very different from each other.[35] The key lies in placing the words of the narrator in the conditions in which they were pronounced. One case among many concerns that of the Hebrew term *mikkedem*, with reference to the Garden, understood by some as the locative term "in the east," and by others—the majority of vulgarizers—as the temporal term "in the beginning." Having chosen the first meaning as the correct one, Huet is faced with the choice between placing

---

[33] J. Le Brun, "Entre la Perpetuité et la *Demonstratio evangelica*," in *Leibniz à Paris, Studia Leibnitiana Supplementa*, XVIII (Wiesbaden: Franz Steiner Verlag, 1978), II, 1–13, 10 ff.

[34] Massimi, 216.

[35] *Tractatus de situ Paradisi terrestris*, here in the Latin translation of 1698, "excudunt Amstelaedami Henr. et vid. Th. Boom...; et Ultrajecti, Guil. vande Water").

Eden in the Far East, or in the region between Palestine and the Persian Gulf: and here he claims that it is necessary to look with the eyes of Moses. Moses wrote near the western boundary of the continent; like the contemporary Jews and Arabs he probably called *sabios* (orientals) the inhabitants of the lower reaches of the Euphrates; in the Bible itself he several times uses the word *kedem* for the area a little to the east of the Tigris: thus there is no doubt that Paradise is to be placed in Mesopotamia. As for the possibility of understanding the passage in both spatial and temporal terms, going along with a presumed ambiguity inspired by God, it should not be forgotten that Jerome translates *a principio* above all in homage to the authority of the Greek paraphrasers Aquila, Symmac and Theodotius; many other Fathers, by contrast, believed that the temples of the ancient church faced east to commemorate the first country of mankind.

With Huet the inquiry into where Paradise was found reaches its most extreme form of meticulous, detailed scholarship, although it does not seem to have been considered to be complete. French Reformed scholarship, exiled into the Protestant states after the Revocation of the Edict of Nantes, is by no means silent; the bitterness over the savage repression experienced over the century, and for the eradication of circles of such a high intellectual level as the academies of Saumur and Sedan, is also nourished in the cult of great figures of Hebrew scholarship, Cameron, Cappel and Bochart. The latter's biography was published in 1692, produced by his pupil Etienne Morin, pastor at Caen and after his expulsion teacher of oriental languages at Amsterdam. The reconstruction of Eden *secundum mentem Bocharti*, based on the memories of more than twenty years earlier, is a clear sign of the vitality of those who had been defeated in the reign of Louis XIV.

Morin's thesis is essentially the same as Huet's, placing Eden at the meeting of the Tigris and the Euphrates; and the visible epicenter of the biography is a great map of the region, similar to that of the *Traité* (figure 1). The reasoning, however, is quite different: Huet's insistence on exegesis, which he showed in the constant work of comparison of the Scriptures' translations, such as to confer on his dissertation the coloring of biblical criticism, are very nearly absent. The main lines of

Figure 1. Anonymous, map of Mesopotamia including the region of earthly Paradise, in *Samuelis Bocharti Geographia Sacra, seu Phaleg et Canaan*, procuravit Petrus de Villemandy, Lugduni Batavorum, apud Cornelium Boutesteyn, et Jordanum Luchtmans; Trajecti ad Rhenum, apud Guillielmum vande Water, 1707.

the text belong essentially to Semitic studies, juxtapositing observations more strictly philological with others of a historical and ethnographical nature, and the route backwards through the interpretations, the method favored by Huet, is substituted by going directly to the analysis of the Hebrew text, considered as the written expression of the language spoken by Adam. In this sense Morin is moving in the temporal mode translated spatially into the engraving that is included in the 1707 edition of Bochart's *Works*, in which the *Life* is republished (figure 2): the interval between the naming of the animals in the Garden—the primordial act of the founding onomatesia of human vocal expression and simultaneously the sign of God's approval of man's dominion over other creatures—and the building of the tower of Babel, which represents the dissolution of that primitive linguistic unity that was similarly a privilege conceded by divine benevolence. After the fracture marked by the tower the ancient idiom survives, through the age of barbarism, as the prerogative of the descendants of the devout, and can be the key to enter into the age before the diaspora, that of Genesis and unity. In the

Figure 2. Anonymous, Adam and Nimrod, in *Samuelis Bocharti Geographia Sacra*, op. cit.

Exercitationes de lingua primaeva, published in Utrecht a couple of years later, Morin faces the question of the original language of humanity, pleading the cause of Hebrew in a project that concerns from the very first the truthful status of the Bible, guaranteed by the intrinsic and transcendent force of the phonemes:

> ...certainly proper nouns have their own efficacy; but when they are drawn out of another language that intrinsic efficacy cannot be sought for, because there can be no certainty that it belongs to the original nouns. It is therefore important to be quite sure of the actual words of the sacred text, so that one can deduce more convincing arguments from them, superior to any objections.[36]

In line with tradition, Morin rejects the idea that language can be innate in man. Although gestures and facial expressions linked to emotions are expressive features common to all humanity, words are not, so that indeed language is learned with difficulty, and the child raised by wild animals would develop an idiom close to their vocal sounds. Language cannot be considered to be born of reason, either, since in the beginning Adam spoke to God and to Eve in a language which was already complete, without forming it progressively through his relationship with things and by comparison with other expressive modes. However, Morin's main interest lies elsewhere, in such questions as, has Adam's language kept its original purity? Does anyone speak it today? According to Gregory of Nyssa, Grotius and Huet, it could not have survived in its integral form, but only in oral traces in the peoples that came after the Flood. Morin is certain that the language of Adam was Hebrew, handed down to his descendents by Shem and by his son Heber, shut into their dwelling on the slopes of Ararat at the time of the construction of the tower and therefore immune to punishment. This con-

---

[36] "Sane suam habent efficaciam nomina; sed cum ex alia lingua petuntur, insita illa efficacia non potest urgeri, quia incertum est an primitivis etiam inesset; itaque expedit certiorem fieri de genuinis Textus sacri verbis, ut ex iis validiora, et omni exceptione majora argumenta firmiter deducantur...." *Exercitationes de lingua primaeva ejusque appendicibus, in quibus multa S. Scripturae loca, diversae in linguis mutationes, multiplices nummorum Israelitarum, et Samaritanorum species, atque variae veterum consuetudines exponuntur,* Ultrajecti, apud Gulielmum Broedelet, 1694, f. 4r.

clusion allows him to follow a third path beyond the opposing schools of Protestant philology, expressed some decades earlier by Louis Cappel and Johann Buxtorf Jr. On the one hand, the introduction of a clear evolutionary dynamic of languages, with the affirmation of the later development of Masoretic vocal characteristics (to which the second half of the book is devoted) and the recognition of a derivation of the Semitic family from Hebrew; on the other, the confident reaffirmation of the divine nature of Hebrew, and of its metaphysical connotations.[37]

Supported by the flexibility of theses whose theme at least was already set out at the moment of writing the dissertation on Paradise, Morin is able to utilize linguistics more effectively to explore the region of Eden, understood as much as a place of apologetic utterance as a testing-ground of an already autonomous sphere of Hebrew studies. Once again, only the placing is of interest, and it is no longer a question of the logical orientation towards the various lexical interpretations, but the consideration of the possible alternatives in their relation to the geographical space. Of the various classifiable opinions the first—from Origen to Francesco Zorzi—believes Paradise to be an allegorical construction: one can only contest it by faith in the literal meaning of the words. The second group, led by the Valentinians, believe it to have a physical reality, but outside this world, in the third heaven, an opinion denied by the presence of the angel on its threshold, a sign of the fact that men could reach it in the flesh. The third opinion, typical of medieval map culture, and rendered improbable by the roundness of the earth, places Paradise girding the world, beyond the oceans. Then gradually the more recent hypotheses: according to Joachim von Watt, or Vadianus Sangallensis, Eden can be superimposed over the entire world. This was a more convincing hypothesis, except for the enigma of the four rivers rising at the center of the Garden. For François du Jon Eden was Mesopotamia, whose inhabitants practiced agriculture from the remotest times, almost as if they wished to recreate the primordial con-

---

37 *Exercitationes de lingua primaeva,* 39 ff. On human language in the period before the Flood see Delumeau, 262 ff.; on the Cappel-Buxtorf polemic which arose out of the *Arcanum punctationis,* see Laplanche, 220 ff.

ditions. Finally with Calvin, and above all with Bochart, we arrive at the exact collocation, on the banks of the Tigris between the cities of Ctesiphon and Apamea.[38] The mapping dimension, thanks to which the Scripture manifests the guarantee of its truthfulness, takes shape by gradually getting nearer to the exact center of the space and the discourse; the search for the rational proof of the Revelation can only mean descending to the knowable level of nature: from the spiritual dimension of allegory, to that of the third heaven, to that of the unknown region beyond the oceans, up to the definition of Eden within a land the size of a small county, what we see is the atomization of the object of study, as in the microscopic analysis of living tissues, in the search for the ultimate components of things. In a further magnification, the lens focuses on the critical point of the identification of the two unknown rivers, the Pishôn and the Gihôn, on which every treatise on Paradise hinges. Here, having arrived at the definition of the area of interest, Morin avoids getting involved in the interpretations of the vulgarizers, to get straight at the production of proof through the use of scientific instruments. These instruments are the ethnographical summaries, from which the ancient memory of a land of delights near the peoples of the Middle East were found, or more often the classical authors, e.g., Pliny's *Natural History* and Strabo's *Geography*. But it is the comparative approach to the Semitic languages, with Hebrew at the center, which confers real sense on the construction and ensure on the basis of the cross-referencing and checking of the etymologies, the certainty of the thesis.

The studies by Huet and Morin, for number of sources and breadth of analysis, are the culminating point of the historical and geographical literature of the earthly Paradise. In them, in fact, the apologetic tensions of intellectual elites disposed to take on religious relativism on a rational terrain, and the projects of language disciplines divided between biblical exegesis and more strictly scientific interests, converge. Sacred geography was a genre which, when grafted onto the study of antiquity, maintained its appeal and continued to provoke polemics

[38] GS, *Dissertatio de Paradiso terrestri secundum mentem S. Bocharti*, 9 ff.

until at least the fourth decade of the eighteenth century. If the research on the placing of Eden testifies to the great rational defensive effort made by Christianity to protect itself against the threat of scepticism, it was also a vigorous demonstration of the need to have the Hebrew text in front of one, at least in order to understand the words, and not simply at a fideistic level. This is a demonstration which could only undermine the authority of the Latin translation, and against which, on the Roman Catholic side, intervention was thought necessary. Of course Huet was also Catholic, but close to the general tendency of Protestant exegetes, and more interested in scholarship than in dogmatic theology. It was more likely from Jesuit circles that drafts for the mapping of Eden emerged, addressed to presenting the question from another point of view. There is an ample Jesuit tradition on the subject. Between the end of the sixteenth and the beginning of the seventeenth centuries some of the most important theologians of the Roman Catholic church touch on it: Pereira, Mariana, Bellarmine, and van den Steen.[39] In 1635 Father Abram, in his voluminous gloss on Virgil's *Georgics*, addresses it. About forty years later we find Athanasius Kircher—polygraph, scientist and great artificer of marvels of the Roman baroque—involved in the Garden, devoting a chapter of his spectacular *Arca Noë* to the question of the destruction of Paradise, and where it was to be found.[40] From the dogmatic point of view, he was not of course one of the most active of the Society of Jesus, which he generally praised propagandistically more for its scientific than for its religious merits. However, some details of his exposition are help to illustrate the change of perspective: the presence of a skeptical influence, starting with the opening acknowledging the fact that the controversy over the placing "is great, and always will be;" the reluctance to examine the Hebrew text, which Kircher nevertheless knows; and the faith in the exegesis of

---

[39] Delumeau, 188.

[40] On the conception of nature involved in Kircher's placing of Eden see I. Cantoni, "'Tempora labuntur irrequieta cyclis': Tempo e cosmologia nella filosofia della natura di Athanasius Kircher," in the volume edited by W. Tega, *Le origini della modernità. Linguaggi e saperi nel XVII secolo* (Florence: Olschki, 1999), II, 361–90, 78–79.

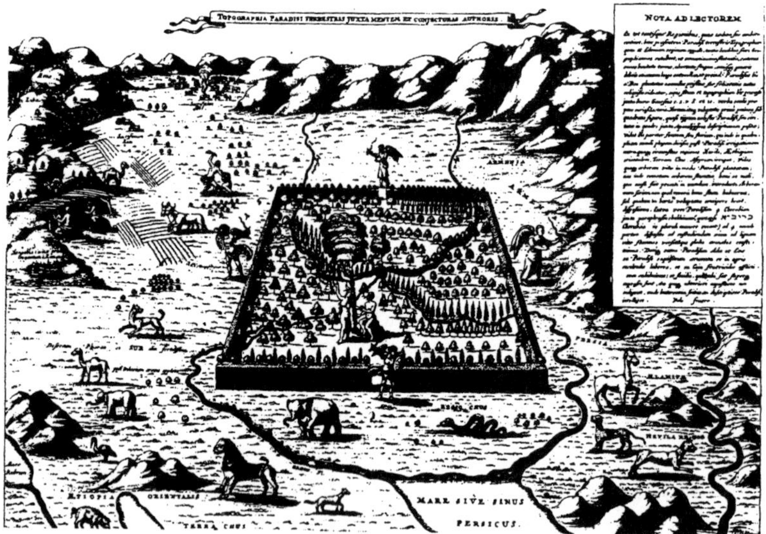

Figure 3. C. Decker, The Earthly Paradise, in A. Kircher, *Arca Noë*, Amstelodami, apud Joannem Janssonium a Waesberge, 1675.

the Vulgate, where he accepts the translation of *mikkedem* as "in the beginning."[41] Above all, the presence of motifs of a clearly allegorical and moral character, entirely absent from the writings of his French contemporaries, in a work that is in any case apologetic in nature, intent on demonstrating the technical feasibility of the ark and of its navigation on the surface of the ocean of the Flood. Probably the dry literalism behind the geographical analysis cannot be accepted in a Catholic context, striking at the bases of a pastoral reading of the Bible, and aiming directly at the affirmation of its immediate understanding. The graphic representation of Paradise itself includes a series of elements foreign to the tradition of sacred geography (figure 3). These elements are the theme of the *hortus conclusus*, charged with moral symbolism, that in the description Kircher defines as being the mirror of the heavenly city

[41] *Arca Noë, in tres libros digesta, quorum I. de rebus quae ante Diluvium, II. de iis, quae ipso Diluvio ejusque duratione, III. de iis, quae post Diluvium a Noemo gesta sunt... explicantur, et demonstrantur*, Amstelodami, apud Joannem Janssonium a Waesberge, 1675, 197 ff.

described in the Apocalypse; the centrality of the reproduction of the angels (in homage to the Chaldee paraphrase, that uses the plural) guarding the entrances, and of the tree of life and of knowledge, figures of the state of grace, of the fall and of its punishment; and the contemporary presence of events that happened later than Genesis, scarcely relevant to the question of geography. These are the signs of a probable difficulty of the Catholic church, towards the last three decades of the seventeenth century, in making the established features of the rational foundation of religion their own, or in Huet's words, of the "demonstration of the Gospel."

This does not mean that these subjects do not come into play in a later age. In a softer version, in keeping with the character's usual balance, in the 1707 *Commentaire* on the Christian Testament, Benedictine Father Augustin Calmet suggests a placing in Armenia; even while making use of the comparative exegesis of the various translations of the Bible, he prefers not to negotiate a linguistic analysis of the Semitic family like those proposed by Huet and the Protestants.[42] This may be the reason for choosing Armenia, isolated from the Semitic linguistic context, and consequently less involved in the controversy on the origin of languages, and simultaneously dear to the evidence of Greek historiography, particularly Xenophon. In addition, a similar framework can be seen in the *Disseratio de situ Paradisi terrestris* of Adrian Reland, an orientalist from Utrecht, which can be dated a few years after Calmet's work, and which takes up both the idea of Eden in Armenia and the ample use of classical sources.[43] A more rigorous appeal to Catholic orthodoxy on the issue of mapping Eden, on the other hand, is made by Jean Hardouin, an aggressive polemicist at the Paris Jesuit College, who in 1723 on the occasion of the publication of a sumptuous edition of Pliny's *ad usum Delphini*, published a disquisitio on Paradise whose title was already an indication of a change of perspective: "Pliny's con-

[42] *Commentaire littéral sur tous les livres de l'Ancien et du Nouveau Testament*, here in the edition of 1724, Paris, chez Emery, Saugrain, Pierre Martin, t. 1, 1; short notes on the text in P. Marsauche, "Présentation de Dom Augustin Calmet (1672–1757): Dissertation sur les possessions du Démon," in Armogathe, 233–53, 240.

[43] *Dissertatio de situ Paradisi terrestris*, in Ugolini, 581–608.

formity to Moses."[44] Here we are not dealing with the concordance of pagan literature with revealed wisdom which Bochart and Huet theorized, but with a matching, of a veiled skeptical flavor, of Moses and Pliny as authors on a more or less analogous level: among the aims of the text, in fact, is the desire to demonstrate that the conservation of the *Historia Naturalis*, the only work of antiquity to mention the rivers of Paradise, is due to Providence.[45] The importance of those few pages on the location of Paradise, in the context of the imposing volume itself, is clear from the little map that follows the frontispiece and the index; the map reserves the first collocation of Eden to Palestine, the sign of a typologizing attitude, and therefore one more markedly pedagogical than Kircher's. The role of the Bible is not to be assimilated to that of the text endowed with history and of the various redactive levels studied at the Saumur Academy, but that of a holy book in every way not historical but confessional; Hardouin states programmatically that he is using the Vulgate "both because it is right for a Catholic to do so, and because on this subject it is extremely accurate, and clearer than anyone else."[46] From such a set of assumptions it is quite as natural to identify the spring in the center of Eden with the spring at the head of the Jordan, as the rhetorical nature of Moses' description of Paradise, recalled to the minds of the people of Israel to exhort it to the reconquest of the Promised Land, which is none other than mankind's primordial seat.[47]

---

[44] *De situ Paradisi terrestris disquisitio, sive de Plinii cum Mose convenientia in Paradisi fluminibus indicandis*, in *Caii Plinii Secundi Historiae Naturalis libri XXXVII... Editio altera emendatior et auctior*, Parisiis, typis Antonii-Urbani Coustelier, I, 1723, 359–68. The text, vulgarized, is republished in 1733 in a sylloge of *Traités géographiques et historiques* edited by A. H. Bruzen de la Martinière; Massimi, *Traités*, 219, and Delumeau, *Traités*, 188, indicate 1716 as the date of first publication, contradicting the *Bibliothèque de la Compagnie de Jésus* of C. Sommervogel, IV, s.v., whose opinion, in the absence of documentary proofs, is to be preferred.

[45] Hardouin, 359.

[46] Hardouin, "quoniam et sic facere catholicum decet, et est ea in hoc argumento perquam accurata, et ceteris omnibus multo apertior."

[47] Hardouin, 362 ff. Hardouin's thesis is taken up again, with not many variations, by the *Histoire du peuple de Dieu, depuis son origine jusqu'à la naissance du Messie*

Father Hardouin's treatise is perhaps the last to be specifically devoted to the place of Paradise; the project of rationalist apologetics, faced with the evident contradictions of its own nature, has by now definitively failed, and with it the subject of sacred geography. It is significant that having begun as an area where faith and critical reason met, it ends its career in the conceptual space of confessional conflict.

(1728), of Isaac-Joseph Berruyer, here consulted in the 1734 edition, Paris, chez J. B. Coignard fils, 17–19. It should be noted that Hardouin and Berruyer, for the christology expressed in the comments on the Gospels, are both together accused of Socinianism in a violent anti-Jesuit campaign, and the *Opera* of the former are placed on the Index in 1739.

Paradise in the Final Scene of *Faust II*

Alberto Destro

Before engaging the subject of this essay directly I would like to give a few brief reminders of some of the essential factors concerning both the plot and the conclusion of Goethe's great drama.[1] Faust is an extraordinarily complex hero, a kind of traveling companion for Goethe during a genesis lasting sixty years or so. It should be obvious that given such a lengthy gestation, a tightly unified project is out of the question. The work reflects the myriad aspects of a rich and varied human experience, and it is through the wealth and many-sidedness of the material flowing into the crucible of a work forever in progress that the complexity of the protagonist can be explained. Yet a conspicuous number of critics have loudly decried the play's lack of unity, leading to a critical debate that has sometimes had scholars expounding the norms by which Goethe should have written *Faust;* happily this tiresomeness now seems to be drying up. Indeed, apart from the slight if perceptible defects in detail which the author did not seem to worry about unduly, what is emphasized these days is the central character's overall consistency, particularly when the encyclopedic variety of his experiences are taken into account. Now, even when we wish to underline the actual inconsistency of some aspects of what happens, the solidity of the construction of Faust's personality remains very much in evidence. An evolution takes place in it, as in any non-schematic version of human reality, but this does not alter the reality of his identity, at the deepest level. We can

---

[1] The following brief bibliographical indications for Faust criticism are in order here: the *Faust-Bibliographie,* ed. Hans Henning, Teil II: *Goethes Faust 2; Sekundärliterature zu Goethes Faust,* in two volumes (Berlin and Weimar, 1970). Also very useful is Karl Robert Mandelkov's *Goethe im Urteil seiner Kritiker,* 4 vols. (Munich, 1975–1984). On a more limited scale but still extremely useful are the anthologies edited by Werner Keller, *Aufsätze zu Goethes "Faust I,"* and *Aufsätze zu Goethes "Faust II"* (Darmstadt, 1974; second editions 1991 and 1992). As far as the critical editions go, while Erich Trunz's classic III volume of the Hamburger Ausgabe is still very useful, essential today is the more recent one by Albrecht Schöne in Vol. VII of the Goethe edition of the Bibliothek Deutscher Klassiker.

therefore indicate some basic characteristics which may be summed up in that almost untranslatable word *Streben,* which marks his true founding figure. *Streben* means to tend, but is normally followed by something definite: one tends to something. In Faust, on the contrary, *Streben* appears to be rendered absolute; it is an attitude of the spirit, a dissatisfaction with the existing state of things and a perennial seeking for something "else," which is always supposed to be better. Faust is a hero who lives this tension. He himself is so much aware of this basic characteristic that he agrees without hesitation to the pact that Mephistopheles proposes, in the certainty that he will never have to satisfy the conditions of the pact (the recognition of the beauty of the passing moment, to satisfy that inexhaustible *Streben*). The whole complex business of the drama registers the various stages of the route that Faust and Mephistopheles follow in the eternal chase after a satisfaction that appears eternally unreachable, or that at any rate is not reached.

These stages in Faust's experience are however constantly marked with guilt. Faust seems to be the coherent demonstration of the apparent truth of the maxim pronounced by God in the Prologue in Heaven, according to which "man errs for as long as he is tending to some goal." The life of Faust (of this Faust, who has abandoned the secluded life of the scholar to throw himself into "life," meaning the life of the senses, though not only this) goes through a great many stages, all of them marked by guilt: the seduction of Gretchen, the murder of the brother and probably the mother of the girl, her abandonment in the moment of her greatest need, and then in the second part, more subtly, the systematic recourse to magic tricks to gain favors from the Emperor's court—from the invention of paper money (backed up by subterranean treasures which are impossible to find), to the use of superhuman forces to allow the Emperor to win the battle against his rival for the imperial throne, to the use (of which however Faust does not seem entirely aware), of a magical-hellish labor force to carry out that land reclamation that represents his last and supreme project. In the anticipation of the vision of the future lands reclaimed from the sea and inhabited by active and prosperous colonists, the blind hundred-year-old Faust finds a satisfaction that to Mephistopheles seems sufficient to carry out the old pact and try to carry off the soul of his hitherto uncontainable victim. Faust is therefore an unusually active hero, but also constantly guilty, right up to the end, right up to the killing of the old Philemon and Baucis; for these two Faust does feel somewhat sorry, as if he was faced with the consequences of an unintentional accident, but does not feel real repentance.

And yet this Faust not only is saved, in the sense that his soul is torn from the claws of Mephistopheles in a grotesque struggle, but he actually goes through an apotheosis in a very special heaven; and it is this we now have to deal with.

The soul (or "the immortal part") of Faust travels through the whole of paradise. Goethe's paradise seems to be separated into two regions which however are apparently continuations of each other. The former, the inferior one, is in rugged, steeply rocky terrain like the landscape in which anchorites found refuge. The blessed travel along it towards the top to get to the second region, the one really up in the heavens, made up of space characterized by a great upward movement of the ranks of angels and the blessed in which we find also Mary, presented as the Queen of the Heavens, and, even, in the last words of her most fervent adorer Doctor Marianus, as the "Goddess." This heaven looks like a space open towards the upper end, without upper limits, and in fact God does not appear at the upper end of this space. He is named, but we do not notice him in this particular paradise. If, in the linguistic approximation of Christian theologies, the supreme goal of paradise is the eternal contemplation of God, and this can be presented as the perfection of satisfaction, the quieting-down of the creature who experiences his return to the creator as his supreme fulfilment, in the paradise that Goethe prepares for Faust there is no trace of this, just as there is no trace of any fulfilment. Fulfilment is provided by the eternal ascending. Towards God? Not necessarily. Rather, the ascending is thought of as of value in itself. If God is the perfection to which the creature tends, this would lead us to conclude that perfectibility is more important for Goethe than perfection, the process of ascending more important than the goal.

This paradise corresponds so well to the *Streben* that constitutes the very essence of Faust's personality, that it reveals itself to be a kind of mythical figure or metaphysical hypostasis. A Faust taken up into a heaven at whose boundaries he would have met the peace of divine contemplation, would not have been himself. But there is more to it than that. When Faust's soul in its initial ascent meets with other groups of the blessed, he overtakes them. His ascending movement is faster (for example when compared to young lads), because he has the advantage of the vast experience gained in this life. This would be incomprehensible unless we interpreted these experiences as statements of the *Streben* that characterizes Faust. The change from an earthly existence to a heavenly one appears to be merely an opening out into a *Streben* infinitely more powerful, to which Faust's personality finally has access after the unsure, imperfect and even guilty attempts made during his life.

To Goethe's reading of paradise we may react in at least two directions. The first, which I personally am not competent to judge, is theological, and turns on the issue of the relation between possession and the conquest of truth (which coincides with beauty, perfection, fulfilment etc.) to reach the source of truth itself, God, in which the soul is traditionally fulfilled. An issue that can never forget that the terms themselves of the dilemma (possession or conquest) are in reality metaphors, imperfect approximations with which we try to formulate two aspects of the relationship of the creature with his creator, which in its essence necessarily escapes us. Nor can we forget that these lexical choices are of philosophical rather than biblical origin (although they have been widely accessible due to the way Greek philosophy has influenced western theology). In the Bible there is no possession of the truth; on the contrary there is a much stronger statement that to the philosopher is virtually incomprehensible, and that is "I am the truth": truth is meant here not as conceptual content or as image expressed in abstract formulas, but as a person. This leads us to the depths of the mystery of incarnation and inevitably a very long way from Goethe, who did not seem to feel much need for the incarnation of a divine savior. So we could ask whether Goethe's paradise is to be entirely rejected from a theological perspective. In my opinion it is not, since we are using categories (such as the possession of truth) which, however problematic in the light of revelation, had and still have a very wide currency in theological thinking, in ecclesiastical praxis and in the mentality of those who call themselves believers. We may easily remember how the solid faith in one's own possession of the truth is the foundation of terribly strong and sure conformist religiosity. In this sense the scepticism towards, or rather the tacit ignoring of, such a perspective on the part of Goethe makes sense once more, and places the religious discourse back into a dimension of unexhausted seeking and tension which seem to partake much more of a substantial religious experience than any idea of possession. But I do not wish to venture any further on this terrain.

I come therefore to the other direction which research can take concerning this singular Goethean paradise, which is more properly historical, or of literary or cultural history. We can ask ourselves about the historical context in which Goethe's idea was born, and therefore about the meaning it has for him and indirectly for us. And here something interesting strikes us at once. As Jochen Schmidt[2] has recently pointed out, here Goethe has in reality invented nothing new, but has taken over and given concrete poetic voice to very ancient conceptions of non-orthodox Christian eschatological meditation, which he encountered already formulated in texts he almost certainly knew about, going back to the early Enlightenment. Two passages in particular, that everything leads us to believe must have been known to Goethe, can be considered precursors of his paradise of over a century later. The first, published in *The Spectator,* the magazine of Joseph Addison (July 7, 1711), argues:

> ...the several Generations of rational Creatures, which rise up and disappear in such quick Successions, are only to receive their first Rudiments of Existence here, and afterwards to be transplanted into a more friendly Climate, where they may spread and flourish to all Eternity.

---

[2] See his essay "Die 'katholische Mythologie' und ihre mystische Entmythologisierung in der Schluss-Szene des Faust II," *Jahrbuch der Deutschen Schiller-Gesellschaft* 34 (1990), 230–256.

> There is not, in my Opinion, a more pleasing and triumphant Consideration in Religion than this of the perpetual Progress which the Soul makes towards the Perfection of its Nature, without ever arriving at a Period in it.[3]

Addison even goes so far as to imagine the attitude of God towards this creation of his: "...it must be a Prospect pleasing to God himself to see his Creation for ever beautifying in his Eyes, and drawing nearer to him, by greater degrees of Resemblance."[4] Addison outlines a picture of Christian paradise in which God is still on his throne, even if eternally unreachable to his creature, unless in an inexhaustible approximation at the limit. The other text Schmidt puts forward is a quotation from Leibniz's *Principles of Nature and of Grace* (1714), conceptually quite near to the words of Addison:

> Ainsi notre bonheur ne consistera jamais, et ne doit point consister dans une pleine jouissance, où il n'y auroit plus rien à désirer, et qui rendroit notre esprit stupide, mais dans un progrès perpétuel à de nouveaux plaisirs et de nouvelles perfections.[5]

Goethe knew and valued *The Spectator* (which ceased publication in 1714), going so far as to recommend it to his sister, in whom he was trying to instill a modern, lively culture. He knew Leibniz's work as well, so that even if we cannot actually prove that he read the *Principles,* it is probable that he did. And in any case the idea of perfectibility as ideal of perfection can be found often in Leibniz's work, even if the textual affinities are not as close as here. Addison and Leibniz are of course valuable not just in themselves as individual authors, but also as representatives of a particular cultural moment, the Enlightenment, if not exactly at its birth, at least still in its expanding and productive phase. The juxtaposition allows us to confirm what criticism has in several ways been able to establish, and that is that Goethe was deeply rooted in the Enlightenment, even though this is not a question central

---

[3] J. Addison, *The Spectator* n. 111, Saturday July 7th, 1711, in Vol. 1 (London: Dent, 1945), 339.

[4] J. Addison, *The Spectator* n. 111, 339.

[5] "In der Vernunft begründete Prinzipien der Natur und der Gnade," in Gottfried Wilhelm Leibniz, *Philosophische Schriften* Bd. 1: *Kleine Schriften zur Metaphysik,* ed. Hans Heinz Holz (Frankfurt, 1986), S. 438.

to our interests here. For the present discussion it may be more relevant to underline the anthropological conception underlying the visions of the three writers, and to what extent they coincide or overlap: a basically optimistic idea, in line with basic Enlightenment beliefs.[6]

The perspective of infinite perfectiblity opening up to man is exciting, and it would perhaps be better to turn upside down the rational scheme followed up to here, and see the images of paradise not as concrete results of, or metaphysical guarantees of, perfectibility—but sim-

---

[6] An important critical problem could be opened up, if the specific nature of Goethe's heterodox paradise (infinite ascent, without ever reaching God) is to be accounted for—in addition to his own extremely personal religious evolution, about which the author speaks in his autogiography *Dichtung und Wahrheit*—by the patristic tradition well known to him, and in any case well documented in the *Unparteyische Kirchen- und Ketzerhistorie* (first published between 1699 and 1715) of Gottfried Arnold, whom Goethe read and studied carefully well before the Enlightenment texts of Addison, Leibniz and others. Since it seems certain that Goethe knew both textual traditions, the link with the more recent texts would appear more cogent from a methodological perspective, which can be connected to the poet's roots in the culture and sensibilities of the Enlightenment. However, if Jochen Schmidt is in favor of a certain dependence on the Addison-Leibniz early Enlightenment tradition, many other scholars take into account only the patristic heterodox tradition, above all Origen. See for example Elizabeth M. Wilkinson, "The Theological Basis of Faust's Credo," *German Life and Letters* 3 (1957), 229–239, and especially Arthur Henkel, "Das Ärgernis Faust," in *Versuche zu Goethe: Festschrift für Erich Heller,* eds. V. Dürr and G. von Molnar (Heidelberg, 1976), 282–304, which strongly favors the identification of Faust's salvation with Origenian apocatastasis. This thesis, which has been well received by critics, is contested strongly by, first, R. D. Zimmerman, "Goethes 'Faust' und die 'Wiederbringung aller Dinge. Kritische Bermerkungen zu einem unkritisch aufgenommenen Interpretationsversuch," *Goethe-Jahrbuch* 111 (1994), 171–185; and Dieter Bremer, "'Wenn starke Geisteskraft [...].' Traditions-Vermittlungen in der Schlusszene von Goethes 'Faust,'" *Goethe-Jahrbuch* 112 (1995), 257–307. Bremer not only persuasively denies the presence of an echo of the Origenian apocatastasis at the end of Faust, but traces the Goethean conception of salvation of the entelecheia to traditions even more remote, going back as far as Heraclitus. Beyond this particular, though very important, problem, we must keep sight of the fact that the Goethian image is defined necessarily, and certainly consciously, against the orthodox and widespread conception of paradise as an Augustinian quietening down or repose in God. The perception of this difference from orthodoxy is part of the signifying structure of the text.

ply as mythical projections of that infinite human perfectibility, which is the real logical prius of Enlightenment thought. But this line of thinking does not strike me as very useful for an understanding in depth of Goethe's paradise, which at bottom does not seem to possess a traditionally transcendent dimension (although it is by no means lacking in a secret religious vein, for long stretches informed with a Spinoza-mediated pantheism).[7]

Yet it seems to me more important to emphasize another point (to which an additional, final point will be added). This is the rigorous individualism of the salvation by ascent of Goethe's paradise. The soul of Faust ascends, and by doing so is purified or perfected, but it is exclusively his business. Any kind of choral or community dimension is quite absent, unless we accept the verses sung by the groups of the blessed who, in certain opera-style Catholic scenographies of heaven, describe the ascending path of the newly blessed one, and who (in the case of the last words of the "blessed lads"), hope in future for help from none other than Faust for their further ascending. It could be said that Faust's soul is only concerned with his own salvation. Other souls (foremost among them that of Gretchen) are concerned with him, and pray for him. He himself seems to march straight on along the road of individual salvation, which seems to be and perhaps really is the only thing he cares about. All this is most shrewdly expressed not through the words or phrases of Faust—whose death we have just witnessed, so that his talking might seem odd or grotesque or frankly comical—but precisely because he says nothing. In the two final scenes the central character no longer speaks, although he is at the center of the stage. Everyone talks about him, but he is silent; an effective expedient to express the cutting away of every social or interpersonal connection of a soul included in an individual process of purification of a considerably paradoxical flavor. I have tried elsewhere to justify in the context of the overall evolu-

[7] For a synthetic overview of Goethe's religiosity and of the numerous parallels that link the final scene of *Faust* to the poetry on religious themes throughout Goethe's life, see Erich Trunz, "Goethes religioes Gedankenwelt, dargestellt auf Grund der Gedichte und des 'Faust'-Schlusses," in his *Weltbild und Dichtung im Zeitalter Goethes. Acht Studien* (Weimar, 1993), 125–144.

tion of the author, this radical, almost paradoxically individualistic shift in the conclusion to *Faust II*.[8] Suffice it here to have pointed out this characteristic feature of blessedness as Goethe understood it, and to stress how difficult it is to reduce it to the Christian tradition, whether of Protestant or Catholic orthodoxy. And in fact, just as it was easy where *Streben* was concerned to point out the parallels to the infinite ascending movements to paradise, in the same way it will not be difficult to see in the living Faust's egocentrism the feature that finds continuation and fulfilment in this totally individual aim at purification in his paradisal journey after death.

There is one final point to examine in this peculiar paradise. The strength that pushes Faust towards ever higher regions in heaven (which means: that takes him to ever higher degrees of perfection) is divine love (subjective genitive). Faust in other words appears to be almost pushed or carried up; his role is mostly passive. This great protagonist of the action throughout the whole play here seems to be the object of an entirely transcendent force that raises him up (in the same way one could stress that the very active living Faust is in reality passively subject to the intimate restlessness of the *Streben*). Now, the force that pushes him up into paradise is a rather impersonal one. We seem to be faced with a kind of salvational automatism, a great irresistible magnet drawing him up to God, a God whom however we never manage to see and who hovers a long way off in the background of the image. At a certain point this love (which we should not forget is in German female: *Liebe*) is polarized in an equally female figure, Mary, who at the end of the enthusiastic address directed at her by "Doctor Marianus" will even be called "Goddess," *Göttin*. The salvific love that draws us near to God seems to emanate from a female figure who assumes divine features and a divine role. But no personification of love really takes place, as is clear from the words that close the play, which name the "Eternal Female/ that draws us upwards." Here the confusion—certainly consciously desired—appears to be total. Love is not a link between people (as it

---

[8] See "L'eroe colpevole o la salvezza tragica di Faust," *Studia theodisca* (1996), 109–126.

would be both in its ordinary sense and in the entire biblical and theological tradition), but a force which seems for a while to emanate out of Mary, but then immediately afterwards is generalized, so that the nonetheless "divine" Mary is shown to be simply a personification of a female principle, of which it is extraordinarily difficult to say anything which does not sound appallingly blasphemous. And if we add to this that love has already been spoken about elsewhere, to be precise at the close of Act II, as a universal cosmogonic and metamorphic force, we can easily see how Goethe here has wished to shuffle his cards a good deal; indeed, he succeeded so well that criticism today is still a long way from giving a rigorous definition of this love. And I certainly do not want to propose one here myself, but will once again simply underline how far it all is from what the biblical and theological tradition, however confusedly, allows us to affirm.

Even here, while we clearly must acknowledge Goethe's distance from Christianity, I think we may point out that however estranged or deformed it is, it does belong to a really religious experience. The "pagan" Goethe shows that he possesses a non-professed, non-canonical, non-conventional, but not unimportant secret religious awareness. Precisely the character of the power of love which I have, a little provocatively, called almost automatic, which raises the rather passive Faust to ever higher degrees of perfection, may be read as a twilight form of consciousness of the fact that human forces on their own are not enough for salvation, that man is not saved by virtue of himself, but that salvation is the fruit of a free meeting with what the Christian tradition calls grace. It is obvious that Goethe knows this idea of grace perfectly well, since he belongs to a generation that still received a solid religious education; he evidently knew the patristic tradition very well, to an extent that would today be almost limited to specialists. But it is also obvious that where he is not interested, he is always able to ignore even central ideas of the Christian message, as for example the incarnation, the Trinity or redemption. If something approximating the idea of grace recurs positively in Goethe's paradise, however confusedly or imperfectly, it can I think be argued that this signals some kind of adherence by the author to such an idea.

I will close with a methodological warning that would threaten to reopen the entire argument attempted so far, if I wished to carry it to its furthest extent. I have spoken of the Goethean paradise with reference to *Faust.* Methodological caution is however necessary, which I shall formulate with a question; are we sure that this is a Goethean paradise, and not just the *Faust* paradise, i.e. of a fictional poetical work, that as such does not personally involve the author? The question is an important one which elsewhere (if these were strictly literary studies) might require clarification in depth. Here I think it can be more or less treated as if it were really Goethe's thinking, by arguing that in any case this was what Goethe wanted to entrust to us. And if he of course knew how complicated the relationship was between a work and its author, he also knew that the reader would perceive the artistic presentation as basically very close to his deepest ideas. Today in addition we know we can read literary fiction suspending judgment as to its fictional character and accepting it—in a very serious game—as if it were a real experience. This much must be enough to justify our continuing to reason over the Goethean paradise, trying to draw out what Goethe thought, or even better, what we ourselves can think about it.

The Paradise of Names: Benjamin's Interpretation of Genesis 1–3 (1916)

Gianfranco Bonola

Although short, the theoretical scope of *Über Sprache überhaupt und über die Sprache des Menschen*[1] must lead us to consider it one of the young Benjamin's most committed and "esoteric" works. Furthermore, the high regard in which the author held this work, and his treatment of it, indicate that for a long period he considered it to be the work that most closely reflected his philosophical position. On the other hand, the work's genesis was fortuitous because, as Benjamin states himself, it was written[2] in response to certain questions raised by Scholem in a letter that today has been lost. It is difficult to surmise the exact purport of Scholem's questions, and his diaries, which have now been published and which contain reflections on language that were committed to paper in the period immediately before 31.10.1916, are no help.[3] These

---

[1] This will be referred to as "ÜS" in the notes. The German text can be found in Walter Benjamin, *Gesammelte Schriften*, edited by R. Tiedemann and H. Schweppenhäuser, vols. I–VII (Frankfurt am Main, 1972–89) (= WB GS); see WB GS II, 140–57. Quotations in English are taken from Walter Benjamin, *Selected Writings*, edited by Marcus Bullock and Michael W. Jennings, Volume 1, 1913–1926 (Cambridge, London: The Belknap Press of Harvard University Press, 1996).

[2] See the passage from the letter to G. Scholem of 11.11.1916, that can now be found in Walter Benjamin, *Gesammelte Briefe*, Bd. I. 1910–1918, edited by Christoph Gödde and Henri Lonitz (Frankfurt am Main, 1995), (= WB GB I) see WB GB I, 343: "A week ago I started a letter to you that went on for eighteen pages. It was an attempt to provide comprehensive answers to some of the not inconsiderable numbers of questions that you had asked me. However, in order to get to grips with the subject matter, I had to rework it into a small treatise, which I am now writing in a definitive form." The essay must therefore have been written between 4 and 11 November 1916.

[3] Scholem's diary entry for this day is the terse: "Benjamin geschrieben." See Gershom Scholem, *Tagebücher nebst Aufsätzen und Entwürfen bis 1923, I. Halbband 1913–1917*, unter Mitarbeit von Herbert Kopp-Oberstebrink, eds. Karlfried Gründer und Friedrich Niewöhner (Frankfurt am Main, 1995). (= GS Tb I), see GS Tb I, 414. Two weeks previously, on 13.October, some reflections on mysticism, language, mathematics and Zion were jotted down; see 407.

reflections only give us an idea of the importance of language because of the wide range of topics over which the two friends' discussions ranged, and because of the strong and vital connection between language and the transcendental sphere that is identified. This sphere is both that of the Messiah and of Scholem's interpretation of Zion, which was the metaphysical cornerstone of his vision of reality.

When Benjamin announced the ambitious title of *Über Sprache überhaupt und über die Sprache des Menschen* to Scholem, he admitted that this reflected a "systematic intention," although he was nevertheless convinced that he would not for the moment be able to properly embark on such an undertaking.[4] Later references in Benjamin's letters confirm the importance of the work,[5] and we learn that from an early stage in his career he attempted several times to reconnect his thought with this seminal work, but to little effect. Benjamin was no longer able to take up the train of thought that runs through this work, which was to remain the culminating point of a moment of great theoretical felicity. In fact we know today that after 1933 there was to be no re-examination of *Über Sprache überhaupt* (which was published only in 1955, in the edition of the *Schriften*[6]). The ideas contained in the work, on the other hand, with which only a very small group of friends of his youth were familiar, would continue to secretly inspire his later sporadic attempts to address the problem of language and would keep these attempts searching and urgent.[7] However, the biblical source on which this work draws must have continued to run deep like a secret underground river that was hidden from public view because it is to the lexis and the biblical visions that Benjamin returns in his last, visionary work, *On the Concept of History*.

[4] The fact that WB wanted to achieve a completely systematic formulation is borne out by the fact that he appears to have also told Scholem that this was only "a first part that would be followed by two others." See Gershom Scholem, *Walter Benjamin—die Geschichte einer Freundschaft* (Frankfurt am Main, 1975), 48.

[5] For example, in letters to Ernst Schoen on 25.2.1917 (See WB GB I, 355).

[6] See Walter Benjamin, *Schriften*, 2 Bde, eds. Th. W. Adorno and Gretel Adorno (Frankfurt am Main, 1955).

[7] As an example we cite the 1928 review for Eva Fiesel, *Die Sprachphilosophie der deutschen Romantik* (Tübingen, 1927), now to be found in WB GS III, 96.

1. Admitted and Denied

When announcing the contents of *Über Sprache überhaupt* in his letter of 11.11.1916 to Scholem that we have already mentioned, Benjamin wrote: "...in this work I am trying to examine the essence of language, as far as possible in immediate relationship to Jewishness and the first chapters of Genesis."[8] In other words, he expressed the hope that he would be supported and encouraged in this by his friend. These brief comments do not, however, give us any clue as to why Benjamin thought it necessary to resort to a text like the Bible, that he had until then made very little use of,[9] in order to get at the root of the problem of language. We find an attempt to offer comprehensive reasons for his use of the Bible in the central part of the essay, which serves as an introduction to the section dedicated to an interpretation of the chapters in Genesis. In this passage[10] Benjamin also states his assumptions regarding the authority and validity he is prepared to recognize in the scriptural text, and the quality and scope of the interpretative work on which he has embarked is also defined. He writes that "in what follows the nature of language is considered on the basis of the first chapter of Genesis," and is at the same time anxious to clear up two possible misunderstandings. His analysis of the "first chapter of Genesis" does not aim to be a straightforward "biblical interpretation." It will rather be a procedure through which he will pursue his objective of defining the nature of language. Although he has resorted to the Bible, he does not intend to subject it to "objective consideration as revealed truth." It will rather be a "discovery of what emerges of itself from the biblical text that will enable him to define the nature of language..." However, after denying that Genesis is authoritative this respect because of its transcendental nature, Benjamin quotes its contents to show that it is necessary to

---

[8] See WB GB I, 343.

[9] Only in a letter to Carla Seligson written on 4.8.1913 from Freudenstadt (See WB GB I, 162s.), had WB drawn attention to biblical themes such as the presence of the Tree of Knowledge in the centre of the Garden of Eden (Gen. 2:9), its forbidden fruits (Gen. 2,17) and the subsequent Fall (Gen. 3:1–7).

[10] See WB GS II, 147.

resort to the Bible. For now, he declares, this is an "indispensable" work of reference because there is objective convergence between the Biblical doctrine of language and the conception of language that he has elaborated: the "fundamental point" on which Benjamin is in agreement with the Bible is "in presupposing language as an ultimate reality, perceptible only in its manifestation, inexplicable and mystical." If we accept these explanations, we must accept that it was only after a period of reflection that Benjamin thought of the Bible as a text that could provide enlightenment and support (perhaps in considerable quantities) to an autonomous theory that had arisen separately from it and which was independent of it.

It is, however, also possible in my opinion that the entire question posed by *Über Sprache überhaupt* was suggested and guided by an initial and perhaps unconscious reaction to the passages of Genesis that deal with language. The essay uses these verses to construct a rich and dense exegesis, the unusual complexity of which arises from a perception of the profundity of the underlying philosophical problem, for which such exegesis is entirely appropriate. Not only does the work explicitly state that "the present argument broadly *follows*"[11] the Bible in the central question that we have just mentioned, but long before the Scriptures are explicitly examined the attentive reader can gather formal evidence and proofs supplied by content that anticipate the theoretical framework that is in the meanwhile set out in the form of pure philosophical reflection. Right from the first pages the connection between the linguistic nature of things and the idea of God is evoked, admittedly by antiphrasis, and a cryptic quotation of Genesis 1:2 even finds its way into the metaphor that illustrates a problematic link.[12] The most important and decisive proof of this dependence on the biblical conception of

[11] Ibid.; my italics.

[12] "The view that the mental essence of a thing consists precisely in its language—this view, taken as a hypothesis, is the great abyss [*Abgrund*] into which all linguistic theory threatens to fall, and to survive suspended precisely over this abyss is its task." See WB GS II, 141, also Gen. 1:2 (in the Luther version) "...und es war finster auf der Tiefe. Und der Geist Gottes schwebet auf dem Wasser." "Tiefe" and "Abgrund" are, of course, synonyms.

language nevertheless occurs when Benjamin goes on to examine human language from a rigorously theoretical point of view after immediately saying that it "speaks in words." He shows that he immediately and obviously takes the term "word," which includes all the grammatical forms, to mean "name." Basing his argument on the undeniable fact that one of the basic functions of human discourse is that of naming things, Benjamin assumes that this is the primary and fundamental function and that human language is essentially a "naming" language. In a simple passage in which no supporting arguments are offered and it is instead tacitly shown to be understood as something obvious, he conceives language as centering on name-giving. This becomes for him the original and constituting dimension of the linguistic fact, the one from which all others derive and upon which they depend. Emphasizing and favoring the name and the naming (rather than the verb and action, or the manifestation of mental states and pleasure/repulsion or something else), and even more the fact that this approach to human language is considered to be obvious,[13] places the complex theorizing of Benjamin *a priori* in a horizon of biblical ascendancy even before the first quotation from the Bible appears in his work.[14] The idea that language is based on and developed by naming leads him to affirm that man, by naming things and animals, expresses and exercises his dominion over nature; even before the Bible is named Benjamin affirms that *"God's creation is completed when* things receive their names from man,"[15] i.e., he mentions two fundamental aspects of Judaeo-Christian anthropology that are based on the Bible.

In order to show how deeply Benjamin is rooted in the biblical scheme of things, it is first necessary to analyze the page on which he examines the link that exists between language and revelation. It is an

---

[13] It is also obvious that the abstract idea of general language, of which human language would be only one possible declension (as WB states at the beginning of the essay), is open to the same criticism as that which has been formulated for the role of the Bible, because even in this case there is a sort of *hysteron proteron*. It reverberates to the essence of what will be human language.

[14] (Gen. 2:19.) See WB GS II, 145.

[15] See WB GS II, 144. My italics.

important[16] passage, the relevance of which to the overall purpose of the essay nevertheless seems to be extremely doubtful unless the author in fact intends, as he himself states a few lines later, to attribute to the Bible the status of "revealed truth." But even if we assume without necessarily accepting it, that this is a completely general and abstract paradigm of revelation, it is nevertheless based *a priori* on biblical revelation and rests wholly on important parts of it. After identifying the concept of revelation as "the most intimate link" between the philosophy of language and the philosophy of religion, Benjamin maintains that his equation of mental being with linguistic being leads to the traditional notion of an "inverse proportionality" between the two, i.e., the more existent and real the mind (and it is obviously God who is the most existent and real), the more it is inexpressible and unexpressed. To summarize his thesis he affirms: "the expression that is linguistically most existent (that is the most fixed) is linguistically the most rounded and definitive; in a word, the most expressed is at the same time the purely mental." It is on precisely this point that he maintains that he agrees with the concept of revelation, "if it takes the inviolability of the word as the only and sufficient condition and characteristic of the divinity of the mental being that is expressed in it." And yet I wonder what this "inviolability of the word" is if not the principle of transcendence that informs the literal nature of the biblical text according to the Judaeo-Christian tradition. But the biblical inspiration does not stop there.

In order to illustrate his conclusion that "the highest mental region of religion" is "at the same time the only one that does not know the inexpressible" because this is the true meaning of "revelation," Benjamin concludes: "For it is addressed in the Name and expresses itself as revelation." In this sentence we have written "Name" with a capital "N" and have thus eliminated the ambiguity of the German, because in this case the force of the verb and the definite article lead us to strongly suppose that this is not a question of the name as a part (albeit a central and paradigmatic one) of human speech but rather a Name by antonomasia, one of the terms that is pregnant with the whole of Juda-

---

[16] See WB GS II, 146.

ism. It indicates God inasmuch as he has manifested himself and it is he who is invoked by man.[17] The end of the paragraph clearly repeats that "the highest mental being, as it appears in religion, rests solely on man and on the language in him," and even seems to offer a grain of Cabalistic wisdom[18] that will underline man's great responsibility in the entire process of redemption. To seal this passage, Benjamin adds a famous expression of Hamann's, which he has underlined himself: "Language, the mother[19] *of reason and revelation, their alpha and omega.*"[20]

The underlying sense of bewilderment is thus heightened: Does this far-reaching discussion of the relationship between linguistic essence and revelation merely reflect the fact that Benjamin resorted to the Scriptures *faute de mieux* only because "the Bible, in regarding itself as a revelation, must necessarily evolve the fundamental 'linguistic facts'"?[21] I do not believe this to be the case. As he has chosen to ally himself with revelation and as, like the Romantics and *kabbalah,* he cannot conceive a revelation not intimately connected with language, Benjamin is caught up by the force of attraction of the Bible and opts for the idea of a "naming" language. In fact, as he wrote initially to Scholem and later tried unsuccessfully to play down in the text, he finds

---

[17] However, even if this interpretation is not accepted, it is obvious that the name (a simple part of speech) takes on such a central position by antonomasia through the Name.

[18] This is also found in other contemporary writings, for example in the essay *Atheistische Theologie* (1914) by Franz Rosenzweig in this form: "But it is no coincidence that that famous central affirmation of the master of the kabbalah: — God says: if you do not bear witness to me, I am not—is expressed as a word of God and exegetical devices are used to claim that it is also present in God's written word; it is God himself who makes himself dependent on Man's bearing witness (it is not human presumption that assumes that God is in such a position), He 'sells himself,' to use a deeply meaningful metaphorical expression, to Man." See FR W III, *Zweistromland*, 696.

[19] It should be remembered that "language," *Sprache,* is feminine in German.

[20] See Johann Georg Hamann, letter to Friedrich Heinrich Jacobi 18 Oct. 1785 [in fact: 28 Oct. 1785], the complete wording of the German test is: "[Bei mir ist weder von Physik noch Theologie die Rede, sondern von] Sprache, die Mutter *der Vernunft und Offenbarung, ihr alpha und omega*" (the italics are WB's, and alter those of Hamann who emphasized only "Offenbarung").

[21] See WB GS II, 147.

himself formulating a conception of language that has "a direct link with Judaism." In other words, it is totally circumscribed by the biblical horizon.

2. Magical Influences from the North

It certainly comes as no surprise that even in a work that is otherwise so lacking in references as *Über Sprache überhaupt*, Benjamin quotes Johann Georg Hamann to back up his case at two different points in the development of his thesis, both of which are closely connected with the Bible. The voice of the "Magus im Norden" was in fact one of the first to be raised in protest against the spread, which had been propitiated German speaking world by Herder, of the Enlightenment's purely humanistic theory of language that is the basis of the view that language is a set of linguistic conventions. This was a bourgeois concept[22] against which Benjamin, in the tradition of the Romantics, but with his own originality, intended to fight. Drawing on that historic moment and on that dispute, Benjamin seems on the one hand to favor Hamann's spirituality, in which the philosophical and religious aspect become inseparably fused in linguistic being, and on the other to embrace its transcendentalism that is manifested in the idea of an easy and spontaneous production of human language in the presence of an original Paradise-like nature that is filled with the divine word of creation. Furthermore, the allusive tone of esoteric wisdom—which was therefore all the more assertive and definitive—of Hamann's extremely learned discourse, addressed to the initiated, could not but please Benjamin. However, if we examine more closely those phrases of Hamann's that Benjamin quotes, we are immediately struck by the discrepancy between the meaning that he manages to pin onto them in their new context and their original meaning, of which Benjamin must have been aware.

---

[22] "This view is the bourgeois conception of language, the invalidity and emptiness of which will become increasingly clear in what follows. It holds that the means of communication is the word, its object factual, and its addressee a human being;" and "Hence, it is no longer conceivable, as the bourgeois view of language maintains, that the word has an accidental relation to its object, that it is a sign for things (or knowledge of them) agreed by some convention." See WB GS II, 144 and 150.

To return to Benjamin, if we discount the possibility that he completely misunderstood Hamann, we must assume that he at least consciously tried to deprive Hamann's words of their power and to reduce their scope. But even if we exclude this possibility, we become aware of subterranean, more complex perspectives that lend force to Benjamin's essay and move its focus even more markedly in the direction of biblical revelation because this is what underpins all of Hamann's speculations (albeit from a Christian point of view).

As we have seen, the first quotation closes the demanding and ambiguous page that illustrates the relationship that unites language and revelation, and at a first reading it simply sounds like a confirmation of what has just been shown: "Language, the mother *of reason and revelation, their alpha and omega,*" says Hamann.[23] This is taken from a long letter that Hamann wrote to Friedrich Heinrich Jacobi between the 22nd and the 28th of October 1785. It is well known and is often quoted because it neatly sums up its author's position.

Furthermore, it can easily be detached from its context, which happens to be very interesting because the talk is of Kant,[24] Herder and above all Spinoza, also in relation to Mendelssohn, against whom Jacobi is about to engage in a public debate on the question of whether Lessing was really a follower of Spinoza.[25] As he felt involved, Hamann became convinced that he needed to intervene in the debate, but not before first defining his own position better. However, it is the most immedi-

---

[23] See WB GS II, 147.

[24] Hamann's theoretical prospective also comes to the fore in another work of the young Benjamin, the *Programm einer kommenden Philosophie*, now to be found in WB GS II, 157–71. This sets itself the task, as was announced in the letter to Scholem of 22.10.1917, of going beyond Kant, not "by destroying the Kantian system" but by remaking it "on granite" and "developing it universally." The passage on Hamann says, "The great transformation and correction that the unilaterally mathematical and mechanical concept of cognisance must undergo can be implemented only if it is linked to language, as Hamann had already tried to do when Kant was still alive" (ibid., 168). These are thus ideas that are at least one year later than the ÜS essay but they are still linked to a systematic philosophical plan.

[25] On 28 August of that year, Jacobi had in fact signed the preface to the work *Über die Lehre des Spinoza in Briefen an den Herrn Moses Mendelssohn*.

ate part of the passage, which Benjamin entirely ignores, and the interlinked biblical verses, which he quotes, that offer surprises. Hamann writes:

> I shall not express an opinion until I have ordered my own thoughts and attempts and for this I require time, patience and reflection. For me, it is not a question of Physics or of Theology but of *language*, the mother of reason and revelation, their alpha and omega. It [i.e. language] is the double-edged sword for all truths and lies.[26] Do not laugh if I say that I must attack the matter from this quarter. It is the same old story with me, but thanks to you, things have been done.[27] (*Gnothi seauton*[28])

The sequence of this association of Hamann's leaves us in no doubt. It is fairly evident (and could not have escaped Benjamin's notice because the Gildemeister edition used by him contains the biblical references in the notes) that Hamann has good cause to call *Sprache* the mother of reason and, even more so, of revelation itself, because he understands the term to be a synonym of (and in terms of content he considers that language is underpinned by) that *Wort Gottes* that is honed and discriminating and is the true "two-edged sword" of Hebrews 4:12 which is quoted here. And there is also a reference, in strict accordance with the New Testament, to the fact that for the Christian Hamann the word of God found its supreme manifestation in the *logos* of the Gospel according to Saint John, by which "All things were made" and that in Christ "the Word was made flesh, and dwelt among us."[29] Benjamin nevertheless acts as if he could calmly treat this dramatic absorption and grafting of language onto Christology as a mere footnote. But how could Benjamin presume to have found support for and confirmation of his own theses from these words of Hamann's without having to

---

[26] See Hebrews 4:12 in Luther's translation: "Denn das wort Gottes ist lebendig vnd krefftig, vnd scherffer denn kein zweischneidig Schwert. Vnd durch dringet, bis das scheidet seele vnd geist, auch marck vnd bein, vnd ist ein Richter der gedancken vnd sinnen des hertzen."

[27] See John 1:3 in Luther's translation: "Alle ding sind durch dasselbige gemacht...."

[28] See *Johann Georg Hamann's, des Magus im Norden, Leben und Schriften*, hrsg. v. C. H. Gildemeister, Bd. 5. *Briefwechsel mit F. H. Jacobi*, 122. This part of the letter was written on 28.10.1785.

[29] See John 1:14.

implicitly recognize the foundations on which they were based, which were at the same time transcendental and Christian? Hamann's words, if they are taken by themselves and are set in their proper context, tell us something else and give language itself an immense scope and metaphysical function. Nevertheless, it is only thus that his words can be taken towards that "metaphysics of language" to which Benjamin veers. This once again shows it to be the child of a basic tenet that he refuses to recognize.

These observations apply all the more to the second, lengthier quotation, which is taken from the *Last depositions of the Knight Rosenkreuz regarding the divine and human origin of language* by Hamann, which is quoted as confirmation of the fact the "creative word" has become "in man the language of cognition and of the name in spirit in bliss."[30] As a gloss on the happy condition of man in the Garden of Eden, Benjamin quotes a passage from Hamann, which he carefully removes from its context:

> Everything that Man originally heard, saw with his eyes... and his hands have touched was... a living word; because God was the word. With this word on his lips and in his heart the origin of language was natural, easy and spontaneous like a children's game...[31]

This quotation must also be set in its proper context and be returned to its biblical substratum.

> Adam was thus of God: and God Himself presented the first born and greatest of our line as the fief holder and heir to the world completed by the word that cam out of his mouth. Angels who were anxious to contemplate his celestial countenance were the ministers and courtiers of the first monarchy. They all exulted the children of God to the chorus of the stars of the morning. Everything had the savour and aspect of a new and fresh thing and the benevolence of the Architect was made manifest, who played and amused Himself with the children of Men. [...]

---

[30] See WB GS II, 151.

[31] See *Des Ritters von Rosenkreuz letzte Willensmeynung über den göttlichen und menschlichen Ursprung der Sprache* (1772), original printed individually at Königsberg at Kanter's and incorrectly dated 1770, now to be found in *Johann Georg Hamann, Sämtliche Werke*, edited by J. Nadler Vol. 3 (Vienna, 1951), 32.

> Each manifestation of nature was a word: the sign, the perceptible image, the pledge of a new secret ineffable union, participation and communication of divine ideas and energies. Everything that Man originally heard, saw with his eyes looked upon and which his hands touched was a living word.[32] God was indeed the Word.[33] With this word in his mouth and heart,[34] the start of language was natural, immediate and as easy as child's play because human nature from dawn to dusk remained as similar to the heavens as the yeast with which small measure any woman is able to raise three measures of flour.[35]
>
> I should continue to matagrabolize[36] at great length, breadth and depth if I did not know that too many sermons tire the hearing as much as the body of the holy orator, I shall therefore content myself today with having found, thanks to a pilgrimage made in sackcloth and ashes,[37] the essence of language, the alpha and omega:[38] the Word and of having named it...

We see that Hamann, too, uses his comments to portray life in the Garden of Eden as life in the sight of and in communion with the Creator. The whole work serves to defend the divine origin of language, but in particular the passage selected by Benjamin is full of quotations

---

[32] See Ia Joh. 1,1: "Das da von anfang war: das wir gehöret haben, das wir gesehen haben mit vnsern augen, das wir beschawet haben, vnd vnser Hende betastet haten, vom Wort des lebens" (Luther translation), where the reference is to Christ and explicitly points to the next verse (das leben, das ewig ist, welches war bey dem Vater, vnd ist vns erschienen) to the prologue of the Gospel of John.

[33] See John 1:1: "und Gott war das Wort."

[34] See Deut. 30:14: "Denn es ist das wort fast nahe bey dir, in deinem Munde, und in deinem Hertzen, das du es thust" where the word is the *torah*. This is, however, also taken up by Paul in Romans 10:8, where the word ("Die ist das wort vom glauben, das wir predigen") explicitly announces and professes faith in Christ.

[35] See Mt. 13,33.

[36] Note of Hamann's: "Matagraboliser, *mataiografobolizein*, Rabelais. [Rabelais 3,22; from mataios (room) grafein (write) and bolizein (throw)=throw out stupidities in writing.]"

[37] Note of Hamann's: *Art Royal du Chevalier de Rosecroix* (London, 1770). 8E,18.

[38] See Revelations 1:8 (Luther's translation): "Ich bin das A vnd das O, der anfang und das ende, spricht der Herr, der da ist, vnd der da war, vnd der da kompt, der Allmechtige," i.e.: "I am Alpha and Omega, the beginning and the ending, saith the Lord, which is, and which was, and which is to come, the Almighty," i.e., the essence of language, the principle of natural intelligibility, is Christ.

from the Bible. These are, however, mostly taken from the New Testament because in this case the overriding purpose is to proclaim a Christocentric interpretation of the Old Testament that is based exclusively on hermeneutic Christian tenets. It is even more difficult than with the previous quotation to ignore, as Benjamin does, the supremely New Testament and Christological tone of the entire passage, especially the way in which the quotation from the Gospel according to Saint John is the linchpin for the whole of Hamann's argument that *Und Gott war das Wort,* which is also central to the Gospel of John. From Hamann's transcendental and Christian point of view, human language could have been harmonious and fortunate in the Garden of Eden only because from the very beginning man had Christ=logos "in his mouth and heart;" in other words, the word made flesh, through which all things have been created, and which has always dwelt with God and is itself divine.[39]

Why then, does Benjamin insert these quotations of Hamann's if Hamann's discourse, to be used in the essay, must be sterilized to the

---

[39] Hamann's insistence on the Greek locution "Alpha and Omega" can be explained by the fact that for him it no longer had the common meaning of symbolizing the "beginning and the end" but in a coded way also represented, on the basis of Revelations 1:8, the christological principle, which for him was indispensable for making the whole of reality intelligible. The elaboration of this intuition can be found in *Aestetica in nuce* (1762), which is ironically translated into a proposal for a concrete procedure: "I speak with you, O Greeks, because you think yourselves wiser than the chamberlains with the Gnostic key; just try to read the *Iliad* after excising, abstraction, the vowels alpha and omega, and then tell me what you think of the poet's understanding and harmonies" (J. G. Hamann, published by Nadler. Quotation from Vol. 2, 207). A little further on he also emphasizes the function of Christ as the encoded hermeneutic key that is indispensable for understanding the Old Testament: "Jesus' witness is therefore the spirit of prophecy" [Note of Hamann's on Revelations 19,10: "the spirit of prophecy is the witness of Jesus"], and the first sign with which He manifests the majesty of His figure of servant and transforms the holy books of the Covenant into a good old wine that clouds the judgement of the masters at table and strengthens the critics' tired stomachs. *Lege libros propheticos non intellecto CHRISTO*—is what the Father of the Church, Saint Augustine of Hippo said—quid tam insipidum et fatuum invenies? Intellige ibi CHRISTUM, non solum sapit, quod legis, sed etiam inebriat" (Ibid., 213).

point of obliterating all links with what was originally its basis and source of demonstrative force? Certainly, taken at literal face value, Hamann's words are completely in harmony with Benjamin's thoughts on language and emphatically corroborate his viewpoint in certain places, but only if one ignores their veiled but inescapable christological implications. But I think that there is more to the matter than this. I have a well founded suspicion that Benjamin quotes Hamann not only in order to honor a thinker who had been a trailblazer along the path of the "metaphysics of language" but also wanted to reward him for the many intuitions that he had been given for his essay from the *Aestetica in nuce.*[40] In fact, without wanting to (or indeed being able to) in any way belittle the overall originality of *Über Sprache überhaupt,* a close comparison of this essay with Hamann's *Aestetica in nuce,* which is never quoted in the work, leads me to conclude that at least a part of the themes that are developed in it were directly suggested by individual passages from this small work of Hamann's. We shall proceed to indicate them as we examine Benjamin's exegesis of Genesis.

3. Logo-ontology

It should by now be apparent that the aim of my analysis is not to examine Benjamin's conception of language, which is the central theme of his essay, but rather to focus on the relationship that is created between this theorizing and the biblical texts that Benjamin examines and interprets. I shall discuss only those aspects of his general theory of language that are strictly necessary for understanding that relationship. But even with such limited aims, we cannot avoid setting out the more general tenets that are stated at the beginning of the work and we must also define some key terms. We will see that the overall scheme that is

---

[40] J. G. Hamann: *Aesthetica in nuce.* (1762) in J. G. Hamann, *Sämtliche Werke,* ed. J. Nadler (Vienna, 1949–57), Vol. 2, 195–217. In this essay there are more references to Genesis than in the other writings of Hamann's on language; in fact, apart from those on which we will dwell we may mention: the creation of light (Gen. 1:3); the creation of Man in God's image (Gen. 1:27); Adam's covering himself with a fig leaf (Gen. 3:7); the coat of skins made for him by God (Gen. 3:21); and the waters above and below the celestial firmament (Gen. 1:7).

traced does not correspond to a traditional system of ontology pure and simple, but is rather a sort of "logo-ontology." The first binding definition is in fact that of "language," which in its most general sense includes "the tendency... toward the communication of the contents of the mind" (140).[41] A fact is then stated: in its various forms language is a phenomenon that is found everywhere. On the basis of another tenet, which Benjamin in fact asks us to postulate: "it is in the nature of each" (event or thing) "to communicate its mental contents," it therefore follows that "There is no event or thing in either animate or inanimate nature that does not in some way partake of language" (141). He in fact then uses a logically consistent counterproof that is reminiscent of the Berkeley's idealism of *esse est percipi*, when he observes that "we cannot imagine a total absence of language in anything" (141); an entity that is totally deprived of language is therefore only an extreme idea that would be unable to communicate itself in any way either to us or to anything else.

Benjamin therefore sustains that a being, at every level, is part of a dimension that links it and is totally invaded by a single form, is invested or crossed by a single structure or, in other words has a single stream running through it that ensures communicative interdependence. This function is recognizable and identifiable and is what Benjamin calls "*Sprache*," language. At first, there appears to be a sort of linguistically based ontology that is in some ways analogous to what was later proposed by H. G. Gadamer ("Sein, das verstanden werden kann, ist Sprache"). Nevertheless, Benjamin is evidently at great pains to ensure that being is not identified wholesale with language when he states: "the mental entity that communicates itself in language is not language itself but something to be distinguished from it" (141). However, throughout the work, statements also crop up that undermine this position that has been won with such effort.[42] A concept of language is energetically

---

[41] From this point on, as most of the references are to Benjamin's text, the page number of the German edition will be given.

[42] "What can be communicated in a spiritual being is his language. Everything is based on this 'is' (which means 'immediately')." See WB GS II, 142.

proposed that promotes its ontological dignity as a medium, a go-between, and an intrinsic value is bestowed on it that gives it a consistency that is as it were significant in itself and that finally emancipates it from any purely instrumental function because "this mental being communicates itself *in* language and not *through* language" (142). Language therefore has a relevance in itself, because it is a communicative space, an expression of the mental being of entities and the place where they become manifest to one another.

However, there are different types of language, which are different in terms of quality and degree of adaptability to the optimum model, which is human language. In nature there is a clear limit to this aspect: when we state that "the languages of things are imperfect," in other words, "(and) they are dumb," we wish, according to Benjamin, to affirm the unquestioned truth that "Things are denied the pure formal principle of language—namely, sound." How, then, do things communicate?

> They can communicate to one another only through a more or less material community. This community is immediate and infinite, like every linguistic communication; it is magical[43] (for there is also magic of matter). (147)

The message that inanimate beings exchange and communicate to man is the immediate expression of their silent presence. Nevertheless, Benjamin continues to affirm that at this level an overall linguistic phenomenon appears, a universal semiosis, a pansemia, that certainly had no small number of antecedents in the universal hermeneutics of the eighteenth century and in the Romantic philosophies of Nature.

Human language finds the deep reason for its excellence in its ability to use that "symbol" of its "community with things [that] is immaterial and purely mental" (147). This enables man to formulate a language made up of words, or, as we have said, to "name" the other entities and to thereby communicate "his own mental being (insofar as it is com-

---

[43] In ÜS Benjamin several times uses the category of "magic" to indicate the mystery that surrounds the nexus that is a fundamental link between reality and language. See above: "if one wishes to call this immediacy magic, the original problem of language is its magic. The well known formula of the magic of language is linked to another one: the infinity of language." See WB GS II, 142s.

municable)" (143). This is a privileged position because, as man has the naming function and its result, the name, which is "the innermost nature of language itself" (144), man becomes the unique case which is unknown to the rest of nature, in which mental being and linguistic being coincide. The result is that the "mental being of man, alone among all mental entities [is] communicable without residue" (144). But having postulated that all language is in itself significant (so that *a fortiori* human language, the optimum stage of language, is all the more so, and serves only secondarily for inter-human communication in the world), Benjamin needs a further referent capable of grasping the absolute significance of which all language is a vehicle. And it is also present *in* human language; it has, as it were, a significance that, by expressing man's mental being, goes beyond all human and merely human communicative horizons. Therefore, the ultimate referent of language must be transcendent. This is what Benjamin wants to show when he affirms that his theory of language, unlike the utilitarian bourgeois one, "knows no means, no object, and no addressee of communication. He says: *in the name, the mental being of man communicates itself to God*" (144). This is the way out that Benjamin proposes in order to overcome the aridity of the bourgeois concept that saw human language as a merely communicative instrument[44] (whose relationship with things is established by human convention and is therefore accidental). At the same time, he does not fall into the trap of the "mystical theory of language," according to which "the word is simply the essence of the thing" (150). However, in order to fully achieve his goal (without conceding anything to any "mystical theory of language"), and in order to safeguard the unequivocal nature of the relationship that links the name to the thing designated, Benjamin has to abandon the register of metaphysical reflection that he has used so far and adopt the powerful metaphors of the Bible in his discourse.[45] He in fact concludes:

---

[44] See note 22 above.

[45] WB's position here is surprisingly similar to that of Rosenzweig, with the foundation of name-giving in revelation; however, as it is possible to show, the third hypothesis (which is an intermediate position between the bourgeois conception and the

> [For according to mystical theory, the word is simply the essence of the thing. That] is incorrect, because the thing in itself has no word, being created from God's word and known in its name by a human word. (150)

It is only at this point on the last page, after he has incorporated into his main arguments what is supplied by the letter of the Judaeo-Christian tradition (which is not juxtaposed, or kept as a parallel demonstrative text), that we can say that his suppositions are really complete:

> The language of an entity is the medium in which its mental being is communicated. The uninterrupted flow of this communication runs through the whole of nature, from the lowest forms of existence to man and from man to God. Man communicates himself to God through name, which he gives to nature and (in proper names) to his own kind; and to nature he gives names according to the communication that he receives from her, for the whole of nature, too, is imbued with a nameless, unspoken language, the residue of the creative word of God, which is preserved in man as the cognisant name and above man as the judgement suspended over him. (157)

This final formulation perhaps makes it easier to appreciate how much Benjamin's message, that a dumb language crosses and permeates all things and beings, may be akin to (or perhaps inspired by) phrases that are present in Hamann's *Aestetica in nuce,* such as the following:

> ...from Creation, which is talk (*Rede*) to the creature via the creature, as one day talks to the next and a night sends news to the next. Their resolving word passes though all climes till the ends of the world and in every dialect (*Mundart*) we hear its voice.[46] The theme is also taken up elsewhere; see 204: "The book of creation contains examples of universal concepts that it has pleased God to reveal to the creature through the creature; the books of the

---

mysticism of language that WB maintains throughout the treatise) is not at all equidistant from the extremes, but is a consequence of the total guarantee of the unequivocal relationship between reality and language, which is the greatest fruit of the "mystical" theory and is therefore above all related to it, and is ultimately a branch that leads back to the mystical theory.

[46] See *Aesthetica in nuce* quotation from p. 198. Hamman's passage echoes Psalm 19:1–4: "The heavens declare the glory of God; and the firmament sheweth his handywork./ Day unto day uttereth speech, and night unto night sheweth knowledge./There is no speech nor language, where their voice is not heard./Their line is gone out through all the earth, and their words to the end of the world."

> Covenant contain examples of secret articles that it has pleased God to reveal to man through man. The Creator's unity is revealed in the dialect of his works, throughout which there is a tone of immeasurable height and depth!"

4. Logo-anthropology

In the same way, according to Benjamin, it is language that constitutes the privileged condition that is reserved to man in the cosmos. After reflecting on man's special prerogative of namegiver to other beings and after going back to the biblical word, which is what more than all else confirms his right to perform this operation and which guarantees the validity of the result (Gen. 2:19: "and whatsoever Adam called every living creature, that was the *name thereof*" [145]), Benjamin now turns, with the circumspection that I have noted, to analyze the first chapters of the book of Genesis. It is at this point that he becomes aware, like others before him, of the profound differences that distinguish the creation of man from the rest of nature, and he may even in this case have been given the idea in the first place by Hamann.[47] Benjamin's exegesis will address itself to the task of showing how the creation of man, in both cases, is distinguished from the creation of nature by the role that language plays (or does not play) in it, and how this is arranged in such a way that the final effect of creation, which is atypical and peculiar, is the bestowal of language upon man.

This is above all evident in the "second version of the story of the Creation, which...reports that man was made from earth."[48] Benjamin stresses that the exceptional nature of this detail is striking. It consists in the fact that "this is in the whole story of the Creation, the only reference to

---

[47] "The creation of his surroundings is to the creation of man as epic poetry is to dramatic poetry. The first comes about through the word, and the second through action. Soul! Be like a tranquil sea! [...] Listen to the advice: Let us make man in our image, after our likeness and let them have dominion.... This is the action and the LORD GOD made Man from a clod of earth.... Compare advice and action, adore together with the Psalmist the mighty Speaker, together with the disciples' evangelist, the gardener who was believed, and with the Apostle of the Hellenistic philosophers and the Talmudic scribes the free potter." See *Aesthetica in nuce*, 200.

[48] See Gen. 2:7.

the material in which the Creator expresses his will, which is doubtless otherwise thought of as creation without mediation" (148). He also stresses that the creation of man is different from other types of creation precisely because "the making of man did not take place through the word: God spoke—and there was."[49] All this must be deeply significant: such a portrayal shows the qualitative difference between the human creature and the rest of creation, and makes man's centrality (and his superiority) hinge on the linguistic fact: "this man, who is not created from the word, is now invested with the *gift* of language and is elevated above nature."

Something analogous that leads to the same conclusions and which leads by another path to the same idea of language can also be found in the detailed account of the creation to be found in Genesis 1. Here again, according to Benjamin, the "manifold rhythm of the act of creation in the first chapter establishes a kind of basic form, from which the act that creates man diverges significantly."

> Admittedly, this passage nowhere expressly refers to a relationship either of man or of nature to the material from which they were created and the question whether the words "He made"[50] envisages a creation out of material must here be left open; but the rhythm by which the creation of nature (in Genesis 1) is accomplished is: Let there be[51]—He made (created)[52]—He named.[53] In the individual act of creation (Genesis 1:3 and 1:14) only the words "Let there be" occur. In this "Let there be" and in the words "He named"[54] at the beginning and the end of the acts the deep and clear relation of the act of creation to language appears each time. With the creative omnipotence of language it begins, and at the end language, as it were, assimilates the created, names it. Language is therefore both creative and the finished; it is word and name... In God, name is creative because it is word, and God's word is cognisant because it is name. "And he saw that it was good"[55]—that is, he had cognised it through name. (148)

---

[49] See Gen. 1, verses 3, 6, 9, 11, 14, 20, 26, 29.

[50] See Gen. 1, verses 21, 27. Luther: "er machte (schuf)."

[51] Luther: "er nannte."

[52] See Gen. 1, verses 5, 8, 10.

[53] Luther: "er nannte."

[54] See Gen. 1, verses 5, 8, 10.

[55] See Gen. 1, verses 4, 10, 12, 18, 21, 25, 31.

In these acts of creation, language is used by God with two different functions: the performative and the naming function. The first has a creative effect and is only of God, while the second will be subsequently also transferred to man. The former uses the "word," the latter the "name." Benjamin then focuses his attention on verse 1:27. This illustrates the creation of man and the divergence is all the more striking in the threefold "He created."[56] It is used three times without any intervention of performative language (the creative word) nor of naming language (the name of man). Benjamin draws the conclusion that in this case again, "God did not create man from the word, and he did not name him." The two accounts of the creation of man therefore concur and work towards obtaining the same effect; Benjamin maintains that in the one case the Bible mentions the material kneaded by God and in the other case care is taken to prevent the creative word from intervening in order to suggest the position of man in relation to language. If man was not created by a simple word, the Creator "...did not wish to subject him to language, but in man God set language, which had served *him* as medium of creation, free" (149). The end of Genesis 2:7, which recounts the other creation, leads to the same conclusion in a more concrete and effective way: God "breathed into his nostrils the breath of life; and man became a living soul."[57] Benjamin was well aware that breath is, as it were, the raw material from which sound and therefore language comes and explains in passing: "God breathes his breath into man: this is at once life and mind and language" (147).[58]

---

[56] See Gen 1:27, Luther: "Vnd Gott schuff den Menschen jm zum Bilde, zum Bilde Gottes schuff er jn. Vnd schuff sie ein Menlin vnd Frewlin," i.e. "So God created man in his own image, in the image of God created he him; male and female created he them" (King James Version).

[57] Luther: "Vnd er blies jm ein den lebendigen Odem in seine Nasen. Vnd also ward der Mensch eine lebendige Seele."

[58] It is curious that even in the *Aesthetica in nuce*, albeit in a different order, there is this triple formula: "A philosopher establishes monastic rules, as did Saul... passion alone gives abstractions and hypotheses hands, feet and wings; to images and signs it gives spirit, life and a tongue.... Where are there swifter arguments? Where the rolling thunder of eloquence and its companion, the monosyllabic flash of lightening are generated." See J. G. Hamann, *Aesthetica in nuce* quotation from p. 208.

He does not elaborate further on this verse, which could open up wide perspectives on the connection between God and man even in terms of the linguistic fact. Nevertheless, he takes up the same theme again with his original exposition of the beginning of Genesis 1:27: "So God created man in his own image." Benjamin's interpretation of it is consistent with the reading of the creation of man that he has so far put forward. There was already an inkling of this in the exegesis of the fact that God rested on the seventh day. According to Benjamin, this occurred when God, having completed the six days' labor, "left his creative power to itself in man" (149), or in other words, left man with language, which he had used to create. However, as man is a simple creature, that language can no longer have any performative function and at the same time "this creativity, relieved of its divine actuality, became knowledge" (149). But what does "God created man in his own image" mean in practical terms? For Benjamin it means that God's creative faculty is reflected in man, where it becomes a cognitive faculty, and once again it is language that ensures this change: "Man is the knower in the same language in which God is the Creator. God created him in his image; he created the knower in the image of the Creator" (149). Two effects are thus outlined: one is exultant, because man's situation is ennobled by the fact that if it what has been said is true and "the mental being of man is language," then this is "the language in which creation took place;" on the other hand, there is one change in scale because man, being incapable of creation, makes use of language in purely cognitive terms: "God made things knowable in their names. Man, however, names them according to knowledge" (148). Thus within the relationship and communion that is cemented by language, the qualitative difference between the human and the divine becomes manifest in the proportionality between word and creation on the one hand and name and knowledge on the other:

> In the word, creation took place, and God's linguistic being is the word. All human language is only the reflection of the word in name. The name is no closer to the word than knowledge is to creation. (149)

5. Knowing, Naming, Translating

From his first origins, therefore, man's essence is linked to his prerogative of stewardship of language, and man's mission is to administer language. He is initiated into this by naming, and by giving names to things and animals he performs the task that has been entrusted to him so that the work of creation be completed. There is, however, no space in this function for free will: the relevance of the human contribution consists in carrying out and giving expression by the name assigned to the dumb significance contained in things, thereby filling the hiatus between a language that was constrained by the silence of simple presence and articulation in sounds. This is the fundamental reason why language, according to Benjamin, is originally rooted uncontroversially in the reality of entities, and this must be recognized and restored by freeing the field from the unsatisfactory dominant linguistic theories without subscribing to inappropriate mystical theories of language.

Benjamin skillfully exploits the possibilities that the Biblical account of the Creation gives him, based as it is on the working word of God: having passed from nothingness to being through the force of a word, entities are in a certain sense materialized words and therefore hold within themselves the mark of the Creator-language that is realized in a larval but constant communicative impulse that man is able to receive. On the other hand, man has a naming language, which is also the precipitate of the divine creative word in a form that is appropriate to man's ontological degree.[59] But when the divine creative word is transferred to man, having become word, the originally active and spontaneous word becomes receptive and cognizant. In man, therefore,

> this knowledge of the thing, however, is not spontaneous creation; it does not emerge from language in the absolutely unlimited and infinite manner of creation. Rather, the name that man gives to language depends on how language is communicated to him. (150)

To guarantee the pertinence of the naming act, which is a solid

---

[59] WB also examines the extreme example of name giving, which is proper names. The proper name is the apex in which man draws even closer to certain characteristics of divine language by naming his children, who are individuals of whom he knows nothing; see WB GS II, 149.

ontological root of the whole of human language, Benjamin locates this initial passive moment, which is not the sense perception of gnoseology but listening to the dumb flowing of things in which one intuits the figure of a familiar dialect: "in one part receptive... it aims to give birth to the language of things themselves, from which in turn, soundlessly, in the mute magic of nature, the word of God shines forth" (150).

At this point Benjamin is at pains to point out that language does not originate at the human level, which it reaches only when it becomes explicit, but in fact arose at the same time as creation as a residue of the divine word that shows how the human element can also be understood in terms of translation. As naming is "translation of the nameless into name," it is rooted in a process of translating the message that the thing in its own way transmits (and is not a mere deciphering of signs that characterize it). It is therefore removed from any residual suspicion of arbitrariness.

In order to achieve this, however, without belittling human language unnecessarily, Benjamin does not only have to elevate the concept of translation to a central position in his general theory of language,[60] but also to imagine a progression of the translation process that goes from inferior to superior languages and which also increases knowledge:

> The translation of the language of things into that of man is not only the translation of the mute into the sonic; it is also the translation of the nameless into name. It is therefore the translation of an imperfect language into a more perfect one, and cannot but add something to it, namely knowledge. (151)

Benjamin puts himself in a very problematic position when he when he continues:

---

[60] The role of translation is just as central in Hamann, although here the movement is one of descent: "Speech is translation—from the language of angels into a language of men, that is, thoughts into words, things into names, images into signs, which can be poetical or kyriological, historical or symbolical or hieroglyphical, philosophical or characteristic." J. G. Hamann, *Aesthetica in nuce*, 199.

> The objectivity of this translation is, however, guaranteed by God. For God created things; the creative word in them is the germ of the cognisant name, just as God, too, finally named each thing after it was created. (157)

Benjamin is close to reducing man's contribution to a paltry amount. That is why he hastens to deny that this is "not the prior solution of the task that God expressly assigns to man himself" which is that of receiving "the unspoken nameless language of things and converting it by name into sounds" (151). Benjamin finds confirmation of his well-founded supposition that God stands surety for man's naming language in a poem by the eighteenth-century painter Müller "Adam's First Awakening and First Blissful Nights,"[61] which, with a gesture that is as provocative as it is typically Jewish, he elevates to the *midrash* of Genesis. Benjamin in fact sees a poetic reflection of "the realization that only the word from which things are created permits man to name them" in Müller's unusual view of the biblical scene of the naming of the animals (Gen. 2:19),[62] in which "God gives each beast in turn a sign, whereupon they step before man to be named. In an almost sublime way, the linguistic community of mute creation with God is thus conveyed in the image of the sign" (152). But this sign, which fascinated Benjamin because of the mystery of the number, seems in other ways to be a step backwards, because it implies in my opinion a level of meaning that is much less than what a "language of things" can convey, although it is "dumb." In the overall design of this succession of languages it also expresses a further proportionality that implicitly explains Gen. 2:7, and which is cemented by a circular relationship: the language of the divine Creator is superior to the cognizant language of man just as the sonorous language of man is superior to the silent language of things; but even in the latter, and to an even greater extent in the former, the trace of the divine creative word is preserved, which is thus revealed to be the ultimate and sole foundation of expressibility.

---

[61] Friedrich Müller, *Adams erstes Erwachen und erste seelige Nächte*, 2nd ed. (Mannheim, 1779), 49.

[62] This is also mentioned in *Aesthetica in nuce*: "that freedom with which the beasts paid homage to Adam, when God brought them to the man to see what he would call them. For whatever he called them, that was their name." J. G. Hamann, *Aesthetica in nuce*, 206.

6. The Paradox of Judgment

Benjamin's reading of Genesis concentrates completely on the theme of language and finds one of its greatest moments of originality when it uses this *clef de lecture* to reinterpret Original Sin. For Benjamin, this derives from language, takes place in language and is visited on language. The reason for the transgression is in fact traced back to the demand to go beyond the Garden of Eden's language of names, the only "fully cognizant" language that man has been given, in order to reach the cognition upon which the knowledge of good and evil is based. Aiming to go beyond in this way meant falling victim to an idle and even impious curiosity (although Benjamin does not explicitly show this aspect) because it implies a demand to investigate (or even to challenge) the reasons for the judgment that God has already pronounced on things when, after creating them, he said that they were good.[63]

The true Fall therefore consists in turning towards "the knowledge to which the serpent seduces, that of good and evil," which knowledge, having no suitable referent, is therefore outside the sphere of the name: "it is vain in the deepest sense null and void and without worth" (152). The true fall also consists in wanting to attribute consistency and validity to this knowledge. There may be something that leads to this misunderstanding (the very name of the Tree of Knowledge) but "this very knowledge is itself the only evil known to the paradisiacal state." Adam's sin lies in the fact that he "abandons the name" and turns to "a knowledge from outside" that gives the lie to the tempter's promise because it is "an unproductive parody of the creative word." Original sin wants to investigate a question that is devoid of actual sense and therefore twists language to investigate in that direction, and actually achieves the result of making language decay by obliging it to exist from that moment in

[63] WB indicates the perfection of creation by quoting the phrase, "And God saw every thing that he had made, and, behold, it was very good" (Gen. 1:31), pronounced on the seventh day. However, this shows that Benjamin did not know the Jewish tradition contained in the Talmud, according to which this "very" is the first manifestation of the negative (inasmuch as "more" implies "less") and gives the gloss, as Rosenzweig reminds us "it is this 'very' that is death" (*Genesis Rabbah* IX,5 to Gen. 1:31). See Franz Rosenzweig, *Der Stern der Erlösung* (The Hague: Marinus Nijhoff, 1976), 173.

the condition of a purely communicative instrument. "In stepping outside the purer language of name, man makes language a means (that is a knowledge inappropriate to him), and therefore also, in one part at any rate, a *mere* sign" (153). The original offense is therefore a sin against the spirit of language because here, for the first time, "name steps outside itself." It thus marks

> the birth of the *human word*, in which name no longer lives intact and which has stepped out of name-language, the language of knowledge, from what we may call its own immanent magic, in order to become expressly, as it were externally, magic. The word must communicate *something* (other than itself). In that fact lies the true Fall of the sprit of language. (153)

As the central ontological structure on which the whole of Benjamin's special anthropology is based hinges on language, the main consequences of Adam's Fall make themselves felt in man's relationship with language. By judiciously linking the theme of language with the ethical question evoked by the naming of the Tree, Benjamin creates two sets of consequences. The sin of our first parents against language has given rise to and spread "the judging word" in both senses of the word: logical and axiological. It has given rise to a discriminating and categorizing judgement (*Urteil*), which produces all cognitive abstraction[64] and generates abstract language, which is abstract not only because it is rootless and remote, but also because it is the opposite of the original naming language.

> The immediacy (which, however, is the linguistic root) of the communicability of abstraction resides in judgement. This immediacy in the communication of abstraction came into being as judgement, when, in the Fall, man abandoned immediacy in the communication of the concrete—that is, name—and fell into the abyss of the mediateness of all communication, of the word as means, of the empty word, into the abyss of prattle.[65] (154)

The inevitable (and already implicit) consequence of the degeneration of language into communicative language will be the Babel of

---

[64] There is agreement with Hamann on this point too: "She [a muse] will dare to purify the natural use of the senses from the unnatural use of abstractions, which mutilate our ideas of things as badly as they suppress and blaspheme the name of the Creator." See *Aesthetica in nuce*, 207.

[65] WB uses the word "prattle" in Sören Kierkegaard's sense. See *Kritik der Gegenwart*, ed. Th. Haecker (Innsbruck, 1914), 44.

tongues with its hazards and fragmentation of communication.

But even judgment (*Gericht*), in the sense of a verdict pronounced on the guilty by a court that examines, judges and punishes the wrongdoing, derives according to Benjamin from the same "judging word" for which "the knowledge of good and evil is immediate." This knowledge is, as it were, inherent to the Tree of Knowledge and there it is "blissful unto itself." But man's demand to have access to it provokes it to manifest itself and fall upon him like a judgment of punishment. This punishment is the expulsion of humanity from the paradise of pure language, alienation from the language of the sphere of the name.

> This judging word expels the first human beings from Paradise; they themselves have aroused it in accordance with the immutable law by which this judging word punishes—and expects—its own awakening as the sole and deepest guilt. (153)

Thus the paradox of the Garden of Eden takes shape, which Benjamin constructs around the true role of the Tree of Knowledge, which is placed at the center of Paradise not in order to communicate knowledge but as a source of temptation, to provoke empty (and impious) questioning that would bring down judgment.

> For... the question as to good and evil in the world after the Creation was empty prattle. The Tree of Knowledge stood in the garden of God not in order to dispense information on good and evil, but as an emblem of judgement over the questioner. This immense irony marks the mythic origin of law. (155)

In fact I think that I can, like Benjamin, reply to those who ask what the "good" really means that God pronounced upon creation, that it actually opens up an abyss; the criterion that separates good from evil is hidden in the abyss of divine transcendence, and merely having touched or evoked it, the mere fact of wanting in some way to accede to it, brings down judgment on the questioner.

By composing this singular work of exegesis, rich as it is in insight and profundity, Benjamin shows that he has consistently used a single, coherent hermeneutic act. He had decided that what others considered to be the obvious ingenuousness of the mythic material in Genesis that was molded by Jewish tradition is in fact a fruitful source, although it had been dismissed by others. And he has given this ingenuity theoretical force. As a result, in perfect although unconscious obedience to a Jewish and Christian tradition going back thousands of years, he makes the logical weaknesses of an archaic text into its strong points and finds the highest significance in the incongruities of a much written and rewritten text. Furthermore, he does not neglect to pronounce rigorous rational deductions and to exploit, in order to create and enrich, the consistencies that the text does offer. On the other hand, making the discourse culminate in paradoxes is one of the main ways in which importance is given to themes that have yet to be untangled.

This procedure is also consistent with the general structure of the discourse of the whole of the work, which itself can be summarized as a single philosophical proposition. The uncritical basis of the biblical creation myth (with its ingenuous assumption of a linguistic dimension that was already present and articulate and shared between God and man/nature) is not treated dismissively but is on the contrary wholly accepted and exploited (in the Judaic tradition). Furthermore, it is used to establish language as an ontological *primum*. With the complete certainty that in language we have an objective reality, the unfathomable mystery of which, as the Romantics teach us, is inevitably rooted in the first beginnings.

Paradise and the Dialogical Relation: Genesis 1–2 in the Commentary of Karl Barth and of Some of His Interlocutors

Alberto Gallas

Introduction

Barth devotes the central part of book III,1 of his *Church Dogmatics,* published in 1945, to the commentary on the first two chapters of Genesis. This volume is divided into three parts. The title of the first part is *The Faith in God the Creator*; the second, *Creator and Covenant,* is the most important part of the volume and is divided into three chapters. Chapter One, "Creation, History and Creation History," is of interest to us since it contains some methodological observations on hermeneutics and the definition of "saga;" Chapter Two, "Creation as the External Basis of the Covenant," deals with Genesis 1; Chapter Three, "The Covenant as the Internal Basis of Creation," concerns Genesis 2. The third and final part of the volume is called *The Yes of God the Creator.*

This essay likewise is divided into three parts. The first is methodological; it is concerned with the concept of "saga," which Barth used to define the typology of narratives of the Creation. The second and third parts examine the commentary on the text itself, in particular the interpretation of the double name Jehovah-Elohim and the man-woman relationship in the Garden of Eden.

In choosing Barth's interlocutors (in a broad sense) I have limited myself to modern authors, and to the two most important among them, Benno Jacob (1862–1945) and Martin Buber (1878–1965). Benno Jacob published a *Commentary on Genesis* in 1934, was Rabbi in Göttingen and later in Dortmund, and emigrated to England in 1939. He attracts our attention since he shares with Calvin the position of the most often-quoted author in a positive sense (about 20 times), and is in second place after Gunkel in absolute terms (the latter is quoted mostly negatively or to minimize the significance of his work in making the biblical text more understandable.) Buber on the other hand is never quoted, but he is important because he—or rather the school he represents, namely dialogical thinking—is the principal interlocutor (indeed Buber himself has claimed this position) for the anthropology which Barth develops with regard to the creation of woman in Genesis. I shall also be taking into consideration a third author, Franz Delitzsch (1813–1890). Delitzsch was an orthodox Lutheran influenced by pietism, and was a professor in Leipzig, Rostock and Erlangen; he is the second modern author most often quoted (in a positive sense) because of the fifth edition of his commentary on Genesis. In his case, however, qualitative and quantitative data do not correspond, since his influence is less relevant for the salient points of Barth's commentary than that of Jacob and Buber.

1. Saga

Barth's choice of the term "saga" to define the nature of the narratives of the Creation (and moreover of the biblical narratives in general), is not based on the analysis of the text and its literary genre, but on his general thinking concerning the possibility of referring in historical terms to an event such as the Creation. Barth asserts that the Creation is history and *Geschichte*, i.e. it is a determined event which happens within space and time. For this reason he does not agree with Augustine, and with those who followed the thesis presented in *De Civitate Dei* XI 6, according to which "non est mundus factus in tempore, sed cum tempore."[1] This history is however different from any other because of the fact that it cannot possess any link (*Zusammenhang*) with previous history.[2] Barth implicitly accepts Troeltsch's definition of history—in the sense that it is a possible object of an account of a historical event, i.e. of *Historie*—and argues that in the absence of this

---

[1] K. Barth, *Kirchliche Dogmatik* [= KD], III,1, Zürich 1945, 75 (English translation: *Church Dogmatics* [= CD], III,1, Edinburgh 1958, 70). According to W. Pannenberg (*Systematische Theologie*, Bd 2, Göttingen 1991, 54) Barth does not understand the real meaning of Augustine in this polemic.

[2] According to this (*Über historische und dogmatische Methode in der Theologie* [1898]) the historical method is characterized by: a critical mentality which produces judgments tending to the real (*Wahrscheinlichkeitsurteile*); the application of analogy; and the presupposition of the existence of a *Korrelation* between each historical fact.

Zusammenhang Creation cannot be called history in a narrow sense.[3] The creation story as primordial history therefore cannot be other than *unhistorisch*. This does not mean an undue concession to historical criticism, but a theological statement tied to the nature itself of the thing.[4] The polemic against modern thought (and against Troeltsch) begins only with a second problem, namely with the meaning to be attributed to the *unhistorisch* nature of the creation story. Modern thought (the mode of understanding history which has prevailed since the end of the 17th century[5]) sees something non-historical (*unhistorisch*) as mythological, as unreal and as something which did not happen in space and time; *unhistorisch* accordingly means *ungeschichtlich*. Barth's thesis is that not all history is *historisch*, i.e., not every event that happened in space and time can be an object of the science of history in the modern sense.[6] In the first place, this is true with regard to the Creation on the grounds mentioned above. Secondly,[7] it also holds for every historical fact in a narrow sense because even ordinary historical facts contain an *unhistorisch* element, however small.[8] Information about the Creation, then, can only take on a different form from that of historiography, the form of a narrative with some of the characteristics of the "saga," which Barth defines as "an intuitive and poetic picture of a pre-historical [*praehistorisch*] reality of history [*Geschichtswirklichkeit*] which is enacted once and for all within the confines of time and space."[9]

Barth was not doing anything new when he chose the term saga. It was probably applied for the first time to the Paradise story by Johann

---

[3] For *Zusammenhang*, see also M. Buber, *Moses*, in *Werke II*, Heidelberg 1964, 20.

[4] KD III,1, 86 [CD III,1, 79] (where there is no historian, there is no history, either).

[5] KD III,1, 89 [CD III,1, 82].

[6] See KD I, 1, 343.

[7] We can only hint at the question here, although it is very important because it could allow us to show evidence of continuity with *Römerbrief II* (RBII) on this point.

[8] KD III,1, 83, 90 [CD III,1, 76–77, 82–83]. (See E. Jüngel, *Barth Studien* [Zürich-Köln-Gütersloch, 1982], 93–95, on general hermeneutics with regard to *Preface* to RBII, XIV).

[9] "Sage [ist] ein divinatorisch-dichterisch entworfenes Bild einer konkret einmaligen, zeitlich-räumlich beschränkten praehistorischen Geschichtswirklichkeit" (KD III,1, 88 [CD III,1, 81]).

David Michaelis in his *Einleitung in die göttlichen Schriften des alten Bundes* of 1787.[10] According to Michaelis, saga is not in opposition to history (*Geschichte*), but is handed down as an oral tradition in a form characteristic to the mentality of a very ancient world (*Vorzeit*). The term is used in the nineteenth century with different nuances, for example by Delitzsch, and in the twentieth century its usage is widespread even among non-specialists such as Freud.[11]

But Barth believes that he himself must undertake the task of defining the meaning of both saga and associated or bordering concepts such as myth, fairy tale, legend and anecdote, on which there had been no agreement among the specialists—he mentions Gunkel, Baumgartner, Rühle, Tillich and Bultmann (though strangely the name of Procksch does not appear). He probably would not have felt isolated in this way if he had had the opportunity to read Buber's book on Moses, published in Hebrew in Jerusalem in 1945 (the same year KD III,1 was published), in English in 1946, and German in 1948.

Buber's first pages are also concerned with the distinction between saga and history (*Geschichte*). The sources which speak of Moses are not historical ones in a proper sense, but fall into the "literary category" (*literalische Kategorie*) of saga[12] that Buber defines as an oral and popular conservation, not tied to an official responsibility (unlike the chronicles) for historical events, i.e. events of vital importance for a tribe (*Stamm*).[13] Saga is different from history because it is born of an experience full of images, and from the "objective enthusiasm" in which they were experienced. Saga contains nonetheless an "authentic historical substance" (*echte Geschichtssubstance*) because in the parts nearest to the events handed down, it conserves the testimony of the encounter of a people with events so powerful that it could not overlook the celestial powers at work in them. The task of criticism is not to trace things back

---

[10] See M. Metzger, *Die Paradieserzählung (Genesis 2,4b–3, 24). Die Geschichte ihrer Auslegung von J. Clericus bis W. M. L. De Wette* (Bonn 1959), 27.

[11] See S. Freud, *Der Mann Moses und die monotheistische Religion: Drei Abhandlungen* [1939], in *Kulturtheoretische Schriften* (Frankfurt 1986), 459.

[12] Buber, *Moses* cit., 16.

[13] Buber, ibid., 18.

to objective data, eliminating the enthusiasm or the pictorial components of the story, but to trace things back as closely as possible to the event. Buber considers it very unlikely that a report by a chronicle writer, free of enthusiasm, can get nearer to the truth than saga does. In order to recognize this trustworthiness of the narrative it is necessary to abandon a narrow (i.e. modern-conceptualistic) conception of reason: "No scientific understanding of history exists but the rational one; but this understanding must begin with the overcoming of small *ratio* by great *ratio*."[14]

The differences from Barth's definition are significant: Buber is not concerned here with the creation story but with events which are to be found within the historical correlation; he does not use the distinction between *Historie* and *Geschichte* to introduce the concept of saga. Instead, he does this by resting on considerations about the "literary category" of the biblical narratives. He emphasizes the suggestive-existential component more than Barth does, i.e., the fact that the saga conserves the history of the reaction of a people to events rather than the history of the events themselves. Buber considers that it is the task of criticism to go back to beyond the form in which the saga has come down to us, while Barth always insists—following the example of M. Kähler—on the impossibility of going beyond the text.[15]

In other relevant respects however, Buber's conception is similar to Barth's. The enthusiastic and pictorial component—Barth here uses the term "divine-poetic"—does not jeopardize the historicity of the story; this is recognized by wider and freer *ratio*, although denied by the anchylosed *ratio* of modern conceptualistic thinking. This component cannot be eliminated, and for this reason the biblical narratives cannot be considered as historicization of myth, but rather as enthusiastic mythicization of history. Buber argues exactly in the same way as Barth,

---

[14] Buber, ibid., 20.

[15] Probably the opposition is here at least partly apparent rather than real since Buber intends to go back to the original nucleus of the saga and not to the facts which are behind the saga. On Barth's "prohibition" on going beyond the text, see G. Eichholz, *Der Ansatz Karl Barths in der Hermeneutik*, in *Antwort. Karl Barth zum siebzigsten Geburtstag* (Zollikon-Zürich, 1956), 61.

that the biblical narratives can neither be considered a historical version of an ahistorical speculation,[16] nor be interpreted according to Eichrodt's concept of historicization of myth.[17]

2. The Theory of Sources

So far we already have some indications as to the positions that Barth and Buber take with regard to the theory of sources. According to Buber, a saga grows in time through a process which enriches and modifies its central nucleus, creating new perspectives around it according to the various religious, political and kinship tendencies. It is an organic process, which Buber thinks is completely different from one that produces a unified story through the welding together of writings belonging to different sources.[18] As for Barth, the way the text is structured already shows that the theological connection between Gen. 1 and Gen. 2 is more relevant than a subdivision on the basis of sources. He accepts the theory of sources, although he criticizes the depreciation of the text that accompanies the theory in authors like Gunkel;[19] he merely makes an informative rather than productive use of it. The saga constructs its images at the same time as it joins different elements together, but it is precisely through this process that the text acquires meaning, and so it should be interpreted in the form in which it has been handed down to us.[20]

On this point we can also compare the positions of Jacob and Delitzsch. Jacob takes an extreme stand, radically denying the theory of sources, not because each part of Genesis is the work of only one author or because it is necessary to exclude the existence of previous sources, but because the redactor has given Genesis a unified form in which, as in a large river, it is impossible to separate the main currents from those of the tributaries.[21] We will see later the importance of this position for

---

[16] KD III,1, 91 [CD III,1, 84].

[17] KD III,1, 95 [CD III,1, 87].

[18] Buber, *Moses*, cit., 19. Buber is thinking of an organic process although in one case he uses the term *Kristallisationsprozeß*.

[19] KD III,1, 87 [CD III,1, 80].

[20] KD III,1, 316 [CD III,1, 277]; see also 321 [281].

[21] B. Jacob, *Das erste Buch der Tora. Genesis* (Berlin, 1934), 10.

the interpretation of the use of the double name Jehovah-Elohim in chapter 2. Finally, Delitzsch also states that his approach to the text is essentially different from the modern one[22] since he considers the text as inspired throughout. The inspiration does not concern the sources but the final text, in which these are elaborated and unified again (*zusammengearbeitet*).[23] Delitzsch's case is particularly interesting because of his evolution over a long period as exegete, during which five different editions of his commentary on Genesis were sent to press. In the first one, published in 1852, he still defended the idea of the "mosaic of the Pentateuch."[24] Afterwards he acknowledged the existence of two Elohistic redactors, and finally in the last edition of 1887, called *Neuer Commentar über die Genesis*, which is used by Barth, he acknowledged that Gen. 2 is more ancient than Gen. 1, accepting thus the theory of sources in general.[25] It is an evolution which took place through "difficult inner struggles" as Gunkel says,[26] from which the "strength of his scientific consciousness emerges, the most glorious proof we can think" of his love for true science (Eduardo Meyer).[27] But in this last edition he also declares an unchanged loyalty to the spirit in which the first edition was conceived twenty-five years before,[28] and confirms the idea that interpretation must respect the form which the text has assumed in the canon.

3. The Double Name

It is in the pages on the double name Jehovah-Elohim—which Jacob, following Rosenzweig and Buber, translates "He-God"[29]—that Jacob criticizes the theory of sources most directly: the use of one or another

---

[22] F. Delitzsch, *Neuer Kommentar über die Genesis* (Leipzig, 1887), 17.

[23] Delitzsch, *Neuer Kommentar*, 35.

[24] Delitzsch, *Einleitung und Commentar zur Genesis* (Leipzig, 1852), 11 and 89.

[25] Delitzsch, *Neuer Kommentar*, 17.

[26] Quoted in H. J. Kraus, *Geschichte der historisch-kritischen Erforschung des Alten Testaments* (Neukirchen-Vluyn, 1982), 230.

[27] Quoted in Kraus, 231.

[28] Delitzsch, *Neuer Kommentar*, 17.

[29] Jacob, *Das erste Buch* cit., 11 and 71.

name, or the two names together, does not depend on the different sources but corresponds to a precise intention, i.e., to the narrative-theological art of an author, who carefully chooses the most adequate solution, taking each case individually. Proof of this should be sought in the Bible itself, in Ex. 9:30, another passage of the Pentateuch in which the double name appears. According to Jacob this passage shows that the struggle between Moses and Pharaoh is really a question of the recognition of Jehovah as the real Elohim. A comparable event occurs in the transition from Gen. 1 to Gen. 2. Chapter 1 tells us who Elohim is: he is the creator of heaven, earth and mankind. In their natural course Things obey the will of God; only for man does duty exist. It is for this reason that the creation story is followed by the story of the promulgation of the commandments in chapter 2. But in order to make it effective, he who imparts the commandment appears in all his majesty and with his own name, Jehovah-Elohim. The story lays down the perspective within which the education of the Israelites and of humanity is to occur. The education of the Israelites consists in knowing and recognizing Jehovah in Elohim again and again; the education of humanity consists in recognizing Elohim in Jehovah.[30] There is a general revelation and a specific one, and the one brings us back to the other. The interpretation of Barth, who also quotes Ex. 9:30, is similar to Jacob's. In this passage Moses says: "As for you and your servants I know that you do not fear Jehovah-Elohim," i.e., according to Barth "you still have not recognized that Jehovah, the God of Israel, is the real God." The meaning of the first two chapters of Genesis is then as follows: Gen. 1 tells the story of natural mankind (the creation as external basis for the covenant); Gen. 2 tells the story of mankind in the perspective of salvation (the covenant as internal basis for the creation). The heathens must learn that Jehovah is *Elohim* (where Barth's emphasis falls on Elohim), while Israelites must learn that the *Jehovah* is Elohim (Barth's emphasis falls on Jehovah).[31]

Jacob and Barth interpret the correspondence between the two pas-

---

[30] Jacob, *Das erste Buch*, 77.

[31] K. H. Miskotte (see *Antwort*, 45) considers the first proposition in a similar way, but denies the second one. However he completely ignores the argument in KD III,1 in his analysis of Barth's thinking.

sages (Gen. 2 and Ex. 9:30) in the same way. The parallel is almost verbatim except for the use of underlining in chiasmus, which Barth prefers from his earliest works, over the usage of the inversion between subject and predicate, which Jacob prefers. For this reason it is difficult not to conclude that on this point Barth owes an unacknowledged debt to Jacob.[32]

But the overall picture into which Barth fits these considerations is different. Like Jacob, he asserts that in order to understand the creation story, the decisive commentary is "the rest of the Old Testament."[33] Barth argues also that the Old Testament sheds light on the basic outlines of the creation story and the direction they tend to take, while it is not able to show where exactly these lines meet each other and where they lead (*Ziel*, focus). These lines nevertheless diverge in the actual history of Israel (in a certain sense in the actual history of the Church as well).[34] Jehovah-Elohim is the name of the God who stipulates a covenant with his people, but this covenant is broken again and again. The Old Testament leaves us with an unresolved enigma at the end. It is only in Jesus Christ that this *Ziel* is met and the lines actually converge. In him the covenant is actually realized, and only thanks to him can it really be the basis for the creation. It is a basis to which Barth attributes a retrospective value, in analogy to the Jewish doctrine according to which God creates the world so that Israel can receive the Torah.[35] His argument is however different from this doctrine, in that God's design would remain enigmatic if the law did not find its realization in Christ, who can be the basis of creation only because that design is realized in him.[36]

---

[32] Barth had already written about the name Jehovah (as the name of the God who makes the covenant) in KD I, 1, 334 ff., without introducing the subject of the double name.

[33] KD III, 1, 69 [CD III,1, 65].

[34] KD III, 1, 366 [CD III,1, 320].

[35] KD III, 1, 49 [CD III,1, 46].

[36] Pannenberg comments: "Barth extended the line 'creation-alliance' beyond the story of the covenant with Israel and developed it to include the new covenant founded in Jesus Christ. The creation of man happened in view of that communion that God would have then realized with man in Jesus Christ, as vice versa the creation represents the starting point of the story of alliance with God in view of Jesus Christ." (*Systematische Theologie* cit., 169).

Can it be still argued that the Old Testament is the decisive commentary on Gen. 1 and Gen. 2? On the one hand the answer must be no, because only the New Testament makes manifest the *Ziel* toward which the story tends. On the other, the answer may be yes, because only the Old Testament allows us to understand the course of the lines which lead to that *Ziel*.[37] In our case only Ex. 9:30 allows us to interpret adequately the double name Jehovah-Elohim. This is precisely the debt which Barth owes to Jacob.

Other differences are to be found in features of the interpretation which are less central, but not without interest. In order to consolidate his distinction between natural history and Hebrew history, the focus of interest of chapters 1 and 2 respectively, Barth recalls Isaak de la Peyrére's 1655 hypothesis. According to this, chapter 1 of Genesis relates the birth of pagan (or "pre-adamite") humanity and chapter 2 the birth of the humanity involved in salvation history.[38] Barth learned of de la Peyrére's thesis through Delitzsch, to whom he refers. It is interesting that Delitzsch mentions de la Peyrére only to demolish his thesis, which he believes is merely functional to the polygenetic hypothesis of the origins of humanity put forward by the French author.[39] Barth does not believe in this hypothesis either, yet to him this disagreement is of secondary importance compared to the theological use he can make of de la Peyrére's intuition. Jacob himself does not refer to de la Peyrére in his pages on the double name, yet he disputes the polygenetic hypothesis which developed in the work of authors like Cordonnière, Gobineau and Pouchet in the second half of the nineteenth century, and then in authors like Houston Stewart Chamberlain at the end of the same century.[40] This polemic is also interesting since here Jacob, in order to re-

[37] The passage in which Barth affirms that the christological reading cannot be the first but only the final word of the interpretation should be read in this sense (KD III,2, 372).

[38] The title of the book by Isaak de la Peyrére (Delitzsch and Barth quote his name as La Peyrére) published in Paris in 1655 is: *Praeadamitae sive exercitatio super versibus duodecimo, decimotertio et decimoquarto capitis quinti epistolae S. Pauli ad Romanos. Quibus inducuntur Primi homines antes Adamum conditi.*

[39] Delitzsch, *Neuer Kommentar*, 75.

[40] His *Die Grundlagen des neunzehnten Jahrhunderts* was published in 1899.

fute polygenesis, refers to "serious science," which in his opinion confirms "the point of view of the Bible about the unity of mankind."[41] Because of the burning actuality of the problem of racism he forgets the principle he reiterated many times over, according to which exegesis should not fall into the temptation to meet science more than halfway.[42] Barth agrees with this principle and declares in the preface that he initially believed he was unable to avoid challenging the natural sciences, but was then convinced of the absolute irrelevance of the scientific *Weltanschauung* to the creation story.[43] In his commentary he remains completely loyal to this conviction.[44] Delitzsch on the other hand often competes with the natural sciences in the first edition,[45] but by the last edition of his study on Genesis has given it up almost completely.[46]

4. Man and Woman

The second theme that deserves special attention is that of the *Vollkommenheit* of mankind. Here the author we must address is Buber. The subject is treated in two stages: first in chapter 1, on the interpretation of Creation in the image of God, and then in chapter 2, on the Creation of Eve, the only living being in whom Adam recognizes a suitable helpmeet.

---

[41] Jacob, *Das erste Buch*, 60 ff.

[42] Ibid., 41; see also 19, 37, 52.

[43] KD III, 1, *Vorwort* [CD III,1, IX]. The motive is interpreted in KD III, 1, 235 [CD III,1, 208]: saga deals with *praehistorisch* and therefore *praenaturhistorisch* relations. Barth however says that it is difficult to locate the confines between science and theology.

[44] Pannenberg underscores Barth's coherence in his *Systematische Theologie*, cit., 88, in which he however critically comments as follows: "It is not sufficient for a Christian theology simply to oppose a naturalistic description to another conception of reality."

[45] Delitzsch, *Einleitung und Commentar* cit., esp. 58, 72, 77.

[46] He writes as follows: "The creation story is not conditioned by the confirmations the natural science can prove or deny" (Delitzsch, *Neuer Kommentar* cit., 40). Nevertheless he considers that the Christian *Weltanschauung* is not compatible with a scientific theory which denies the original unity of the mankind (ibid., 37 ff.).

From the outset I must mention that Barth denies the idea of an original "state" of perfection and innocence.[47] Saga cannot intend to represent our origins as objects of "nostalgia;"[48] in the sober way it describes the Garden of Eden, it distinguishes itself from the Muslim tradition.[49] Barth prefers to speak of a "relationship" rather than a "state." He keeps his distance from the Reformation, denying that through sin man lost his resemblance to God (*imago Dei*).[50] According to Barth the meaning of *imago Dei* is explained in a simple and clear way by verse 27 itself, without resorting to the fruits of the surprising creativity manifested by the human spirit over the centuries, in its attempts to interpret this passage.[51] "Male and female created he them": it is precisely in the fact that man is created not according to gender distinction as with animals, but in the man-woman duality, that its being created in the image of God consists. God is actually *in himself* "relation," as the plural form of verse 26 ("Let us...") shows, which Barth interprets as a "dialogue [*Gespräch*] of God with Himself";[52] and the human being is like God because he exists not only in the coexistence among unlike beings, like animals, but in the polar tension, in the *Gegenüber* between me and you. For this reason he is capable of being a partner of God, too: he is the sole living thing whose nature inherently owns the capacity of dialogue which inherently and originally belongs to God.[53]

---

[47] KD III,1, 351 [CD III,1, 307].

[48] KD III,1, 239 [CD III,1, 212]. Consequently Barth does not agree with the idea that paradise always "opens a passage" again and again in history, for example in Jesus, in Francis, in Christian communism or socialism. The idea is sustained by Ragaz in the first volume of his commentary on the Bible which appeared two years after KD III,1. (See L. Ragaz, *Die Bibel—eine Deutung. Die Urgechichte: Moses* [1947] [Fribourg-Brig, 1990], 38.)

[49] KD III,1, 317 [CD III,1, 278].

[50] KD III,1, 224ff. [CD III,1, 200–201].

[51] See KD III,1, 216 [CD III,1, 192].

[52] KD III,1, 204 [CD III,1, 182 translates incorrectly: "There takes place a divine *soliloquy*"]. For the Trinitarian interpretation in Luther, see WA XLII, 43.

[53] This argument has found remarkable consensus. Westermann refers to names such as J. J. Stamm, F. Horst, K. L. Schmidt. He however contests the originality of the argument: "Therefore you should speak not of the interpretation given by Karl Barth

Gen. 2 further develops this subject, which is introduced briefly in Gen. 1, with an effect of clarification which Barth considers is deliberately desired by the redactor who has united the two narratives. This text also attributes to God a reflection which He makes to Himself ("It is not good..."),[54] and the parallel to 1:26[55] seems so strong that Barth considers that the LXX and the Vulgate were right to translate the second part of the verse with the plural form *poiesomen*, and *faciamus*. God reflects here that the human being who is perfect, fulfilled and whole, *der ganze Mensch*, is not the human being who exists in solitude. A solitary being could not represent the subject of that partnership which will develop in the history of the covenant, which as we have seen is here the intimate reason of the story, in contrast to chapter 1. In order to be able to respond to God as partner of the covenant, the human being must be made in such way that the partnership represents that very dimension that makes it complete. It must be *bundesfähig*,[56] "formally prepared for grace" in its very nature.[57] In order to become a perfect man, Adam must enter into dialogue with a being like himself, who is standing before him—a being which "is to him a Thou as truly as he is an I, and he is to it a Thou as truly as it is an I."[58] The human subject is not single but a couple; the man and the woman are in reciprocal relation. This vision of the human being as a living being who can

---

but rather of an interpretation sustained by him in this particular way," i.e., that the *imago* does not refer to something the human being possesses but to its very nature. But the text by W. Riedel (1902) which Westermann quotes to illustrate this observation is not very convincing. On the contrary he fails to mention Bonhoeffer to whom Barth refers in particular. (See C. Westermann, *Genesis*, Bd. I [Neukirchen 1974], 208 ff.). Bonhoeffer's authorship of the concept of "analogical relationships" is not acknowledged by J. Trach in *Theologische Realenziklopädie* (see the entry for *Analogie*), which attributes it to Barth.

[54] KD III,1, 330 [CD III,1, 289].

[55] KD III,2, 370 [CD III,1, 324].

[56] Jüngel uses the expression *bündnisfähig*.

[57] KD III,1, 331 [CD III,1, 290]. This does not mean that Barth now accepts the *Anknüpfungspunkt*; see Jüngel, *Barth Studien*, 52 ff.

[58] KD III,1,331 [CD III,1, 290] ("das für ihn Du ist, so weiß er Ich ist und für das er selbst Du ist, so gewiß er selbst Ich ist").

realize him/herself completely only through dialogue with the other which is standing before him/her constitutes the "Magna Charta der Humanität."[59] Barth then goes on to observe that in Gen. 2 the purpose of the man-woman relation does not seem to be procreation,[60] unlike what normally happens in the Old Testament, with the single exception of the Song of Songs.[61] The Song is the key which the Old Testament offers to understand Gen. 2. In both texts the enthusiasm of the man for the woman (and vice versa)[62] is an erotic one. How have these two "erotic" texts been accepted into the canon? The question is traditional for the Song, but according to Barth it must also be asked for Gen. 2. Surely the redactor knew the desperate problematic inherent in erotic relations?[63] Of course he did. However, he also knew the relationship between God and Israel, which induced him to see the relationship between the sexes in a positive light as well:[64] the continuously-broken covenant, on which the prophets ponder when they speak of Israel as a prostitute, is also the covenant which is always being reconstructed and loyally maintained. Both the creation story in Gen. 2 and the Song correspond to this eschatological perspective, i.e., to Israel's expectation of a fulfilled form of its relationship with Jehovah.[65] The two texts trace some lines which converge in focal point, in a reality. But as we have seen with Ex. 9:30, this focal point lies beyond the Old Testament and consists in the relationship between Jesus Christ and his

---

[59] For the definition, see KD III,2, 351. Here Barth sums up the interpretation on Gen. 2:18–25 which he develops in KD III,1. It is said later in KD III, 2, 273 that every humanism which does not do justice to co-humanity is inhuman.

[60] On this point he might find support in Calvin (the commentary on verse 18, OC XXIII, 46–48) but not in Luther.

[61] According to Luther, on the other hand, Eve is created mainly for the purpose of reproduction, see WA XLII 87. Thus, Eve becomes "necessary" for the ministry of the *oeconomia* only after sin (ibid., 88).

[62] Barth notes that the woman indeed takes the initiative in the Song.

[63] Similar considerations can already be found in E. Thurneysen, "Das Verlorene Paradies. Eine Predigt nach Pfingsten," *Zwischen den Zeiten*, 5 (1927), 1–10.

[64] KD III,1, 359 [CD III,1, 314].

[65] KD III,1, 365 [CD III,1, 319].

community of which Eph. 5:25–27 speaks.[66] Here the expectation becomes reality and the enigma of the Old Testament—"where do these lines lead?"—is resolved. To believe that this *Ziel*, this "reality" in which the lines converge, is effective and real is however no longer a question for exegetes, but one of faith.[67]

The procedure followed by Barth is analogous to what we have seen above regarding the double name. He avoids treating the texts allegorically or spiritually; the text should be read literally.[68] The Old Testament is the best commentary on itself, since precisely thanks to the internal reading (in this case based on the Song of Songs) it is possible to individualize the lines along which the stories try to guide the reader. These lines are *already* present in the Old Testament.[69] But the transition from the perception of these lines to that of the actual reality is possible only on the basis of a christological reading.

While the considerations about eroticism are Barth's own, he refers to three authors—Kohlbrügge, Wilhelm Vischer and Bonhoeffer—for the dialogical reading of the relationship between man and woman. With Kohlbrügge we are dealing with a declaration of affection for an author who was held in esteem by Barth's entourage; already in the '20s the review *Zwischen den Zeiten* was calling attention to him, to rescue him from the oblivion to which he had been abandoned by academic

---

[66] "Husbands, love your wives, even as Christ also loved the church, and gave himself for it; that he might sanctify and cleanse it with the washing of water by the word, that he might present it to himself a glorious church, not having spot, or wrinkle, or any such thing; but that it should be holy and without blemish."

[67] KD III,1, 228 [CD III,1, 202] (on Gen. 1:26 ff., but it can be applied to our passage).

[68] See KD III,1, 363 [CD III,1, 317], against the *bildlich* reading of the erotic relationship between man and woman. The same criterion is confirmed in other contexts: KD III,1, 139, 163, 244, 253 [CD III,1, 125, 146, 216, 224]; differently in KD III, 1, 201 [CD III,1, 179]. (See also Barth's criticism of the Platonic reading by Jacob, *Das erste Buch*, 84 in KD III,1, 276 [CD III,1, 243]).

[69] KD III,1, 368 [CD III,1, 322].

theology.[70] In Vischer's case, and Bonhoeffer's, the reference is more appropriate because both of them use the category of dialogue (*Gegenüber, Ich-Du, Begegnung...*) which Barth makes his own.[71] Barth contents himself with quoting these authors without going back to that philosophical movement from which they—and Barth himself—drew inspiration, i.e., the stream of "dialogical thinking" (*dialogisches Denken* or *dialogischer Personalismus*) which was particularly vital during the '20s. However, he compensates for this omission in the second volume of the book (KD III,2) published in 1948, in which, starting from the interpretation of Gen. 2:18–25, he further develops the idea of dialogue in the pages devoted to the *Humanität*, the *humanum* of mankind, meant as *Mitmensch*, i.e., as a living being whose nature is intrinsically dual (*Zweisamkeit*). The "being with the other," the "being in the encounter,"[72] in a word co-humanity, is primarily the relationship between man and woman.[73] Here he challenges Buber, who will answer the provocation in 1954.

According to Barth there are four fundamental categories to this dialogical anthropology: the encounter implies the looking the other in the eye,[74] talking and listening to one another,[75] mutual solidarity (*Beistand*),[76] and finally that all this occurs "willingly"[77] and comes freely from the bottom of the heart.[78] It is this fourth point that is increasingly

[70] See the letter from Thurneysen to Barth dated June 6th, 1919 (*Karl Barth-Eduard Thurneysen Briefwechsel*, Bd. I, 1913–1921, [Zürich, 1973], 308), and *Zwischen den Zeiten*, 2 (1924), 64 (in one of the notes in this book Kohlbrügge is remembered as one of the "voices which the theology of the nineteenth century neglected wrongly and to its own detriment").

[71] Barth takes the very formula "analogical relation" from Bonhoeffer.

[72] With regard to this "duality" see KD III,2, 291, in which it is emphasized that the dialogical relationship is established primarily in the singular, i.e., "with the other" and not "with others." From here duality is born.

[73] See for example KD III,4 (1951), 184 (where Barth criticizes homosexuality severely).

[74] KD III,2, 299.

[75] KD III,2, 302.

[76] KD III,2, 312.

[77] KD III,2, 318.

[78] KD III,2, 334.

important for him: he defines it as the "mystery of humanity." It really represents "the highest step" which man can reach.[79] Yet it belongs to man's natural dimension. Co-humanity is a subject which belongs to the doctrine of creation, and not to that of reconciliation. This does not coincide with the *agape*, so it is concerned with humanity's common inheritance, not one specific to believers. There is small wonder then, Barth continues, if the subject of co-humanity has developed outside Christianity and the Church, with results sometimes different or worse, but sometimes similar or better than those that Christians have had. Idealism (with its concept of the absolute, the universal and the abstract subject) and Nietzsche (with the ideal of a humanity "without co-humanity," "Humanität ohne den Mitmenschen")[80] are the examples of the first case; those of the latter case are the pagan Confucius, the atheist Feuerbach and finally the Jew Buber. These last three belong to the number of "the wise among the wise" who have attained results regarding co-humanity very similar to those of Christian theology. Denying this similarity would be a sign of jealousy (here Matt. 20:15 is quoted: "Do you begrudge my generosity?") or of fear that, in admitting the value of worldly wisdom, grace is diminished. But Barth affirms that every convergence in the conception of man should be accepted joyfully. Only at one point does he have reservations: when he asks himself whether, beyond all the first three categories of dialogical anthropology—the looking the other in the eye, the talking and listening to one another, and mutual solidarity—there will still be room in wisdom of the world for the fourth and decisively important one, i.e., the "willingness" mentioned above. He does not give a univocal answer to this question; instead he uses interrogatives and complicated hypotheses and resorts frequently to litotes, double negation, adverbs of probability such as "likely" and "accidentally," which leave the reader a certain

[79] KD III,2, 318.

[80] KD III,2, 277 and *passim*.

amount of freedom to choose where to put the dominant emphasis.[81] However, he univocally denies that—even if one must admit that worldly wisdom has not arrived at the final stage represented by "willingness"—this happened *de jure* and not *de facto*. A partial discrepancy between Christian wisdom and the best of worldly wisdom in the field of anthropology, if it exists (as is likely), is contingent and historical, but not necessary or inevitable.

These are the pages in which Buber takes his stand in a short essay of 1954 in which he reconstructs the principal lines of the history of dialogical thinking since the end of the 18th century.[82] Buber recognizes in Barth the advantage of having used the categories of dialogical thinking, while maintaining the originality and force of his own personal perspective on the one hand, and not pretending to "annex" such categories to Protestantism on the other, as Gogarten had so simple-mindedly done in his time. Rather, he has tried to do justice to the "spirit which blows outside of Christianity." Buber lead us to understand that Barth was inspired directly by his book *You and Me* of 1923. This argument is dubious on several counts, because Barth's contact with dialogical thinking was multiple, and in the beginning not based on Buber but on the cousins Hans and Rudolf Ehrenberg and Eugen Rosenstock (but probably not on Rosenzweig), i.e., on the founding group of the Würzburg publishing house Patmos. The interest that Barth's talk at Tambach at the end of 1919[83] had aroused led Patmos to contact him, and actually to publish the talk in 1920. In addition Barth,

---

[81] (Wir können) "ruhig dahin gestellt sein lassen, ob und inwiefern sie (=unchristliche Denker) uns ihrerseits bis in die letzten und entscheidenden Konsequenzen dieser Konzeption, nämlich wirklich bis zu jenem 'gerne,' wirklich zu jener Freiheit des Herzens zwischen Mensch und Mensch als der Wurzel und Krone des Humanitätsbegriffs folgen werden. Würden sie es nicht tun—und es sieht nun doch nicht so aus, ob dies bei Konfuzius, bei Feuerbach, bei Buber sicher der Fall wäre—dann wäre ja wohl sichtbar, daß *duo cum faciunt idem non est idem*" (KD III,2, 334).

[82] Buber, *Nachwort. Zur Geschichte des dialogischen Prinzips* (Heidelberg, 1984), 299–320.

[83] See the letter from Barth to Thurneysen dated October 28th, 1919, in *K. Barth-E. Thurneysen Briefwechsel*, 348.

at least from 1924 on, knew the philosophy of Ferdinand Ebner,[84] another representative of dialogical thinking whose first important work (*Pneumatological Fragments*) was published in September 1920. It is true, however, that Barth considered Buber the most significant representative of this current of thought, since he is the only one quoted in KD.[85]

After recognizing Barth's worth, Buber criticizes him on two counts: first, he finds an incongruency in Barth when the latter asks whether the worldly wise are capable of "following" the concept of co-humanity, typical of Christian theology, to the end. Buber replies: "if the worldly wise do not follow Christian theology, it is because they do not take the same way but arrive at similar conclusions, following their own way." Secondly, he interprets the passages where Barth leaves open the question as to whether worldly wisdom has reached the height of the "willingness," as if his interlocutor were meant to give a negative answer: Barth would assert that that "willingness" in fact cannot be found in Buber's work (nor in Confucius's nor Feuerbach's). Buber sees himself therefore as the object of a direct criticism to which he must reply. This confrontation, Buber says, takes place not between single thinkers but between thinkers who represent two different worlds of faith: Barth that of Protestantism and Buber that of Chasidism. His answer can be therefore very short and limit itself to indicating an experience. For the Chasidim, Buber says, "the willingness of the liberty of the heart is not the consequence, but intimate premise, foundation of the foundation." To realize this it would be enough for Barth to see how "here in Jerusa-

---

[84] In 1924 Barth reviewed in *Zwischen den Zeiten* Brunner's book on Schleiermacher, *Die Mystik und das Wort*, which gives much importance to Ebner's philosophy.

[85] On the relations between Barth and Buber, see D. Becker, *Karl Barth und Martin Buber—Denker in dialogischer Nachbarschaft? Zur Bedeutung Martin Bubers für die Anthropologie Karl Barths* (Göttingen, 1986), 60–66. Here the analysis of *Ich und Du* that Barth made in the Winter term 1943/44 is indicated (ibid., 20 ff.). According to Becker probably there do not exist any documents which can confirm that the two knew each other; but E. Busch published in his biography of Barth a fragment of a letter of Barth of 1950 to the son, Christoph, in which Barth mentions to have attended a conference by Buber's.

lem the Chasidim express the liberty of their heart through the other: they dance."[86] With this word "dance" the short history of dialogical thinking closes.

Conclusion

The modern authors whom Barth quotes most frequently with approbation have in common a different approach to the text from the critical historical method. The authors to whom Barth feels closer read the text from inside of a tradition. Delitzsch declares: "I believe in the Resurrection and draw the consequences from there" (quoted by W. Vischer in *Zwischen der Zeiten* 5 [1927], 388). Barth often quotes his commentary, but does not draw inspiration from him on highly salient points. His influence is therefore not comparable to that which his master Beck exercised on the *Römerbrief* I.[87]

Jacob claims for his own commentary that it is the work of "a son of that people for whom the Torah was written," i.e., written in the living tradition of Israel. This is the premise that enables us to understand the text, first at the linguistic level and then at the hermeneutic level, and in order to avoid that debasement "from the outside" that considers the Old Testament a preliminary stage (*Vorstufe*) of the New Testament.[88] In Jacob Barth finds cues for many detailed arguments, but above all for the interpretation of the double name (Jehovah-Elohim), an interpretation which connects very well with his reading of the relation between Gen. 1 and Gen. 2. Even if Barth developed a christological interpretation and used the categories of the "time of expectation" and "time of the remembering" (and "promise" and "conclusion") to indicate the two Testaments, his exegesis satisfies all Jacob's conditions for a common front between Hebrews and Christians, namely the recognition of Judaism as the originator of Christianity and the defense of the perma-

---

[86] Buber, *Nachwort*, 319.

[87] On the relation between Delitzsch and Beck, see Kraus, *Geschichte der historisch-kritischen Erforschung* cit., 231–235; see also A. Gallas, "Barth e il mondo cristiano. Dalle conferenze di Safenwil alla II edizione del 'Römerbrief,'" *Cristianesimo nella storia*, 8 (1987), 557–589.

[88] Jacob, *Das erste Buch*, 10.

nent value of the Old Testament. It is probably sufficient to remember that in 1941 Barth clashed with Brunner for having supported the reading in the present tense of the sentence "salvation is of the Jews" (John 4:22).[89] Moreover, Barth is convinced that to understand the creation story the decisive comment is "the rest of the Old Testament":[90] the most significant cases are the established relation between Gen. 2 and Ex. 9:30 and the use of the Song of Songs. In the whole of his commentary on the narratives of the creation story, there are 606 quotations from the Old Testament. The obvious divergence, on the other hand, consists in the christological reading—in whose light it seems doubtful that the Old Testament can effectively be the "decisive commentary"—and in the use of the New Testament, which is quoted 179 times (including the application of Matt. 19:4 to Gen. 2:23[91] that had been explicitly criticized by Jacob). Buber did not write any commentary on the first chapters of Genesis, but Barth agrees with him on two points of great importance: on the concept of "saga," and on the dialogical interpretation of the anthropology (according to these, the perfection and happiness which characterize the human condition during the stay in the Garden of Eden consist in the harmony of the man-woman relation in conformity with God's will, harmony which is transformed into a conflictual relation through sin). In the first case we are not dealing with a direct influence, since Barth did not know Buber's book on Moses in which the latter explained his concept of saga; in the second, Barth joins with a broad movement of which Buber was one of the best representatives, though neither the only one, nor the leader of the school, nor always playing the avant-garde role. Nevertheless Barth considers him as the most representative, and for this reason he was the only one who was explicitly quoted.

With regard to his first important work about biblical texts (the *Römerbrief*), in KD III,1 Barth follows the original text much more closely and avoids pushing its actualization to extremes; he does not use

---

[89] Busch, *Karl Barth. Una biografia*, 279.

[90] KD III,1, 69 [CD III,1, 64].

[91] Jacob, *Das erste Buch*, 100; see KD III,1, 347 [CD III,1, 304].

the thinking of any particular author as a general key to his reading (with the exception of *Römerbrief II,* where he quotes for example Kierkegaard and the idea of infinite qualitative difference as a general key to the interpretation of Paul's thought). He remains instead loyal to the program of his first writings, of a reading of the text based on a conception of history broader than that of modern thinking (in Throeltsch's sense).